Veneroni's Complete Italian Grammar

Giovanni Veneroni

BIBLIOLIFE

VENERONI'S

COMPLETE

ITALIAN GRAMMAR:

CONTAINING THE

BEST AND EASIEST RULES;

TO WHICH ARE ADDED,

AN INTRODUCTION TO ITALIAN VERSIFICATION;

EXTRACTS FROM THE ITALIAN POETS;

&c. &c.

THE WHOLE ACCENTED ON A NEW PLAN, TENDING TO FACILITATE THE PRONUNCIATION OF LEARNERS.

TWENTIETH EDITION,

CAREFULLY CORRECTED, AND CONSIDERABLY IMPROVED,

BY P. L. ROSTERI.

LONDON:

LONGMAN, BROWN, AND CO.; WHITTAKER AND CO.; HAMILTON, ADAMS, AND CO.; SIMPKIN, MARSHALL, AND CO.; DULAU AND CO.; SOUTER AND LAW; AND AYLOTT AND JONES.

1846.

PREFACE.

When we reflect on the number of great men that Italy has produced since the glorious age of Leo X.; as well as on the pleasure and instruction to be obtained by visiting that beautiful country; and consequently the necessity of understanding the Italian language, to make such visit profitable; and further, when it is considered, that the authors of Italy constitute a fund of every kind of elegant and polite literature, it is not surprising that the Grammars, written to promote the knowledge of this language, have so greatly multiplied; for, without a proper acquaintance with its idiom, all the treasures of Italian learning and literature, all the discoveries and inventions of genius and industry in that nation, would be lost to the rest of mankind.

The original editor undertook to present to the English student, and in an English dress, Veneroni's Italian Grammar; a work justly considered as far surpassing all other introductions to that elegant language; but with such corrections, improvements, and additions, as were necessary to render it conformable to the English idiom. These improvements consisted of an Introduction to Syntax; an Essay on Italian Poetry

A 2

or Versification; the different Compositions in Verse, and Poetical Licenses; a Treatise on Compound Words, Capitals and Punctuation; and, finally, a Discourse on Expletives, the energy and beauty of which constitute a great part of the merit of most languages.

Some new Grammatical Observations on the Italian Language have likewise been added, with remarks on the Letters of the Alphabet; new Dialogues, Phrases, &c., &c.; and the Italian words are also properly accented, to facilitate the pronunciation to learners. It may be presumptuous to say, that it is impossible that any better introduction to the Italian language should *ever* appear; but it may safely be affirmed, that it will be long before VENERONI's GRAMMAR of the Italian Language can be superseded.

ADVERTISEMENT

TO

THE TWENTIETH EDITION.

In the present edition of this highly esteemed ITALIAN GRAMMAR the accentuation has been carefully attended to, and many useless repetitions removed. Some notes have also been added, and such corrections made as modern modes of speech require. The whole Work has been also thoroughly revised; and it is hoped it has been rendered worthy of the approbation so long bestowed upon it.

P. L. ROSTERI.

LONDON,
November, 1845.

INTRODUCTION

TO THE

ITALIAN TONGUE.

———

THE most expeditious, and certainly the only sure way to understand, write, and speak the Italian, and indeed all other languages, is, to acquire the knowledge of them on the principles of Grammar.—In order, therefore, to facilitate this acquirement, more especially as it respects Ladies, and those persons unacquainted with the Latin, I shall first, in this INTRODUCTION, explain the necessary TERMS and DEFINITIONS of Grammar in general:—this being thoroughly studied and understood, I shall then proceed to explain, in the best manner I can, the Rules of the ITALIAN GRAMMAR in particular.

AN EXPLANATION OF THE TERMS OF GRAMMAR.

The first terms of Grammar are the Letters. There are twenty-two letters in the Italian tongue, viz. *a, b, c, d, e, f, g, h, i, j, l, m, n, o, p, q, r, s, t, u, v, z.*

The Italians do not make use of *k, w, x* and *y.*

The letters are divided into vowels and consonants.

The vowels are, *a, e, i, j, o, u.* They are called vowels from their forming a perfect sound without the assistance of any other letter, as *a* is pronounced single; *e*, the same; and in like manner the other vowels.

The consonants are the remaining letters, *b, c, d, f, g, h, l, m, n, p, q, r, s, t, v, z.* We give them the name of

B

consonants, because we cannot pronounce them without the help of a vowel, either before or after them. See their pronunciation from page 24.

H, at the beginning of a word, is not considered properly a letter, and therefore is never pronounced in Italian; yet, the use made of it, in the middle of words, is greater than most people imagine. See what we say of it in treating of the pronunciation of consonants.

It is the mixture of the letters that generally forms the different words, which every language is capable of producing; and that some order may be observed in the infinite number of words, they have been reduced to ten parts of speech, though most Italians reckon no more than eight.

A speech is composed of sentences.

Sentences are composed of words.

Words of syllables, and syllables of letters.

Letters are certain marks or characters, which serve to form the syllables and words, as *a, b, c, d, e, &c.*

A syllable is a word, or part of a word, pronounced with a single sound, and composed of one, two or three letters, as *astròlogo*, an astrologer, is composed of four syllables, *a-stro-lo-go*, the second of which is composed of three letters, and the rest of two. *A-mo*, I love, is composed of two syllables; the former of a single letter, and the latter of two.

Sometimes a word contains but one syllable, and then we call it a monosyllable (a term of Greek derivation), that is to say, having but one syllable; as *re*, a king; *me*, me; *te*, thee, &c.

A sentence is composed of several words, forming a complete sentence; as *per ben parláre Italiano, bisógna parlare e pronunziare Toscanamente*; to speak good Italian, we must speak and pronounce as they do in Tuscany (¹).

---

¹ The learner should guard, however, against a fault too prevalent in Tuscany, and principally amongst the lower class, that of pronouncing *ce, ci*, and *ge, gi*, too softly; and *ca, co, cu*, with a kind of aspiration. The Romans pronounce these syllables more correctly, and perhaps from this only, arises the well-known proverb, "*Lingua Toscana in bocca Romana.*"

A speech or discourse is composed of ten parts; these are—the Article, Noun, Adjective, Pronoun, Verb, Participle, Adverb, Preposition, Conjunction, and Interjection. Every word is reducible to either one or other of these parts of speech, the particulars of which will be found in the following explanation :—

AN EXPLANATION OF THE PARTS OF SPEECH.

In order easily to understand a language, we should endeavour to obtain a perfect knowledge of the parts of speech, and their meaning; otherwise it is impossible ever to understand or speak it correctly. According to the preceding order, I should begin with the article; but, that I may be the better understood, I shall commence with the noun.

OF NOUNS.

A Noun is a word which serves to name and distinguish some thing: as, *Dío*, God; *ángelo*, an angel; *uòmo*, a man; *cièlo*, heaven; *tèrra*, earth; *cavállo*, a horse; *libro*, a book; *cappèllo*, a hat; *távola*, a table; *páne*, bread; *víno*, wine, &c.

There are two sorts of nouns ; one is called a noun-substantive, and the other a noun-adjective.

The noun-substantive is that which subsists by itself, or which by itself alone so clearly expresses the thing named, that we immediately understand it ; as, heaven, earth, a king, a horse, a book ; for we know the meaning of the words, heaven, earth, king, &c.

The noun-adjective is a word which denotes the qualities of the substantive ; as, great, *gránde;* fine, *bèllo;* little, *piccolo;* red, *rósso;* we know not what is great, fair, little or red, unless we join a substantive to it ; as, a great book, *un gran libro;* a fine book, *un bèl libro;* a little book, *un piccolo libro;* a red book, *un libro rósso;* a great hat, *un gran cappèllo;* a fine hat, *un bèl cappèllo;* a little hat, *un piccolo cappèllo;* a red hat, *un cappèllo rósso.*

Every noun is either of the masculine or the feminine gender, there being no neuter in Italian.

The masculine gender is marked by the article *il* or *lo*, in English, *the*

The feminine gender is marked by the article *la*, in English, also *the*.

All nouns, before which we may place *il* or *lo*, are of the masculine gender; and those before which we place *la*, are of the feminine gender; example, *il líbro*, the book; *il fuòco*, the fire; *lo spècchio*, the looking-glass; are of the masculine gender: *la tèrra*, the earth; *la cámera*, the room; *la pénna*, the pen; are of the feminine gender

₊ Observe, that the noun-substantive is but of one gender: that is to say, either masculine or feminine; as *Dío*, God; *cièlo*, heaven; *giardíno*, garden; are always of the masculine gender, and never of the feminine. *Tèrra*, the earth; *cámera*, a room; are feminine, and never masculine.

The noun-adjective ought to agree with the substantive: when it terminates in *o*, it is masculine; and when it terminates in *a*, it is feminine. Take notice, that all nouns-adjective masculine ending in *o*, may become feminine, by changing *o* into *a*.

bèllo, bèlla ([*]),	handsome.
píccolo, píccola,	little.
buòno, buòna,	good.
sánto, sánta,	holy.

There are some nouns-adjective, which, without changing their termination, are of both genders; and they are those which in Italian end in *e* in the singular number, as *illústre, ammirábile, fácile,* &c. One may say,

un uòmo illústre,	an illustrious man.
una dònna illústre,	an illustrious woman.
uno spírito ammirábile,	a wonderful wit.
una bellézza ammirábile,	a wonderful beauty.
un libro fácile,	an easy book.
una leziòne fácile.	an easy lesson.

₊ Observe, that all nouns-adjective which end in *e* in Italian, are of the common gender.

---

[*] See the N. B. at the end of page 23.

The nouns before which *il* or *lo,* and *la* (*the*) must not be placed indifferently, but only one of them, are nouns-substantive; as, *il sóle,* the sun; *la lúna,* the moon; *il giardíno,* the garden; *il frútto,* the fruit; *la virtù,* virtue; *la prudènza,* prudence.

Nouns that can change *o* into *a* are also adjectives; thus of *dòtto,* learned, you may form *dòtta,* learned; but of *lúna, giardíno, tèrra, &c.* which are nouns-substantive, you cannot form *lúno, giardína, tèrro, &c.*

A noun is also of the singular and plural number.

The singular number is used where we speak of one thing only; as, the prince, *il príncipe;* the body, *il còrpo;* the horse, *il cavállo;* where we speak but of one prince, of one body, and of one horse.

The plural number is used when we speak of more than one; as, the princes, *i príncipi:* the bodies, *i còrpi;* the horses, *i caválli:* here we speak of several princes, several bodies, and several horses.

The little words of two or three letters, as *il* or *lo, la,* in English, *the; i, gli,* and *le,* which signify *the* in the plural, and are placed before nouns to mark the gender, number and case, are called Articles.

OF THE ARTICLES.

The ARTICLE is a declinable word, of one, two or three letters, which is put before the nouns to show their gender and number.

The gender and number have been explained already.

But, not to perplex the memory, I have inserted the explanation of the cases after the parts of speech, as it will be time enough then to learn them; and it is sufficient, at present, to know that the English article is *the,* and that it is used both in the singular and plural number.

You cannot always know the gender, number or case of nouns, except by the article which precedes them. If one should ask, for instance, what gender the word *piède,* a foot, is of, it would be impossible to know, without prefixing an article to it: the articles *il* and *lo* denote the masculine, and *la* the feminine ; so that in saying *il piède*, the foot, the article *il* shows it is of the masculine gender.

In like manner, if a person should ask of what number any other word is, the question could not always be resolved, without putting the articles *il, lo, i* or *gli*, before it, to mark the singular or the plural number.

*** Observe, that when an article comes before a word beginning with a vowel, the last letter of the article must be cut off; that is to say, you retrench the vowel at the end of the article, and in the place of it you put an apostrophe, which is made thus ('). Example; in prefixing an article to *amóre, onóre, ánima*, you must not pronounce or write *lo amóre, lo onóre, la ánima*; but *l'amóre, l'onóre, l'ánima, &c.*

In this manner you retrench the vowel in other cases; *dell' amóre, dell' onóre, dell' ánima; all' amóre, all' onóre, all' ánima; dall' amóre, dall' onóre, dall' ánima.*

OF PRONOUNS.

A PRONOUN, which the Italians call *Pronome* or *Vicenome*, is a declinable part of speech ; so named, because it is used instead of a noun. There are seven sorts of pronouns ; namely,

Pronouns

Personal,	Interrogative,
Conjunctive,	Relative,
Possessive	Improper, or
Demonstrative,	Indefinite.

Of Pronouns Personal.

The pronoun personal marks the three persons ; namely, the first, second and third, as well in the singular as plural.

The first person is he or she, who speaks ; and it is expressed by I, *io* ; we, *nói.*

The pronoun personal *io*, marks the first person singular; as, I speak, *io párlo;* I sing, *io cánto;* I believe, *io crédo; nói* marks the first person plural; as, we speak, *nói parliámo,* &c.

The pronouns personal I, *io;* we, *nói;* belong as well to the masculine gender as to the feminine; so that a woman as well as a man says, I sing, *io cánto;* I see, *io védo;* we sing, *nói cantiámo;* we see, *nói vediámo,* &c.

The second person is that to whom we speak; and it serves also for the masculine and feminine; viz. thou, *tu,* in the singular number; you, *vói,* in the plural; example, thou speakest, *tu párli;* thou dost sing, *tu cánti:* you speak, *vói parláte;* you sing, *vói cantáte,* &c.

The third person is that of whom we speak; namely, he, *egli* or *ésso,* for the masculine; she, *élla* or *essa,* for the feminine; and, in the plural, the masculine makes *églino,* they; the feminine, *élleno;* as, he speaks, *egli párla;* he sings, *egli cánta;* she speaks, *élla párla;* they speak, *églino* or *éssi párlano,* m. *élleno* or *ésse párlano,* f.

*** Observe, that there are only *I* and *we* for the first person: there are also only *thou* and *you* for the second; consequently, every sentence in which there is neither *I, we, thou* nor *you,* must be of the third person; as, the king is willing, *il re vuòle;* the master teaches, *il maèstro insègna,* &c.; both these sentences belong to the third person, because they have neither *I, we, thou* nor *you.*

Of Pronouns Conjunctive.

Although conjunctive pronouns are only an *inflection* of the personal pronouns, and ought not to be treated of separately, we will, however, make a separate class of them, to follow the general custom of grammarians, which we are far from approving.

The pronouns conjunctive in Italian are *mi,* me *or* to me; *ti,* thee *or* to thee; *si,* himself *or* to himself, herself *or* to herself; *ci,* us *or* to us; *vi,* you *or* to you; *lóro,* them *or* to them.

The pronouns conjunctive have a very great resemblance and affinity with the pronouns personal, as they are always put before the verb, except *lóro;* but with this difference, that the pronouns personal make the action of the verb, before which they are placed, and the pronouns conjunctive receive it; example, *io cánto,* I sing; *vói parláte,* you speak : it is the pronouns *I* and *you* which make the action of the verbs *sing* and *speak,* before which they are placed; and consequently they are pronouns personal. But when we say *Dio mi véde,* God sees me, it is *God* constitutes the action of the word *sees,* and *me* receives it. In like manner when we say, *io vi prégo,* I pray you; *vói ci consideráte,* you consider us; I wish to know which are the words in these two phrases that constitute the action of the verbs *pray* and *consider?* It is *I* that pray; therefore *io,* I, is the pronoun personal; and *vi,* you, is the pronoun conjunctive.

In the second phrase, *vói ci consideráte,* you consider us; it is *vói,* you, that is the pronoun personal, and causes the action of the verb *consider;* but the word *ci,* us, that receives it, is the pronoun conjunctive, &c.

Of Pronouns Possessive.

Pronouns possessive mark the possession of a thing; the pronouns possessive are, *my, thy, his* or *her, their, our, your:* example, *my horse; thy hat; his* or *her book; my room; thy daughter; his house; our judgment; our intention; your wit; your pen; my children; my land; thy pleasures; thy actions; his glass; his chaise; our horses; our towns; your clothes; your hands; their father; their kindred.* Properly speaking, possessive pronouns are only those which are employed instead of, and without, the substantive; as, *this is my book:* here *my* is not a possessive pronoun, but a possessive adjective. *Whose book is this? mine :.* here *mine* is a pronoun. In Italian we have no different words to express the possessive pronouns and possessive adjectives, as in French and English; consequently, as they have the same sound, care must be taken not to confound them.

Of Pronouns Demonstrative.

The pronouns demonstrative serve to point out, as it were, a particular person or thing, or persons or things; as, *this* and *that*; *these* and *those*; example, *this coach*; *this woman*; *that man*; *these books*; *those pictures*, &c.

Of Pronouns Interrogative.

The pronoun interrogative is used in asking a question; there are but three in English, namely, *who?* *which?* *what?* example, *what would you have? who is there? what woman is that? what do you mean? which man do you mean?*

Of Pronouns Relative.

A pronoun relative has reference to a thing or person spoken of before; as, *which, who, that,* when they are not interrogatives; example, *the book that I read; the master who teaches; the lesson which I study.*

Of Pronouns Indefinite.

The indefinites are, *every, every one, all, any;* or *nobody, none, several, some, other,* &c. They are also called improper, because, strictly speaking, they are not pronouns.

*** Note, that these pronouns improper are very much like adjectives, being most of them both of the masculine and feminine gender in Italian; but as there is no such distinction as masculine and feminine in the English pronouns improper, there can be no example of them given here; so that I refer beginners to the third chapter concerning pronouns, where it will be rendered more intelligible.

The pronouns indefinite or improper have also their distinction of singular and plural number; but this, as well as the gender, cannot be explained here by examples; it shall be done with more convenience and perspicuity in its proper place.

OF VERBS.

THE Verb and the Noun are the two principal parts of speech.

The Noun serves to name any thing.

The Verb serves to denote every action that may be performed, by expressing the person performing, and the tense or time when performed; as, *to laugh; to love; to sleep; to run; to nourish; to die; to sing; to teach; I love, we love; I laugh, we laugh,* &c. : *I will love, we will love; I will laugh, we will laugh,* &c.

The Verb has neither masculine nor feminine gender; but is distinguished by three *times* or *tenses,* viz. the *present;* the *preterperfect,* or time past; the *future,* or the time to come.   Generally before the verb, there is a pronoun personal; as, *I sing, he sings; we sing, you sing, they sing.   I sang, he sung; I will sing, ye shall sing.*   In which examples, the difference of the time of performing the action is obvious.

The change of time or tense is, in the grammatical phrase, known by the name of *conjugation.*

The conjugation of verbs is composed of four parts, viz. of moods, tenses, persons and number.

OF MOODS.

A MOOD is a grammatical term, used to express the internal operation of the mind and will, and the different ways and manners of acting.

Now this may be done after five manners or moods, and these moods are called indicative, imperative, optative, subjunctive, and infinitive.

The Indicative or Demonstrative, as others call it, is the first mood: it shows and declares simply and absolutely, and without any condition, the thing signified by the verb; as when I say, *I sing, I have sung, I will sing,* one may plainly perceive that there are, in these three examples, the time present, past, and to come, without our being obliged to inquire, whether this verb depends on some particle or mark, as *that, provided that,* &c. in which case, the verb would not be in the indicative, but in the subjunctive.

The Imperative marks the action of the verb in commanding and forbidding : example, *sing you, do not sing ; go thou, do not go.* It is obvious that, in the foregoing examples, the person speaks either in the way of command or prohibition ; and, of course, in the imperative.

The Optative expresses the action of the verb by wishing and desiring ; as, *would I had five hundred pounds a-year! could I but go to Rome! had I but that, how happy should I be!*

The Subjunctive or Conjunctive, is so called, because it is generally used with conjunctions before it : such as, *that, although, to the end that, provided that :* example, *my master is willing that I do my duty ; although he says that I may write ; provided that he come ; he desires that I may sing.* The verbs, *do, say, write, come,* and *sing,* which follow the conjunctions, are of the subjunctive mood.

The manner of applying conjunctions to verbs will be illustrated when we come to speak of the syntax of verbs, in the second part of this Grammar, to which we refer the reader.

The Infinitive represents the action of the verb, without marking either the number or person ; as, *to love, to write ;* one cannot tell by what number of persons this action, *to love* or *to write,* is to be done, nor who is to do it.

OF TENSES.

VERBS have properly but three tenses ; the present, the preter, and the future.

The Present denotes a thing done at the very time we are speaking ; as, *I sing, you sing,* &c.

The Preter, or time past, denotes an action which is no longer present ; as, 1. *I was singing :* 2. *I sung :* 3. *I have sung :* 4. *I had sung.*

These four examples plainly show that an action may be passed in four different manners, which is the reason that there are four different tenses which mark the time past; they are,

1. The preterimperfect.	3. The preterperfect.
2. The preterperfect definite.	4. The preterpluperfect.

The Preterimperfect serves for the actions which were present at a certain time; example, *I was singing when you came in :* the words, *I was singing,* show that the action of singing was doing when you came in.

The English language has not a proper and *exclusive* form corresponding to the Italian or Latin preterimperfect, but in the phrase, *I was singing when you came in :* although the expression, *I was singing,* may be employed also in other instances besides this, it does, however, in this instance convey the idea of the imperfect Italian present: that is, the English definite sense must be translated into the Italian imperfect, when it conveys, as to time, the same idea as the expression, *I was singing,* does in the above-quoted instance.

The Preterperfect definite marks and defines the time, the year, or the day, when the action was done; as, *I sung yesterday; I spoke to the king last year.*

We also make use of this tense, in telling or relating any action: example, *last year the king took the field; he made himself master of several towns, and conquered whole provinces; he defeated the enemy, who made a vigorous defence; he struck a terror into his neighbours, and at last forced them to accept of such a peace as he pleased to prescribe.* All the verbs of this example are in the preterperfect definite.

Those who do not understand Latin, have some difficulty to distinguish the preterimperfect from the preterperfect definite: in order to comprehend this matter, attend to the two following observations :—

⁂ 1. That the preterimperfect may be applied to a time past, or to that which is still in being. By the time still in being, or not quite past, we are to understand a day, a night, a week, a month, a year, the age we live in.

By the past time, or that which is no more, we understand yesterday, the day before yesterday, last week, last month, last year, last century.   Hence we may use the preterimperfect thus: *I was writing to-day; I was singing this week; I was reading this month.* On the contrary, the preterperfect definite is applied to the time past, and never to that still in being : we may say, *I wrote yesterday; I read last week;* but we must not say, *I wrote to-day: I did read to-day.*

2. But to make the difference between the preterimperfect and the preterperfect definite more plain and intelligible to ladies, it is sufficient to know, that the first person of the preterimperfect is always terminated in *vo* or *va*, in Italian ; as *amáva,* I was loving ; *cantáva,* I was singing ; *godéva,* I was enjoying, &c. The preterperfect definite never has that termination : as, *amái,* I loved ; *godéi,* I enjoyed, &c.

The Preterperfect expresses actions perfectly past ; as, I have sung, *ho cantáto;* I have enjoyed, *ho godúto.*

Observe, that we always make use of a verb and participle to express the preterperfect or compound tense ; as, I have written, *ho scritto.* It is obvious, that *ho* is the verb, and *scritto* the participle. These are expressed in Italian as well as in English ; but in Latin they make use of a single verb only.

We generally use the preterperfect to express an action done at a time which is still in being and not entirely elapsed, as, *I have given; I have written; I have spoken to-day, this morning, this week, this month, in my life-time,* &c.; and not as some people, who confound the preterperfect definite with the preterperfect, saying, *I gave, I spoke to-day, this month,* &c. because *to-day, this month,* &c. are times still in being, which we ought to express by the preterperfect, *I have given, I have spoken,* &c. *to-day, this month,* &c.

The Preterpluperfect denotes not only an action perfectly past, but likewise shows that it was over, before another action of which we are speaking, began ; example, *I had supped, when you were singing; I had done writing, when you entered.*

Here it appears plainly that there are four preterites, or past tenses ; viz. two simple, and two compound.

The simple are the preterimperfect and the preterperfect definite, which in Italian are expressed by a single verb, with a pronoun personal before it; as, *leggéva*, I was reading; *leggévi*, thou wast reading; *leggéva*, he was reading; *léssi*, I read; *leggésti*, thou readest; *lésse*, he read. In these examples, there is no more than one verb.

The two compound preterites are the preterperfect and the preterpluperfect; which are always expressed by a verb and a participle, as, I have written, *ho scritto;* thou hast written, *hai scritto;* he has written, *ha scritto,* &c.; I had given, *io aveva dato;* thou hadst given, *tu avevi dato;* he had given, *egli aveva dato,* &c.

The Future is a tense that signifies something to come; as, I will sing, *canterò;* I will speak, *parlerò,* &c. It is either simple or compound; simple in the examples above mentioned; compound when I say, I shall have read, *avrò lètto;* I shall have written, *avrò scritto,* &c.

OF PERSONS.

The tenses of verbs are composed of three Persons.

The first is always expressed by *I* in the singular number, and by *we* in the plural; as, *I sing, we sing.*

The second person is marked by *thou* in the singular, and *you* in the plural; as, *thou singest, you sing.*

The third is *he* or *she* in the singular, and *they* in the plural; as, *he* or *she speaks, they speak.*

OF NUMBERS.

The tenses of the verbs have also two Numbers, the singular and the plural; singular, *I love, thou lovest, he loveth;* plural, *we love, ye* or *you love, they love.*

OF PARTICIPLES.

The Participles are so called, because, although they are verbs, they partake of the nature and quality of adjectives; as, *amáto, amáta,* loved; *ornáto, ornáta,* adorned: one may say, *I loved,* and *I have loved; I adored, I have adored:* which are verbs; we also say, *a man beloved, a woman loved, a God adored;* then those words, *loved, beloved, adored,* &c. are nouns adjective, and consequently, participles, from their partaking of the nature of adjectives and verbs, and from their serving to form the preterperfect.

⁂ Observe, that whenever two verbs follow one another in the same phrase, and the first is one of the tenses of the verbs *to have* or *to be,* the second is a participle, as, *I have seen, you have spoken, he has written, I am loved, we are commended:* the words *seen, spoken, written, loved, commended,* are participles.

The former five parts of speech, namely, the Article, Noun, Pronoun, Verb, and Participle, change their terminations in Italian: example, *il cavállo del príncipe è bèllo,* the prince's horse is handsome: *i caválli dei príncipi sono bèlli,* the princes' horses are handsome. By these two examples, you may see the change of the articles, nouns, and verbs. By the two following you will observe a change of the pronouns and participles.

La vòstra lèttera è scrítta in una manièra affettuósa e famigliáre.	Your letter is written in an affectionate and familiar style.
Le vòstre lèttere sono scrítte in tèrmini affettuósi e famigliári.	Your letters are written in affectionate and familiar terms.

The other four parts of speech admit of no alteration: as, *bène,* well, which is an adverb; *con,* with, a preposition; *che,* that, a conjunction; *oimè,* alas, an interjection: these are constantly pronounced and written in the same manner; and it may be observed, that these words have neither gender, number, case nor time.

OF ADVERBS.

Adverbs are words that help to express in a better manner what the verb denotes, and add more or less force and significancy to it; as *well, ill, more, plainly, better, hardly:* example, when I say, *I teach,* this expression shows what I do, that is, *I teach;* but it does not point out the manner how I teach. To convey this meaning, I add an adverb; thus, *I teach plainly.* We have already observed, that adverbs have neither gender, number, nor case.

There are a great many kind of adverbs; but I shall here only give examples of two or three of the most common.

Adverbs of time; such as, *when, yesterday, to-night, to-day, to-morrow, late, soon, a long while, always, never,* &c.

Adverbs of place; as, *where, here, there, above, below, towards, far, near,* &c.

Adverbs of quantity; as, *how much, how many, much, as much, little,* &c.

OF PREPOSITIONS.

Prepositions, like Adverbs, have neither gender, number nor case; they are always prefixed to nouns, articles and verbs, and therefore are called prepositions, from the Latin word *præponere,* to set before; as, *upon, near, before, without, out, in, against, for;* as, *upon the house, near the palace, in the garden, against reason, in court, before the king,* &c.

⁕ Observe, that there is a great difference between the adverb and preposition; for the adverb requires nothing after it, but the sense of it is complete without the addition of another word: example, *he teaches well, you speak learnedly, you write fast,* &c. But, on the contrary, the preposition always requires some word to follow it; for example, *you are before me, it is upon the table, they are in the garden,* &c.

⁕ Observe, also, that the prepositions sometimes become adverbs, when we speak absolutely, and there is neither article, noun, nor pronoun, after the prepositions; for instance, *my brother walks before, he will come after, they are behind, she is near.*

In these four examples, *before, after, behind,* and *near* are adverbs; but if we said, *my brother walks before his company, he will come after us, the servant is behind us, she is near us;* then, *before, after, behind, near,* are prepositions.

OF CONJUNCTIONS.

The Conjunctions serve to join and connect words and sentences together; such as, *and, or, but, though, that, as, provided that, in short,* &c. Example, *Peter* and *Paul, black* or *white: I promised it to you,* but *you must give it me again.*

OF INTERJECTIONS.

The Interjections are words that make sense of themselves, and serve to express any violent emotion; as, *alas! fie! courage! halt! hush!*

AN EXPLANATION OF THE CASES*.

The variation of articles, nouns, and pronouns, is called a Declension.

The change of verbs is called a Conjugation.

A declension has six variations, which are called Cases; viz. nominative, genitive, dative, accusative, vocative and ablative.

The case, or variation of nouns, is known only by the articles.

I must here repeat what I have before observed when treating of the articles, viz. when an article happens to precede a word beginning with a vowel, the vowel at the end of the article is retrenched, and an apostrophe is placed in its stead.

The articles of the nominative are, *the,* both in the singular and plural in English; as, *the sun, the earth, the ladies.*

This case is called the nominative, from *nominare,* to

---

* *A great part of this Treatise of Cases is applicable only to the learned, and to some foreign languages, such as French, Italian, &c.; for the English have no variation in the noun except the genitive, as,* man, man's, *and none at all in the article, since they only make use of the little signs or particles, to distinguish the cases; as* of, to, for, from, &c.

name; because it declares the name of any thing with
the article *the*, and this article, with the following noun
makes the nominative; as, *the sun, the moon, the earth,
the horses, the men, the women*.

The articles of the genitive are, *of the*, and *of*; for instance, *of the sun, of the moon, of the earth, of London*.

We give the name of the genitive to this case, because
it shows the author or cause of the noun of which we
speak; for example, when we say, *the heat of the sun*;
in this example, *of the sun*, is the genitive case, because
the sun is the author and the cause that produced the
name *heat*; and so, in the following example: *the length
of the street, the father's son, the fruit of the tree, the
beauty of Paris*.

The word genitive comes from the Latin *gignere*,
which signifies to produce.

The dative is marked by the articles *to the* and *to*,
for the singular and plural; example, *to the sun, to the
prince, to London, to the men, to the houses*, &c.

The dative serves to make known to whom, or to
what, we give or address the thing spoken of: as, *to
give alms to the poor; to write to the king, to the queen,
to London, to Rome*. The word dative comes from *dare*,
to give.

The accusative is like the nominative, and the articles
are the same: as, *the sun, the earth, the women*.

The word accusative is derived from the Latin *accu-
sare*, to accuse.

The only difference between these two cases is, that
the nominative is before the verb, and the accusative
after it.   •

To distinguish the nominative from the accusative,
you have only to remember, that the nominative names
the person or thing that makes the action of the verb,
and the accusative accuses or names that which receives
it: example, *the king loves the queen*.

The king is the nominative case, because it is the king
that makes the action of loving; and *the queen* is the
accusative, because it is the queen that receives the
action of loving from the king.

⁎ Note, that the accusative is generally put after

verbs active and prepositions ; as, *I behold the sun, with the princes, for the king*, &c.

The vocative is always distinguished by the interjection *O ;* it is used in calling out to a person : example, *O Peter, O Paul*, &c. Most commonly we put no article at all to express the vocative ; as, *Sir, Madam, Mary, Peter*, &c.

The word vocative comes from the Latin *vocare*, to call.

The ablative, in English, is expressed by the articles *from the, from* and *by*.

The ablative is generally put after the verbs passive. Now, the ladies, and those who do not understand Latin, will easily know what a verb passive is, being always composed of two verbs ; the first of which is some tense of the verb *essere*, to be, and the other a participle : so that these two together make a verb passive, after which the ablative case is put : example, *I am esteemed by the king*.

The ablative is also used after the following verbs, *to take away, to receive, to obtain, to separate*, &c.

Examples :

To take from the . . . hands.
I have received from the prince.
He is separated from . . me.
I came from . . . . . Italy.

The last words are in the ablative case.

The word ablative derives its origin from the Latin *ablatum*, which signifies, taken away ; *I am beloved by the prince. I have received a hundred pounds from the prince.*

This is the same thing as if I should say, *I have received from the prince, his love, and a hundred pounds.*

When the pupil is sufficiently versed in the foregoing particulars, and understands the meaning of tenses, genders, numbers, and persons, he may then be exercised in the parts of speech contained therein :

For Example,

The soldiers who fight bravely for their king are esteemed and praised by the whole kingdom.

The is a definite article of the plural number, of the masculine gender, and the nominative case.

Soldiers, is a noun substantive, of the same number, gender, and case.

Who, a pronoun relative of the plural number, and nominative case.

Fight, a verb of the pres. indic. and 3rd person plural.

Bravely, an adverb.—*For,* a preposition.

Their, a pronoun possessive.

King, a noun substantive, masculine, in the accusative singular.

Are, a verb in the third person plural, and present indicative.—*Esteemed,* a participle.

Are esteemed, a verb passive, of the third person plural, and present indicative.

And, a conjunction.—*Praised,* a participle.

Are praised, a verb passive, of the third person plural, and present indicative.

By, a preposition.—*All,* a pronoun indefinite.

Kingdom, a noun substantive, masculine.

By the whole, in the ablative ; because *are esteemed,* and *are praised,* are both verbs passive, and require an ablative case after them.

METHOD OF FINDING OUT THE WORDS IN A DICTIONARY.

Nouns substantive are to be found by their singular number, and not by their plural; therefore you must not look for *heavens, horses,* &c., but *heaven, horse,* &c. Nouns adjective are sought for by the masculine, and not by the feminine : for example, to know the Italian of *fine,* you must look for *bèllo,* and not *bèlla.*

The method of finding out verbs in a dictionary, is by their infinitives. In English, the infinitive is known by the participle *to* placed before the verb, as *to love, to sing.* In Italian, the infinitives terminate in *áre, ére,* or *íre.* So that if I want to know the infinitive of *amiámo, cediámo, sentiámo* I must not look for *ámo, crédo, sènto,* but for *amáre, crédere, sentíre,* and so form them according to the rules of each conjugation.

The augmentatives and diminutives, or nouns increased or diminished in their signification, are very rarely given in dictionaries; the rules, therefore, for their formation, will be found explained where the noun is treated of.

THE

COMPLETE ITALIAN MASTER.

PART I.

THE first thing necessary to be acquired is, the ITALIAN PRONUNCIATION; this is confined to some syllables which the Italians pronounce differently from the English, as may be seen at the end of this discourse, where the whole difficulty of the Italian pronunciation is included in a period of seven lines.

OF THE ITALIAN PRONUNCIATION.

The Italian language contains twenty-two letters, which are pronounced by the Tuscans in the following manner: in some other parts of Italy they pronounce the letters *b, c, d, g, p, t, z,* as with a single *e* after them, saying *be, tche, de,* &c.: but the pronunciation of TUSCANY, which is the most correct, is, as nearly as can be expressed in writing, as follows:

A		*aa,*	M		*èmmay,*
B		*bee,*	N		*ènnay,*
C		*tchee,*	O		*o,*
D		*dee,*	P		*pee,*
E	Pronounced	*a,*	Q	Pronounced	*coo,*
F		*èffay,* (p. 24)	R		*èrray,*
G		*dgge,*	S		*èssay,*
H		*acca,*	T		*tee,*
I		*e,*	U		*oo,*
J		*ee,*	V		*voo,*
L		*èllay.*	Z		*dzaita.*

Hence it appears that the Italian pronunciation is very different from the English; and we must be careful to sound the letters, as nearly as possible, as they are marked in the preceding alphabet.

The Italians have no such letter as *k, x, w* or *y*; at least they never make use of them, except in writing foreign names, as *Stockholm, Xenócrate*, &c., and then they pronounce the former word as if it were a *c* instead of *k*, and the latter as if it were an *S* instead of the letter *X*. You are also at liberty to write *Stocolm* and *Senócrate*.

The letters are divided into vowels and consonants, as has been already remarked in the Introduction.

VOWELS.

OF THE PRONUNCIATION OF THE VOWELS.

THE vowels, which are *a, e, i* or *j, o, u*, are pronounced *ah, a, e, ee, o, oo.*

A is always sounded open and broad, like *a* in the English word *arm, art;* thus *amo*, I love, *amante*, lover, &c.; when *a* is accented at the end of a word *à*, it has a quicker, louder and sharper tone than otherwise; thus in *calamità*, calamity, the *a* must be pronounced sharper and louder than in *calamíta*, a loadstone.

E is never mute in Italian, as it often is in French, but it has two sounds, one close and one open; *e close* sounds like *ai* in *pain*, as in *pena*, pain; *legge*, law; *venti*, twenty, &c.; it is generally close in Italian words derived from the Latin, in which the *i* in Latin was changed into *e* in Italian; as *sélva*, from *sylva*, wood; *pésce*, from *piscis*, fish, &c. &c.; *e* is always close at the end of words of more than one syllable; example, *Arse di spème, e pèrde il cor dolènte*; he was inflamed with hope, and his heart is overwhelmed with grief.

E has an open sound, like *e* in *let;* as *tèma*, a theme; *lègge*, he reads; *vènti*, winds, &c. See NB. at p. 23.

E is open before *st* in nouns substantive, as *fèsta*, a festival; *vèste*, a garment; *arrèsto*, an arrest.

N. B. Exceptions to the above rule are, *césto*, a tuft of grass; *destíno*, destiny; *destrézza*, dexterity; *mestízia*, sadness.

Mele, with an open *e*, pronounced *malay*, signifies *honey*; and with *e* close, signifies *apples*.

I is pronounced like *ee* in the English word *feet*; as *diritto*, direct, pronounce *dereetto*; *cimiterio*, a churchyard, pronounce *tchemeetareo*.

O, as well as the vowel *e*, has also two sounds, one *close*, like *o* in *note*, as in *foro*, hole; *tòrta*, tart, &c.; *open*, as *o* in *not*, in *fòro*, the bar; *torta*, twisted, &c.

OF *O* CLOSE.

O (like *E*) is generally close in Italian words derived from the Latin, in which the *u* of the Latin word was changed into *o* in the Italian; as *dolce*, from the Latin *dulcis*, sweet; *molto*, from *multum*, many; *volgo*, from *vulgus*, vulgar, &c. &c., which words pronounce, softening the *o* a little, *dolche, molto, volgo*.

O is close when accented, in words ending in *óne, óra, óre, óso*; as *orazióne*, prayer; *qualóra*, whenever; *Signóre*, Sir; *amoróso*, amorous.

O is also close before *l, m, n, r*; as *volére*, to be willing; *tómba*, a grave; *baróne*, baron; *córte*, a court. N. B. Except when preceded by *i* or *u*.

O is close before *gn*; as *Bologna*, which pronounce *Bolonnia*; *bisogno*, want, pronounce *bisonnio*, &c. &c.; and it is also close before *s* in adjectives; as *amoróso*, amorous, &c.

OF *O* OPEN.

O is pronounced open when preceded by *i* or *u*; as *chiòma*, head of hair, pronounce *keomah*; *Giòve*, pronounce *Jovey*; *cuòre*, a heart, pronounce *core*. The final *ò*, when accented, is likewise open, as *amò, parlò*, &c.; and so it is in all monosyllables, as *fo, so, vo*, &c.

O is also open before *s* in substantives; as *ròsa*, a rose; *spòsa*, a spouse.

U is pronounced like *oo* in English; example, *pubblicazióne*, pronounce *pooblecatseónay*.

N. B. Before we proceed with the pronunciation of letters and syllables, we must observe that there is in Italian, as well as in English, an *accent* or *stress* on a peculiar syllable of every word; but it has no fixed place, and it is only marked by this accent (`) when it falls on the last vowel of a word, as in *farò, necessità, virtù*.

Most Italian words have the *stress* or *tonic accent*, on the last syllable but one, as in *ple-bè-o, no-ió-so, ab-bièt-to*, &c. Thus to avoid any doubt, we will mark with this accent (´) all the vowels on which the stress is to be laid, and we will make use of this accent (`) on the *e* and *o* when open.

CONSONANTS.

OF THE PRONUNCIATION OF CONSONANTS.

THE consonants *b, d, f, l, m, n, p, r,* are pronounced as in English.

Some of the consonants vary from the English pronunciation, especially *c, g, z,* to which may be added *h, t,* and *s,* and upon each of which there are several particulars to be observed.

C, before the vowels *a, o, u,* and before the consonants *l, r,* is pronounced the same as in English; as *cása*, a house; *còllo*, a neck; *cúra*, care; *Cristo*, Christ; *clemènza*, clemency; *crudèle*, cruel.

C, before the vowels *e* or *i*, sounds like *che* and *chi* in the English words *cherry* and *chick;* examples:

		Pronounce
Césare,	Cæsar,	*Chésare*
Cecità,	blindness,	*checheetà*
Città,	a city,	*chittà*

If two *cc's* come before the vowels *e* or *i*, the former is sounded as *t*, and the latter like *che* in *cherry;* example, *accènto*, an accent, pronounce *atchènto; bráccio*, an arm, pronounce *brátcheo*.

When after *ci* there is a vowel, as *cia, cie, cio, ciu*, it must be pronounced as one syllable, so as to lose, in some measure, the sound of the vowel *i;* examples, *Fráncia, cièlo, bácio*, pronounce *Fránchea, cheáylo, bácheo*.

The syllables *sce, sci*, are pronounced *sha, she;*

example, *scemáre*, to diminish, pronounce *shaymáray;* *lasciáre*, to leave, pronounce *lashéaray*.

Ch is used instead of, and pronounced like, the letter *k*, which the Italians never use but in foreign names; as *Bochsa*, pronounce *Boksa*.

The syllables *che*, *chi*, whether in the beginning or at the end of a word, are pronounced *ka*, *ke:* example: *cherubíno*, a cherubin: *chiódo*, a nail; *giovènchi*, heifers: pronounce *kayroobeeno*, *keódo*, *giovènkee*.

F is used by the Italians instead of *ph*, as *Efeso*, Ephesus; *filòsofo*, philosopher; *frase*, phrase.

G before the vowels *a, o, u*, and before consonants, is pronounced as in English; example: *gábbia*, a cage; *gòbbo*, hunchbacked; *gústo*, taste; *grádo*, a degree; *grído*, a cry.

G before *e, i*, is pronounced as in the English words *geography, gin*, as in *gèlo, giro*.

When after the syllable *gi* there is another vowel, as *gia, gio, giu*, the *g* is pronounced like an English *j;* as in *giardíno, giórno, giúdice*, pronounce *jardíno, jórno, júditchay*.

When two *g*'s precede the vowels *e, i*, the first *g* is pronounced as a *d*, and the last as a *g;* for example: *oggètto*, an object: *òggi*, to-day; read *odgètto, òdgi*.

G before *li* is pronounced like *ll* in the French word *fille*, or like the *ll* in the English words *million, brilliant;* first, in the different inflections of the article and pronoun *il, lo;* secondly, in the pronoun, *egli, eglino;* thirdly, when it is followed by a vowel, and forms a diphthong, as in *vaglio, maglio*.

The syllables *gna, gne, gni, gno, gnu*, are pronounced something like *nniar, nnie, nni, nnio, nniu;* for example: *guadagnáre*, to gain; *agnèllo*, a lamb; *ignùdo*, naked; *incògnito*, unknown; read *guadanniare, anniéllo, inniúdo, incónnieeto*. In short *gn*, before a vowel, retains the same sound as in the French words, *Allemagne, Boulogne, montagne*. The words *negligènza*, negligence; *negligènte*, negligent; *negligere*, to neglect; *Anglicáno*, Briton; and *Anglia* (poet.), England, are sounded hard, as in English.

The syllables *ghe, ghi*, are pronounced like *gue* and

c

gui in the English words *guest* and *guinea ;* as *bottéghe,*
shops, sound *bottéguay; luòghi,* places, sound *luògui.*

The letter *h* is never aspirated, nor pronounced at the
beginning of words ; as, *ho,* I have, &c.   But according
to the modern orthography, all words are written without an *h,* except the three persons singular, and the
third person plural, of the present indicative of the verb
avére ; and this in order to distinguish the verb *ho* from
the sign of the vocative *O,* or from *o* the conjunction ; as
likewise *hái,* from *ái,* the article, in the dative plural
masculine gender, *ái signóri,* to the lords or gentlemen ;
ha from the dative indefinite, *a Piètro,* to Peter ; and
lastly *hánno* from *anno,* which signifies a year.

The letter *j* was considered sometimes as a consonant,
and sometimes as a vowel ; but according to the present
orthography, it is only considered as a vowel when used
instead of *ii ;* as the plural of names ending in *io* in the
singular, as in *princípj, tempj ;* where it is pronounced
long ; almost as a double *i.*

S, in the beginning of words, is pronounced as in
English ; for example: *salúte, sóle, sále, singoláre,
sèrvo, sópra.*

Sa, in these words, *casa,* house ; *còsa,* a thing ; *rósa,*
gnawed, must be pronounced like the first syllable of
salúte, that is to say, strong.

The same may be said of all adjectives ending in *óso ;*
as *glorióso,* glorious ; *vittorióso,* victorious ; as well in
the singular as in the plural, masculine and feminine.
It is generally pronounced as in the English words
misery, desire, &c., when preceded by an open *ò,* as in
spòso, esòso, except in the word *ripòso.*

S will take the same sound in the adjectives terminating in *ese,* and in words in *uso,* except *fúso,* a
spindle, where the *s* must be sounded as in *salúte.*

Così, in like manner, is pronounced with a strong
hissing sound, the same as in *casa* and *cosa.*

S, between two vowels, is generally sounded like a *z ;*
as *sa, se, si, so,* read and pronounce them as if they were
written, *za, ze, zi, zo ;* but in all words that have *si*
added to them, as *scrivesi,* they write, *s* preserves its
natural sound.

In the following words the syllable *ti* is pronounced hard : as, *simpatia*, sympathy ; *natio*, native, or genuine ; *mallattia*, illness ; *questióne*, question ; *molèstia*, trouble ; and a few verbs, as *tiène, potiáte, patiámo, patiáte*, which are to be acquired only by practice.

V, in Italian, is pronounced as in English.

Z, like *s*, has two sounds ; in some words as *ds* in *Windsor*, in others as *ts* in *nits*. It is like *ds* or *dz* in all words in which the *z* is used both in Italian and English, as in

gazzétta	gazette, Pronounce	*gadzétta*
Lázzaro	Lazarus	*Ládzaro*
zèffiro	zephyr	*dzèffero*
zodíaco	zodiac	*dzodéaco*
zòna	zone	*dzòna*, &c. &c.

Z is also pronounced like *dz* in the following words :

grézzo	clownish	Pron. *gredzzo*
gazza	magpie	*gadza*
mèzzo	middle	*medzzo*
rézza	gauze	*rédzza*
zeba	goad	*dzaba*
zèlo	zeal	*dzalo*
Zenofónte	Xenophon	*Dzenofòntay*
zèta	Z	*dzayta*
zendádo	tiffany	*dzendádo*
zénzero	ginger	*dzénzaro*
ziffera	cipher	*dzeffara*

Z (single as well as double) is pronounced like *ts* in all words in which it is followed by two vowels, the first being *i*, as *Fázio; grázia*, grace ; *spázio*, space ; *azióne*, action ; *zio*, uncle, &c. &c. ; pronounce *Fatsio, gratsia, spatsio, atsionay, tsio*. It is also pronounced as *ts* when preceded by *l* or *r*; as in

calza	stocking	Pron. *caltsa*
fòrza	force	*fòrtsa*
sbalzo	a jump	*sbaltso*
tèrzo	third	*tèrtso*, &c. &c.

Exceptions—*garzóne*, a boy; *scòrza*, bark; and *òrzo*, barley; in which the *z* has rather a softer sound.

All the other *Z*'s (single and double) are pronounced like *ts* when before or after an *e* or *o* close, as in

Arezzo	Arezzo	Pron. *Aretso*
avvézzo	accustomed	*avvetso*
bellézza	beauty	*belletsa*
fazzolétto	handkerchief	*fatsolétto*
gentilézza	gentility	*gentilétsa*
pèzzo	a piece	*pètso*
pózzo	a well	*pótso*
prèzzo	prize	*prètso*
ribrézzo	fear	*ribrétso*
zeppo	block	*tseppo*
Mazéppa	Mazeppa	*Matzeppah*

All words with *z*, pronounced either like *dz* or *ts*, require a slight pause or stress on the *d* or *t*, thus *mèzzo*, *gentilézza*, *nòzze*, pronounce *mèd-zo*, *gentilét-sa*, *nòt-se*, &c.

Observe, finally, that great attention must be paid to double consonants between vowels; thus: *secco*, dry; *cadde*, he fell; *fummo*, we were; *carro*, cart; *fatto*, fact; *Avvènto*, Advent, &c., must receive a fuller sound than *seco*, with him; *cade*, he falls; *fumo*, smoke; *caro*, dear; *fato*, fate; *evento*, event.

A COLLECTION OF WORDS AND SYLLABLES, MOST DIFFICULT TO BE PRONOUNCED.

BEFORE you proceed to this collection, attend to the pronunciation of the syllables, *cia, cie, cio, ciu ; sce, sci, scio, sciu ; gia, gie, gio, giu ; gli, glia, glio.*

Ce, ci, pronounce as *che, chi,* in *cherry* and *chick.*

Ciceróne, céci, cecilà, cénere, céna, cenáre, cérchio, cíbo, cillà, citáre, accènto, bácio, ciaschedúno, cièlo, cioè, ciúrma.

Che, chi, pronounce *ka, kee.*

Che díte? che fáte? che voléte? chi cercáte? chi voléte? chi domandáte?

Ge, gi, pronounce, *dge, dgi ;* and *gli* as *lli* in *million, William,* &c.

Gèsto, gènio, gèlo, gènte, gíro, giúdice, maggióre, leggiádro, giórno, gióvane, Giúgno ; fíglio, pigliáre ; gionchíglia, fòglio, orgòglio.

Gna, gne, gni, gno, gnu, pronounce *nniar, nnia, nniee, nnio, nnioo,* in one syllable, as we have already observed when treating of the pronunciation of consonants.

Bagnáre, guadagnáre, légna, ingegnerò, magnífico, pégno, légno, signóre, ingégno, ignúdo.

Scia, sce, sci, scio, sciu, pronounce, *shea, sha, she, sho, shiu. Sciática, scégliere, discifráre, disciògliere, asciútto.*

Sa, se, si, so.

Pronounce the *s* as in *hiss* in the words *salúte, casa, còsa, ròsa, róso, virtuóso, così.*

c 3

U, pronounce *oo*.

Tu, virtù, pugnàre, púgno, matúro, funèsto, múro, brúno.

U, before *o*.

When those two vowels form but one syllable, the *u* must be pronounced almost insensibly.

Buòno, fuòco, giuòco, figliuòlo, figliuòla.

Except from this rule *túo, súo, suòcero, suòcera, virtuóso,* &c., because the *u* and *o* are two syllables.

The Florentines, in the words *buòno, fuòco*, &c., pronounce the *u* rather stronger than the Romans, who indeed sound those words in such a manner as if there were no *u* at all.

Z or *zz*, pronounce *ts*.

In the words *nòzze, fazzolétto, pózzo, pazzía, pázzo, ragázzo,* &c.

Z or *zz*, pronounce *dz*.

In the words *mèzzo, Lázzaro, zòna, zodiaco, zigríno, rózzo, sozzo,* &c.

Z, pronounce like *ts* soft,

In words ending in *anza, enza, onza;* example: *ignoránza, diligènza, Magónza.*

To acquire the true Italian accent, it will be necessary attentively to read over the following lines, in which all the difficulties lie in the syllables marked with a star: whoever has learned to pronounce these properly, will soon be master of the Italian pronunciation.

AN EXERCISE FOR ITALIAN PRONUNCIATION.

Ciaschedúno sa, che cóme non v' è còsa, ché più dispiáccia a Dio, che l' ingratitúdine ed inosserváanza de' suòi precètti; così non v'è niènte che cagióni maggiormènte la desolazióne dell' univèrso, che la cecità e supèr-

bia degli uòmini, la pazzía de' Gentíli, l'ignoránza, e l' ostinazióne de' Giudèi e scismátici.

"Every one knows, that as there is nothing which displeases God more than ingratitude, and the neglect of his commandments: so there is nothing that occasions the desolation of this world more than the blindness and pride of men, the folly of the Gentiles, the ignorance and obstinacy of Jews and schismatics."

A RECAPITULATION OF THE ITALIAN PRONUNCIATION.

	Pron.	Example.	Pron.
A	ah	*arte*	arte
C *ca*	cah	*cása*	kasa
cc	tche	*accènto*	attchènto
ce	che (³)	*céna*	chena
che	ka	*che*	ka
chi	kee	*chi*	ke
ci	chi (⁴)	*città*	chittà
cia	chia	*ciascúno*	chiascoono
cie	chie	*cièlo*	chielo
cio	tchio	*bácio*	bacheo
cru	croo	*crudèle*	croodaylay
E (*close*)	pen	*pena*	paynah
(*opèn*)	ta	*tèma*	tamah
G *ga*	gar	*gábbia*	gábbiah
ge	dge	*gènio*	dgaynio
ghe	gue	*bottéghe*	bottégey
ghi	gui	*luòghi*	luògui
gi	dgi	*gíro*	dgeero
gia	ja	*giardíno*	jardino
gie	je	*gièlo*	Jaylo
gio	jo	*Giòve*	Jòvay
giu	joo	*giústo*	joosto
glo	glo	*glòria*	glòreeah

---

³ As in che-rish.   ⁴ As in chi-valry.

	Pron.	Example.	Pron.
gli	lli	*pigliáre*	pilliaray
gna	nniar	*regnáre*	renniaray
O (*close*)	pole	*volére*	volayray
(*open*)	raw	*ròsa*	rawza
S (*strong*)	san	*sánto*	sánto
(*soft*)	sa	*guísa*	gwesah
sce	shiay	*scèna*	shanah
sci	shi	*lasciáre*	lasheahray
U	oo	*virtù*	veertóo
V	viv	*vívere*	veveray
vv		*avveníre*	a-veneere
Z as *s*	sa	*diligènza*	delegentsa
ts	fats	*Fázio*	Fatzio
dz	dze	*Zèffiro*	dzef'erow

N. B. Notwithstanding the foregoing copious illustration of this essential part of the Italian language, a natural and correct pronunciation can only be acquired by an attentive ear to the lessons and accentuation of an experienced master, a native of Italy.

CHAPTER I.

OF ARTICLES

IN GENERAL (').

THERE are two sorts of articles: one Definite, the other Indefinite.

The Definite marks the gender, number and case of the nouns which it precedes, as

The prince,	*il príncipe*
Of the prince	*del príncipe.*
To the prince,	*al príncipe.*
From or by the prince,	*dal príncipe.*
The princes,	*i príncipi.*
Of the princes,	*déi príncipi.*
To the princes,	*ái príncipi.*
From or by the princes,	*dái príncipi.*
The earth, land or ground,	*la tèrra.*
Of the earth,	*délla tèrra.*
To the earth,	*álla tèrra.*
From or by the earth,	*dálla tèrra.*
The earths,	*le tèrre.*
Of the earths,	*délle tèrre.*
To the earths,	*álle tèrre.*
From or by the earths,	*dálle tèrre.*

The articles *il* or *lo, la, del, dello, della, al, allo, alla,*

See BOTARELLI's EXERCISES, p. 14.

dal, dallo, dalla, i, gli, le, are called Definite articles, because they mark and define the masculine or feminine gender, and the singular or plural number of nouns to which they are prefixed.

The Definite articles have six cases, the nominative, genitive, dative, accusative, vocative and ablative.

The Indefinite article may be put before the masculine, as well as the feminine gender, before the singular, as well as the plural number.

The Indefinite articles (or more properly prepositions) in Italian are the following monosyllables :

di, a (or *ad* before a vowel), and *da.*

Although it would be more proper to call these monosyllables *prepositions,* we shall adopt the name used by other grammarians in conformity with custom.

Di may be put before a noun masculine as well as feminine ; as *úna coróna di re,* a king's crown ; *úna libbra di páne,* a pound of bread ; the words *re* and *páne* are masculine : *un cappèllo di páglia,* a straw hat ; *tre libbre di cárne,* three pounds of meat ; the words *páglia* and *cárne* are of the feminine gender.

The Indefinite article *di* is also put before the plural as well as the singular number ; example : *úna coróna di fióri,* a crown of flowers ; *un tóndo di pisèlli,* a plate of pease.

The Indefinite article has but three cases, the genitive, dative and ablative.

Of is expressed in Italian by *di ; to* by *a* (or *ad* before a vowel) ; *from* by *da.*

OF THE DEFINITE ARTICLES.

The English language has but one definite article, namely, *the*, which serves for both numbers.

The Italian has three, viz. *il* and *lo* for the masculine, and *la* for the feminine.

The article *il* is prefixed to masculine nouns beginning with a consonant, and makes *i* in the plural; as *il pádre, i pádri; il fratéllo, i fratélli; il líbro, i líbri; il cièlo, i cièli.*

The article *lo* makes the plural *gli*, and is put before two sorts of nouns, viz. before masculine nouns beginning with *s* and followed by a consonant; as, *lo stúdio, lo spírito, lo scolàre; gli stúdj, gli spíriti, gli scolári; lo spècchio, gli spècchi.*

If the letter *s* be followed by a vowel, we must make use of the article *il* and not *lo*; as *il soldáto, il sacraménto, il signóre, il sècolo, il supèrbo*, and not *lo soldáto, lo signóre*, &c.

When the article *lo* stands before nouns beginning with a vowel, we then retrench the vowel, and insert an apostrophe; examples: *l'amóre, l'onóre, l'ingégno*, and not *lo amóre, lo onóre, lo ingégno; gli amóri, gli onóri,* (°) *gl' ingégni*, in the plural. The same may be said in regard to the article *la* for the feminine. We have also touched upon this subject in the Introduction to the Italian tongue.

The article *la* serves for the feminine, and makes *le* in the plural; as,

la cása	*le cáse*	the houses
la méssa	*le mésse*	the masses
la cámera	*le cámere*	the rooms
la stráda	*le stráde*	the streets
la chièsa	*le chièse*	the churches
la tèrra	*le tèrre*	the earths
la pòrta	*le pòrte*	the doors
la stélla	*le stélle*	the stars

(°) See the °₌° two notes at p. 36.

Declension of the Masculine Articles il *and* lo.

I do not put the accusative, because it is the same as the nominative ; nor the vocative, because it is expressed by *O* in both languages.

Sing.	Nom.		*il* | *lo*	the
	Gen.		*del* | *dello*	of the
	Dat.		*al* | *allo*	to the
	Abl.		*dal* | *dallo*	from *and* by the
Plur.	Nom.		*i* | *gli*	the
	Gen.	*dei* or *de'*	*dégli*	of the
	Dat.	*ai, a'*	*ágli*	to the
	Abl.	*dai, da'*	*dágli*	from *or* by the

We do not use in the plural the articles *li, delli, alli, dalli,* as the ancients did. Yet they may be used in verse.

*** Note, to write correctly, we must not abridge the article *lo* in the plural, unless the following noun begins with an *i ;* therefore you must write *gl' ingégni, gl' incèndj,* with an apostrophe, and *gli amóri, gli onóri,* without one. Nevertheless you are to take but one syllable of the article and the subsequent vowel : so that you must pronounce *glia-móri, glio-nóri,* and not *gli-a-móri, gli-o-nóri.* In this respect the Italian language is extremely delicate.

———

Declension of the Feminine Article la.

Sing.	Nom.	*la*	the
	Gen.	*délla*	of the
	Dat.	*álla*	to the
	Abl.	*dálla*	from the
Plur.	Nom.	*le*	the
	Gen.	*délle*	of the
	Dat.	*álle*	to the
	Abl.	*dálle*	from *or* by the

*** You must not abridge *la* in the plural, unless the

following word begins with an *e*; and therefore we write *l'eminènze, l'esecuzióni*, with an apostrophe, and *le ánime, le invenzióni, le ómbre, le últime*, without one. And yet we write *le effigie*, in the plural, to distinguish it from the singular, because this noun has the same termination in both numbers: you are to observe the same in regard to the word *esèquie*.

Declension of the Article il *with a masculine noun, whose first letter is a consonant.*

Sing.	Nom.	*il libro*	the book
	Gen.	*del libro*	of the book
	Dat.	*al libro*	to the book
	Abl.	*dal libro*	from *or* by the book
Plur.	Nom.	*i libri*	the books
	Gen.	*dei libri*	of the books
	Dat.	*ai libri*	to the books
	Abl.	*dai libri*	from *or* by the books

The Declension of the Article lo *before a masculine noun, whose first letter is an* s *followed by a consonant.*

Sing.	Nom.	*lo spècchio*	the glass (mirror)
	Gen.	*déllo spècchio*	of the glass
	Dat.	*állo spècchio*	to the glass
	Abl.	*dállo spècchio*	from the glass
Plur.	Nom.	*gli spècchi*	the glasses
	Gen.	*dégli spècchi*	of the glasses
	Dat.	*ágli spècchi*	to the glasses
	Abl.	*dágli spècchi*	from the glasses

The Declension of the Article la *before a feminine noun beginning with a consonant.*

Sing.	Nom.	*la cása*	the house
	Gen.	*délla cása*	of the house
	Dat.	*álla cása*	to the house
	Abl.	*dálla cása*	from the house
Plur.	Nom.	*le cáse*	the houses
	Gen.	*délle cáse*	of the houses
	Dat.	*alle cáse*	to the houses
	Abl.	*dálle cáse*	from the houses

The article *la* is also prefixed to feminine nouns beginning with an *s*, followed by a consonant; as, *la stráda, le stráde*, the streets, &c.

_____

The Declension of the Article lo, *with an* apostrophe *or* elision.

Sing.	Nom.	*l' amóre*	the love
	Gen.	*dell' amóre*	of the love
	Dat.	*all' amóre*	to the love
	Abl.	*dall' amóre*	from the love
Plur.	Nom	*gli amóri*	the loves
	Gen.	*dégli amóri*	of the loves
	Dat.	*ágli amóri*	to the loves
	Abl.	*dágli amóri*	from the loves

*** Observe, that the English have no variation in their articles for the plural; they say, *the men, the women;* the Italians have an article for each gender in the plural, *gli uómini, le dónne, i líbri, le stélle.*

The Declension of the Article la, *with an* apostrophe.

Sing.	Nom.	*l' ánima*	the soul
	Gen.	*dell' ánima*	of the soul
	Dat.	*all' ánima*	to the soul
	Abl.	*dall' ánima*	from the soul
Plur.	Nom.	*le ánime*	the souls
	Gen.	*délle ánime*	of the souls
	Dat.	*álle ánime*	to the souls
	Abl.	*dálle ánime*	from the souls

OF THE INDEFINITE ARTICLE.

The Indefinite article has but three cases, or, to speak more properly, the prepositions which are most commonly placed before articles are three, and serve, as we have already mentioned, for the singular and plural, for the masculine and feminine.

Gen.	*·di*	of
Dat.	*a* (or *ad* before a vowel)	to
Abl.	*da*	from *or* by

The following example will show, that nouns declined by the Indefinite article have no article in the nominative, accusative or vocative.

Nom.	*Róma*	Rome
Gen.	*di Róma*	of Rome
Dat.	*a Róma*	to Rome
Acc.	*Róma*	Rome
Voc.	*o Róma !*	o Rome!
Abl.	*da Róma*	from Rome

The Indefinite article is used in declining the nouns that have no article in the nominative; such as the names, of angels, *d' ángeli ;* of men, *d' uòmini ;* of cities, *di città ;* of months, *di mési ;* as also the pronouns personal, demonstrative, interrogative, and relative; for example, *London, January, February, March, April; me, thee, him, we, you; this, that, those, these; who,* &c.

Who or *which,* in Italian *quále,* may be declined by the Definite articles : for we say, *il quále* and *la quále, del quále* and *della quále.*

The Indefinite article may also be prefixed to all other sorts of nouns, as I have already observed : for we say, *una libbra di pane,* a pound of bread ; *un cappèllo di paglia,* a straw hat ; *una tazza d' argènto,* a silver cup ; *un vestíto di pánno,* a cloth suit.

If the Indefinite article of the genitive, *di,* precedes a noun beginning with a vowel, we must make an elision to it, and add a *d* to that of the dative *a ;* ex. nominative, *Antònio ;* genitive, *d' Antònio ;* dative, *ad Antònio ;* accusative, *Antònio ;* ablative, *da Antònio.*

*** Observe, that in speaking of any part of the body, it is more elegant to make use of the indefinite than the definite article : hence we say, *mi trarrà l' ánima di còrpo,* he will tear my soul from my body ; *mi tòglie il libro di máno,* &c., he takes the book out of my hand, &c.

The Indefinite article is also put before infinitives, and signifies *to ;* as, it is time to speak, to sleep, to read, to study, to write, to love, to go ; *è tempo di parláre, di dormíre, di lèggere, di studiáre, di scrivere, d' amáre, d' andáre ;* but we make an elision when the verbs begin with a vowel ; as, *d' amáre, d' andáre.*

*** Note. Whenever you meet with *of* or *to* in English, remember they are the indefinite articles ; and then you must make use of the indefinite articles *di* or *a,* (or *ad* before a vowel) in Italian.

REMARKS ON THE ARTICLES.

First, the word *him* or *it* before a verb is always expressed by *lo*; as, I see him or it, *io lo védo*; we know it, *noi lo sappiámo*; 1 know it, *io lo so*.

Secondly, *her* or *it* before a verb is expressed by *la*; examples : I know her, *io la conósco*; I do not know her, *non la conósco*.

Thirdly, *them* before a verb is expressed by *li* for the masculine, and by *le* for the feminine; example : *io li védo*, or *io le védo*, according to the gender.

Fourthly, the pronouns *lo, la, li, le*, must be always put after the adverb *ècco*, and also after the infinitives and gerunds ; as, there he is, *èccolo*; there she is, *èccola*; there they are, *èccoli*, for the masculine, and *èccole*, for the feminine. To see him, we must say, *per vedérlo*, because *vedére* is in the infinitive : in like manner, to express seeing him, we must not say, *lo vedèndo*, as is done in French, but *vedèndolo*, because *vedèndo* is a gerund, and the Italian rule requires that these words, *lo, la, li, le*, should always follow the infinitive and gerund, as also the word *ècco*, as in English, but never precede them, as in French.

⁎ Remember that we have been speaking of the words *lo, la, li, le*, and not of the articles *lo, la, li, le*, and that, a little above, we said the words, *lo, la, li, le*, because these words *lo, la, li, le*, when they precede verbs, are not articles, but relative pronouns. They are articles only when they precede nouns or pronouns.

Fifthly, the preposition *in* is sometimes expressed in Italian by *in*; as, in Paris, *in Parígi*; in France, *in Fráncia*; in a room, *in una cámera*; in a fire, *in un fuòco*; in all the earth, *in tútta la tèrra*; in a drinking glass, *in un bicchière*; in a bottle, *in una bottiglia*.

When the preposition *in* is followed by the article *the*, or by a pronoun possessive, as, *in the, in my, in thy, in his*; we must render it by *nel, nello, nella, nei, negli, nelle, nel mio, nel tuo, nel suo* : example : in the garden, *nel giardíno*, and not *in il giardíno*.

Say, *nello*, and not *in lo spírito*, because *spírito*, beginning with an *s* followed by a consonant, takes the article *lo*.

In the house,	*nélla cása*
In the gardens,	*nei giardíni*
In the fires,	*nei fuòchi*
In the spirits,	*négli spíriti*
In the houses,	*nélle cáse*
In my garden,	*nel mio giardíno*
In thy book,	*nel tuo líbro*
In his or her bed,	*nel suo lètto*
In his or her room,	*nella sua cámera*
In his or her books,	*nei* or *ne' suòi líbri*
In his or her rooms,	*nélle sue cámere*

When *in* precedes the pronoun possessive of the masculine gender, in the plural it is usually expressed by *ne'* instead of *nei*; as, in my books, *ne' mièi líbri*; which is practised to avoid a harshness of sound.

Sixthly: You see, by these examples, that *in the* is expressed in Italian by *nel* or *néllo*, in the masculine, by *nélla*, in the feminine.

Nel is placed before the same nouns that we put the article *il*, and in the plural it makes *nei* or *ne'*, in the.

Néllo is put before the same nouns that we put the article *lo*, and in the plural it makes *négli*.

Nélla is put before the same nouns as the article *la*, and in the plural it makes *nélle*.

We may express *in* by *in*, when it is before a pronoun possessive feminine, by transposing the pronoun possessive to the end of the phrase; as, in my room, *in cámera mia*; in your house, *in cása vòstra*; in his or her shop, *in bottéga sua*; but this rule is only for feminine nouns, and not masculine.

Seventhly: When after the preposition *with*, which in Italian is expressed by *con*, we find the article *the*, or a pronoun possessive, as, with the, with my, with thy, with his, instead of saying, *con il, con lo, con la*, say rather *col, colla, coi, con gli, con le* or *colle*; example: with the prince, *col príncipe*; plural, *coi príncipi*.

With the hand,	*colla máno*
With the hands,	*con le máni*

With the scholar,	*collo scoláre*
With the princesses,	*colle príncipesse*
With the scholars,	*con gli scolári*
With my book,	*col mio líbro*
With my pen,	*colla mía pénna*
With your friends,	*co' vòstri amíci*
With my books,	*co' mièi líbri*

Col makes in the plural, *coi* and *co'*.

Collo makes *con gli*; *colla* makes *colle*, or *con le*.

Nevertheless, when the following words begin with the letter *s* and another consonant, it is more elegant to write *con lo* and *con gli*; thus you will say, *con lo strále, con lo scolare, con gli stúdj*; and *col* or *coll'*, when the word begins with a single consonant, or with a vowel.

Eighthly: When the preposition *with* is followed by a pronoun possessive, and this by a noun of quality or kindred; as, with your majesty, with your highness, with your excellency, with his brother, with her mother, with her sister; *with* must then be rendered by *con*, as, *con vòstra maestà, con sua altézza, con vòstra eccellènza, con suo fratèllo, con sua mádre, con sua sorèlla*, without using the article.

⁎ Observe, we may also make use of *col* and *colla*, by transposing the pronouns possessive after the noun, and say, *colla maestà vòstra, coll' eccellènza sua, col fratèllo suo, colla mádre sua*, &c.

Ninthly: If the pronouns possessive are in the plural, then we must express *with* by *co'* for the masculine, and by *colle* for the feminine; example: with my brothers, *co' mièi fratèlli*; and not *con mièi fratèlli*; with my sisters, *colle mie sorèlle*, and not *con mie sorèlle*; if you choose to insert the article, you must use the same transposition, and say; *coi fratèlli mièi, coi parènti vòstri, cólle sorèlle tue, colle mádri nòstre*, &c.

⁎ Note. Some writers prefer saying, *con lo, con la, con gli, con le*, instead of *collo colla, cogli, colle*.

CHAPTER II.

OF NOUNS.

ITALIAN Nouns have but five terminations, viz. those of the five vowels, *a, e, i, o, u.*

They have but two genders, the masculine and the feminine.

Italian Nouns have no variation of cases like the Latin; and it is the article only that distinguishes the case; example: nom. *il signóre*; gen. *del signóre*; dat. *al signóre*; acc. *il signóre*; voc. *o signóre*; abl. *dal signóre.* Nom. plur. *i signóri*; gen. *dei signóri*; dat. *ai signóri,* &c.

*** Take notice, as a general rule, that all masculine nouns make their plural in *i*; example: *il pápa,* the pope, *i pápi*; *il pádre,* the father, *i pádri*; *il libro,* the book, *i libri,* &c.

OF NOUNS ENDING IN *a*.

Nouns ending in *a* are feminine, and form their plural in *e*; as, *la cása,* the house; *le cáse,* the houses; *la chièsa,* the church; *le chièse,* the churches; *la carròzza,* the coach; *le carròzze,* the coaches.

Exceptions.—First. All nouns ending in *ca* and *ga,* have an *h* in the plural between the *c* or *g* and the final vowel, to avoid the change of sound; as, *la mánica,* the sleeve, *le mániche*; *la piága,* the wound, *le piághe.*

Secondly. Nouns ending in Italian in *tà,* and in English in *ty,* never change their Italian terminations in the plural; as, *la calamità,* calamity; *le calamità,* calamities; *l' autorità,* authority; *le autorità,* authorities; *la carità,* charity; *le carità,* charities.

*** Yet observe, that those nouns are syncopated or shortened, and their real termination is in *ade* or *ate,* according to the most ancient writers. In the plural they change their termination into *i;* thus we say, *beltáde* or *beltáte*, in the singular, and *beltádi* or *beltáti* in the plural. I do not remember ever to have seen these nouns written in the plural with a *t*. Though the Italians sometimes make use of the termination in *ade*, yet it is better to say *bontà* than *bontáde*, and *generosità* than *generositáde*, &c.

Thirdly : Nouns masculine ending in *a* form their plural in *i ;* as, *poèta, poèti; profèta, profèti.*

All Nouns ending in *e*, whether masculine or feminine, substantive or adjective, form their plural in *i ;* example: *il pádre*, the father; *i pádri*, the fathers: *una mádre*, a mother; *le mádri*, the mothers; *prudènte, prudènti*, prudent.

Exceptions.—First. *Mille*, a thousand, which makes in the plural *mila*.

Secondly. The five following nouns : *re*, a king; *spècie*, a sort; *superficie*, a superficies; *effigie*, an effigy ; *l' esèquie*, the funeral ; which have no change of termination in the plural; for we say, *il re, i re ; la spècie, le spècie ; la superficie, le superficie ; l' effigie, le effigie ; l' esèquie, le esèquie :* without curtailing the article of the two last nouns in the plural to distinguish it from the singular *l' effigie, l' esèquie.*

Observe, that we seldom make use of the word *esèquie* in the singular.

I have taken no notice here of the noun *rèquie*, repose, coming from the Latin word *requies*, because I never saw an instance in which it was used in the plural. However, it would admit of no variation in the plural, any more than the word *re*, &c.

Moglie, wife, makes *mogli* in the plural.

RULES FOR FINDING THE GENDER OF NOUNS IN *e.*

First. Nouns ending in *me* are masculine; example : *il costúme,* the custom ; *il fiúme,* the river ; *il ráme,* the copper ; *il vèrme,* the worm.

There are two nouns in *me,* feminine, viz. *la fáme,* hunger, and *la spème,* hope.

Secondly. There are but four nouns in *re,* feminine ; viz. *la fèbbre,* the fever ; *la mádre,* the mother ; *la tórre,* the tower ; *la pólvere,* the dust or powder.

All the nouns in *ore* are masculine ; as, *il fióre,* the flower ; *il calóre,* heat ; *il furóre,* rage ; *lo splendóre,* splendor ; *il cuòre,* the heart ; *il predicatóre,* the preacher, &c.

There are four nouns in *re* of both genders, viz. *il* and *la cárcere,* the prison ; *il* and *la cénere,* the ashes; *il* and *la fólgore,* the lightning ; *il* and *la lèpre,* the hare.

Thirdly. Of the Italian nouns ending in *ine, ione,* and *one,* some are masculine and some feminine ; as, *l' órdine,* m. the order; *la grándine,* hail ; *la prigióne,* the prison ; *il bastóne,* the stick ; we say, *il fíne,* when we take it for *aim* or *design ;* and *la fíne,* when we mean the *end ;* though in the latter signification it is usual also to say, *il fíne* and *la fíne.*

Fourthly. The following nouns in *nte* are feminine ; namely, *la gènte,* the people ; *la patènte,* the patent; *la sorgènte,* the source ; *la corrènte,* the current ; *la ménte,* the mind ; and perhaps some few more : all the other nouns ending in *nte* are masculine, as *il dènte,* the tooth ; *il pónte,* the bridge; *il mónte,* the mount; *il gigánte,* the giant, &c. We are speaking here only of nouns-substantive, not of adjectives.

There are three nouns in *nte,* which have two genders, viz. *il* and *la fánte,* a servant; *il* and *la frónte,* the forehead ; and *il* and *la fonte,* a fountain.

Fifthly. The other different terminations in *e* keep the same gender as in French and Latin ; example : *il pésce,* the fish ; *la vóce,* the voice : *la cróce,* the cross ; *il latte,* the milk ; *la lòde,* the praise ; except

La grégge, a flock or herd. We say likewise, *il grégge.*

OF NOUNS IN i.

The Italian language has but few nouns terminating in *i*; they are the same in the plural as in the singular, and are distinguished by the articles; namely,

Singular.		Plural.
il dì,	the day,	i dì, the days,
il Lunedì,	Monday,	i Lunedì
il Martedì,	Tuesday,	i Martedì
il Mercoledì,	Wednesday,	i Mercoledì
il Giovedì,	Thursday,	i Giovedì
il Venerdì,	Friday,	i Venerdì
la diòcesi,	a diocese,	le diòcesi
il barbagiánni,	an owl,	i barbagiánni
l' ecclìssi,	an eclipse,	le ecclìssi
l' èstasi,	an ecstasy,	le èstasi
la perífrasi,	a periphrasis,	le perífrasi
l' ènfasi,	an emphasis,	le ènfasi
la metamòrfosi,	a metamorphosis,	le metamòrfosi
la crìsi,	a crisis,	le crìsi
la tèsi,	a thesis,	le tèsi
la Gènesi,	Genesis,	
un pári,	an equal,	i and le pári

The last noun is of all genders and numbers; and we say, *un pári vòstro*, such a man as you; *una pári vòstra*, such a woman as you; implying respect.

Gènesi has no plural, and is of all genders. In Dante we meet with *lo Gènesi*, but the generality of good writers say *la Gènesi*.

There are also some proper names in *i*, as *Giovánni*, *Parígi*, *Nápoli*; and the numeral nouns, as *dièci*, *úndici*, *dódici*, *trédici*, *quattórdici*, *quíndici*, *sédici*, *vénti*.

OF NOUNS IN o.

Nouns ending in *o* are masculine, except, first, nouns of women, as *Sáffo*, *Elo*. Second, the word *máno*, which is feminine, and makes the plural in *i*; for example, *il fratèllo*, the brother; *i fratèlli*, brothers; *il fazzolétto*, the handkerchief; *i fazzolétti*; *la máno*, the hand, *le máni*; *uòmo*, man, makes *uòmini* in the plural.

₊ Note, that nouns-substantive in *aro*, more elegantly change their termination into *aio*; thus we say,

> *Gennáro*   and *Gennáio*,   January.
> *Febbráro*   and *Febbráio*,   February.
> *Calzoláro* and *calzoláio*,   a shoemaker.
> *Mortáro*   and *mortáio*,   a mortar.

There are some nouns in *o* which terminate in the plural more elegantly in *a* than in *i*, and then they become feminine in the plural; they are as follow:

l' anèllo,	*le anèlla,*	the rings
il bráccio,	*le bráccia,*	the arms
il budèllo,	*le budèlla,*	the bowels
il calcágno	*le calcágna,*	the heels
il cérchio,	*le cérchia,*	the circles, hoops
il ciglio,	*le ciglia,*	the eyebrows
il còrno,	*le còrna,*	the horns
il díto,	*le díta,*	the fingers
il ditèllo,	*le ditèlla,*	the armpits
il filo,	*le fíla,*	the threads
il frútto,	*le frútta,*	the fruit
il gèsto,	*le gèsta,*	the actions, feats
il grído,	*le grída,*	the cries
il gúscio,	*le gúscia,*	the shells
il ginòcchio,	*le ginòcchia,*	the knees
il lábbro,	*le lábbra,*	the lips
il lenzuòlo,	*le lenzuòla,*	the sheets (of a bed)
il légno,	*le légna,*	the sticks
il mélo,	*le méla,*	the apples
il mèmbro,	*le mèmbra,*	the limbs
il múro,	*le múra,*	the walls
il migliáio,	*le migliáia,*	the thousands
il míglio,	*le míglia,*	the miles
l' orécchio,	*le orécchia,*	the ears
l' òsso,	*le òssa,*	the bones
il páio,	*le páia,*	the pairs

il pómo,	*le póma,*	the apples
il púgno,	*le púgna,*	the fists
lo stáio,	*le stáia,*	the bushels
il ríso,	*le rísa,*	the laughters
l' uóvo,	*le uóva,*	the eggs
il rúbbio,	*le rúbbia,*	the measures
il vestigio,	*le vestigia,*	the footsteps

Nouns of two syllables, ending in *co* and *go,* take an *h* in the plural, in order to avoid a change of pronunciation: examples; *il fuòco,* the fire ; *i fuòchi,* the fires ; *il luògo,* the place : *il luòghi,* the places.

Two are excepted.

Il pòrco, the pig ; *i pòrci,* the pigs.
Il Grèco, Greek ; *i Grèci,* Greeks.

The other nouns in *co* and *go,* of more than two syllables, do not take an *h* in the plural ; as, *amíco, amíci,* friends ; *domèstico, domèstici,* domestics ; *canònico, canònici,* canons ; *cattòlico, cattòlici,* Catholics ; *mèdico, mèdici,* physicians ; *mendíco, mendíci,* beggars.

The following are exceptions :

Albèrgo,	*albèrghi,*	dwellings
Antíco,	*antíchi,*	ancients
Beccafíco,	*beccafíchi,*	fig-peckers
Bifólco,	*bifólchi,*	labourers
Catafálco,	*catafálchi,*	scaffolds
Diálogo,	*diáloghi,*	dialogues
Fiamíngo,	*Fiamínghi,*	Flemings
Recíproco,	*recíprochi,*	reciprocals
Siniscálco,	*siniscálchi,*	high-stewards
Tedésco,	*Tedéschi,*	Germans
Tráffico,	*tráffichi,*	tradings

Astròlogo, astrologer, makes *astròloghi* and *astròlogi ;* and *mònaco,* a monk, *mònachi* and *mònaci.*

Nouns ending in *io* form their plural in *ii, j,* or *i,* as follows :

Those in which the *io* is long, the *i* of *io* being accented, and making a dissyllable, retain the two syllables in the plural, changing *o* into *i* ; thus, *natío, pío, zío, mormorío* make in the plural *natíi, pii, zii, mormorii.*

D

Those in which the io is long, without the i being accented, change io into j. Examples :

Singular.	Plural.	
tèmpio,	tempj,	temples
princìpio,	principj,	principles
segretário.	segretarj,	secretaries
libráio,	libraj,	booksellers
mugnáio,	mugnaj,	millers
rasóio,	rasoj,	rasors
asciugatóio,	asciugatoj,	towels

But those in cio, gio, ccio, ggio, chio, ghio and glio, having the io short, the plural is formed by simply omitting the final o, as follows :

Singular.	Plural.	
bacio,	baci,	kisses
láccio,	lacci,	knots
impáccio,	impacci,	hindrances
refúgio,	refugi,	refuges
rággio,	raggi,	rays
spècchio,	specchi,	looking-glasses
òcchio,	occhi,	eyes
figlio,	figli,	sons
consiglio,	consigli,	counsels

OF NOUNS IN u.

The Italian language has but few nouns in u; and they do not change their termination in the plural. Examples :

la grù,	a crane,	le grù
la gioventù,	youth,	le gioventù
la servitù,	servitude,	le servitù
la tribù,	a tribe,	le tribù
la virtù,	virtue,	le virtù
la schiavitù,	slavery,	le schiavitù

REMARKS ON SOME NOUNS.

₊ When the letter l is found in Latin and French after f, b, p, we must change l into i. Examples, fleur, fióre ; blanc, biánco ; blanche, biánca ; plein, pièno ; temple, tèmpio ; plomb, piómbo.

*** Note, the Italians never put a *c* or *p* before a *t*, but the *p* or *c* is changed into *t* and sometimes into *z* ; examples : doctus, *dòtto* ; doctor, *dottóre* ; act, *átto* ; aptitude, *attitúdine* ; adoption, *adozióne*.

Ph is changed into *f* ; example : philosopher, *filòsofo* ; Ephesus, *Efèso* ; *x* is changed into *s* or *ss*, and sometimes into *c* ; as Xerxes, *Sèrse* ; Alexander, *Alessándro* ; excellent, *eccellènte*.

OF THE AUGMENTATIVES.

The Italians, more than other nations, have this peculiarity in their language, that they can augment or diminish the signification of the nouns, by only adding certain syllables to the end of them, which they call *augmentatives* or *diminutives*.

Augmentatives are words which, by the increase of a syllable, increase also in their signification.

There are two sorts of augmentatives ; the first terminates in *one*, to express any thing great and large ; as, *cappèllo*, a hat, which, by changing *o* into *one* makes *cappellóne*, a large hat ; *sála*, a hall, change *a* into *one*, and you make *sálone*, a large hall ; *frate*, a friar, *frátone*, a fat overgrown friar ; *casa*, a house, *casóne*, a great house ; *libro*, a book, *libróne*, a large book ; and so of the rest.

*** Observe, that the augmentatives ending in *one* are always masculine, though the nouns from whence they are formed be feminine ; example, *una pòrta*, *un portóne* ; *la cámera*, *il camérone*.

The other augmentatives are formed by changing the last letter of the word into *accio*, for the masculine, and into *accia* for the feminine ; but then these augmentatives declare the thing to be contemptible ; as,

Cappèllo, a hat ; *cappeláccio*, an ugly hat.
Sála, a hall ; *saláccia*, a dirty hall.
Cása, a house ; *casáccia*, a dirty house.

Nouns terminating in *ame* denote plenty or abundance of any thing common ; as, *gentáme*, abundance of people ; *ossáme*, abundance of bones.

Observe, nevertheless, that in those terminations there

are nouns which are not augmentatives ; for instance, in *one* we find *bastóne*, a stick ; in *áme*, *stáme*, worsted ; in *áccio* and in *áccia*, *láccio*, a halter ; *fáccia*, a face, &c.

OF DIMINUTIVES.

Although the diminutives are increased by the addition of one or more syllables, yet the addition lessens the signification of their primitives.

There are two sorts of diminutives ; one of kindness and flattery, another of compassion.

The diminutives of kindness and flattery have their terminations in *ino, etto, ello*, for the masculine : and in *ina, etta, ella*, for the feminine ; examples : from *pòvero*, poor, come *poverino, poverétto, poverèllo*, a poor little man ; *poverina, poverétta, povcrèlla*, a poor little woman.

The diminutives of compassion end in *uccio, uzzo, icciuòlo*, for the masculine, and in *uccia, uzza, icciuòla*, for the feminine ; example : from *uòmo* is formed *omúccio, omúzzo, omicciuòlo*, a poor little man. See note ("ᵘ.)

•₊• Note, the diminutives convey no meaning of contempt like the augmentatives ; so that to express a little old man, you may use indifferently *vecchiétto, vecchino, vecchiettino, vecchiarèllo, vecchiarellino*, except the termination *uccio* and *uzzo ;* as, *vecchiúzzo, cassúccia ;* as also *casina, casétta,* to express a small house.

•₊• Observe, also, that the diminutives in *ino* and *ina* have something of tenderness, and persuasive flattery in them ; examples : the pretty little prince, *il principino ;* the pretty little princess, *la principessina ;* in her pretty little room, *nel suo bèl camerino*.

Cáne, a dog, has its diminutive *cagnolino*, a pretty little dog ; of *fiore, fiorellino ; fiume, fiumicello,* &c.

Távola,	makes	*tavolino,*	a little table.
Cása,	a house,	*casina,*	a small house.
Cámera,	a room,	*camerétta,*	a little room.

Berrétta, berrettino, a little cap (for men) ; which show that several feminine nouns in *a* make their diminutives in *ino*.

OF NOUNS ADJECTIVE.

The adjectives always agree with their substantives in gender, number, and case.

There are two sorts of adjectives, one terminated in *o*, the other in *e*. The adjectives in *o* serve for the masculine ; example : *bèllo, sánto, dòtto, rìcco, pòvero :* these adjectives, and all others ending in *o*, form their plural in *i ;* as, *bèlli, sánti, dòtti, rìcchi, pòveri.*

To make these adjectives of the feminine gender, you must change *o* into *a*, as *bèllo, bèlla ; dòtto, dòtta ; rìcco, rìcca :* and in the plural you must change *a* into *e ;* as *bèlle, dòtte, rìcche.*

The other adjectives, ending in *e*, are of the masculine and feminine gender, without changing their termination, and they form their plural in *i*, as well for the masculine as feminine ; examples : *un uòmo prudènte, úna dònna prudènte ; due uòmini prudènti, due dònne prudènti.*

From the adjectives we may form comparatives and superlatives.

OF COMPARATIVES(').

The English comparatives are adjectives, before which are put the particles, *more, less, better, worse,* &c.

The Italian comparatives have before them, *più, méno* or *mèglio :* as, *più dòtto*, more learned ; *méno dòtto*, less learned ; *più bèlla*, more handsome ; *méno bèlla*, less handsome.

The comparatives serve to compare one thing with another : *the sun is larger than the earth ; your sister is better dressed than your niece.* In these examples we compare the sun with the earth, the sister with the niece.

There are four Italian comparatives, which end in *ore ;* they may also be expressed by *più, grande, piccolo,*

' See Exercises, p. 19.

D 3

or *cattivo* except *miglióre*, for *più buono*; and they are comparatives without the help of the particle *più*; viz.

maggióre,	greater,	*più gránde*
minóre,	less,	*più píccolo*
peggióre,	worse,	*più cattivo*
miglióre,	better,	*più buòno*

To which may be added, *superióre*, superior, and *inferióre*, inferior or lower.

Observe, that the Italians never make use for *peggióre* and *miglióre*, of the words *pèggio* and *mèglio*, but when they want to express the French words *pire* and *mieux*, that is, *worse* and *better*, taken as adverbs. When the comparative is to agree with the substantive, they say *peggióre* and *miglióre*.

*** Observe also, that there can be no comparison made without the word *than*, and that this word is not expressed in Italian by *che*, but by the articles of the genitive, *di*, *del*, *dello*, *della*, *dei*, *degli*, *delle*.

When the word *than*, placed after the comparative, is followed by an article, or a pronoun possessive, as *than the; than my, than thy, than his, than ours, than yours, than theirs*, &c., the word *than* is expressed by the definite articles, *del*, *dello*, *della*, *dei*, *degli*, *delle*. Examples:

Clearer than the sun,	*più chiáro del sóle.*
Whiter than the snow,	*più biánco della néve.*
More learned than the scholar,	*più dòtto dello scoláre.*
Longer than the days,	*più lúnghi dei giórni.*
More beautiful than the stars,	*più bèlle delle stelle.*
Clearer than the glasses,	*più chiari degli spècchi.*
Larger than my book,	*più gránde del mio libro.*
Broader than my hand,	*più lárgo della mia máno.*
Richer than your relations,	*più ricchi dei vostri parènti,*

*** But if the word *than* is not followed by an article or pronoun possessive, then it is expressed by the indefinite article *di*. Examples:

More learned than Cicero,	*più dòtto di Ciceróne.*
More esteemed than I,	*più stimáto di me,*
Larger than the whole earth,	*più gránde di tútta la tèrra.*
Richer than this man,	*più rícco di quést' uòmo.*

If after *than* there happen to be a pronoun possessive, followed by a noun of quality or kindred in the singular, *than* is expressed by the indefinite article *di*. Example:

Handsomer than my brother, my sister, your excellency, &c. *più bèllo di mio fratèllo, di mia sorèlla, di vostra eccellènza,* &c. We may likewise make use of the definite article; but in that case we must place the pronoun, and the noun substantive, according to what has been observed at the end of the first chapter; and we must say, *più bèllo del fratèllo mio, della sorèlla mia, dell' eccellènza vòstra,* &c.

* If the pronoun possessive be in the plural number, as *my brothers, their aunts, their highnesses,* we must use the definite articles *de'* and *delle;* example: more powerful than my brothers, *più potènti de' mièi fratèlli, delle mie zie, delle altézze loro.*

* If the word *than* is followed by an adjective, or by a verb, an adverb or a preposition, it is rendered by *che.* Examples:

More white than yellow,	*più biánco che giállo.*
More poor than rich,	*più pòvero che rícco.*
He writes more than he speaks,	*scríve più che non parla.*
It is better late than never,	*è mèglio tárdi che mái.*

When the Italians require to heighten their comparisons, they make use of *vie più, assái più, mólto più,* a great deal, or much more; as also of *vie méno, assai méno, mólto méno,* a great deal or much less.

Examples: Cæsar is much more esteemed than Pompey.

Césare è vie più stimáto di Pompèo.
Césare è assai più stimáto di Pompèo.
Césare è molto più stimáto di Pompèo.

Pompey was much less happy than Cæsar.

Pompèo è stato vie méno, assai méno, molto méno felice di Césare.

When both the objects are in the nominative case, the comparative *than* cannot be expressed by *che* before the

D 4

last, without repeating the verb, but by *di*, &c.; but when the objects compared are in the accusative case, that is to say, after an active verb, then the comparative *than* must be expressed by *che* before the last object. Example : I esteem you more *than* your brother ; *stimo più voi che vostro fratèllo.*

*** See the Second Part of this Grammar, in the chapter of the concord of nouns, the rule concerning the comparison, when it is made by *as much as, so,* &c.

OF SUPERLATIVES([*]).

The English superlative is only a noun adjective, to which is prefixed the article *most*, in order to heighten the sense ; as, *most learned, most honoured.*

The Italian superlative is formed from the noun adjective, by changing the last letter into *issimo* for the masculine, and into *issima* for the feminine ; thus from *gránde*, great, you form *grandissimo*, very great; from *bèlla*, handsome ; *bellissima*, very handsome.

The most, is expressed by *il più, la più;* as, the fairest or most fair, *il più bèllo, la più bèlla, i più bèlli, le più bèlle ;* the largest, *il più grande.*

*** Observe, that by changing the last letter of adjectives, in *issimaménte*, the superlative adverbs are composed ; as, from *dòtto*, learned, *dottissimaménte*, most learnedly ; from *rícco*, rich, *ricchissimaménte*, most richly ; from *prudènte*, prudent, *prudentissimaménte*, most prudently.

You are also to take notice, that the positive is sometimes used in the Italian language, instead of the superlative ; as, *è la bèlla delle bèlle ;* as if one were to say, she is the fair of the fair.

There is also another sort of superlative ; for we say, *un uòmo dòtto dòtto*, to signify a very learned man.

OBSERVATIONS ON SOME NOUNS.

Observe, that the six following words, *uno, bèllo, gránde, sánto, quéllo, buòno*, are abridged or retrenched before masculine nouns beginning with a consonant, and we only write,

Un, bèl, gran, san, quel, buòn; as un libro, bel cáne, gran fuòco, san Michèle, quel bastóne, buon figliuòlo.

Before the feminine nouns we write,

Una, bèlla, gran, sánta, quélla, buòna.

None but *gran* is shortened before feminines.

⁎⁎⁎ See, in the Second Part, the chapter concerning words which are to be abridged.

Fráte signifies a friar, or brother of a religious order.

In this sense we abridge the word *fráte*, before the proper names of men, and only use *fra*; as, *fra Piètro*, brother Peter; *fra Páolo*, brother Paul; *fra Agostino*, brother Augustine; *fra Giovánni*, brother John.

We must remember also, that *fra* before numeral nouns, signifies *in*; examples: *fra un ánno*, in a year; *fra due mesi*, in two months: *fra quíndici giórni*; in fifteen days.

NUMERAL NOUNS.

One,	*Un, úno, úna.*
Two,	*due.*
Three,	*tre.*
Four,	*quáttro.*
Five,	*cinque.*
Six,	*sèi.*
Seven,	*sètte.*
Eight,	*òtto.*
Nine,	*nòve.*
Ten,	*dièci.*
Eleven,	*úndici.*
Twelve,	*dódici.*
Thirteen,	*trédici.*
Fourteen,	*quattórdici.*
Fifteen,	*quíndici.*
Sixteen,	*sédici.*
Seventeen,	*diciassètte.*
Eighteen,	*diciòtto.*
Nineteen,	*diciannòve.*
Twenty,	*vénti.*

Twenty-one,	*ventúno.*
Twenty-two,	*vénti-dúe.*
Twenty-three, &c.	*venti-tre, &c.*
Thirty,	*trénta.*
Forty,	*quaránta.*
Fifty,	*cinquánta.*
Sixty,	*sessánta.*
Seventy,	*settánta.*
Eighty,	*ottánta.*
Ninety,	*novánta.*
Hundred,	*cènto.*
Two hundred,	*dugènto.*
Three hundred,	*trecènto.*
Thousand,	*mille.*
Two thousand,	*due míla.*
A million,	*un milióne.*
A score,	*una ventína.*
Half a score,	*una diecína.*
A dozen,	*una dozzína.*
A score and a half,	*una trentína.*

ORDINAL NOUNS.

First,	*Primo.*
Second,	*secóndo.*
Third,	*tèrzo.*
Fourth,	*quárto.*
Fifth,	*quínto.*
Sixth,	*sèsto.*
Seventh,	*sèttimo.*
Eighth,	*ottávo.*
Ninth,	*nòno.*
Tenth,	*dècimo.*
Eleventh,	*undècimo.*
Twelfth,	*duodècimo.*
Thirteenth,	*dècimotèrzo.*
Fourteenth,	*dècimoquárto.*
Fifteenth,	*dècimoquínto.*
Sixteenth,	*dècimosèsto.*
Seventeenth,	*dècimosèttimo.*
Eighteenth,	*dècimottávo.*

Nineteenth,	*dècimonòno.*
Twentieth,	*ventèsimo.*
One-and-twentieth,	*ventèsimo primo.*
Thirtieth,	*trentèsimo.*
Fortieth,	*quarantèsimo.*
Fiftieth,	*cinquantèsimo.*
Sixtieth,	*sessantèsimo.*
Seventieth,	*settantèsimo.*
Eightieth,	*ottantèsimo.*
Ninetieth,	*novantèsimo.*
Hundredth,	*centèsimo.*
Thousandth,	*millèsimo.*
Last,	*último.*

The proportional numbers are, *sémplice, dóppio, triplicáto, quadruplicáto, centuplicáto*, single, double, threefold, fourfold, a hundredfold.

The distributive nouns are *uno a uno*, one by one ; *due a due*, two by two.

In French and English all ordinal numbers may be formed into adverbs, but in Italian they have only *primieraménte* and *secondariaménte.*

To express thirdly, fourthly, &c. they say *in tèrzo luògo, in quárto luògo*, &c. in the third place, in the fourth place, &c.

A Method by which those who understand FRENCH *may learn a great many* ITALIAN *words in a short time.*

Though Italian is said to be a corruption of the Latin, yet it has a greater conformity and resemblance with the French than with any other language ; for French words, with a little variation, are all Italian, as may be seen by the following examples ; only we must observe that the French syllable *cha* is already expressed in Italian by *ca*, rejecting *h.* Example : *Charbon, charité, chasteté, chapon, charette, chandelle, chapeau;* the Italians say, *Carbóne, carità, castità, cappóne, carrétta, candéla, cappèllo.*

To acquire a great number of Italian words in a short time, observe the following rules :

FRENCH TERMINATIONS WHICH IN ITALIAN END IN A.

French words ending in *ance*, as constance, vigilance, &c. in Italian end in *anza; costánza, vigilánza,* &c.

Those in *ence* in French, as clémence, diligence, prudence, end in Italian in *enza; clemènza, diligènza, prudènza.*

AGNE makes AGNA.

montagne,	*montágna*
campagne,	*oampágna*

OGNE makes OGNA.

Catalogne,	*Catalógna*
charogne,	*carógna*

IE makes IA.

comédie,	*commèdia*
tragédie,	*tragèdia*

OIRE makes ORIA.

gloire,	*glòria*
victoire,	*vittòria*

TÉ makes TÀ.

pureté,	*purità*
libéralité,	*liberálità*

[See what has been said in the exceptions of nouns terminating in *a*.]

URE makes URA.

aventure,	*avventúra*
imposture,	*impostúra*

FRENCH TERMINATIONS WHICH IN ITALIAN END IN E.

AL makes ALE.

cardinal,	*cardinále*
.mal,	*mále*

ABLE makes EVOLE.

charitable,	*caritatévole*
honourable,	*onorévole*
louable,	*lodévole*

AIS, names of nations, ESE.

Anglais,	*Inglése*
Français,	*Francése*
Hollandais,	*Olundése*

ANT makes ANTE.

vigilant,	*vigilánte*
amant,	*amánte*

ENT, adjective, ENTE.

prudent,	*prudènte*
diligent,	*diligènte*

EUR makes ORE.

honneur,	*onóre*
chaleur,	*calóre*

IER makes IÈRE.

cavalier,	*cavalière*
perruquier,	*parrucchière*

ION makes IÓNE.

union,	*unióne*
portion,	*porzióne*

ISON makes GIONE.

raison,	*ragióne*
prison,	*prigióne*

ON makes ONE.

charbon,	*carbóne*
canon,	*cannóne*
baron,	*baróne*

ONT makes ONTE.

front,	*frónte*
pont,	*pónte*

UDE makes UDINE.

inquiétude,	*inquietúdine*

ULIER makes OLÁRE.

régulier,	*regoláre*
particulier,	*particoláre*

FRENCH TERMINATIONS WHICH IN ITALIAN END IN O.

AGE makes AGGIO.

page,	*pággio*
équipage,	*equipággio*

AIN makes ANO.

vilain,	*villáno*
humain,	*umáno*

AIN and IEN (names of nations) make ANO and INO.

Italien,	*Italiáno*
Romain,	*Románo*
Napolitain,	*Napoletáno*
Parisien,	*Parigíno*

AIRE makes ARIO.

salaire,	*salário*
téméraire,	*temerário*

EAU makes ELLO.

chapeau,	*cappèllo*
manteau,	*mantèllo*

ENT (substantive) ENTO.

sacrement,	*sacraménto*

EUX makes OSO.

généreux,	*generóso*
gracieux,	*grazióso*

IN makes INO.

vin,	*vino*
jardin,	*giardino*

IF makes IVO.

actif,	*attivo*
passif,	*passico*

C makes CO or CCO.

porc,	*pòrco*
Turc,	*Túrco*
Grec,	*Grèco*
franc	*franco*
bec	*becco*
sec	*secco*

CHANGE OF TERMINATIONS OF VERBS AND PARTICIPLES.

ER makes ARE.

aimer,	*amáre*
parler,	*parláre*

ENDRE makes ENDERE.

prendre,	*prèndere*

rendre,	*réndere*

IR makes IRE.

partir,	*partire*
sentir,	*sentire*
finir	*finire*

The participles in é make *ato*; aimé, *amáto*; orné, *ornáto*; chanté, *cantáto*; parlé, *parláto*.

The participles in *i* make *ito*; dormi, *dormíto*; senti, *sentíto*; parti, *partíto*; menti, *mentíto*.

There are a great many Italian words which have no kind of analogy or resemblance with the French; as, *le ciglia*, the eyebrows; *fazzolétto*, a handkerchief; *gòbbo*, crook-backed; *chiamáre*, to call; *scherzáre*, to joke; and many others, which prevent these rules from being general.

OTHER TERMINATIONS OF THE ITALIAN NOUNS, DERIVED FROM THE LATIN.

The Latin ablative generally makes the Italian nominative; as, *calóre, onóre, pèttine, vérgine*.

The neutral nominatives change their last syllable into *o*; as, sacerdotium, *sacerdozio*, &c. But if the last syllable of the nominative begins with a consonant, the consonant continues, and the vowel *o* is added to it; examples: *tempus*, say *tèmpo*; *cornu*, *còrno*; retaining the *p* and *n*, which are the first letters of the last syllable of the nominative *tempus*, *tèmpo*, and the nominative, *cornu*, *còrno*.

The neutral nominatives in *en* drop the letter *n*; as, nomen, *nóme*; flumen, *fiúme*; changing also the letter *l* into *i*, as has been already observed, when we treated of nouns ending in *u*.   (P. 50.)

The greatest part of the Latin infinitives, of the second and third conjugation, make the Italian infinitives; as, *dolére*, *tenére*, *solére*, *temére*, *vedére*, *crédere*, *lèggere*, *difèndere*.

CHAPTER III.

OF THE PRONOUNS.

THE pronouns are either personal, conjunctive, possessive, demonstrative, interrogative, relative, or indefinite.

OF PRONOUNS PERSONAL([*]).

The pronouns personal are *io* and *noi* (*I* and *we*) for the first person, and they serve for the masculine and feminine.

Tu and *voi* (*thou* and *you*) for the second, and these serve also for the masculine and feminine.

Egli or *esso* (*he*) for the third person of the masculine gender, and makes *églino* or *essi* (*they*) in the plural.

Ella or *essa* (*she*) for the third person in the fem. gender, form in the pl. *elleno* or *esse*, but *esse* is preferable.

---

* See EXERCISES, p. 22.

The pronouns personal are declined by the article indefinite, *di, a, da.*

The Declension of Pronouns Personal.

First Person.

Sing.	Nom.	I,	*io.*
	Gen.	of me,	*di me.*
	Dat.	to me,	*a me,* or *mi.*
	Acc.	me,	*me,* or *mi.*
	Abl.	from me,	*da me.*
Plur.	Nom.	we,	*noi.*
	Gen.	of us,	*di noi.*
	Dat.	to us,	*a noi,* or *ci.*
	Acc.	us,	*noi,* or *ci.*
	Abl.	from *or* by us,	*da noi.*

With me, is rendered by *con me,* or *méco. Me,* after the imperatives, is expressed by *mi;* as, speak to me, *parlátemi;* tell me, *ditemi;* send me, *mandátemi;* write to me, *scrivétemi.*

Us, after the imperative, is rendered by *ci;* examples: tell us, *diteci;* give us, *dáteci;* show us, *mostráteci.* In these examples, *us* is not a pronoun personal, but conjunctive, as will be shown hereafter.

Second Person.

Sing.	Nom.	thou,	*tu.*
	Gen.	of thee,	*di te.*
	Dat.	to thee,	*a te,* or *ti.*
	Acc.	thee,	*te,* or *ti.*
	Abl.	from thee,	*da te.*
Plur.	Nom.	you *or* ye,	*voi.*
	Gen.	of you,	*di voi.*
	Dat.	to you,	*a voi,* or *vi.*
	Acc.	you,	*voi,* or *vi,*
	Abl.	from you,	*da voi.*

With thee is rendered by *con te,* or *teco; you,* after imperatives, by *vi,* and not by *voi,* as, Be contented, *contentátevi;* show yourself, *mostrátevi;* hide yourself, *nascondétevi;* dress yourself, *vestítevi;* thee or thyself, is expressed after imperatives by *ti;* as, *móstrati,* show thyself.

Third Person. For the masculine.

Sing. Nom. he,   *egli* or *esso.*
    Gen. of him,   *di lui* or *di esso.*
    Dat. to him,   *a lui, a esso,* &c. or *gli.*
    Acc. him,   *lui,* or *lo* and *il* (poet.).
    Abl. from him,   *da lui.*

Plur. Nom. they,   *églino,* or *essi.*
    Gen. of them,   *di loro,* or *di essi,* &c.
    Dat. to them,   *a loro,* or *loro,* and *gli.*
    Acc. them,   *loro,* or *li.*
    Abl. from them,   *da loro.*

₊ Remember that the pronoun *him,* or *to him,* when joined to a verb, is always rendered in Italian by *gli,* and *her* by *le,* as you will see in the pronouns conjunctive.

Third Person. Feminine.

Sing. Nom. she,   *ella,* or *essa.*
    Gen. of her,   *di lei,* or *di essa,* &c.
    Dat. to her,   *a lei,* or *le.*
    Acc. her,   *lei,* or *la.*
    Abl. from *or* by her,   *da lei.*

Plur. Nom. they,   *elleno,* or *esse.*
    Gen. of them.   *di loro,* or *di essi,* &c.
    Dat. to them,   *a loro,* or *loro.*
    Acc. them,   *loro,* or *le.*
    Abl. from or by them,   *da loro.*

Though there are instances of *lui, lei,* and *loro* being used in the nominative, yet it is better to say *egli párla, ella cánta,* than *lui párla, lei cánta;* because *lui* or *lei* are not to be used in the nominative, but in the other cases. *Esso,* plural *essi,* &c. for the nominative and the other cases. We therefore say, with him, *con lui*, or *con esso* ; for her, *per lei*, or *per essa* ; for them, *per loro* or *per essi* ; with him, *con lui* or *seco* ; with her, *con lei* or *seco*.

Of the Pronoun se, *one's self,* himself *or* herself.

There is another personal pronoun, which serves indifferently for the masculine and feminine ; it is *se*, one's self ; it has no nominative.

Gen. of one's self, himself, or herself,   *di se.*
Dat. to one's self, &c.   *a se,* or *si.*
Acc. one's self, &c.   *se,* or *si.*
Abl. from *or* by one's self, &c.   *da se.*

It is often joined with the pronoun *stésso*, or *stéssa*, and in that case it is more elegant ; *per se stésso*, by, or for himself ; *per se stéssa*, for herself.

OF CONJUNCTIVE PRONOUNS.

The conjunctive pronouns bear a great resemblance to the personal pronouns : the personal pronouns are,

I, thou, he, she ; we, ye, they.

There are seven pronouns conjunctive, viz. *to me,* or *me ; to thee,* or *thee ; to himself,* or *himself ; to herself,* or *herself ; to him,* or *him ; to us,* or *us ; to you,* or *you ; to them,* or *them.*

They are expressed in Italian by

mi, ti, si, gli, or *le, ci, vi, loro.*

It is easy to remember that the pronouns conjunctive, *me, thee, one's self, himself,* or *herself ; to him, them,* or *to them,* &c. are always rendered in Italian by *mi, ti, si, gli,* or *le, loro.* Example : this pleases me, *questo mi piáce ;* so he said to him, *così gli disse ;* God sees thee, *Dio ti véde ;* the sun rises, *il sole si léva ;* I will tell him, *io gli dirò ;* I will tell her, *io le dirò ;* I will see him, *io lo vedrò ;* I will see her, *io la vedrò ;* I promise them, *prométto loro ;* as well for the masculine as the feminine.

✱ The pronoun conjunctive *loro* is always put after the verb in Italian, as it is in English ; for instance, you will tell them, *diréte loro.*

The pronoun conjunctive, to him, is expressed in Italian by *gli*, and to her, by *le;* example : I speak to him, *io gli párlo;* I speak to her, *io le párlo.* We likewise make use of *gli* in the plural, to signify *loro;* but observe, we must put *gli* when before the verb ; as, *io gli ho intéso dire cose mirábili;* and *loro* when after, as, *ho vedúto far loro cose mirábili;* return them their book, *rendéte loro il loro libro.*

The pronouns *we* and *ye* are expressed in Italian by *noi* and *voi,* when they precede the verbs whose action they make, and to which they are nominatives : as, we pray, *noi preghiàmo;* you sing, *voi cantáte.* *We* is the nominative of *to pray,* of which it makes the action ; and so *ye* is the nominative of *to sing ;* then *we* and *ye* are pronouns personal.

When *we* and *ye,* in Italian *noi* and *voi,* precede verbs to which they are not the nominative, and there is some other word which goes before, and makes the action of the verb, then they are pronouns conjunctive, and must be expressed by *ci* and *vi,* in English *us* and *you;* example : the master speaks to us, *il maèstro ci párla,* and not *noi párla :* because the master makes the action, and is the nominative to the verb. In like manner, to render in Italian, *we speak to you,* we must say, *noi vi parliámo,* and not *noi voi parliámo;* because *we* is the nominative, and makes the action of the verb, and not *you,* which, instead of making it, receives it. Yet we may say, *il maèstro párla a noi, noi parliámo a-voi.*

⁎ One of the chief difficulties to learners of the Italian language is, to express the pronouns conjunctive *mi, ti, ci, gli, ci, vi,* when they are followed by the particles *lo, la, li, le,* or *ne.*

But to explain this, observe you must express them here as follows, changing the letter *i* of the pronoun conjunctive into *e;* as to say, *to me of it,* instead of *mi ne,* you must say *me ne;* in like manner, instead of *mi lo,* you are to say *me lo,* pronouncing the two syllables short. And the same is to be observed in all the following conjunctive pronouns :

Me, *mi ;* me of it, *me ne,*	it,	to me,	*me lo,* mas.
	it,	to me,	*me la,* fem.
	them,	to me,	*me li, me le,* m. & f.
Thee, *ti ;* thee of it, *te ne.*	it,	to thee,	*te lo,* mas.
	it,	to thee,	*te la,* fem.
	them,	to thee,	*te li, te le,* m. & f.
Himself, *si ;* himself of it, *se ne.*	it,	to himself,	*se lo,* mas.
	it,	to himself,	*se la,* fem.
	them,	to himself,	*se li, se le,* m. & f.
To him, *gli ;* to him of it, *gliene.*	it,	to him,	*glielo,* mas.
	it,	to him,	*gliela,* fem.
	them,	to him,	*glieli, gliele,* m. & f.
Us, *ci ;* us of it, *ce ne.*	it,	to us,	*ce lo,* mas.
	it,	to us,	*ce la,* fem.
	them,	to us,	*ce li, ce le,* m. & f.
You, *vi ;* you of it, *ve ne.*	it,	to you,	*ve lo,* mas.
	it,	to you,	*ve la,* fem.
	them,	to you,	*ve li, ve le,* m. & f.

To them, *loro ;* to them of it, *ne loro ;* putting always *loro* after the verb.

If the verbs are in the infinitive or the gerund, the pronoun conjunctive must be placed after, as follows : to tell me, *per dirmi ;* to tell me of it, *per dírmene ;* to give it to me, *per dármelo ;* in telling it me, *dicèndomelo ;* to give it to us, *per dárcelo ;* so as to make, as it were, but one word of it, remembering that we must always pronounce short, *melo, mene, telo, tene, celo, celi, cele,* and the rest after the same manner.

Other examples concerning the pronoun conjunctive *loro,* them.

I promise them,	*promètto loro.*
To promise them some,	*per promètterne loro.*
In promising them some,	*promettèndone loro.*

After imperatives, and before infinitives and gerunds, the pronouns are never personal, but conjunctive ; examples : give us, *dáteci ;* to see you, *per vedérvi ;* in speaking to you, *parlándovi.*

After verbs, when a question is asked, the pronouns are personal, and not conjunctive ; example : have you ? *avéte voi ?* shall we sing ? *canterémo noi ?*

The poets always use *ne*, instead of *ci*, to express the pronoun conjunctive, *us*, as in Guarini's *Pástor Fido*.

Perchè, crudo destin, ne disunísci tu, s'amór ne stringe ?
E tu perchè ne stringi, se ne párte il destín, pèrfido amóre ?

Why, cruel fate, dost thou part us, if love unites us ? And thou, treacherous love, why dost thou unite us, if fate parts us ?

OF PRONOUNS POSSESSIVE ([10]).

The English have no article in the nominative before pronouns possessive, but the Italians have ; as, my, *il mio, la mia*, fem. ; plur. *i mièi, le mie*, fem.

There are six pronouns possessive, viz. *il mio, il túo, il súo, il nòstro, il vòstro, il loro* ; my, thy, his, our, your, their : in the plural they make *i mièi, i tuòi, i suòi ; i nòstri, i vòstri, i lóro*.

The feminine pronouns possessive are, *la mia, la túa, la súa, la nòstra, la vòstra, la lóro* ; in the plural, *le mie, le túe, le súe, le nòstre, le vòstre, le lóro*.

Loro, as you see, never changes, but is always *loro* ; it is put before the masculine, as well as the feminine ; before the singular, as well as the plural number.

The pronouns possessive are declined by the definite article *il* for the masculine, and by *la* for the feminine.

To render them easy to decline, I shall give the following example :

Sing. Nom. my book,   *il mio libro.*
     Gen. of my book,   *del mio libro.*
     Dat. to my book,   *al mio libro.*
     Abl. from *or* by my book, *dal mio libro.*
Plur. Nom. my books,   *i mièi libri.*
     Gen. of my books,   *de' mièi libri.*
     Dat. to my books,   *a' miei libri.*
     Abl. from *or* by my books, *da' miei libri.*

Decline all the other masculines in the same manner, and the feminines by the article *la* ; as *la mia sèrva*,

---

([10]) See Bottarelli's Exercises, p. 24.

d. lla mia serva, alla mia serva, dalla mia serva, le mie serve, delle mie serve, alle mie serve, dalle mie serve.

⁎ Note, you must not use the definite article when the pronouns possessive precede nouns of quality, but the indefinite articles, *di, a, da* ; examples :

Your majesty,	*vòstra maestà.*
Of your majesty,	*di vòstra maestà.*
To your Majesty,	*a vostra maestà.*
From your majesty,	*da vostra maestà.*

⁎ Remember also, that names of kindred conform to this rule ; thus we say, *mio pádre, di mio pádre, a mio padre, da mio padre ; mia mádre, di mia mádre, a mia mádre, da mia mádre ; mio fratèllo, di mio fratèllo, a mio fratello, da mio fratello ; mia sorèlla, di mia sorèlla, a mia sorella, da mia sorella ; mio maríto,* &c.

If the nouns of quality or relation be in the plural, we must make use of the definite article *i* or *le, de', dei,* or *delle ;* examples :

Your brothers,	*i vòstri fratèlli,* or *i fratèlli vòstri.*
Of your brothers,	*de'* or *dei vòstri fratèlli,* or *de' fratelli vostri.*
To your brothers,	*a' vostri fratelli.*
From your brothers,	*da' vostri fratelli.*
Your sisters,	*le vòstre sorèlle,* or *le sorèlle vòstre.*
Of your sisters,	*delle vostre sorelle.*
To your sisters,	*alle vostre sorelle.*
From your sisters,	*dalle vostre sorelle.*
Their highnesses,	*le altézze loro,* or *le loro altézze.*
Of their highnesses,	*delle altézze loro.*
To their highnesses,	*alle altezze loro.*
From their highnesses,	*dalle altezze loro.*

Though the definite article sometimes occurs in ancient and modern authors before nouns of kindred in the singular number, yet we ought not to imitate them ; according to the old proverb, *tu vivendo bonos, scribendo sequere peritos.*

Observe, that when the pronoun possessive is accompanied by the pronoun demonstrative, we do not put the article in the nominative. We do not say, *il quésto mio libro*, but *quésto mio libro*. In all other cases we make use of the indefinite article; thus we say, *di quésto vòstro libro, a quélla nòstra cása*, &c.

OF PRONOUNS DEMONSTRATIVE.

The pronouns demonstrative are *this, that, these, those*.

They are called pronouns demonstrative, because they serve to point out or demonstrate any thing or person : as, *this book, that man, that woman*, &c.

We make use of *quésto, quésti, quésta, quéste*, in showing a thing near at hand ; and *quél, quéllo, quélli, quéi, quélla, quélle*, in showing or speaking of a thing at a distance.

Costúi, colúi, costèi, colèi, are also pronouns demonstrative, and never used but in speaking of a rational being ; as, of a boy, a man, a woman, &c. and not of a horse, a dog, &c. : examples : It is for this man, do not give it to that, *è per costúi, non lo dáte a colui ;* pay this woman, and send away that, *pagáte costèi, e rimandáte colèi ;* you may also say, *è per quésto, non lo dáte a quéllo ; pagáte quésta, rimandáte quélla.*

Colúi, costúi, colèi, costèi, are used (in prose) to imply contempt.

Costúi and *costèi* form in the plural *costóro*, these men or women : *colúi* and *colèi* make in the plural *colóro*, they or those men or women.

We seldom make use of *colóro* or *costóro*, either in the feminine or in the masculine for the nominative.

We make use of *costúi, colúi, costèi, colèi, costóro, colóro*, when they are the last words of a sentence, but seldom in the beginning or middle of it.

We frequently meet with *cotésto* and *cotésta*, and they signify *that man* or *thing, that woman* or *thing ;* but you are to observe that there is a difference between *quésto* and *cotésto.* Foreigners, and sometimes the Italians themselves, are mistaken in the use of these two pronouns. We ought never to use *cotésto* and *colésta*, but in speaking of a thing which is on, under or about the person whom we address. Therefore you may say, *cotésto vostro ábito*, for, that coat of yours; but not *cotesto mio ábito*, for, this coat of mine.

*** Observe, *quésti* and *quégli* are often used for the singular number; as, this man was happy, that unfortunate, *quésti fu felice, quegli sfortunáto;* but it is used only in speaking of a rational being, as of a man, a woman, an angel, &c. and not in speaking of an animal, or any inanimate things, for then we are to make use of *quésto* and *quel* or *quello*.

*** Note, *what* is often expressed by *il che;* but in that case it must refer to some antecedent phrase: example; my father is dead, which obliges me to go, *mio pádre è mòrto, il che mi òbbliga a partíre.* In the beginning of a sentence we must say, *ciò che;* example: that which pleases me I have not, *ciò che mi piáce, non l' ho.*

OF PRONOUNS INTERROGATIVE.

The pronouns interrogative serve to ask questions, and are as follow: who? what? which? *chi? che? quále?* Examples:

Who is it?	*chi è?*
Who told you so?	*chi v' ha détto ciò?*
What will you have?	*che voléte?*
What are you doing?	*che fáte?*
What book is it?	*che libro è?*
What house is it?	*che casa è?*

What? *che?* of what? *di che?* to what? *a che?* from what? *da che?*

*** *Che* is often used for *quále?* and then the phrase is more elegant; example: what man is that? *che vòmo è?* what business have you? *che affári avéte?* instead of saying, *qual uòmo è? quáli affári avéte?*

OF PRONOUNS RELATIVE([11]).

There are three pronouns relative in English,
That, who, and *which.*

That, when it is a relative pronoun, is expressed in
Italian by *che,* or by *il quále* in the masculine, and by
la quále in the feminine ; example : *il libro che io lèggo,*
the book that I read ; *la casa che ho,* the house that I
have.

I said when it is a pronoun relative, because when it
is a conjunction or adverb it is rendered by *che ;* you
must therefore say, *crédo che andrò,* &c. I believe I
shall go, &c.

Who, except it be interrogative, is also expressed by
che ; examples : the master who teaches, *il maèstro che
insègna :* the fools who laugh, *gli sciòcchi che ridono.*
But if it be interrogative, it is rendered by *chi.*

Of whom or *whose* is expressed by *di chi* or *di cui.*

To whom is expressed by *a chi* or *a cui.*

From whom by *da chi* or *da cui.*

Which, masc. is expressed by *il quále ;* of which *del
quále ;* to which, *al quále ;* from which, *dal quále ;*
which, plural, *i quáli ;* of which, *dei quáli ;* to which,
ai quáli ; from which, *dai quáli.*

Which, feminine, *la quále, della quále, alla quále,
dalla quále ;* in the plural, *le quáli,* &c.

⁎ Observe, that the pronouns relative, *that, who,
which,* are also expressed by *che ;* thus, instead of saying, *quále, quáli, il quále, i quáli, la quále, le quáli ;* we
may say and write *che,* which is more received.

⁎ The purest authors place the pronoun *cui* between
the definite article and the noun. See the following
examples : but observe, that you will never find this
pronoun in the nominative.

Whose fair face, il cui bèl viso or *vólto,* or *il di cui bel
viso,* for *il bel viso di cui.*

Whose beauties, le cui bellézze, or *le di cúi bellézze,*
for *le bellézze di cui.*

To whose father, al cui pádre, or *al di cui pádre,* for
al pádre di cui.

([11]) See Bottarelli's Exercises, p. 26.

From whose brother I have received, *dal cui*, or *dal di cui fratèllo ho ricevúto.* See *Boccáccio, Lodovico Dólce, Menzíni, Dávila,* and cardinal *Bentivòglio,* who frequently use these expressions.

The French relative *dont, of which,* or *of whom,* is rendered in Italian by *di cui.*

Dont le, il di cúi, or *il cúi.*

Dont la, la di cui, or *la cui.*

Dont les, i di cui, or *i cui,* for the masculine.

Dont les, le di cui, or *le cui,* for the feminine.

** *Lo, la, li, le,* are pronouns conjunctive, when before verbs.

Him, as we have already observed in the chapter of articles, is rendered by *lo;* example : I see him, *io lo védo;* you know him, *voi lo conoscéte.*

If the verb begins with a vowel : there must be an elision : as, I caress him, *io l' accarézzo.*

Her is expressed by *la;* examples : I know her, *io la conósco;* you want her, *voi la voléte.*

Them is expressed by *li* for the masculine, and by *le* for the feminine ; as, I see them, *li védo* or *le védo.*

** Remember that the conjunctive pronouns, *lo, la, li, le,* must be transposed after infinitives, gerunds, and the word *ècco,* here or there is, and not put before, as in French.

Esso, he, himself or it, is a personal pronoun which can be constructed also as a demonstrative : it makes in the plural, *essi,* themselves ; *essa,* she, herself or it, makes *esse,* themselves, fem.

OF IMPROPER OR INDEFINITE PRONOUNS.

These pronouns are called *indefinite* or *improper,* because, in fact, they are not properly pronouns, but have a great resemblance to adjectives as well as to pronouns. They are the following :

Tútto, tútti, m. *tútta, tútte,* f. all or every ; *ógni,* each or every ; *áltro, áltra,* other, *áltri, áltre,* others ; *quálche,* some ; *chiúnque,* whosoever ; *qualchedúno, qualchedúna,* some one ; *alcúno,* some one, man or thing ; *alcúna,* some one, woman or thing ; *ciaschedúno, ciaschedúni,* masc. *ciaschedúna, ciaschedúne*, fem. every one ; *nessúno* nobody ; *il medésimo* or *il medémo, lo stésso*, masc. *la medésima, la medéma, la stéssa, l' istéssa*, fem. the same ; *ciascúno*, masc. *ciascúna*, fem. each or every one ; *altrúi, altri*, others, &c.

Verúno, verúna, not one man or woman, is used for the affirmative as well as for the negative.

Tútto, comprehends a totality, and agrees with the thing spoken of; examples : all the world, *tútto il móndo*, or *tútto 'l móndo ;* all the men, *tútti gli uómini ;* the whole earth, *tútta la tèrra ;* all the women, *tútte le dònne*.

. We must use *tútto* and *tútta* when the word *all* is followed by an article or a numeral noun : as, all the world, *tútto 'l móndo ;* all the earth, *tútta la tèrra ;* all three, *tútti e tre*.

But if after the word *all* there be no article, we must use *ogni ;* examples : all men who say so, speak wrong, *ogni uòmo che dice quésto, párla mále ;* all women who, *ogni dònna che.*

Observe, nevertheless, that this pronoun (*tútte*) is used without the article, and is of great elegance, especially in verse.

> *Che* tútte *altre bellézze indiètro vánno.*
> *Sciòlti da* tútte *qualitidi umáne.*

. *Ogni* is put with the singular number, and never with the plural ; and it is indeclinable. It is used before masculines as well as feminines, and especially when the pronoun *all* may be rendered by each or every ; examples : all or every scholar, *ogni scoláre ;* for all or every thing, *per ogni cosa.*

There are some examples of *ogni* in the plural. Crescenzi, 236, says, *apprèsso la fèsta d'ogni sánti*, after the feast of All Saints. Fiammetta, 29, *i mièi affánni ogni áltri trapássano.* But such examples are so uncommon, that they hardly deserve notice.

Altro makes in the plural *altri ; altra*, feminine, makes *altre*. Oblique cases can be constructed by *altrúi ;* as, gen. *altrúi* or *d' altrúi ;* dat. *altrúi* or *ad altrúi ;* acc. *altrúi ;* abl. *altrúi* or *da altrúi.*

Altro, when it is not followed by a noun, signifies *another thing.*

Altri is sometimes put for the singular number; as, *áltri piánge, áltri ride,* one weeps, another laughs.

⁎ *Quálche* is only placed before the singular, and never with the plural: it is not right to say, *quálche signóri, quálche signore,* some gentlemen, some ladies; you must say, *alcúni signóri, alcúne signóre.*

Qualsivòglia, whatever, is likewise used as an improper noun: *qualsivòglia libro,* whatever book; *qualsivòglia céra,* whatever wax.

CHAPTER IV.

OF THE VERBS ([12]).

Whatever relates to the verbs, will be rendered much easier to learn by attending to the following remarks:

IMPORTANT REMARKS ON THE CONJUGATIONS.

Before you begin to learn the conjugations, it will be proper to observe, that all the verbs may be conjugated without the pronouns personal, *io, tu, égli, noi, voi, églino;* you are therefore at liberty to form them with or without the pronouns; and it will be right in you to follow the Latin rule,

Supprimit orator, quæ rusticus edit ineptè.

⁎ You must also observe, that the tenses marked with a star, in the conjugation of the verb *avére, to have,* are terminated and conjugated after the same manner in all the other verbs; thus we say in the preterimperfect of the verb *avére,*

Avéva or *avévo* ([13]), *avévi, avéva, avevámo,* &c.

---

[12] See Bottarelli's Exercises on the Verbs, p. 40.

[13] The termination in *o* for the first person of the preterimperfect is commonly used in colloquial discourse, and in familiar letters, yet in serious and respectful style the termination in *a* is more correct.

All verbs follow the same rule ; examples :
Amávo or *amáva, amávi, amáva, amavámo,* &c.
Credévo or *credéva, credévi, credéva, credevámo,* &c.
Sentívo or *sentíva, sentívi, sentíva, sentivámo,* &c.

And in like manner all other tenses that are distinguished by a star, except the single verb *èssere,* to be.

Note. In the Italian language, as in Latin, we do not make use of any personal pronouns before verbs, except when two or three different persons are expressed by the same word ; as the subject of the third person both of the singular and plural may be a man or a woman, two men, or two women, it admits very frequently of the pronoun, when there is no antecedent which points clearly to the subject.

CONJUGATION OF THE AUXILIARY VERB AVÉRE, *to have.*

INDICATIVE.

PRESENT.
Singular.

I have,	*io ho* (see p. 26, l. 3), or	*ho.*
Thou hast,	*tu hái,*	*hái.*
He has,	*ègli ha,*	*ha.*

Plural.

We have,	*nói abbiámo,* or	*abbiámo.*
You have,	*vói avéte,*	*avéte.*
They have,	*églino hánno,*	*hánno.*

PRETERIMPERFECT.

I had,	*io avéva,* or *avévo* ([13]).
Thou hadst,	*tu avévi.*
He had,	*ègli avéva.*
We had,	*noi avevámo.*
You had,	*voi aveváte.*
They had,	*églino avévano.*

PRETERPERFECT DEFINITE.

I had,	*io èbbi.*
Thou hadst,	*tu avésti.*
He had,	*ègli èbbe.*

We had,	*noi avémmo.*
You had,	*voi avéste.*
They had,	*églino èbbero.*

PRETERPERFECT.

I have had,	*io ho avúto.*
Thou hast had,	*tu hái avúto* (see note [21]).
He has had,	*égli ha avuto.*
We have had,	*noi abbiámo avuto.*
You have had,	*voi avéte avuto.*
They have had,	*églino hánno avuto.*

PRETERPLUPERFECT.

I had had,	*io avéva avúto.*
Thou hadst had,	*tu avévi avuto.*
He had had,	*égli avéva avuto.*
We had had,	*noi avevámo avuto.*
You had had,	*voi aveváte avuto.*
They had had,	*églino avévano avuto.*

FUTURE.

I shall *or* will have,	*io avrò.*
Thou shalt have,	*tu avrái.*
He shall have,	*égli avrà.*
We shall have,	*noi avrémo.*
You shall have,	*voi avréte.*
They shall have,	*églino avránno.*

IMPERATIVE.

The Imperative has no first person singular in Italian.

Have thou,	*ábbi tu.*
Let him have,	*ábbia égli.*
Let us have,	*abbiámo noi.*
Have you,	*abbiáte voi.*
Let them have,	*ábbiano églino.*

E 3

OPTATIVE AND SUBJUNCTIVE.

I join them together, because their tenses are similar.

PRESENT.

That I may have,	*ch' io ábbia.*
That thou mayest have,	*che tu ábbi* or *ábbia.*
That he may have,	*ch' égli ábbia.*
That we may have,	*che noi abbiámo.*
That you may have,	*che voi abbiáte.*
That they may have,	*ch' églino ábbiano.*

FIRST PRETERIMPERFECT.

That I had,	*°ch' io avéssi.*
That thou hadst,	*che tu avéssi.*
That he had,	*ch' égli avésse.*
That we had,	*che noi avéssimo.*
That you had,	*che voi avéste.*
That they had,	*ch' églino avéssero.*

SECOND PRETERIMPERFECT.

I should have,	*io avrèi.*
Thou shouldst have,	*tu avrésti.*
He should have,	*égli avrèbbe.*
We should have,	*noi avrémmo.*
You should have,	*voi avréste.*
They should have,	*églino avrèbbero.*

PRETERPERFECT.

That I have had,	*ch' io ábbia avúto.*
Thou hast had,	*che tu ábbi avuto.*
He has had,	*ch' égli ábbia avuto.*
We have had,	*che noi abbiámo avuto.*
You have had,	*che voi abbiáte avuto.*
They have had,	*ch' églino ábbiano avuto.*

PRETERPLUPERFECT.

It is compounded of the first preterimperfect sub-junctive and the participle.

If I had had,	*se io avéssi avúto.*
If thou hadst had,	*se tu avéssi avuto.*
If he had had,	*s' égli avésse avuto.*

If we had had,	se noi avéssimo avuto.
If you had had,	se voi avéste avuto.
If they had had,	s' églino avéssero avuto.

SECOND PRETERPLUPERFECT.

It is compounded of the second preterimperfect subjunctive and the participle.

I should have had,	io avrèi avúto.
Thou shouldst have had,	tu avrésti avuto.
He should have had,	égli avrèbbe avuto.
We should have had,	noi avrémmo avuto.
You should have had,	voi avréste avuto.
They should have had,	églino avrèbbero avuto.

FUTURE.

It is compounded of the future of the indicative and the participle.

When I shall have had,	quand io avrò avúto.
Thou shalt have had,	—— tu avrái avuto.
He shall have had,	—— égli avrà avuto.
We shall have had,	—— noi avrémo avuto.
You shall have had,	—— voi avréte avuto.
They shall have had,	—— églino avránno avuto.

INFINITIVE.

PRESENT.

| To have, | avére. |

PRETERPERFECT.

| To have had, | avére avúto. |

PARTICIPLES.

| Had, | avúto, avúta; plural, avúti, avúte. |

E 4

GERUNDS.

Having, *or* in having,	avèndo. coll' avére. nell' avere. in avere.
Having had,	avèndo avúto.

*** We often use the verb *avére*, with the particle *da*, or *a*, instead of the verb *dovére*; examples : I have to do, *ho da fáre;* being to speak, *avèndo a dire;* instead of *dèvo fáre, dovèndo dire.*

By the generality of tenses of the verb *avére*, you plainly perceive how necessary it is to be perfectly acquainted with them in order to attain a speedy knowledge of all the rest, since there is such an entire conformity between them, except in the present, preterperfect definite, and the subjunctive.

*** Upon first learning the Italian language, the interrogation creates some difficulty ; and we are at a loss how to express *shall I have ? have we ? hast thou ? has he ?* yet there is nothing more easy ; for it is merely by putting the pronouns personal after the verbs, as in English, and we shall never mistake in saying *avrò io? abbiámo noi ? hai tu ? ha égli ?* And if we would express ourselves with greater elegance and ease, we ought not to mention the pronouns at all ; examples : shall I have this ? *avrò quésto ?* does he do well ? *fa bène ?* shall we sing ? *canterémo ?*

When we speak negatively, we must use the word *non ;* examples : I have not, *non ho;* you must not know, *non dovéte conóscere ;* thou hast not, *non hai ;* he has not, *non ha.*

In the like manner to express, I have some, thou hast some, he has some, say, *ne ho, ne hai, ne ha,* &c.

And to express, I have none, thou hast none, he has none, &c. you may say, *non ne ho, non ne hai, non ne ha.*

But to express, have I none ? hast thou none ? we say, *non ne ho io ? non ne hai tu ?*

CONJUGATION OF THE AUXILIARY VERB ÈSSERE, *to b*

INDICATIVE.

PRESENT.

I am,	*io sòno,*	or	*sòno.*
Thou art,	*tu sèi,*		*sèi.*
He is,	*égli è,*		*è.*
We are,	*noi siámo,*		*siámo.*
You are,	*voi siète,*		*siète.*
They are,	*églino sóno,*		*sóno.*

PRETERIMPERFECT.

I was,	*io èra,* or *èro,*		*èra, èro* ([13]).
Thou wert,	*tu èri,*		*èri.*
He was,	*égli èra,*		*èra.*
We were,	*noi eravámo,*		*eravámo.*
You were,	*voi eraváte,*		*eraváte.*
They were,	*églino èrano,*		*èrano.*

PRETERPERFECT DEFINITE.

I was,	*io fúi,*	or	*fúi.*
Thou wert,	*tu fósti,*		*fósti.*
He was,	*égli fù,*		*fù.*
We were,	*noi fúmmo,*		*fúmmo.*
You were,	*voi fóste,*		*fóste.*
They were,	*églino fúrono,*		*fúrono.*

PRETERPERFECT.

It is compounded of the present indicative, *io sòn*
and its own participle *státo* or *státa ;* pl. *stati* or *state.*

I have been,	*io sòno státo* or *státa.*
Thou hast been,	*tu sèi stato* (see note [26]).
He has been,	*égli è stato.*
We have been,	*noi siámo stati* or *state.*
You have been,	*voi siète stati.*
They have been,	*églino sóno stati.*

If we speak in the feminine, we must say, *sòno státa, sèi státa, è státa; siámo státe, sièle státe, sóno státe;* and so on in all the compound tenses.

PRETERPLUPERFECT.

I had been,	*io èra státo,* or *státa.*
Thou hadst been,	*tu èri státo.*
He had been,	*égli èra státo.*
We had been,	*noi eravámo stati,* or *state.*
You had been,	*voi eraváte stati.*
They had been,	*églino èrano stati.*

FUTURE.

I shall *or* will be,	*io sarò.*
Thou shalt be,	*tu sarái.*
He shall be,	*égli sarà.*
We shall *or* will be,	*noi sarémo.*
You shall be,	*voi saréte.*
They shall be,	*églino saránno.*

IMPERATIVE.

Be thou,	*sii tu,* or *sia tu.*
Let him be,	*sia égli.*
Let us be,	*siámo noi.*
Be you,	*siáte voi.*
Let them be,	*siano,* or *sieno églino.*

OPTATIVE AND SUBJUNCTIVE.

PRESENT.

That I may be,	*ch'io sia.*
Thou mayest be,	*che tu sii* or *sia.*
He may be,	*ch' égli sia.*
We may be,	*che noi siámo.*
You may be,	*che voi siáte.*
They may be,	*ch' églino siano,* or *sieno.*

FIRST PRETERIMPERFECT.

That I were *or* might be,	*ch' io fóssi.*
Thou wert,	*che tu fóssi.*
He were,	*ch' égli fósse.*
We were,	*che noi fóssimo.*
You were,	*che voi fóste.*
They were,	*ch' églino fóssero.*

SECOND PRETERIMPERFECT.

I should *or* would be,	*io sarèi.*
Thou shouldst be,	*tu sarésti.*
He should be,	*égli sarèbbe.*
We should be,	*noi sarémmo.*
You should be,	*voi saréste.*
They should be,	*églino sarèbbero.*

PRETERPERFECT.

It is compounded of the present conjunctive *io sía*, and the participle *státo* or *státa*, of the same verb.

That I have been,	*ch' io sía státo* or *státa.*
Thou hast been,	*che tu súi,* or *sía stato.*
He has been,	*ch' égli sia stato.*
We have been,	*che noi siámo stati,* or *state.*
You have been,	*che voi siáte stati.*
They have been,	*ch' églino síano stati.*

PRETERPLUPERFECT.

It is compounded of the first preterimperfect subjunctive, and the participle.

If I had been,	*se io fóssi státo.*
Thou hadst been,	*se tu fóssi stato.*
He had been,	*s' égli fósse stato.*
We had been,	*se noi fóssimo stati.*
You had been,	*se voi fóste stati.*
They had been,	*s' églino fóssero stati.*

SECOND PRETERPLUPERFECT.

It is compounded of the second preterimperfect subjunctive and the participle.

I should *or* would have been,	*io sarèi státo.*
Thou shouldst have been,	*tu sarésti stato.*
He should have been,	*égli sarèbbe stato.*
We should have been,	*noi sarémmo stati.*
You should have been,	*voi saréste stati.*
They should have been,	*églino sarèbbero stati.*

FUTURE.

When I shall have been,	*quand' io sarò státo.*
Thou shalt have been,	*tu sarái stato.*
He shall have been,	*égli sarà stato.*
We shall have been,	*noi sarémo stati.*
You shall have been.	*voi saréte stati.*
They shall have been,	*églino saránno stati.*

INFINITIVE.

To be,   *èssere.*

PRETERPERFECT.

To have been,   *èssere státo.*

PARTICIPLES.

Been, *státo,* for the masculine; *státa,* for the feminine.
Plural, *státi,* . . . . . *státe.*

GERUNDS.

Being, *or* in being, { *essèndo,* or *coll' èssere, nell' essere. in essere, per essere.*
Having been,   *essèndo státo.*

The verb *èssere* has no need of any other auxiliary verb; and we must never put any of the tenses of the verb *avére* before the participle *státo;* as for, I have been, you must say, *sono státo*, and not *ho stato*; I had been *èro stato*, and not *avévo stato*. Notice this well, since this is an instance in which foreigners are apt to commit mistakes.

OF THE REGULAR CONJUGATIONS.

The Italian verbs have three different terminations in the infinitive; that is to say,

In $\begin{Bmatrix} are \\ ere \\ ire \end{Bmatrix}$ as $\begin{cases} parláre, amáre, cantáre, saltáre. \\ véndere, crédere, temére, cèdere. \\ servíre, sentíre, dormíre, mentíre. \end{cases}$

For which reason I shall give but three conjugations:
Amáre, will serve as a rule for the verbs in *are*.
Crédere, for the verbs in *ere*.
Sentíre, for the verbs in *ire*.

It is proper here to observe, that the infinitives of verbs derived from the Latin retain the same quantity as they have in Latin. For instance, the verb *cantáre*, in Latin, has the second syllable long; and it has also the same syllable long in Italian. On the contrary, *crédere*, *créscere*, having the second syllable short in Latin, have it also short in Italian. If you observe this rule in pronouncing infinitives you will avoid the mistakes which most learners of the Italian language are apt to commit. The rule, however, has some exceptions. See page 111.

*** Some Italian grammarians give four conjugations instead of three: they make two branches of the verbs in *ire*, viz. those which change *ire* for the present indic. into *o, i, e, iamo, ite, ono*, and those into *isco, isci, isce, iamo, ite, iscono*. See p. 143.

An Easy Method of learning to Conjugate the Verbs.

I have reduced all the tenses of the verbs to seven, four of which are general, and have the same terminations in all the verbs; and the other three, by changing the one letter in the third person, may be likewise made general, and all conjugations reduced to one.

The general tenses are the Preterimperfect, the Future, the first and second Preterimperfect Subjunctive.

The Preterimperfect is terminated, in all the verbs, in
va or *vo*, *vi*, *va* ; *vámo*, *váte*, *vano*.

The Future Indicative is terminated in
rò, *rái*, *rà* ; *rémo*, *réte*, *ránno*.

The Imperfect Subjunctive in
ssi, *ssi*, *sse* ; *ssimo*, *ste*, *ssero*.

The Second Imperfect, *or* Conditional, in
rèi, *rèsti*, *rèbbe* ; *rémmo*, *rèste*, *rèbbero*.

Change *re* of the verbs *amáre*, *crédere*, *sentíre*, (and generally of all the other verbs) into *va* or *vo*; and *rò* into *ssi* and *rei*, &c. and you will find the imperfect, the future indicative, the first and second imperfect subjunctive of all the other verbs, without any exception; which will greatly assist the learner.

⁂ Note. The future, and the second imperfect, of the verbs in *áre*, are terminated in *erò* and *erèi*, and not in *arò* and *arèi*. Therefore in these tenses, after having made the change of *re* into *rò* for the future, and into *rèi* for the second imperfect, you must also change the vowel that precedes *rò* and *rèi*, and say *amerò*, *amerèi*; and so of the other verbs terminated in *áre*.

From this rule must be excepted the verbs in *are* of only two syllables, as *dare*, *stare*, *fare*, which retain the letter *a*, and make *darò*, &c. instead of *derò*, &c.

The present indicative, the preterperfect definite, and the present subjunctive, are the only tenses necessary to be learned; for the other four, given above, are general.

In order to form those three tenses, you must cut off the last syllable of the infinitive, and then change the last vowel which remains. For the present indicative, change it into o, through all the conjugations: thus of *amáre*, *crédere*, *sentíre*, you make *ámo*, *crédo*, *sèntu*. For the preterperfect definite of the indicatives change it into *ai* in the first conjugation; thus of *amáre*, you form *amái*; but when you come to those of the second conjugation, you must change it into *ei;* thus of *crédere*, you make *credéi;* verbs of the third conjugation have it changed into *ii;* thus *sentíre* makes *sentíi.* As for the present subjunctive, the vowel that remains is changed into *i* in the first conjugation, and into *a* in the others; thus, *ámi, créda, sènta.*

PRESENT.

$$(^{14}) \left\{\begin{array}{l} are \\ ere \\ ire \end{array}\right\} \text{ into } \left\{\begin{array}{llllll} o, & i, & a, & iámo, & áte, & ano. \\ o, & i, & e, & iámo, & éte, & ono. \\ o, & i, & e, & iámo, & íte, & ono. \end{array}\right.$$

*** Take notice, that in the singular you are to change the letter in the third person only.

PRETERPERFECT DEFINITE INDICATIVE.

$$\left.\begin{array}{l} are \\ ere \\ íre \end{array}\right\} \text{ into } \left\{\begin{array}{llllll} ái, & ásti, & ò, & ámmo, & áste, & árono. \\ éi, & ésti, & è, & émmo, & éste, & érono. \\ ii, & isti, & ì, & immo, & iste, & irono. \end{array}\right.$$

PRESENT SUBJUNCTIVE.

$$\left.\begin{array}{l} are \\ ere \\ ire \end{array}\right\} \text{ into } \left\{\begin{array}{llllll} i, & i, & i, & iámo, & iáte, & ino. \\ a, & a, & a, & iámo, & iáte, & ano. \\ a, & a, & a, & iámo, & iáte, & ano. \end{array}\right.$$

*** Observe, that through each of the conjugations there is no change made in the singular.

THE PARTICIPLES ARE,

$$\left.\begin{array}{l} are \\ ere \\ ire \end{array}\right\} \text{ into } \left\{\begin{array}{lllll} áto, & áta, & \text{sing.} & áti, & áte, \text{plur.} \\ úto, & úta, & & úti, & úte. \\ íto, & íta, & & íti, & íte. \end{array}\right.$$

---

[14] Change the termination, *áre, ére, íre,* with the letters and syllables opposite to them, and you will find the present, the preterperfect definite, and the present of the subjunctive, of all the regular verbs.

FIRST CONJUGATION OF THE VERBS IN *are,*

INDICATIVE.

PRESENT.

I love,	*ám-o.*
Thou lovest,	*ám-i.*
He loves,	*ám-a.*
We love,	*am-iámo.*
You love,	*am-áte.*
They love,	*ám-ano.*

I shall omit the personal pronouns, *io, tu, egli,* &c.

PRETERIMPERFECT.

I did love,	*am-áva* or *am-ávo* ([13]).
Thou didst love,	*am-ávi.*
He did love,	*am-áva.*
We did love,	*am-avámo.*
You did love,	*am-aváte.*
They did love,	*am-ávano.*

PRETERPERFECT DEFINITE.

I loved,	*am-ái.*
Thou lovedst,	*am-ásti.*
He loved,	*am-ò.*
We loved,	*am-ámmo.*
You loved,	*am-áste.*
They loved,	*am-árono.*

The poets frequently use *amár* and *amáro,* for *amárono;* and so of all the verbs in *áre.*

PRETERPERFECT.

This tense is composed of the participle *amáto,* and the present indicative of the auxiliary verb *avére.*

I have loved.	*ho am-áto.*
Thou hast loved,	*hái am-ato,* (see note [12].)
He has loved,	*ha am-ato,*
We have loved,	*abbiámo am-ato.*
You have loved,	*avéte am-ato.*
They have loved,	*hánno am-ato.*

PRETERPLUPERFECT.

This tense is composed of the participle *amáto*, and the imperfect of the auxiliary verb *avére.*

I had loved,	*avéva am-áto.*
Thou hadst loved,	*avévi am-ato.*
He had loved,	*avéva am-ato.*
We had loved,	*avevámo am·ato.*
You had loved,	*aveváte am-ato.*
They had loved,	*avévano am-ato.*

FUTURE.

I shall *or* will love,	*am-erò* (final *ò*, open).
Thou shalt love,	*am-erái.*
He shall love,	*am-erà.*
We shall love,	*am-erémo.*
You shall love,	*am-eréte.*
They shall love,	*am-eránno.*

Formerly *amarò* was used; but it is now the practice to write *amerò*, and so of all the verbs in *are.*

IMPERATIVE.

Love thou,	*ám-a (tu).*
Let him love,	*ám-i (égli).*
Let us love,	*am-iámo (noi).*
Love you,	*am-áte (voi).*
Let them love,	*ám-ino (églino).*

OPTATIVE AND SUBJUNCTIVE.

PRESENT.

That I may love,	*ch' io ám-i* or *che ami,* &c.
Thou mayest love,	*che tu am-i.*
He may love,	*ch' égli am-i.*
We may love,	*che noi am-iámo.*
You may love,	*che voi am-iáte.*
They may love,	*che eglino ám-ino.*

N. B. You may use the pronouns personal in the singular of this tense, *io, tu, égli,* in order to distinguish the persons, which are all terminated in the same manner; but it is superfluous to put them in the plural, the persons being sufficiently distinguished by their terminations. The same rule is applicable to the following preterimperfect, and to the present optative, and subjunctive of the second and third conjugation.

FIRST PRETERIMPERFECT.

That I might *or* could love,   *ch' io am-ássi.*
   Thou mightest love,   *che tu am-ássi.*
   He might love,   *che am-ásse.*
   We might love,   *che am-ássimo.*
   You might love,   *che am-áste.*
   They might love,   *che am-ássero.*

When the conjunction *si,* in French, governs the indicative imperfect, it governs the same tense of the subjunctive in Italian: as *si vous m'aimiez, je vous payerais d'un parfait retour;* if you loved me, &c. *se voi m'amaste,* &c. and not *se voi m'amavate;* and so in all the verbs, because, when we speak by way of wish or desire, we should make use of the subjunctive or optative.

SECOND PRETERIMPERFECT.

I should *or* would love,   *am-erèi.*
Thou shouldst love,   *am-erésti.*
He should love,   *am-erèbbe.*
We should love,   *am-erémmo.*
You should love,   *am-eréste.*
They should love,   *am-erèbbero.*

PRETERPERFECT.

It is composed of the participle *amáto,* and the present subjunctive of the auxiliary verb *avére.*

That I have loved,   *ch' io ábbia am-áto.*
   Thou hast loved,   *che ábbi amato.*
   He has loved,   *ch' égli ábbia amato.*

That we have loved,	*che abbiámo amato.*
You have loved,	*che abbiáte amato.*
They have loved,	*che ábbiano amato.*

PRETERPLUPERFECT.

It is composed of the participle *amáto*, and the first preterimperfect subjunctive of the auxiliary verb *avére.*

If I had loved,	*se io avéssi am-áto.*
Thou hadst loved,	*se tu avéssi amato.*
He had loved,	*se avésse amato.*
We had loved,	*se avéssimo amato.*
You had loved,	*se avéste amato.*
They had loved,	*se avéssero amato.*

SECOND PRETERPLUPERFECT.

It is composed of the participle *amáto*, and the second preterimperfect subjunctive of the auxiliary verb *avére.*

I should have loved,	*avrèi am-áto.*
Thou shouldst have loved,	*avrésti amato.*
He should have loved,	*avrèbbe amato.*
We should have loved,	*avrémmo amato.*
You should have loved,	*avréste amato.*
They should have loved,	*avrèbbero amato.*

FUTURE.

It is composed of the participle *amáto*, and the future indicative of the auxiliary verb *avére.*

When I shall have loved,	*quand' avrò am-áto.*
Thou shalt have loved,	*avrái amato.*
He shall have loved,	*avrà amato.*
We shall have loved,	*avrémo amato.*
You shall have loved,	*avréte amato.*
They shall have loved,	*avránno amato.*

INFINITIVE.

To love,	*am-áre.*
To have loved,	*avére am-ato.*

PARTICIPLES.

Loved, *am-áto*, mas.   Loved, *am-áta*, fem.

GERUNDS.

Loving *or* in loving { *amándo, coll' amáre, con amare,*
{ *nell' amare, in amare.*
Having loved,   *avéndo amato.*

REMARKS ON THE VERBS IN áre.

All the verbs ending in *áre* are conjugated in the same manner as *amáre*, except four, which only deviate from this rule in some of their tenses ; they are, *andáre*, to go ; *dáre*, to give ; *fáre*, to make ; *stáre*, to stay or stand. You will find their conjugations at p. 104.

₊ Note. The verbs terminating in the infinitives in *cáre* and *gáre*, take an *h* in those tenses where the *c* and *g* would otherwise meet with the vowels *e* or *i;* that is to say, in the present indicative, imperative, optative, future indicative, and the second preterimperfect subjunctive ; which are the tenses I shall give as examples, in the verbs *peccáre* and *pagáre*.

Peccáre, to sin : present, *pècc-o, pècc-hi* (and not *pècci,*), *pècc-a, pecc-hiámo, pecc-áte, pècc-ano,* I sin, &c.

Future, *pecc-herò,* I shall sin ; *pecc-herái, pecc-herà, pecc-herémo, pecc-heréte, pecc-heránno,* and not *pecc-erò, pecc-erái,* &c.

Imperative, *pècc-a, pècc-hi, pecc-hiámo, pecc-áte, pec-chino,* sin thou, let him sin, &c.

Optative, *che pècc-hi, pecc-hi, pecc-hi; pecc-hiámo, pecc-hiáte, pècc-hino,* that I may sin, &c.

Pecc-herèi, I should sin ; *pecc-herésti, pecc-herèbbe, pecc-herémmo, pecc-heréste, pecc-herèbbero.*

Pagáre, to pay ; present, *pág-o, pág-hi, pág-a, pa-ghiámo, pag-áte, pág-ano,* I pay, &c.

Future, *pag-herò, pag-herái, pag-herà ; pag-herémo, pag-heréte, pag-heránno,* I shall *or* will pay, &c.

Imperative, *pág-a, pág-hi ; pag-hiámo, pag-áte, pág-hino,* pay thou, let him pay, &c.

Optative, *che pág-hi, pag-hi, pag-hi; pag-hiámo, pag-hiáte, pág-hino,* that I may pay, &c.

The second preterimperfect, *pag-herèi, pag-herésti, pag-herèbbe; pag-herémmo, pag-heréste, pag-herèbbero,* &c. that I should pay, &c.

The other tenses are conjugated like *amáre.*

CONJUGATION OF THE VERBS PASSIVE.

Before we proceed to the second conjugation, it is necessary to know that the verbs passive are merely the participles of verbs active, conjugated with the verb *èssere:* example,

Èssere amáto, *to be loved.*

INDICATIVE.

PRESENT.

I am loved,	*sòno am-áto.*
Thou art loved,	*sèi amato.*
He is loved,	*è amato.*
We are loved,	*siámo amati.*
You are loved,	*siète amati.*
They are loved,	*sóno amati.*

PRETERIMPERFECT.

I was loved,	*èra* or *éro amáto.*
Thou wert loved,	*èri amato.*
He was loved,	*èra amato.*
We were loved,	*eravámo amati.*
You were loved,	*eraváte amati.*
They were loved,	*èrano amati.*

PRETERPERFECT DEFINITE.

I was loved,	*fúi amáto.*
Thou wert loved,	*fósti amato.*
He was loved,	*fù amato.*
We were loved,	*fúmmo amati.*
You were loved,	*fóste amati.*
They were loved,	*fúrono amati.*

94 VERBS.

PRETERPERFECT.

I have been loved,	*sòno státo am-áto.*
Thou hast been loved,	*sèi stato amato.*
He has been loved,	*è stato amato.*
We have been loved,	*siámo stati amati.*
You have been loved,	*siète stati amati.*
They have been loved,	*sóno stati amati.*

PRETERPLUPERFECT.

I had been loved,	*èra státo am-áto.*
Thou hadst been loved,	*èri stato amato.*
He had been loved,	*èra stato amato.*
We had been loved,	*eravámo stati amati.*
You had been loved,	*eraváte stati amati.*
They had been loved,	*èrano stati amati.*

FUTURE.

I shall *or* will be loved,	*sarò am-áto.*
Thou shalt be loved,	*sarài amato.*
He shall be loved,	*sarà amato.*
We shall be loved,	*sarémo amati.*
You shall be loved,	*saréte amati.*
They shall be loved,	*saránno amati.*

I shall proceed no further with the conjugation, because it is merely a repetition of the verb *sòno*, joined to the participle *amáto.*

*** Observe, that the participles and adjectives change their gender and number after the tenses of the verb *èssere;* examples:

I am loved, { *sòno am-áto,* for the masculine / *sòno amáta,* for the feminine } singular.

We are loved, { *siámo amáti,* for the mas. / *siámo amáte,* for the fem. } plural.

You are learned, { *siète dòtto,* / *siète dòtta,* } for the singular. / { *siète dòtti,* / *siète dòtte,* } for the plural.

Observe, that in the construction of the passive, the Italians make use of *da* or *dal,* and *per* (by), which

answer to the French *du* and *par;* with this difference
that the French use *du*, when the verb expresses an
operation of the mind, and *par*, when it expresses an
operation of the body, or of the mind and body
whereas the Italians always put *da* or *dal:* thus they
say *Pietro è amáto dal súo principe*, and not *per il sú*
principe; which French learners are apt to confound.

SECOND CONJUGATION, OF THE VERBS IN ere.

INDICATIVE.
PRESENT.

I believe,	*créd-o.*
Thou believest,	*créd-i.*
He believes,	*créd-e.*
We believe,	*cred-iámo.*
You believe,	*cred-éte.*
They believe,	*créd-ono.*

PRETERIMPERFECT.

I did believe,	*cred-éva* or *evo* ([13]).
Thou didst believe,	*cred-évi.*
He did believe,	*cred-éva.*
We did believe,	*cred-evámo.*
You did believe,	*cred-eváte.*
They did believe,	*cred-évano.*

PRETERPERFECT DEFINITE.

I believed,	*cred-éi.*
Thou believedst,	*cred-ésti.*
He believed,	*credè* (final è, close).
We believed,	*cred-émmo.*
You believed,	*cred-éste.*
They believed,	*cred-érono.*

PRETERPERFECT.

I have believed,	*ho cred-úto.*
Thou hast believed,	*hái creduto.*
He has believed,	*ha creduto.*
We have believed,	*abbiámo creduto.*
You have believed,	*avéte creduto.*
They have believed,	*hánno creduto.*

PRETERPLUPERFECT.

I had believed,	avéva cred-úto.
Thou hadst believed,	avévi creduto.
He had believed,	aveva creduto.
We had believed,	avevámo creduto.
You had believed,	avepáte creduto.
They had believed,	avévano creduto.

FUTURE.

I shall or will believe,	cred-erò.
Thou shalt believe,	cred-erái.
He shall believe,	cred-erà.
We shall believe,	cred-erémo.
You shall believe,	cred-eréte.
They shall believe,	cred-eránno.

IMPERATIVE.

Believe thou,	créd-i.
Let him believe,	créd-a.
Let us believe,	cred-iámo.
Believe you,	créd-éte.
Let them believe,	créd-ano,

OPTATIVE AND SUBJUNCTIVE.

PRESENT.

That I may believe,	ch' io créd-a.
Thou mayest believe,	che tu créd-a.
He may believe,	ch' égli créd-a.
We may believe,	che cred-iámo.
You may believe,	che cred-iáte.
They may believe,	che créd-ano.

PRETERIMPERFECT.

That I might or could believe,	ch' io cred-éssi.
Thou mightest believe,	che tu cred-éssi.
He might believe,	che cred-ésse.
We might believe,	che cred-éssimo.
You might believe,	che cred-éste.
They might believe.	che cred-éssero.

SECOND PRETERIMPERFECT.

I should believe,	*cred-erèi.*
Thou shouldst believe,	*cred-erésti.*
He should believe,	*cred-erèbbe.*
We should believe,	*cred-erémmo.*
You should believe,	*cred-eréste.*
They should believe.	*cred-erèbbero.*

PRETERPERFECT.

That I have believed,	*ch' io ábbia cred-úto.*
Thou hast believed,	*che tu ábbi creduto.*
He has believed,	*ch' égli ábbia creduto.*
We have believed,	*che abbiámo creduto.*
You have believed,	*che abbiáte creduto.*
They have believed,	*che ábbiano creduto.*

PRETERPLUPERFECT.

If I had believed,	*se io avéssi cred-úto.*
Thou hadst believed,	*se tu avéssi creduto.*
He had believed,	*se avésse creduto.*
We had believed,	*se avéssimo creduto.*
You had believed,	*se avéste creduto.*
They had believed,	*se avéssero creduto.*

SECOND PRETERPLUPERFECT.

I should have believed,	*avrèi cred-úto.*
Thou shouldst have believed,	*avrésti creduto.*
He should have believed,	*avrèbbe creduto.*
We should have believed,	*avrémmo creduto.*
You should have believed,	*avréste creduto.*
They should have believed,	*avrèbbero creduto.*

FUTURE.

When I shall have believed,	*quand' avrò cred-úto.*
Thou shalt have believed,	*avrái creduto.*
He shall have believed,	*avrà creduto.*
We shall have believed,	*avrémo credut*
You shall have believed,	*avréte creduto*
They shall have believed,	*avránno credu*

F

INFINITIVE.

To believe,   *crédere.*

Believing, *or* in believing,   *cred-èndo, col créd-ere,* &c.

Believed, *cred-úto,* masc.   Believed, *cred-úta,* fem.

Conjugate in like manner the following verbs, which are the only verbs in *ere* that follow the rule of *créd-ere.*

₀ Note, that all the regular verbs in *ere* have two terminations in the preterperfect definite, as they make

éi, ésti, è ; émmo, éste, érono,
or
étti, ésti, ètte ; émmo, éste, èttero.

	Infinitive.	Preterp. Def.		Participle.
beat,	*báttere*	*éi*	*ètti*	*úto.*
drink,	*bévere* or *bére*	*éi* or	*ètti*	*úto.*
yield,	*cèdere*	*éi*	*ètti*	*úto.*
cleave,	*fèndere*	*éi*	*ètti*	*úto.*
fret,	*frèmere*	*éi*	*ètti*	*úto.*
groan,	*gèmere*	*éi*	*ètti*	*úto.*
enjoy,	*godére*	*éi*	*ètti*	*úto.*
reap,	*miètere*	*éi*	*ètti*	*úto.*
feed,	*páscere*	*éi*	*ètti*	*úto.*
To hang,	*pèndere*	*éi*	*ètti*	*úto.*
retch,	*rècere*	*éi*	*ètti*	*úto.*
receive,	*ricévere*	*éi*	*ètti*	*úto.*
shine again,	*rilúcere*	*éi* without a participle.		
sit down,	*sedére*	*éi*	*ètti*	*úto.*
shine,	*splèndere*	*éi*	*ètti*	*úto.*
glide,	*sèrpere*	*éi*	*ètti*	*úto.*
creak,	*stridere*	*éi*	*ètti*	*úto.*
fear,	*temére*	*éi*	*ètti*	*úto.*
sell,	*véndere*	*éi*	*ètti*	*úto.*

All the other verbs in *ere* are irregular.

The regular verbs end with two vowels in the preterperfect definite; as *am-ái, cred-éi, sent-ii*.

All the irregular verbs, in the same tense, end with the vowel *i;* and this vowel *i* is preceded by a consonant; as *èbbi, credètti, scrissi*. Thus *crédere*, which makes *credéi* and *credètti*, is both regular and irregular.

You will find, in the chapter of the irregular verbs in *ere* short (p. 124) a very easy method of learning the irregularity of the verbs, which I have reduced to one general rule.

THIRD CONJUGATION, OF THE VERBS IN ire.

INDICATIVE.

PRESENT.

I hear,	*sènt·o*.
Thou hearest,	*sènt-i*.
He hears,	*sènt-e*.
We hear,	*sent-iámo*.
You hear,	*sent-íte*.
They hear,	*sènt-ono*.

PRETERIMPERFECT.

I did hear,	*sent ìva* or *ivo* ([13]).
Thou didst hear,	*sent-ìvi*.
He did hear,	*sent-iva*.
We did hear,	*sent-ivámo*.
You did hear,	*sent-ìváte*.
They did hear,	*sent-ivano*.

PRETERPERFECT DEFINITE.

I heard,	*sent-ii*.
Thou heardst,	*sent-isti*.
He heard,	*sent-ì*.
We heard,	*sent-ìmmo*.
You heard,	*sent-íste*.
They heard,	*sent-irono*.

I have heard,	*ho sent-íto.*
Thou hast heard,	*hái sentito.*
He has heard,	*ha sentito.*
We have heard,	*abbiámo sentito.*
You have heard,	*avéte sentito.*
They have heard,	*hanno sentito.*

PRETERPLUPERFECT.

I had heard,	*avéva sent-íto.*
Thou hadst heard,	*avévi sentito.*
He had heard,	*avéva sentito.*
We had heard,	*avevámo sentito.*
You had heard,	*aveváte sentito.*
They had heard,	*avévano sentito.*

FUTURE.

I shall *or* will hear,	*sent-irò.*
Thou shalt hear,	*sent-irái.*
He shall hear,	*sent-irà.*
We shall hear,	*sent-irémo.*
You shall hear,	*sent-iréte.*
They shall hear,	*sent-iránno.*

IMPERATIVE.

Hear thou,	*sènt-i.*
Let him hear,	*sènt-a.*
Let us hear,	*sent-iámo.*
Hear you,	*sent-íte.*
Let them hear,	*sènt-ano.*

OPTATIVE AND SUBJUNCTIVE.

PRESENT.

That I may hear,	*ch' io sènt-a.*
Thou mayest hear,	*che tu sènt-a.*
He may hear,	*ch' égli sènt-a.*
We may hear,	*che sent-iámo.*
You may hear,	*che sent-iáte.*
They may hear,	*che sènt-ano.*

PRETERIMPERFECT.

That I could *or* might hear,	*che sent-issi.*
Thou mightest hear,	*che tu sent-issi.*
He might hear,	*che sent-isse.*
We might hear,	*che sent-issimo.*
You might hear,	*che sent-iste.*
They might hear,	*che sent-issero.*

SECOND PRETERIMPERFECT.

I should hear,	*sent-irèi.*
Thou shouldst hear,	*sent-irésti.*
He should hear,	*sent-irèbbe.*
We should hear,	*sent-irémmo.*
You should hear,	*sent-iréste.*
They should hear,	*sent-irèbbero.*

PRETERPERFECT.

That I have heard,	*ch' io ábbia sent-íto.*
Thou hast heard,	*che ábbi sentito.*
He has heard,	*che égli ábbia sentito.*
We have heard,	*che abbiámo sentito.*
You have heard,	*che abbiáte sentito.*
They have heard,	*che ábbiano sentito.*

PRETERPLUPERFECT.

If I had heard,	*se io avéssi sent-íto.*
Thou hadst heard,	*se tu avéssi sentito.*
He had heard,	*se avésse sentito.*
We had heard,	*se avéssimo sentito.*
You had heard,	*se avéste sentito.*
They had heard,	*se avéssero sentito.*

SECOND PRETERPLUPERFECT.

If I should have heard,	*avrèi sent-íto.*
Thou shouldst have heard	*avrésti sentito.*
He should have heard,	*avrèbbe sentito.*
We should have heard,	*avrémmo sentito.*
You should have heard,	*avréste sentito.*
They should have heard,	*avrèbbero sentito.*

FUTURE.

When I shall have heard,	quand' avrò sent-ito.
Thou shalt have heard,	avrái sentito.
He shall have heard,	avrà sentito.
We shall have heard,	avrémo sentito.
You shall have heard,	avréte sentito.
They shall have heard,	avránno sentito.

INFINITIVE.

To hear, or to feel, *sent-ire*. Participle, heard, *sent-ito*. Gerund, in hearing, *sent-èndo*.

Conjugate in the same manner the following verbs, which are the only verbs in *ire* that conform to the rule of *sent-ire*.

	Infinitive.	Pres.	Pret. Def.	Particip.
open,	aprìre	ápro	aprìi	apèrto
boil,	bollìre	bóllo	bollìi	bollìto
consent,	consentìre	consènto	consentìi	consentìto
convert,	convertìre	convèrto	convertìi	convertìto
cover,	coprìre	còpro	coprìi	copèrto
sew,	cucìre	cúcio	cucìi	cucìto
sleep,	dormìre	dòrmo	dormìi	dormìto
fly,	fuggìre	fúggo	fuggìi	fuggìto
lie,	mentìre	mènto	mentìi	mentìto
die,	morìre	mòro	morìi	mòrto
depart,	partìre	párto	partìi	partìto
repent,	pentìrsi	mi pènto	mi pentìi	pentìtosi
ascend,	salìre	sálgo	salìi	salìto
follow,	seguìre	séguo	seguìi	seguìto
serve,	servìre	sèrvo	servìi	servìto
suffer,	soffrìre	sòffro	soffrìi	soffèrto
come or go out,	sortìre	sòrto	sortìi	sortìto
dress,	vestìre	vèsto	vestìi	vestìto
come or go out,	uscìre,	èsco	uscìi	uscìto
hear,	udìre	òdo	udìi	udìto

To (brace spanning the above list)

All the other verbs in *ire* are irregular in the present tense, which they make in *isco;* as you will observe in the Chapter of Irregulars in *ire ;* examples :

Diger-ire   diger-isco   diger-ii   diger-ito, &c.
Langu-ire   langu-isco   langu-ii   langu-ito, &c.

N. B. When you have learned to conjugate these five verbs, *avére, éssere, amáre, crédere, sentíre,* you may be said to be master of almost all the rest ; the termination of the tenses and persons being the same, especially in the regular verbs ; but, in order to be perfect in your conjugations, it is not sufficient to know those verbs in the order of the tenses, that is, beginning with the present indicative, and proceeding to the preterimperfect, as children do ; but it is necessary to know each tense of the indicative and optative, &c. by heart. Your teacher will instruct you upon this head ; but should he not, or if you learn Italian without a master, your method must be, to conjugate two or three of those verbs, or all five at the same time. This will enable you to learn them with greater ease ; to retain them better in your memory, and to express yourself more readily. In order to conjugate the two auxiliary verbs together, you may, for instance, repeat,

Ho un cavállo, e ne sòno contènto ; I have a horse, and am satisfied with it.

And thus you may exercise yourself through every tense and person of the whole conjugation.

With regard to the other three, you will receive much benefit if you conjugate them by other similar verbs. For instance : I buy my goods, sell them cheap, and serve my friends faithfully ; *cómpro le mie mercanzie, le véndo a buòn mercáto, e sèrvo con fideltà i mièi amíci.* The verb *compráre* is conjugated like *amáre ; véndere,* like *crédere ; servíre* like *sentíre.* If you practise this mode of conjugation, you will find that in a very little time you will be able to speak and write with great ease ; for in the Italian language they write as they speak, and speak as they write ; here, however, you will find a Book of Exercises ([15]) highly necessary and useful.

[15] See Bottarelli's Exercises, with references to the rules of this Grammar.

OF THE IRREGULAR VERBS
OF THE FIRST CONJUGATION.

There are in each conjugation some verbs which do not conform to the common rule, and on that account are called irregulars.

There are but four verbs of the first conjugation, which in some of the tenses depart from the rule of the verb *amáre*, viz.

ANDÁRE, DÁRE, FÁRE, STÁRE.

The verb *fáre* is, properly speaking, an irregular of the second conjugation, since it is only the Latin verb *Fácere* syncopated or abridged. Yet I place it here in compliance with the method of other grammarians.

Observe, that these verbs are irregular; some in the present, some in the preterperfect-definite, and others in the future tense.

*** Remember also, that when a verb is irregular in the present of the indicative, it retains its irregularity in the imperative and present of the subjunctive.

ANDÁRE,

The verb *andáre* is irregular only in the present tense ([16]).

INDICATIVE.
PRESENT.

I go,	**vádo* or *vo.*
Thou goest,	*vái.*
He goes,	*va.*
We go,	*andiámo.*
You go,	*andáte.*
They go,	*vánno.*

PRETERIMPERFECT.

I was going, thou wast going, &c. *Andáva, andávi, andáva; andavámo, andaváte, andávano.*

---

[16] In the subsequent pages, the tenses which have a star are the only irregular ones; the others are regular.

PRETERPERFECT DEFINITE.

I went, thou wentest, he went; we went, you went, they went. *Andái, andásti, andò; andámmo, andáste, andárono.*

PRETERPERFECT.

I have gone,	*sòno andáto.*
Thou hast gone,	*sèi andato.*
He has gone,	*è andato.*
We have gone,	*siámo andati.*
You have gone,	*siète andati.*
They have gone,	*sóno andati.*

If we are to speak in the feminine, we should say, *sòno andáta, sèi andata, è andata; siámo andate, siète andate, sóno andate.*

I was gone, thou wast gone, he was gone; we were gone, you were gone, they were gone.

PRETERPLUPERFECT.

I had gone, thou hadst gone, he had gone; we had gone, you had gone, they had gone.

Era andáto, èri andato, èra andato; eravámo andati, eraváte andati, èrano andati.

FUTURE.

I shall *or* will go, thou shalt go, he shall go; we shall go, you shall go, they shall go.

*Andrò, andrái, andrà; andrémo, andréte, andránno.

IMPERATIVE.

Go thou, let him go; let us go, go ye, let them go.

*Vai or va', váda; andiámo, andáte, vádano.

OPTATIVE AND SUBJUNCTIVE.

PRESENT.

That I may go,	**ch' io váda.*
Thou mayest go,	*che tu váda.*
He may go,	*ch' égli váda.*
We may go,	*che andiámo.*
You may go,	*che andiáte.*
They may go,	*che vádano.*

PRETERIMPERFECT.

That I might *or* could go, thou mightest go, he might go ; we might go, you might go, they might go.

Che andássi, andássi, andásse ; andássimo, andáste, andássero.

SECOND PRETERIMPERFECT.

I should go, thou shouldst go, he should go ; we should go, you should go, they should go.

* *Andrèi, andrésti, andrèbbe ; andrémmo, andréste, andrèbbero.*

Preterp.　That I have gone, *che sía andáto.*

Preterpl.　If I had gone, *se fóssi andáto.*

Future.　When I shall be gone, *quando sarò andáto.*

INFINITIVE.

To go, *andáre.*　Participle, gone, *andáto.*　Gerund, in going, *andándo.*

₊ Note, that the preposition *a* or *ad* must be put after the verb *andáre*, and all the other verbs of motion, when they precede an infinitive ; examples :

Let us go and see, *andiámo a vedére.*

Go to supper, *andáte a cena.*

You shall go, and expect me, *andréte ad aspettármi.*

Let us send to say yes, *mandiámo a dire, di sì.*

The French are frequently mistaken in this respect, because they are accustomed to put the infinitive, without a preposition, after the verbs of motion.

DÁRE.

Dáre is irregular only in the present and preterperfect definite.

INDICATIVE.

PRESENT.

* I give, thou givest, he gives ; we give, you give, they give ; *do, dái, dà ; diámo, dáte, dánno.*

Preterimperf.　I did give, thou didst give, he did give ; we did give, you did give, they did give : *dáva, dávi, dáva ; davámo, daváte, dávano.*

PRETERPERFECT DEFINITE.

*I gave,	dièdi,	or dètti.
Thou gavest,	désti.	
He gave,	dìcde,	or dètte, diè.
We gave,	démmo.	
You gave,	déste.	
They gave,	dièdcro,	or dèttero.

The poets use dièr, diéron and diérono, instead of dièdero.

Perfect comp.	I have given,	ho dáto.
Preterplup.	I had given,	avéva dato.
*Future,	I shall give,	darò.

IMPERATIVE.

*Give thou, let him give; let us give, give you, let them give: dai or da', dia; diámo, dáte, diano.

OPTATIVE AND SUBJUNCTIVE.

*Present. That I may give, &c. che dia, che tu dia, ch' égli dia; che diámo, che diáte, che diano.

*Preterimp. That I might give, that thou mightest give, that he might give, &c. che déssi, tu déssi, désse; déssimo, déste, déssero.

*Second Imperf. I should give, &c. darèi, darésti, darèbbe; darémmo, daréste, darèbbero.

INFINITIVE.

Present,	To give,	dáre.
Gerund,	In giving,	dándo.
Participle,	Given,	dáto.

FÁRE.

Fáre, formerly *facere*, has its irregularity in the present and the preterperfect definite, &c. &c.; and requires the *t* to be doubled in the participle.

INDICATIVE.

PRESENT.

* I do, thou dost, he does ; we do, you do, they do ; *fo, fái, fu ; facciámo, fáte, fánno*.

Preterimp. I was doing, &c. *facéva, facévi, facéva*, &c.

* Preter-def. I did, thou didst, he did ; we did, you did, they did : *féci, facésti, féce ; facémmo, facéste, fécero*.

Preterp. I have done, *ho fátto*.

Preterplup. I had done, *avéva fátto*.

* Future. I shall do, &c. *farò, farái, farà ; farémo. faréte, faránno*.

IMPERATIVE.

* Do thou, let him do ; let us do, do you, let them do : *fai* or *fa', fáccia ; facciámo, fáte, fácciano*.

OPTATIVE.

PRESENT.

* That I may do, or that I do, thou mayest do, he may do; we may do, you may do, they may do : *che fáccia, che tu fáccia, ch' égli fáccia ; che facciámo, che facciáte, che fácciano*.

Preterimp. That I might do, thou mightest do, he might do ; we might do, you might do, they might do : *che facéssi, facéssi, facésse ; facéssimo, facéste, facéssero*.

* Second Imp. I should do, thou shouldst do, he should do ; we should do, you should do, they should do : *farèi, farésti, farèbbe ; farémmo, faréste, farèbbero*.

INFINITIVE.

* To do, *fáre*. Gerund, in doing, *facèndo*. Participle, done, *fátto*.

STARE.

Stáre signifies *to be, to dwell, to stand, to stay;* it is irregular in the presents, preterperfect definite, in the future, &c.

INDICATIVE.

PRESENT.

* I stand, *or* I am, *sto;* thou standest, *stái;* he stands, *sta; stiámo, státe, stánno.*

Imperf. I did stand, &c. *stáva.*

* Preter-def. I stood, thou stoodest, he stood, &c, *stètti, stésti, stètte; stémmo, stéste, stèttero.*

Preterp. I have stood, &c. *sòno státo.*

Preterpl. I had stood, &c. *èra stato.*

* Future. I shall *or* will stand, &c. *starò, starái, starà; starémo, staréte, staránno.*

IMPERATIVE.

* Stand thou, *stai* or *sta';* let him stand, *stia;* let us stand, *stiámo;* stand you, *státe;* let them stand, *stíano,* or *stíeno.*

OPTATIVE AND SUBJUNCTIVE.

PRESENT.

That I may stand, thou mayest stand, he may stand, &c. *ch' io stía, che tu stía, ch' égli stía; che stiámo, che stiáte, che stíano* or *stíeno.*

* Imperfect. That I might *or* could stand, *che stéssi;* thou mightest stand, *che tu stéssi;* he might stand, *che stésse;* we might stand, *che stéssimo;* you might stand, *che stéste;* they might stand, *che stéssero.*

* Second Preterimp. I should stand, thou shouldst stand, he should stand, &c. *starèi, starésti, starèbbe; starémmo, staréste, starèbbero.*

INFINITIVE.

To stand, *stáre.* Gerund, standing, *stándo.* Participle, stood *or* been *státo.*

Observations on the four Irregular Verbs,

ANDÁRE, DÁRE, FÁRE, STÁRE.

These four verbs form the second person of the present tense in *ai*; as, *vái, dái, fái, stái*; and the third person plural in *anno*, and not in *ano*, like the regulars; examples : *vánno, dánno, fánno, stánno*; the regular verbs make it in *ano*; as *ámano, cántano, párlano*, &c.

The future indicative does not terminate in *erò*, but in *arò*; we must therefore say, *farò, darò, starò*; except the verb *andáre*, which makes *andrò*. Observe, nevertheless, that the verbs *stáre*, and *dáre*, become regular when they are compounded; as, *accostáre, sovrastáre, secondáre, comandáre.* We say in the second person of the present tense, *accòsti, sovrásti, secóndi, comándi*, and not *accostái, sovrastái, secondái, comandái*, this being the first person singular of the preterperpect definite of those verbs. In a word, they follow the rule of the regular verb through all its tenses. The same cannot be said of the verb *fáre*, which continues its irregularity, though compounded : therefore we must say *disfo, disfacciámo, disfèci, disfacésti*, &c.

The regular verbs in *are* make their subjunctive in *i*; as *ámi, párli, cánti, sálti.* The four irregulars form theirs in *a*; as, *váda, dia, fáccia, stía.*

Dáre and *stáre* make the preterimperfect subjunctive *déssi*, and *stéssi*, and not *dássi* and *stássi.*

In the second preterimperfect they make *andrèi, darèi, farèi, starèi.*

Note, the verb *dáre* is conjugated like the verb *stáre*, only by changing the *st* into *d*; *do, sto*; *dáva, stáva*, &c.

OF THE IRREGULAR VERBS IN ERE.

There are two sorts of verbs in *ere*, one of which has the penultima, or the last syllable but one, long; as,

    Cadére, Dovére, Sapére, Volére.

The other the penultima short; as,

    Crédere, Lèggere, Scrìvere, Pèrdere.

There are no more than twenty-two verbs which have the infinitives in *ere* long, viz.

	Infinitive.	Pres.	Pret. def.	Part.
115	*Cadére* - to fall,	*cúdo,*	*cáddi,*	*cadúto.*
111	{*Calére* - care for, a verb impersonal. {*Capére* - contain.			
116	*Dovére* - owe,	*dèvo,*	*dovéi,*	*dovúto.*
117	*Dolérsi* - grieve,	*mi dòlgo,*	*mi dòlsi,*	*dolútosi.*
118	*Giacére* - lie down,	*giáccio,*	*giácqui,*	*giaciúto.*
* *	*Godére* - enjoy,	*gòdo,*	*godéi,*	*godúto.*
76	*Avére* - have,	*ho,*	*èbbi,*	*avúto.*
120	*Parére* - appear,	*páio,*	*párvi,*	*parúto.*
119	*Piacére* - please,	*piáccio,*	*piácqui,*	*piaciúto.*
121	*Persuadére* - persuade,	*persuádo,*	*persuási,*	*persuáso.*
113	*Potére* - be able,	*pòsso,*	*potéi,*	*potúto.*
121	*Rimanére* - remain,	*rimángo,*	*rimási,*	*rimásto.*
112	*Sapére* - know,	*so,*	*sèppi,*	*sapúto.*
* *	*Sedére* - sit,	*sièdo,*	*sedéi,*	*sedúto.*
122	*Solére* - be accustomed,	*sòglio,*	*soléi,*	*sòlito.*
119	*Tacére* - be silent,	*táccio,*	*tácqui,*	*taciúto.*
122	*Tenére* - hold,	*tèngo,*	*ténni,*	*tenúto.*
* *	*Temére* - fear,	*tèmo,*	*teméi.*	*temúto.*
123	*Valére* - be worth,	*váglio,*	*válsi,*	*valúto.*
123	*Vedére* - see,	*védo,*	*vidi.*	*vedúto.*
114	*Volére* - be willing,	*vòglio,*	*vòlli,*	*volúto.*

* * The three verbs marked with two stars are regular; the figures in the margin, refer to the pages in which the other verbs are found conjugated at full length.

The compounds of these verbs make *ere* long also; as, *Ricadére, Riavére,* &c.

Of these twenty-two verbs there are but three regular, viz. *Godére, Sedére,* and *Temére;* and they are conjugated like *Crédere.*

Of the other verbs which make their infinitive in *ere* long, some are irregular in the present, others in the preter-definite and future, and some in the participle.

The conjugation of the verb AVÉRE has been given already. CALÉRE and CAPÉRE are little in use.

CONJUGATION OF THE IRREGULAR VERBS IN ÉRE
LONG.

I begin with *sapére, potére* and *volére*, because they
frequently occur in discourse.

SAPÉRE, *to know.*

* Present. *So, sái, sa; sappiámo, sapéte, sánno:* I
know, thou knowest, he knows; we know, you know,
they know.

Imperf. *Sapéva, sapévi, sapéva; sapevámo, sapeváte,
sapévano:* I did know, thou didst know, he did know;
we did know, you did know, they did know.

* Preter-def. *Sèppi, sapésti, sèppe: sapémmo, sapéste, sèppero:* I knew, thou knewest, he knew; we
knew, you knew, they knew.

Preterperfect. *Ho sapúto, hái sapúto, ha sapúto, &c.*

* Future. *Saprò, saprái, saprà; saprémo, sapréte,
sapránno:* I shall know, thou shalt know, he shall
know; we shall know, you shall know, they shall know.

IMPERATIVE.

* *Sáppi, sáppia; sappiámo, sappiáte, sáppiano:* know
thou, let him know: let us know, know you, let them
know.

OPTATIVE AND SUBJUNCTIVE.

* *Che sáppia, sáppia, sáppia; sappiámo, sappiáte,
sáppiano:* that I may know, thou mayest know, he may
know; we may know, you may know, they may know.

* Imperfect. *Che sapéssi, sapéssi, sappésse; sapéssimo,
sapéste, sapéssero:* that I might know, thou mightest
know, &c.

* Second Imp. *Saprèi, saprésti, saprèbbe; saprémmo,
sapréste, saprèbbero:* I should or would know, thou
shouldst know, he should know; we should know, you
should know, they should know.

INFINITIVE.

Sapére, to know.   Gerund, *Sapèndo,* knowing.   Participle, *Sapúto,* known.

POTÉRE, *to be able.*

INDICATIVE.

* Present. *Pòsso, puòi, può; possiámo, potéte, pòssono:* I can *or* am able, thou canst, he can ; we can, you can, they can.

Imperf. *Potéva, potévi,* &c. I could, &c.

Pret.-def. *Potéi, potésti, potè; potémmo, potéste, potérono;* I could, thou couldst, he could ; we could, you could, they could.

Preterp. *Ho potúto,* I have been able.

* Future. *Potrò,* I shall be able.

No imperative.

OPTATIVE AND SUBJUNCTIVE.

* *Che pòssa, pòssa, pòssa ; possiámo, possiáte, pòssano:* that I may be able, thou mayest be able, he may be able ; we may be able, you may be able, they may be able.

Imp. *Che potéssi, potéssi, potésse ; potéssimo, potéste, potéssero;* that I might be able, thou mightest be able, he might be able ; we might be able, you might be able, they might be able.

* Second Imp. *Potrèi, potrésti, potrèbbe,* &c.

N. B. In conjugating the verb *potére,* to be able, we do not say in the future *poterò,* and in the second preterimperfect *poterci ;* because *poterò* and *poterèi* are the future and second preterimperfect of the verb *potáre,* to prune.

The vowel *e* is frequently dropped between a mute and a liquid consonant : thus, instead of *caderèi, saperèi, cederò,* we say, *cadrèi, saprèi, cedrò :* this, however, is only used when the *e* is short ; but we never say *mádra* for *madèra; anacòrta* for *anacorèta,* &c.

INFINITIVE.

Potére. Gerund, *Potèndo.* Participle, *Potúto.*

VOLÉRE, *to be willing.*

* Present. *Vòglio, vuòi, vuòle; vogliámo, voléte, vò-glíono;* I will *or* am willing, thou art willing, he is willing; we are willing, you are willing, they are willing.

Imperf. *Voléva, volévi, voléva: volevámo, volevále, volévano;* I was willing, thou wast willing, &c.

* Preter-def. *Vòlli, volésti, vòlle; volémmo, voléste, vòllero:* I was willing, thou wast willing, &c.

Preterperf. *Ho volúto,* I have been willing, &c.

* Future. *Vorrò, vorrái, vorrà; vorrémo, vorréte, vorránno;* I shall be willing, thou shalt be willing, he shall be willing; we shall be willing, &c.

No imperative.

OPTATIVE AND SUBJUNCTIVE.

* *Che vòglia, vòglia, vòglia; vogliámo, vogliáte, vò-gliano;* that I may be willing, thou mayest be willing, he may be willing; we may be willing, you may be willing, they may be willing.

Imperf. *Voléssi, voléssi, volésse; volésimo, voléste, voléssero;* that I were willing, thou wert willing, he were willing; we were willing, you were willing, they were willing.

* Second Imp. *Vorrèi, vorrésti, vorrèbbe; vorrémmo, vorréste, vorrèbbero.* I should *or* would be willing, thou shouldest *or* wouldest be willing, &c.

Inf. *Volére.* Gerund, *Volèndo.* Participle, *Volúto.*

REMARKS ON THE VERBS TERMINATING IN ERE LONG.

⁎ 1. Remember that *volére* makes in the preterperfect definite, *vòlli, volésti, vòlle; volémmo, voléste, vòllero;* and not *vòlsi, volésti, vòlse; volémmo, voléste, vòlsero;* because *vòlsi, vòlse, vòlsero,* comes from the verb *vòlgere,* to turn. Yet we find *vòlsi, vòlse,* and *vòlsero,* in several authors, which can only be considered as a poetical licence.

✱ Observe, that it is sometimes an elegance to use the verb *volére*, instead of *dovére*. For instance : *ma su di ciò non si vuòl con áltri ragionáre*, for *non si dève*, we must not.

2. The verbs terminated in the infinitive in *lere*, as *volére, dolére, solére, valére*, and their compounds, have a *g* before the letter *l* in the first person singular, in the first and third plural, in the present, and in all the persons of the present subjunctive ; as,

> *Vòglio, vuòi, vuòle ; vogliámo, voléte, vògliono.*
> *Dòglio, duòli, duòle ; dogliámo, dolète, dògliono.*
> *Sòglio, suòli, suòle ; sogliámo, solète, sògliono.*
> *Váglio, váli, vále ; vagliámo, valéte, vágliono.*

3. The verbs terminated in the infinitive in *nére* and *níre*, as, *rimanére, tenére, veníre*, have also a *g* in the first person singular, and in the third plural ; but not in the first person plural ; as,

> *Tèngo, tièni, tiène ; teniámo, tenéte, tèngono.*
> *Rimángo, rimáni, rimáne ; rimaniámo, rimanéte, rimángono.*
> *Vèngo, vièni, viène ; veniámo, venite, vèngono.*

They have also a *g* in the first, second and third person of the present subjunctive in the singular, and in the third of the plural.

4. All the verbs ending in *lére, nére, níre*, require double *r* in the future, and in the second imperfect tenses.

Examples.			
Volére	*vòglio,*	*vorrò,*	*vorrèi.*
Tenére,	*tèngo,*	*terrò,*	*terrèi.*
Veníre,	*vèngo,*	*verrò,*	*verrèi.*

And not *Volerò, tenerò, venirò*, &c.

✱ Except *finíre, puníre, svèllere*, to root up ; which follow the common rule, and make *finirò, punirò, svellerò ;* and in the present, *finísco, punísco, svèllo.*

CADÉRE, *to fall.*

Cádo, cádi, cáde ; cadiámo, cadéte, cádono : I fall, thou fallest, he falls ; we fall, you fall, they fall.

Imperf. *Cadéva, cadévi, cadéva; cadevámo, cade-váte, cadévano:* I was falling, &c.

* Preter-def. *Cáddi, cadésti, cádde; cadémmo, ca-déste, cáddero;* I fell, thou didst fall, he fell; we fell, you fell, they fell.

Preterp. *Sòno cadúto, sèi cadúto, è cadúto; siámo cadúti, siète cadúti, sóno cadúti:* I have *or* am fallen, thou hast *or* art fallen, &c.

Preterpl. *Era cadúto, èri cadúto, èra cadúto; era-vámo cadúti, eraváte cadúti, èrano cadúti:* I had *or* I was fallen, thou hadst *or* wast fallen, &c.

Future. *Caderò, caderái, caderà; caderémo, cade-réte, caderánno,* or *cadrò,* &c.   I shall fall, thou shalt fall, he shall fall, &c.

Imperative. *Cádi,* fall thou; *cáda,* let him fall; *ca-diámo,* let us fall; *cadéte,* fall you; *cádano,* let them fall.

Optative. *Che cáda, cáda, cáda; cadiámo, cadiáte, cádano:* that I may fall, that thou mayest fall, &c.

Imperf. *Cadéssi, cadéssi, cadésse; cadéssimo, cadéste, cadéssero;* that I might fall, thou mightest fall, &c.

Second Imperf. *Caderèi, caderésti,* or *cadrèi,* &c. I should fall.

Infinitive. *Cadére.* Gerund, *cadèndo.* Participle, *cadúto.*

DOVÉRE, *to owe.*

Dovére is conjugated through all its tenses, like *cré-dere.* It is irregular only in the present, by putting an *e* for an *o;* **dèvo, dèvi, dève; dobbiámo, dovéte, dèvono,* and *dèbbono:* I owe, thou owest, he owes; we owe, you owe, they owe.

Imperf. *Dovéva, dovévi,* &c. I did owe, &c.

Preter-def. *Dovètti, dovésti, dovètte: dovémmo, do-véste, dovèttero,* or *dovei, . . . dove,* &c. I owed, &c.

Preterp. *Ho dovúto, hái dovúto, ha dovúto:* I have owed, &c.

* Future. *Dovrò, dovrái, dovrá,* I shall *or* will owe, &c.

* Imperative. *Dèvi, débba; dobbiámo, dovéte, dèb-bano:* owe thou, let him owe; let us owe, owe you, let them owe.

* Optative and Subjunctive. *Che dèbba, dèbba, dèbba ; dobbiámo, dobbiáte, dèbbano:* that I may owe, thou mayest owe, he may owe, &c.

Imperf. *Dovéssi,* that I might owe, &c.

* Second Imp. *Dovréi, dovrésti, dovrèbbe ; dovrémmo, dovréste, dovrèbbero :* I should owe, &c.

Infinitive. *Dovére.* Gerund, *dovèndo.* Part. *dovúto.*

DOLÉRSI, *to grieve, to complain.*

Dolérsi is a reciprocal verb, conjugated with the pronouns conjunctive, *mi, ti, si,* in the singular number, and with *ci, vi, si,* in the plural.

All verbs having the particle *si* after the infinitive, must be conjugated like *dolére ;* as, *pentírsi,* to repent ; *ricordársi,* to remember, &c.

INDICATIVE.

* I grieve,	*io mi dòlgo,* or *dòglio.*
Thou grievest,	*tu ti duòli.*
He grieves,	*égli si duòle.*
We grieve,	*noi ci dogliámo.*
You grieve,	*voi vi doléte.*
They grieve,	*églino si dòlgono.*

Imper. *Mi doléva, ti dolevi, si doléva, ci dolevámo, vi dolaváte, si dolévano ;* I grieved, &c.

PRETER DEFINITE.

* I grieved,	*mi dòlsi.*
Thou grievedst,	*ti dolésti.*
He grieved,	*si dòlse.*
We grieved,	*ci dolémmo.*
You grieved,	*vi doléste.*
They grieved,	*si dòlsero.*

Preterperf. *Mi sòno dolúto,* I have grieved, &c.

Preterpluperf. *Mi èra dolúto,* I had grieved, &c.

* Future. *Mi dorrò, ti dorrái, si dorrà ; ci dorrémo, vi dorréte, si dorránno ;* I shall grieve, &c.

---

* *Duòliti,* grieve thou, *dòlgasi,* let him grieve ; *dogliámoci, dolétevi, dòlgansi,* let them grieve.

OPTATIVE AND SUBJUNCTIVE.

* Present. *Che mi dòlga, ti dòlga, si dòlga* or *dó-glia; ci dogliámo, vi dogliáte, si dòlgano:* that I may grieve, thou mayest grieve, &c.

Imperf. *Che mi doléssi,* that I might grieve, &c.

* Second Imperf. *Mi dorrèi,* I should *or* would grieve, &c.

INFINITIVE.

Dolérsi, to grieve.   Gerund, *Dolèndosi,* grieving. Participle, *Dolútosi,* grieved.

** Remember that *dolére* signifies also to be ill, and then it is a verb impersonal, having only the third personal singular; as,

I have the headach,	*mi duòle la tésta.*
Thou hast the headach,	*ti duole la testa.*
He has the headach,	*gli duole la testa.*
She has the headach,	*le duole la testa.*
We have the headach,	*ci duole la testa.*
You have the headach,	*vi duole la testa.*
They have the headach,	*duole loro la testa.*

GIACÉRE, *to lie down;* PIACÉRE, *to please;* TACÉRE, *to hold one's tongue.*

These three verbs are conjugated alike.

* Indicative. Present tense. *Giáccio, giáci, giáce; giaciámo, giacéte, giácciono;* I lie down, &c.

Imperf. *Giacéva,* I did lie down, &c.

* Preter-def. *Giácqui, giacésti, giácque; giacémmo, giacéste, giácquero:* I lay down, &c.

Preterperf. We do not say, *sòno státo giaciúto,* I have laid down; but *sono stato a giacére,* &c.

Future. *Giacerò,* I shall lie down, &c.

* Imperative. *Giáci, giáccia; giaciámo, giacéte, giácciano:* lie thou down, let him lie down, &c.

* Optative and Subjunctive. *Che giáccia, giáccia, giáccia ; giaciámo, giaciáte, giácciano :* that I may lie down, &c.

Imperf. *Che giacéssi,* that I might lie down.

Second Imperf. *Giacerèi,* I should *or* would lie down.

Infinitive, *Giacére.* Gerund, *giacèndo.* Participle, *giaciúto.*

---

* PIACÉRE. *Piáccio, piáci, piáce ; piaciámo, piacéte, piácciono ;* I please, thou pleasest, he pleases ; we please, you please, they please.

Imp. *Piacéva, vi, va ; vámo, váte, vano :* I pleased, thou pleasedst, &c.

* Preter-def. *Piácqui, piacésti, piácque ; piacémmo, piacéste, piácquero :* I pleased, thou pleasedst, he pleased ; we pleased, you pleased, they pleased.

Preterperf. *Ho piaciúto,* &c. I have pleased.

Future. *Piacerò,* &c. I shall please.

Imp. *Piáci, piáccia ; piaciámo, piacéte, piácciano :* please thou, &c.

Subjunctive. *Che piáccia, a, a ; iámo, iáte, iano :* that I may please.

Imp. *Che piacéssi,* that I might please, &c.

Second Imperf. *Piacerèi,* I should please.

Infinitive. *Piacére.* Gerund, *piacèndo.* Participle, *piaciúto.*

---

* TACÉRE. *Táccio, táci, táce ; taciámo, tacéte, táccicono :* I hold my tongue, thou holdest thy tongue, he holds his tongue ; we hold our tongues, &c.

Imp. *Tacéva, vi, va ; vámo, váte, vano :* I did hold my tongue, thou didst, &c.

* Preter-def. *Tácqui, tacésti, tácque ; tacémmo,* &c. I held my tongue, &c.

Preterperf. *Ho taciúto,* I have held my tongue.

Future. *Tacerò, tacerái, tacerà ; tacerémo, taceréte, taceránno :* I shall hold my tongue, &c.

Imperative. *Táci, táccia ; taciámo, tacéte, tácciano :* hold thy tongue, let him hold his tongue, &c.

* Subjunctive. *Che táccia, a, a ; taciámo, taciáte, tácciano :* that I may hold my tongue, &c.

Imperf. *Che tacéssi, tacéssi, tacésse :* that I might hold my tongue, &c.

Second Imp. *Tacerèi, tacerésti, tacerèbbe,* &c. I should hold my tongue, &c.

Infinitive. *Tacére,* to hold one's tongue. Gerund, *tacèndo,* holding one's tongue, &c. Participle, **taciúto.*

PARÉRE, *to seem.*

* Indicative, Present. *Páio, pári, páre ; paiámo, paréte, páiono :* I seem *or* appear, thou seemest, he seems ; we seem, &c.

Imp. *Paréva,* I appeared, &c.

* Preter-def. *Parvi, parésti, párve ; parémmo, paréste, párvero :* I seemed, &c.

* Future. *Parrò, parrái, parrà :* I shall seem, &c.

* Imperative. *Pári, páia ; paiámo, paréte, páiano :* seem thou, let him seem ; let us seem, seem you, let them seem.

₊ Remember what has been already remarked, that when a verb has any irregularity in the present of the indicative, it has the same in the present of the imperative and subjunctive.

* Optative and Subjunctive. *Che páia, páia, páia ; paiámo, paiáte, páiano :* that I may seem, thou mayest seem, he may seem.

Imp. *Che paréssi, paréssi, se ; ssimo, ste, ssero :* that I might seem, &c.

Second Imp. *Parrèi,* I should *or* would seem, &c.

Infinitive. *Parére,* to seem. Gerund, *parèndo,* seeming. * Participle, *parso,* seemed.

Parére is also an impersonal reciprocal verb, that has only the third person singular, when it signifies *it seems ;* as, it seems to me, *mi páre* or *parmi.*

	to thee,	*ti pare.*
	to him *or* her,	*gli pare* or *le pare.*
It seems	to us,	*ci pare.*
	to you,	*vi pare.*
	to them,	*pare loro.*

In like manner through all the tenses : it seemed *or* appeared to me, mi *paréva.* Preter-def. *mi párve.*

₊ Remember that no more than four verbs in *ere* long, are irregular in the participle ; namely, *parére, párso ; persuadére, persuáso ; rimanére, rimasto* or *rimáso ; solére, sòlito ;* all the other verbs are regular, making it in *úto.*

PERSUADÉRE, *to persuade.*

Indicative, Present. *Persuádo, persuádi, persuáde ; persuadiámo, persuadéte, persuádono :* I persuade, &c.

Imperf. *Persuadéva, vi, va ; vámo,* &c. I persuaded, thou persuadedst, &c.

* Preter-def. *Persuási, persuadésti, persuáse ; persuadémmo, persuadéste, persuásero,* I persuaded, &c.

Future. *Persuaderò, rái, rà ; rémo, réte, ránno.*

Imperative. *Persuádi, a ; iámo, éte, ano :* persuade thou, &c.

Optative. *Che persuáda, a, a ; iámo, iáte, ano :* that I may persuade, &c.

Imperf. *Che persuadéssi,* that I might persuade.

Second Imp. *Persuaderèi,* I should *or* would persuade.

Infinitive. *Persuadére,* to persuade. Gerund, *persuadèndo,* persuading. * Participle, *persuáso,* persuaded.

RIMANÉRE, *to remain.*

₊ Remember the rules of the verbs in *lére, nére, rire.*

* Indicative, Present. *Rimángo, rimáni, rimáne ; rimaniámo, rimanéte, rimángono :* I remain, thou remainest, &c.

Imperf. *Rimanéva,* I was remaining.

* Preter-def. *Rimási, rimanésti, rimáse ; rimanémmo, rimanéste, rimásero :* I remained, &c.

Preterperf. *Sono rimásto* or *rimaso :* I have remained, &c.

G

* Future. *Rimarrò, rimarrái, rimarrà,* I shall remain, &c.

* Imperative. *Rimáŋi, rimánga; rimaniámo, rimanéte, rimángano:* remain thou, let him remain, &c.

* Optative. *Che rimánga, rimánga, rimánga; rimaniámo, rimaniáte, rimángano:* that I may remain.

Imperf. *Che rimanéssi;* that I might remain.

* Second Imp. *Rimarrèi, rimarrésti,* I should *or* would remain.

Infinitive. *Rimanére,* to remain. Gerund, *rimanèndo,* remaining. Participle, *rimasto* or **rimáso,* remained.

SOLÉRE, *to be wont, or used to.*

* Indicative, Present. *Sòglio, suòli, suòle: sogliámo, soléte, sògliono,* I am wont, &c. or *Sòn sòlito,* I am wont; *sèi sòlito,* thou art wont; *è sòlito,* he is wont; *siámo sòliti,* we are wont; *sièie sòliti,* you are wont; *sóno sòliti,* they are wont.

And in like manner through all the tenses; as, *èra sòlito,* I was wont; *non èra sòlito,* I was not wont, &c.

Imp. *Soléva,* &c. I was accustomed, &c.

Preterperfect-def. *Fùi sòlito,* &c.

* Imperative. *Suòli, sòglia; sogliámo, soléte, sògliano:* be thou wont, let him be wont, &c.

* Optative and Subjunctive. *Che sòglia, sòglia, sòglia; sogliámo, sogliáte, sògliano:* that I may be wont, &c.

Che soléssi, that I might be wont, &c.

Second Preterimperf. *Sarèi sòlito,* I should *or* would be wont, &c.

Infinitive. *Solére,* to be wont. Gerund, *solèndo, essèndo sòlito,* being wont. Participle, *sòlito,* wont.

TENÉRE, *to hold.*

* Indicative, Present. *Tèngo, tièni, tiène; teniámo, tenéte, tèngono:* I hold, thou holdest, he holds; we hold, you hold, they hold.

Imp. *Tenéva*, I did hold *or* was holding.

* Preter-def. *Ténni, tenésti, ténne ; tenémmo, tenéste, ténnero :* I held, thou heldest, he held ; we held, you held, they held.

Preterperf. *Ho tenúto,* &c.

* Future. *Terrò, terrái, terrà ; terrémo, terréte, terránno :* I shall hold, thou shalt hold, he shall hold, &c.

* Imperative. *Tièni, tènga ; teniámo, tenéte, tèngano :* hold thou, &c.

* Optative and Subjunctive. *Che tènga, tenga, tenga ; teniámo, teniáte, tèngano :* that I may hold, &c.

Imper. *Che tenéssi, tenessi, tenesse ; ssimo, ste, ssero :* I might hold, thou mightest hold, &c.

* Second Imp. *Terrèi, terrésti, terrèbbe ;* I should *or* would hold.

Infinitive. *Tenére,* to hold. Gerund, *tenèndo,* holding. Participle, *tenúto,* held.

VALÉRE, *to be worth.*

* Indicative, Present. *Váglio, váli, vále ; vagliámo, valéte, vágliono :* I am worth, thou art worth, he is worth ; we are worth, you are worth, they are worth.

* Imperf. *Valéva, valévi, valéva,* &c. I was worth, thou wast worth, he was worth, &c.

* Preter-def. *Válsi, valésti, válse ; valémmo, valéste, válsero :* I was worth, thou wast worth, he was worth, we were worth, &c.

Preterperf. *Ho valúto.*

* Future. *Varrò, varrái,* &c. I shall be worth, &c.

* Imperative. *Váli, váglia* or *valga ; vagliámo,* &c. be thou worth, let him be worth ; let us be worth, &c.

* Optative. *Che váglia* or *valga, vaglia, vaglia ; vagliámo, vagliáte, vágliano* or *válgano :* that I may be worth, &c.

Imperf. *Che valéssi,* &c.

Second Imp. *Varrèi,* &c.

Infinit. *Valére.* Gerund, *valèndo.* Participle, *valúto.*

VEDÉRE, *to see.*

Indicative, Present. *Védo, védi, véde ; vediámo, vedéte,*

védono : I see, thou seest, he sees ; we see, you see, they see.

Imperf.   *Vedéva, vi, va ; vámo, váte, vano :* I did see, &c.

* Preter-def.   *Vidi, vedésti, vide ; vedémmo, vedéste, vídero :* I saw, thou sawest, he saw ; we saw, you saw, they saw.

Preterperf.   *Ho vedúto* or *visto,* &c. I have seen, &c.

* Future.   *Vedrò, rái, rà ; rémo, réte, ránno :* I shall see, thou shalt see, he shall see, &c.

Imperative. *Védi, véda ; vediámo, vedéte, védano :* see thou, let him see ; let us see, see you, let them see.

Optative.   *Che véda* or *végga, véda, véda ; vediámo, vediáte, védano* or *véggano :* that I may see, that thou mayest see, that he may see, &c.

Imperf.   *Che vedéssi,* that I might see, &c.

* Second Imperf.   *Vedrèi,* I should see, &c.

Infinitive.   *Vedére.* Gerund, *vedèndo.* Participle, *vedúto* or **visto,* seen.   They say also *véggo* or *véggio, veggiámo,* and *veggèndo* instead of *védo, vediámo, vedèndo.*

OF THE VERBS IN ERE SHORT.

Of all the verbs in *ere* short, there are none regular, except those which I have put just after the verb *crédere.*

All the rest, of which there is a great number, are irregular ; some in the present tense, most of them in the preterperfect-definite, some in the future, and almost all in the participle.

A New and General Rule, to learn in a short time all the Irregular Verbs in ERE short.

We are taught by an axiom in philosophy, that *frustra fit per plura, quod potest fieri per pauciora.* And it is in conformity with this maxim, that I have reduced all the irregular verbs in *ere* short, to one single rule.

These five verbs *conóscere,* to know ; *créscere,* to grow ; *náscere,* to be born ; *nuòcere,* to hurt (*morally*), *rómpere*, to break, form the preterperfect definite, and the participles, as follow :

Preter-def.	Participle.
Conóbbi, &c.	*Conosciúto.*
Crébbi, &c.	*Cresciúto.*
Nácqui, &c.	*Náto.*
Nòcqui, &c.	*Nociúto.*
Rúppi, &c.	*Rótto.*

Generally speaking, all the other verbs ending in the infinitive in *ere* short, form the preterperfect-definite in *si*, and the participle in *so, to,* or *sto.*

†‡† Though this rule might suffice for all the preter-perfect definites of verbs terminated in *ere* short, yet we may also observe, that the same verbs may be ter-minated in thirteen different ways, which will make, however, but one and the same rule.

⁎⁎ You will see in the terminations, which are placed in direct lines, that there is a star at the end of some of them, and there are others without that mark, The star at the end is intended to show that those verbs make the participle in *to;* the verbs that have no star make the participle in *so,* or in *esso.*

TERMINATIONS OF THE VERBS IN ERE SHORT.

The verbs in *ere* short are terminated in the in-finitive :—

([17]) 128   1. In *cere;* as, *vincere, tòrcere, cuòcere.*   ⁎

        131   2. In *dere;* as, *árdere, chiúdere, ridere.*

        132   3. In *gere;* as, *piángere, spingere, lèggere.*   ⁎

        133   4. In *gliere;* as, *cògliere, sciògliere, tògliere*   ⁎

        134   5. In *áere;* as, *tráere,* obs. now *trárre, &c.*   ⁎

        135   6. In *lere;* as, *svèllere.*

---

[17] The figures in the margin refer to the pages where the verbs of a similar termination are conjugated.

135   7. In *mere;* as *imprímere, opprímere.* Preter-def. *imprèssi, opprèssi.*   Participle, *imprèsso, opprèsso.*

136   8, In *nere;* as, *pónere,* obs. now *pórre, ripónere,* obs. now *ripórre.*   Participle, *ripósto.*

132 and 137   9. In *ndere;* as, *prèndere, rèndere, rispóndere, nascóndere.*   Participle, *préso, réso* or *rendúto, rispósto, nascósto* or *nascóso.*

138   { 10. In *pere;* as, *rómpere,* makes in the perfect defin. *rúppi,* in the participle, *rótto.*
        11. In *rere;* as, *córrere, concórrere.*
        12. In *tere;* as, *méttere, mísi, mésso.*

139   13. In *vere;* as, *scrívere, vívere.*

₊ Change all these terminations into *si,* and you will find the preterperfect definite of them all, in which consists the greatest irregularity; example: to find the preter-definite of *víncere, tòrcere, árdere, prèndere, piángere, rispóndere,* only change their terminations, *cere, dere, gere, ndere,* into *si,* and you will find *vínsi, tòrsi, ársi, prési, piánsi, rispósi.*

₊ Observe, that the verbs written with two *gg's* before the penultima, drop them, and double the *s* in the preterperfect definite, and the *t* in the participle; example, *lèggere, règgere,* &c.   To form the preterperfect definite, we must change the termination *ggere* into *ssi,* and for the participle into *tto,* and we shall find *lèssi, rèssi, lètto, rètto,* &c.

Take notice, likewise, that the verbs terminating in *gliere,* always retain the *l,* and only lose *giere* in the preterperfect definite; the same rule serves for the participle; examples: *cògliere, sciògliere, scégliere, tògliere,* &c. take from those words, *giere,* there remains *col, sciol, scel, tol;* and by adding *si* to them in the preterperfect definite, and in the participle *to,* we shall find *còlsi, sciòlsi, scélsi, tòlsi; còlto, sciòlto, scélto, tòlto,* &c.

₊ To conjugate these verbs with ease, remember that there are always three irregular, and three regular persons, in the preter-definite.

The three irregular persons are the first and third singular, and the third plural, which are very easy to be formed, if we only observe, that the first person is always terminated in *i*; *vínsi, ársi, piánsi;* change *i* into *e*, and it is the third singular; *vínse, árse, pianse;* and by adding *ro* to the latter it becomes the third plural, *vínsero, ársero, piánsero;* and so of the rest. Example :

prési, scríssi,	*prése, scrísse,*	*présero, scríssero.*
rési, lèssi,	*rése, lèsse,*	*résero, lèssero.*

The three regular persons are, the second singular, and the first and second plural. There is frequently more difficulty in finding out these than the irregular persons, because we confound one with the other. Now, the true way to avoid being mistaken in this point is, to remember that the second person singular of the preter-definite in all verbs, as well regular as irregular, is formed from the infinitive, by changing *re* into *sti*; as, *víncere, vincésti, árdere, ardésti; piángere, piangésti,* except the verb *èssere.*

The first person plural is also formed from the infinitive by changing *re* into *mmo*; as, *amáre, amámmo; vedére, vedémmo : lèggere, leggémmo.*

The second person plural of the preterperfect definite is formed in all the verbs from the second of the singular, by changing its final *i* into *e*; as, *vincésti, vincéste; ardésti, ardéste; piangésti, piangéste.* Thus we shall find, *vínsi, vincésti, vinse; vincémmo, vincéste, vínsero; ársi, ardésti, arse; ardémmo, ardéste, ársero.*

These observations should be carefully remembered, as being very necessary for conjugating the irregular verbs.

*** We must also remember, that the verbs terminated in *áere* and *vere*, as *tráere, scrívere,* double the letter *s* in the preterperfect definite, and the letter *t* in the participle ; examples: *trássi, scríssi; trátto, scrítto.*

The above rule would be sufficient for learning the irregularity of the verbs in *ere* short; yet, for the greater conveniency of learners, I have thought proper to explain these thirteen terminations more at large, in order to obviate all the difficulties that may occur.

OF THE VERBS TERMINATED IN CERE.

The verbs in *cere* form the preterperfect definite, by changing *cere* into *si*, and the participle into *to*; as,

CUÒCERE, to bake, to cook. Pres. *cuòco, cuòci, cuòce; cociámo* (¹⁸), *cocéte, cuòcono;* I bake, thou bakest, &c.

Imp. *Cocéva, vi, va; vámo, váte, vano;* I baked, &c.

* Preter-def. *Còssi, cocésti, còsse; cocémmo, cocéste, còssero;* I did bake, thou didst bake, &c.

Preterp. *Ho còtto,* I have baked.

Preterplup. *Avéva còtto,* I had baked.

Fut. *Cocerò, rái, rà; rémo, réte, ránno:* I shall bake.

Imper. *Cuòci, cuòca; cociámo, cocéte, cuòcano;* bake thou, let him bake, &c.

Opt. *Che cuòca.* Imp. *Che cocéssi.* Second Imp. *cocerèi.* Infinitive. *cuòcere.* Part. *còtto. Ger. cocèndo.

CONDÚCERE, obs. CONDURRE, to conduct. Present, *Condúco, condúci, condúce; conduciámo, conducéte, condúcono;* I conduct, thou conductest, &c.

Imperf. *Conducéva, vi, va,* &c. I was conducting.

Preter-definite. *Condússi, conducésti, condússe; conducémmo, conducéste, condússero;* I conducted, &c.

* Fut. *Condurrò, rái, rà,* &c. I shall conduct, &c.

Imperative. *Condúci, condúca,* &c. conduct thou, &c.

Optative. *Che condúca.* Imperf. *Che conducéssi.* 2nd Imp. *Condurrèi.* Part. *Condótto. Ger. Conducèndo.

RILÚCERE, to shine. Present, *rilúco, rilúci, rilúce; riluciámo, rilucéte, rilúcono;* I shine, &c. Imperfect, *rilucéva,* &c. I was shining, &c.

---

¹⁸ Observe, that words containing *uo,* as in *cuòcere, muòvere, uòmo, nuovo,* &c. lose their *u* when, through their inflection, the *tonic accent* passes on another vowel, or when a double consonant follows: the conjugation of *cuòcere* will offer ample and clear examples.

Preter-definite. *Rilússi, rilucésti, rilússe ; rilucémmo, rilucéste, rilússero :* I shined, thou didst shine, he shined.
Future. *Rilucerò,* I shall shine, &c.
Imperative. *Rilúci, rilúca ; riluciámo, rilucéte, rilúcano :* shine thou, let him shine, &c.
No Optative. Subjunctive. *Che rilúca, rilúca, rilúca ; riluciámo, riluciáte, rilúcano ;* that I may shine, &c.
Imperfect. *Rilucéssi,* &c. that I might shine, &c. Second Imperfect. *Rilucerèi,* &c. I should shine, &c.
No Participle. Gerund. *Rilucèndo,* shining.

VÍNCERE, to win. Present. *Vinco, vínci, vínce ; vinciámo, vincéte, víncono :* I win, thou winnest, he wins, &c. Imperfect. *Vincéva,* I was winning. * Preter-definite. *Vinsi, vincésti, vínse ; vincémmo, vincéste, vínsero :* I won, &c. Preterperfect. *Ho vinto,* I have won. Future. *Vincerò,* I shall win. Imperative. *Vinci, vínca,* &c. win thou, let him win, &c.
Optative and Subjunctive. *Che vinca, vinca,* &c.
Imperfect. *Che vincéssi.* Second Imperfect. *Vincerèi.*
Participle. *Vinto.* Gerund. *Vincèndo.*

TÒRCERE, to twist. Present. *Tòrco, tòrci, tòrce ; torciámo, torcéte, tòrcono :* I twist, thou twistest, he twists ; we twist, &c. Imperfect. *Torcéva,* I was twisting. * Preter-definite. *Tòrsi, torcésti, tòrse ; torcémmo, torcéste, tòrsero.* Future. *Torcerò.*
Imperative. *Tòrci, tòrca,* &c. twist thou, let him twist, &c.
Optative. *Che tòrca.* Imperfect. *Che torcéssi.* Second Imperfect. *Torcerèi.* Participle. *Tòrto.* Gerund. *Torcèndo.*

CONÓSCERE and CRÉSCERE, change *scere* into *bbi,* to form the preter-definite, and make the participle in *sciúto ;* as,
Present. *Conósco, conósci, conósce ; conosciámo, conoscéte, conóscono :* I know, &c. Imperfect. *Conoscéva.*

G 5

Preter-definite. *Conóbbi, conoscésti, conóbbe; conoscémmo, conoscéste, conóbbero:* I knew, &c. Future, *conoscerò,* &c. Imperative. *Conósci, conósca,* &c. know thou, let him know, &c.

Optative. *Che conósca.* Imperfect. *Che conoscéssi.* Second Imperfect. *Conoscerèi.* Participle. **Conosciúto.*

CRÉSCERE. Present. *Crésco, Crésci,* &c. *crescéte, créscono:* I grow, thou growest, he grows; we grow, you grow, they grow. Imperfect. *Crescéva,* I was growing. Preter-definite. *Crébbi, crescésti, crébbe.* Future. *Crescerò,* I shall grow.

Imperative. *Crésci, crésca,* &c. grow thou, let him grow, &c.

Optative. *Che crésca.* Imperf. *Che crescéssi.* Second Imperf. *Crescerèi,* I should grow, &c. Participle, **cresciúto.* Gerund. *Crescèndo.*

NÁSCERE and NUÒCERE make the preterperfect definite in *qui.*

NÁSCERE, to be born. Present. *Násco, násci, násce; nasciámo, nascéte, náscono;* I am born, thou art born, he is born; we are born, you are born, they are born. Imperfect. *Nascéva,* I was born. Preter-definite. *Nácqui, nascésti, nácque; nascémmo, nascéste, nácquero:* I was born. Future. *Nascerò,* I shall be born.

Optative. *Che násca.* Imperfect. *Che nascéssi.* Second Imperfect. *Nascerèi.* Participle. **Náto.* Gerund. *Nascèndo.*

NUÒCERE, to hurt (morally) ([18]). Present. *Nuòco, nuòci, nuòce; nociámo, nocéte, nuòcono:* I hurt, &c. Imperfect. *Nocéva,* I did hurt. Preter-definite. **Nòcqui, nocésti, nòcque; nocémmo, nocéste, nòcquero:* 1 did hurt, or I hurt, &c. Future. *Nocerò,* &c.

Imperative. *Nuòci, nuòca,* hurt thou, let him hurt, &c.

Optative. *Che nuòca.* Imperfect. *Che nocéssi.* Second Imperf. *Nocerèi.* Participle. **Nociúto.* Gerund, *Nocèndo.*

OF THE VERBS IN DERE.

The verbs in *dere* form the preterperfect definite in *si*, and the participle in *so:* as,

A'RDERE, to burn. Present. *A'rdo, árdi, árde; ardiá- mo, ardéte, árdono:* I burn, thou burnest, &c.

Imperfect, *Ardéva,* I was burning. *Preter-definite, ársi, árdesti, árse; ardémmo, ardéste, ársero:* I burnt, he burnt, &c. Future. *Arderò,* I shall burn, &c.

Imperative. *A'rdi, árda; ardiámo, ardéte, árdano:* burn thou, let him burn, &c.

Optative. *Che árda, árda, árda; ardiámo, ardiáte, árdano:* that I may burn, &c. Imperfect. *Che ardéssi.* Second Imperfect. *Arderèi.* Participle. *A'rso,* burnt. Gerund. *Ardèndo,* burning *or* in burning.

I shall give no more tenses of the verbs than the present, the preterperfect definite, and the participles, none but these being irregular.

CHIÚDERE, to shut. *Chiúdo.* *Chiúsi.* *Chiúso.* And so of the rest, except,

CHIÈDERE, to ask; which makes in the preter-def. *Chièsi,* and the participle, *Chièsto,* and not *chièso.*

PÈRDERE, makes in the preter-definite, *perdéi* or *perdètti,* and *pèrsi:* in the participle, *perdúto,* and *pèrso.*

RÍDERE, to laugh. *Rído.* *Rísi.* *Ríso.*

RÓDERE, to gnaw. *Ródo.* *Rósi.* *Róso.*

Observe, that all these verbs have the preter-definite in *ei* and *etti.* It is more elegant to say, *chiudéi, perdéi,* &c. than *chiúsi, pèrsi,* &c. This is to avoid the ambiguity that might arise between *chiúsi, pèrsi,* the first person of the preter-definite, and *chiúsi, pèrsi,* as nouns adjective plural.

The participle of the verbs in *dere* short, is always terminated in *so.* Except the verbs *chièdere* and *pèrdere,* which make *chièsi* and *pèrsi, chièsto* and *perdúto* or *pèrso.*

*** You perceived, after the conjugation of the verb *crédere*, that *cèdere* is a regular verb; its compounds are not; for they form the preter-definite in *essi*, and the participle in *esso*.   Examples :

SUCCÈDERE, to succeed. *Succèdo.* **Succèssi.* **Succèsso.*

CONCÈDERE, to agree, to grant, or yield to. *Concèdo.* **Concèssi.* **Concèsso.*

I apprehend that those two verbs, as well as *pèrdere*, to lose, are regular and irregular, since we may likewise say, *Succedéi* or *succedètti. Succedúto. Concedéi, concedètti. Conceduto. Perdéi, perdètti. Perdúto :* and in like manner all the compounds of the verbs *cèdere* and *pèrdere.*   Some prefer the regular termination.

OF THE VERBS IN ENDERE.

The verbs in *endere* form the preter-definite in *ei* and *si*, and the participle in *so*.   Example :

ATTÈNDERE, to attend. *Attendéi* or **attési.* **Attéso.*

PRÈNDERE, to take. *Prendéi,* **prési.* **Préso.*

RÈNDERE, to render. *Rendéi,* **rési.* *Réso.*

This verb also forms the participle in *uto,* as *Rendúto ;* but it is better to use *Réso.*

Fèndere, to cleave, and *pèndere,* to hang, are regular. In the preter-definite they make *Fendéi* or *fendètti, Pendéi* or *pendètti,* in the participle, *fesso* and *peso.*

Take notice, nevertheless, that the compounds of these two verbs are irregular, and they make the preter-definite in *esi,* the participle in *eso,* like *Difèndere,* to defend, **difèsi,* **diféso ; Appèndere,* to hang, or fix up, **appési,* **appéso,* &c.

OF THE VERBS IN GERE.

The verbs in *gere* make the preter-definite in *si,* and the participle in *to ;* as,

CÍNGERE, to gird. *Cingo.* Preter-definite. **Cinsi, cingésti, cinse,* &c.   Participle. **Cinto.*

Spíngere, to push. *Spíngo. *Spínsi. *Spínto.

Pòrgere, to offer. Pòrgo. *Pòrsi. *Pòrto.

U'ngere, to anoint. U'ngo. *U'nsi. *U'nto.

Spárgere, to shed. Present. Spárgo. Preter-definite. *Spársi. Participle. *Spárso.

To which we may also add Estínguere. Estínguo. *Estínsi. *Estínto.

Èrgere, to erect. *Ergo. *Ersi. *Erto.

All these verbs have the preter-definite in ei and ètti, but regularly their participle is in to. Immèrgere, dispèrgere, tèrgere, an obsolete verb (but poetical), and some others of the like sort, have it in so. Both these participles are formed of the first syllable of the present indicative joined to the syllable to or so. For instance, of Cíngere we make Cínto, of Spárgere, Spárso. If the infinitives of those verbs are accented on the second syllable, the participle is then formed on the two first syllables added to to or so.

Thus from Immèrgere is formed Immèrso, of Disgiúngere, Disgiúnto, &c.

₊ Remember that the participle of the verb spárgere, is spárto and spárso, not spargiúto, except in poetry for the sake of rhyme, or to serve the measure of the verse, and even then we ought to use it as little as possible.

Observe, that verbs which have a vowel before gere must be written with two gg's and that they double the letter s in the preter-definite; as,

Fríggere, to fry; Friggo. Fríssi, friggésti, &c. Frítto.

Lèggere, to read; Lèggo. Lèssi, leggésti, &c. Participle, Lètto.

Take care not to say, friggiúto or leggiúto.

OF THE VERBS IN GLIERE.

Observe, that besides the irregularity in the preter-definite, and the participles of verbs ending in glíere, they are also contracted or abridged in the infinitive, and in the future and second imperfect tenses; as,

Cògliere or Còrre, and Cor, to gather. Future. Corrò. Second Imperfect. Corrèi.

The verbs in *gliere* change their terminations into *lsi,* to form the preter-definite ; and in *lto,* to make the participle.   The conjugating of *cògliere, còlsi, còlto,* will serve as a rule for those verbs that are of the same termination.

* Indicative.   Present. *Còlgo* and *cóglio,* I gather ; *cògli, còglie ; cogliámo, cogliéte, còlgono.*   Imperfect. *Cogliéva,* I was gathering.   *Preterperfect-definite. *Còlsi, cogliésti, còlse, cogliémmo,* &c. I gathered.   Future. *Corrò,* &c.   I will *or* shall gather.

* Imperative.   *Cògli, còlga* or *còglia ; cogliámo, cogliéte, cògliano* or *còlgano :* let him gather.

Optative. *Che còglia* or *còlga,* &c.   Imperfect. **Che cogliéssi.*   Second Imperfect. **Corrèi.*   Participle. **Còlto.*

TòGLIERE or TòRRE.   Present. *Tòlgo or *tòglio.* Preter-definite. **Tòlsi, togliésti,* &c.   Future. **Torrò.*

Optative. * *Tòlga.*   Imperfect. *Togliéssi.* * Second Imperfect. *Torrèi.*   Participle. *Tòlto.*

SCIòGLIERE or SCIòRRE, to loosen.   Present. **Sciòlgo,* or *sciòglio.*   Preterperfect-definite. **Sciòlsi, sciogliésti.*   Participle. *Sciòlto.*

SCéGLIERE, to choose, is not abridged in the infinitive, like the above verbs : it forms in the present, *scélgo, scégli, scéglie ; scegliámo, scegliéte, scélgono.* *Preterperfect-definite. *Scélsi.* *Participle. *Scélto.*

OF THE VERBS IN HERE.

If there were any such thing in the Italian language as a verb terminated in *here,* it would be *tráhere,* to draw, with its several compounds.   But the present orthography is to write them without an *h.*

This verb is also contracted in the infinitive.

Of *Tráere* we form *trárre* or *trár.*   *Trássi* is the preter-definite, and *Trátto* the participle.

* Indicative. Present. *Tràggo, tròi, tròe; traiámo, traéte, tràggono*: I draw, &c. Imperfect. *Traéva.*
*Preterperfect-definite. *Tràssi, traésti*, &c. * Future. *Trarrò, trarrai, trarrà*, &c.

* Imperative. *Tròi, trágga; traiámo* or *traggiámo, traéte, tràggano.*

* Optative. *Che trágga.* Imperfect. *Che traéssi.*

* Sec. Imp. *Trarrèi.* Participle. *Trátto.* Gerund. *Traèndo.*

Observe the same rule in its compounds. *Contráere, attráere, distráere*, &c. which make *contrárre, attrárre, distrárre*, &c. They form the preter-definite in *ssi*, as *Contrássi; Attrássi; Distrássi,* and the participle in *tto*, as, *Contrátto; Attrátto; Distrátto*, &c.

OF THE VERBS IN LERE.

Of all the verbs in *lere*, there is only the verb *svèllere*, to pluck, that changes *e* into *si*, to form the preterperfect-definite, and into *to* for the participle. Preterperfect-def. *Svèlsi, svellèsti.* Future. *Svellerò.* Participle. *Svèlto.*

OF THE VERBS IN MERE.

PRÈMERE, SÚMERE, and their compounds, are the only regular verbs for this rule.

Prèmere, to press. Present. *Prèmo.* Preterperfect-definite. *Preméi* or *premètti,* and *prèssi.* obs. Participle. *Premúto.*

Its compounds in *imere* make the preterperfect-definite in *ssi*, and the participle in *sso;* as,

*Opprímere, *Opprèssi. Opprèsso.*

*Imprímere, *Imprèssi. Imprèsso.*

Súmere is obsolete: its compounds make *súnsi, súnto,* as *Assúmere, *assúnsi, assúnto ; Consúmere* (now *consumáre*), *consúnsi, consúnto* and *consumáto.*

OF THE VERBS IN NERE.

Pónere, obs., is also irregular, with its compounds. It changes the infinitive into *órre*, so that we say, *pórre*, to put ; *dispórre*, to dispose, &c. instead of, *pónere*, and *dispónere*. We may change *nere* or *rre*, into *si*, for the preter-definite, and into *sto* for the participle ; saying, **Pósi, Dispósi ; Pósto, Dispósto*, &c.

The preter-definite may also terminate in *ei*, as *ponéi*, *disponéi*, &c. But the participle always makes *sto*. Nay, it would be very wrong to say, *esposáto, disposáto*, and this should be carefully minded, because foreigners are apt to commit this error. The French are led into it by the turn of their language ; and other nations, by frequently meeting with the word *posáto* in printed books. But you are to take notice, that this word is derived from the verb *posáre*, and not from *pónere* or *pórre*. For the same reason we do not say, *posái* for *pósi*, this word being used only for the first person of the preter-definite of the same verb *posáre*. Consequently, we must never say *disposái, disposasti*, &c. *esposái, esposasti*, &c. for the verbs are the compounds of *pónere* and not *posáre*.

*** Remember the two remarks made on the verbs ending in *lere, nere, nire*, which take the letter *g* in the present, and change *le, ne, ni*, into *r* in the future, &c.

* Present. *Póngo, póni, póne ; poniámo, ponéte, póngono :* I put, &c. Imperfect. *Ponéva.*

* Preterperfect-definite. *Pósi*, or *ponéi*, obs. *ponésti, póse ; ponémmo, ponéste, pósero.* Future. *Porrò.*

* Imperative. *Póni, pónga ; poniámo, ponéte, póngano.*

Optative. *Che pónga, a, a ; poniámo, poniáte, póngano.*

Imperfect. *Che ponéssi.* Second Imperfect. *Porrèi.*
*Participle. *Pósto.* Gerund. *Ponèndo.*

Conjugate its compounds after the same manner.

OF THE VERBS IN ONDERE.

By changing *ondere* into *si*, or *re* into *i*, as in the case of regular verbs, you form the preterperfect definite. The participle is in *osto*, *uso*, or *oso*.

RISPÓNDERE, to answer. Present. *Rispóndo, rispóndi, rispónde; rispondiámo, rispondéte, rispóndono.* Imperfect. *Rispondéva.* * Preterperfect-definite. *Rispósi, rispondésti, rispóse; rispondémmo, rispondéste, rispósero.* Future. *Risponderò.*

Imperative. *Rispóndi, rispónda; rispondiámo, rispondéte, rispóndano.*

Optative. *Che rispónda, da, da; rispondiámo, rispondiáte, rispóndano.* Imperfect. *Che rispondéssi.* Second Imperfect. *Risponderèi.* * Participle. *Rispósto.*

NASCÓNDERE, to hide. Present. *Nascóndo.* * Preterperfect-definite. *Nascósi.* Participle. *Nascósto.*

The verb FÓNDERE, to melt, does not make the preter-definite in *osi*, but in *usi* or *ei*. You must therefore say *Fondei* or *fúsi, fondésti, fondè* or *fúse; fondémmo, fondéste, fondérono* or *fúsero.*

₊ Note, that *fúsi, fúse,* &c. is not so much used at present, except in compounds; as in the verb *confóndere, diffóndere,* &c. which in the preter-definite makes *confúsi* and *confondéi; diffúsi, diffondéi,* &c. and in the participle, *confúso, diffúso,* &c.

Though in the preterdefinite we meet with *confúsi*, and *diffúsi*, yet it would be better to make use of *confondéi*, and *diffondéi.* This is on account of the ambiguity in those words, when they form the first person of the preter-definite, and when they are nouns adjective, as we have observed of *chièsi* and *pèrsi.*

The participle of the verb *fóndere* makes *fúso*, and sometimes *fondúto.*

TÓNDERE, to shear, does not make *tósi*, but *tondéi, tondésti, tondè.* Participle, *tondúto,* and not *tóso*, the latter being abridged from *tosáto,* which comes from the verb *tosáre.*

OF THE VERBS IN PERE.

Rómpere, to break, is, with its compounds, the only irregular verb of this termination ; in the present it forms *Rómpo, rómpi, rómpe ; rompiáno, rompéte, rómpono.* Imperfect. *Rompéva.* * Preterperfect-definite. *Rúppi, rompésti, rúppe ; rompémmo, rompéste, rúppero.* Future. *Romperò.* * Participle. *Rótto.*

OF THE VERBS IN RERE.

Córrere, with its compounds, to run, is also the only verb that ends in *rere* short ; it makes the preter-definite in *si*, and the participle in *so*; as,

Córrere, to run. Present. *Córro, córri, córre ; corriámo, corréte, córrono.* Imperfect. *Corréva.* Preterperfect-definite. *Córsi, corrésti, corse ; corémmo, corréste, córsero.* Future. *Correrò.* Imperative. *Córri, córra,* &c.

Optative. *Che córra, córra, córra ; corriámo, corriáte, córrano.* Imperfect. *Corréssi.* Second Imperfect. *Correrèi, correrésti,* &c. * Participle. *Córso.* Gerund. *Corrèndo.*

Accórere, to run to. Preter-defin. *Accórsi.* Participle. *Accórso ;* and all the other compounds in the same manner.

OF THE VERBS IN TERE.

Méttere, to put, does not make in the preter-definite *Méssi* or *misi, mettésti, mésse* or *mise ; mettémmo, mettéste, méssero* or *misero :* I put, thou puttest, &c. Participle. *Mésso.*

Prométtere, to promise, makes *proméssi* and *promisi.* Participle. *Promésso.*

Riflèttere, to reflect, is irregular only in the participle. We do not say in the preter-definite *riflettéi* or *riflèssi*, obs. The participle makes *riflettùto;* but this word is grown obsolete. It is customary now to use the participle of the verb *fáre*, joined to the word *riflessióne.* As, having reflected, *avèndo fatto riflessióne;* I have reflected upon that, *io ho fatto riflessione sópra ciò,* &c.

RISCUÒTERE, to receive money. *Riscòssi. Riscòsso.*

SCUÒTERE, to shake, makes **Scòssi. Scòsso.*

PERCUÒTERE, to strike, makes *Percòssi* or *percotéi.* Participle. *Percòsso.*

OF THE VERBS IN UCERE.

The verbs *Prodúcere, Addúcere, Ridúcere, Indúcere, Sedúcere, Condúcere, Dedúcere, Tradúcere,* which mean, to produce, to allege, to reduce, to induce, to seduce, to conduct, to deduct, to translate, have been contracted in the infinitive into *Prodúrre, Addúrre,* &c. Their preterdefinite is *Prodússi, Addússi;* Fut. *Produrrò, Addurrò.* Sec. Imp. *Produrréi,* &c. All the other tenses are conjugated after the termination *ucere,* and their participle is terminated in *otto,* as *Prodótto, Addótto,* &c.

Some other verbs, terminating in *úcere,* do not change the infinitive. Therefore we must take care to say *rilúcere,* but never *rilúrre,* and so of the rest.

OF THE VERBS IN VERE.

To form the preterperfect definite of verbs in *vere,* you must change *vere* into *ssi,* or *si.* The participles are different.

MUÒVERE, to move (see note [18]). Preter-definite. *Mòssi.* Participle. *Mòsso.*

SCRÍVERE, to write. *Scríssi, scrivésti, scrisse; scrivémmo,* &c. Participle. *Scritto.*

VÍVERE, to live. **Vissi, vivésti, visse.* Participle. *Vissúto* or *vivúto,* obs.

Assòlvere, to absolve, having a consonant before *vere*, makes in the preterperfect-definite, *Assòlsi* or *assolvei*, *assolvésti*, *assòlse*, &c.   Participle. *Assolúto* or *assòlto*.

Risòlvere, to resolve. Present. *Risòlvo*. Preter-perfect-definite, **Risòlsi, risolvésti;* or *risolvéi* and *ri-solvètti*. Participle. *Risolúto*.

*** Remember, that the optative of verbs ending in *ere* and in *ire* is formed of the first person indicative, by changing *o* into *a*; as, *Vedére, védo, véda; Scrívere, scrívo, scriva; Cògliere, còlgo, còlga; Crédere, crédo, créda; Dormíre, dòrmo, dòrma; Sentíre, sènto, sènta; Finíre, finisco, finisca; Dire, dico, dica*. And so of all the other verbs, except *Essere, Sapére, Avére*, and *Dovére*.

IRREGULARS OF THE THIRD CONJUGATION.

In the third conjugation there are six verbs more irregular than the rest, viz. *Dire*, to say; *Moríre*, to die; *Salíre*, to ascend; *Udíre*, to hear; *Veníre*, to come; *Uscíre*, to go out.

Díre, *to say*.

I apprehend the verb *Dire* is only an abridgment of *dicere*, which was used by the ancients. I give it, how-ever a place among the irregulars of the third conjuga-tion, in order to comply with the custom of other gram-marians.

* Present. *Dico, dici, dice; diciámo, dìte, dicono :* I say, thou sayest, he says.

Imperfect. *Dicéva, vi, va; vámo, váte, vano.*

* Preterperfect-definite. *Dìssi, dicésti, dìsse; dicém-mo, dicéste, dissero :* I said, thou didst say, he said, &c.

Preterperfect. *Ho détto*, I have said.

Preterplup. *Aveva detto*, I had said.

Future. *Dirò*, I shall say.

* Imperative. *Di', dica; diciámo, díte, dícano :* say thou, let him say ; let us say, &c.

* Optative. *Che dica, dica, dica; diciámo, diciáte, dicano:* that I may say, thou mayest say, he may say, &c.

Imperfect. *Che dicéssi.* Second Imperfect. *Dirèi.*

* Participle. *Détto.* Gerund. *Dicèndo.*

Moríre, *to die.*

Morire has no irregularity, but by making the present tense in two different manners.

* Indicative. Present. *Muòio, muòri, muòre; moiámo, morite, muòiono;* or *mòro, mòri, mòre,* &c. I die, thou diest, he dies; we die, you die, they die.

Imperfect. *Moriva, vi, va; vámo, váte, vano.*

Preterperfect-definite. *Morii, moristi, morì; morimmo, moriste, morirono,* and not *mòrsi,* which comes from *mòrdere.*

Preterperfect. *Sòno* or *sòn mòrto,* I am dead.

Future. *Morrò* and *morirò,* I shall *or* will die.

* Imperative. *Muòri, muòia; moriámo, morite, muòiano:* die thou, let him die, &c.

* Optative and Subjunctive. *Che muòia, muòia, muòia; moiámo, moiáte, muòiano.*

Imperfect. *Che morissi.* Second Imperfect. *Morrèi* and *morirèi.*

Participle. *Mòrto.* Gerund. *Morèndo.*

Salíre, *to come* or *go up.*

Salíre is irregular, like *moríre;* because its present tense is formed in two ways.

* Indicative. Present. *Sálgo* or *ságlio,* obs. *sali, sale; sagliámo* or *salghiámo, salite, sálgono* or *ságliono:* I go up, &c. Imperfect. *Salíva,* &c.

Preter-definite. *Salii, salísti, salì; salimmo, saliste, salírono:* I went up. Future. *Salirò,* I shall go up.

* Imperative. *Sali, salga; sagliámo, salíte, sálgano;* go thou up, let him go up, &c.

* Optative. *Che salga, salga, salga,* &c.

Imperfect. *Che salissi, salissi, salisse.*

Second Imperfect. *Salirèi, salirésti.*

Participle. *Salito.*   Gerund. *Salèndo.*

Be particularly careful not to say *saliámo*, instead of *sagliámo* or *salghiámo;* because the former word comes from the verb *saláre*, to salt, and not from *salíre*, to mount.

Udíre, *to hear.*

The irregularity of *udire* is only in the present tense, by changing *u* into *o*, in the first, second and third person singular, and in the third person plural.

* Indicative.   Present. `Odo, òdi, òde; udiámo, udíte, òdono;* I hear, thou hearest, he hears; we hear, you hear, they hear.

Imperfect. *Udíva, vi, va; vámo, váte, vano.*

Preterperfect-def. *Udíi, udísti, udì; udímmo, udíste, udírono:* I heard, &c.

Future. *Udirò, rái, rà; rémo, réte, ránno:* I shall or will hear, thou shalt hear, he shall hear.

* Imperative. `Odi, òda; udiámo, udíte, òdano.*

* Optative. *Che òda,* that I may hear.

Imperfect. *Che udíssi,* that I might hear.

Second Imperfect. *Udirèi.* Participle. *Udíto.* Gerund. *Udèndo.*

Veníre, *to come.*

* Indicative.   Present. *Vèngo, vièni, viène; veniámo, veníte, vèngono:* I come, thou comest, he comes; we come, you come, they come.

Imperfect. *Veníva,* I did come.

* Preterperfect-def. *Vénni, venísti, vénne; venímmo, veníste, vénnero:* I came, thou camest, he came; we came, you came, they came.

Preterperfect. *Sòno venúto.*   Future. *Verrò,* I shall come.

* Imperative. *Vièni, vènga; veniámo, veníte, vèngano:* come thou, let him come; let us come, &c.

* Optative.   Present. *Che vènga.*   Imperfect. *Che veníssi.*

Second Imperfect. *Verrèi.* Participle. *Venúto.* Gerund. *Venèndo.*

All the compounds of *Venire*, as *pervenire*, *rivenire*, &c. are conjugated in the same manner; and so are all the other compounded verbs.

UscíRE, *to come* or *go out*.

Uscíre is irregular, only by changing *u* into *e* in the present, viz. in the first, second, and third person singular, and the third plural.

* Indicative. Present. '*Esco, èsci, èsce; usciámo, uscíte, èscono:* I come or go out, thou comest or goest out, he comes or goes out; we come or go out, you come or go out, they come or go out.

Imperfect. *Uscíva,* I was going or coming out.

Preterperfect-definite. *Uscíi, uscísti, uscì; uscímmo, uscíste, uscírono;* I came or went out, thou camest or wentest out, he came or went out; we came or went out, &c.

Preterperfect. *Sòno uscíto,* I am come or gone out.

Future. *Uscirò, uscirái, uscirà,* &c.

Imperative. *Esci, èsca; usciámo, uscite, èscano.*

* Optative. *Che èsca, esca, esca; usciámo, usciáte, èscano.* Imperfect. *Che uscíssi.*

Second Imperfect. *Uscirèi.* Participle. *Uscíto.* Gerund. *Uscèndo.*

Aprire, to open, makes in the preterperfect-definite, *Aprii* or *apèrsi.* Participle. *Apèrto.*

Coprire, to cover, makes in the preterperfect-definite, *Coprii* or *copèrsi.* Participle. *Copèrto.*

The third conjugation of the verbs terminated in the infinitive in *ire*, has another sort of verbs irregular only in the present, which are formed from the infinitive, by changing *ire* into *isco;* as, *Ardire,* to dare, of which I have given the following conjugations, to serve as a rule for the rest.

OF THE VERBS IN ISCO.

In order to lay down a general rule for the verbs that have the termination in *isco* in the present tense, observe, that some of them do not follow *ardisco,* and they differ only from the verb *sentire* in the preterperfect-definite, and in the participle.   They are as follow :

Present.		Preterperf.	Particip.
Aprire,	*ápro,*	*aprii & apèrsi,*	*apèrto.*
Apparire,	*apparisco,*	*apparii & ap-pársi.*	*appárso.*
Coprire,	*cópro,*	*coprii & copèrsi,*	*copèrto.*
Comparire,	*comparisco,*	*comparii & com-pársi.*	*compárso.*
Offerire,	*offerisco & offro,*	*offerii & offèrsi,*	*offèrto.*
Proferire,	*proferisco,*	*proferii & prof-fèrsi.*	*proffèrto.*
Soffrire,	*sòffro,*	*soffrii, soffèrsi,*	*soffèrto.*
Seppellire,	*seppellisco,*	*seppellii,*	*sepólto & seppellíto.*

I have made a collection of the regular verbs in *ire,* which are conjugated like *sentire,* as you have already seen in this chapter, page 102, where we treated of the third conjugation of verbs.   All the other verbs not contained in that, and in the preceding collection, form the present in *isco,* and ought to be conjugated like *ardisco.*   In this collection there are even some verbs that are also irregular; as, *Consentire, Mentire, Partire,* when the latter signifies, to divide.   We meet with *consentisco, mentisco,* and *partisco.*   When the latter signifies, to share, I should prefer *partisco* to *párto.*   On the contrary, when it denotes, to go away, you must say, *párto,* and not *partisco. Bollire, Convertire, Soffrire,* also make the first person of the present indicative in *isco.*

*** Before you read over words terminating in *isco,* remember the two remarks concerning the irregularity of the present tense.

The first teaches you that the irregularity of the present indicative is continued in the present imperative and subjunctive.

By the second you learn, that the first and second persons plural of the present tense are never irregular.

ARDÍRE, *to dare.*

Indicative. Present. *Ardísco, ardísci, ardísce; ab-biámo ardíre, ardíte, ardíscono:* I dare.

Imperfect. *Ardíva,* I did dare; *ardívi, va, &c.*

Preterperfect-def. *Ardíi, ardísti, ardì; ardímmo, ardíste, ardírono:* I durst, &c.

Preterperf. *Ho ardíto.* Future. *Ardirò.*

Imperative. *Ardísci, ardísca; ardiámo, ardíte, ardíscano;* dare thou, let him dare; let us dare, &c.

Optative. *Che ardísca, ardísca, ardísca; che abbiámo ardíre, che abbiáte ardíre, ardíscano;* that I may dare, thou mayest dare, he may dare, &c.

Imperfect. *Ardíssi.* Second Imperfect. *Ardirèi.*

Participle. *Ardíto.* Gerund. *Avèndo ardíto.*

Conjugate the following words after the same manner:

Abborríre,	isco	ii	ito		abhor.
Abolíre,	isco	ii	ito		abolish.
Arricchíre,	isco	ii	ito		enrich.
Arrossíre,	isco	ii	ito		blush.
Bandíre,	isco	ii	ito		banish.
Bianchíre,	isco	ii	ito		whiten.
Capíre,	isco	ii	ito		comprehend.
Colpíre,	isco	ii	ito		strike.
Compatíre,	isco	ii	ito		excuse *or* bear with.
Concepíre,	isco	ii	ito		conceive.
Digeríre,	isco	ii	ito		digest.
Eseguíre,	isco	ii	ito	to	execute.
Finíre,	isco	ii	ito		finish.
Fioríre,	isco	ii	ito		blossom *or* bloom.
Gradíre,	isco	ii	ito		approve of.
Impazzíre,	isco	ii	ito		grow mad.
Incrudelíre,	isco	ii	ito		grow cruel.
Languíre,	isco	ii	ito		languish.
Obbedíre,	isco	ii	ito		obey.
Patíre,	isco	ii	ito		suffer.
Spedíre,	isco	ii	ito		make haste.
Tradíre,	isco	ii	ito		betray.
Ubbidíre,	isco	ii	ito		obey.
Uníre,	isco	ii	ito		unite.

H

⁎ Note, that the Italian poets do not always observe this irregularity, for they say indifferently *òffro* and *offrisco; múgge,* and *muggisce; lángue* and *languisce; fère* and *ferisce;* as may be seen in Guarini's *Pastór Fido,* and in Tasso's *Amínta.*

> *Múgge in mándra l' arménto.*   Pastor Fido.
> *Qual árme féra, qual dia vita, quále*
> *Sáni e ritórni in vita.*

There are also some verbs that end in *are,* and in *ire;* as,

Coloráre or *colorire,*	to colour.
Inanimáre or *inanimire,*	to animate.
Inacerbáre or *inacerbire,*	to exasperate.
Induráre or *indurire,*	to harden.

Poets also frequently use the verbs *ire* and *gire,* instead of *andáre.* This is all that needs be remarked in regard to irregular verbs.

OF THE VERB IRE, *to go.*

The following tenses are all that occur in good writers:

Indicative.   Imperfect. *I'va,* he did go; *ivano* or *ivan,* they did go.   Future. *Irò, irái, irà; irémo, iréte, iránno* or *irán.*

Imperative,	*I'te,*	go you.
Infinitive,	*I're* or *ir,*	to go.
Parti iple,	*I'to,*	gone.

The other tenses are not used.

OF THE VERB GIRE, *to go.*

There are no more than the following tenses in use:

Present. *Gite,* you go.

Imperfect. *Givo, givi, giva* or *gia; givámo, giváte, givano:* I did go, &c.

Preter-def. *Gisti,* gi' or *gio; gimmo, giste, girono.*

Imperative. *Gite,* go you.

Optative.   Imperfect. *Che gissi, gissi, gisse; gissimo, giste, gissero:* that I might go.

Infinitive. *Gire* or *gir.*   Participle. *Gito.*

There is still something to be said in regard to verbs neuter, reciprocal and impersonal.

OF THE VERBS NEUTER.

The Verbs Neuter are those which, in their compound tenses, are never or seldom conjugated with the verb *èssere*, to be: as, *I speak, I sleep, I tremble*, &c. we may indeed say, *I have spoken, I have slept, I have trembled;* but not *I am spoken,* &c. But to express myself more properly, verbs neuter are those which make a complete sense of themselves, and do not govern any case after them like the verbs active; for instance, I enter, I tremble; *io éntro, io trèmo.* Observe, however, that we meet with some verbs neuter which may govern an accusative; as *io vívo una lúnga vita; io dòrmo un lúngo sonno; io córro un gran rischio,* &c.

It is necessary to be acquainted with the nature of a verb neuter, in order to avoid mistakes or errors in the participles, as may be seen in the Second Part, where we treat of the Syntax of Participles.

OF RECIPROCAL VERBS.

The name of Reciprocal Verbs is given to such as are conjugated through all their tenses with the pronouns conjunctive *mi, ti, si, ci, vi, si,* in the same manner that *dolére* is conjugated in the irregulars of the second conjugation; examples:

Indicative. Present. *Mi pènto, ti pènti, si pènte; ci pentiámo, vi pentíte, si pèntono:* I repent, &c.

Imperf. *Mi pentíva, ti pentívi, si pentíva; ci pentivámo, vi pentiváte, si pentívano:* I did repent, &c.

Preterperfect-def. *Mi pentíi, ti pentísti, si pentì, ci pentímmo, vi pentíste, si pentírono:* I repented, &c.

Preterperfect. *Mi sòno pentíto,* I have repented.

Future. *Mi pentirò,* I shall repent.

Imperative. *Pèntiti tu, pèntasi égli; pentiámoci noi, pentítevi voi, pèntansi églino.*

Subjunctive. *Che mi pènta,* that I may repent, &c

H 2

Indicative. Present. *Mi ricòrdo, ti ricòrdi, si ricòrda;* and so of the rest.

₊ Note, all the verbs active may become reciprocals ; example :

I love myself,	*io mi ámo.*
Thou lovest thyself,	*tu ti ámi.*
He loves himself,	*égli si áma.*
We love ourselves,	*noi ci amiámo.*
You love yourselves,	*voi vi amáte.*
They love themselves,	*églino si ámano.*

And so of all the other tenses, and all the other verbs.

Yet we are to observe, that the pronouns *mi, ti, si, ci,* which give the reciprocality to the verbs, may be placed either before or after them : but in the imperative, infinitive, gerund and participle, they ought to be placed after the verb ; example : *ámami,* love me ; *amándomi,* loving me ; *amársi,* to love oneself ; *amátosi,* loved by oneself : and so in all the other verbs.

OF IMPERSONAL VERBS.

There are three sorts of impersonal verbs, which have only the third person singular.

The first are properly impersonals of themselves ; as,

Accáde,	it happens.
Básta,	it is enough, *or* it suffices.
Bisógna,	it must, *or* it is necessary.
Piòve,	it rains.
Tuòna,	it thunders.

The second are derived from verbs active, preceded by the particle *si,* which renders them impersonals ; as, *si ama,* they love ; *si dice,* they say.

The third, which have a greater affinity with reciprocal verbs, are conjugated with the pronouns conjunctive, *mi, ti, gli* or *le ; ci, vi, loro ;* as, *mi duòle, ti duòle, gli duòle,* &c.

The impersonal verbs of themselves are,

Accáde, it happens.	*Névica,* it snows.
Avviène, it falls out.	*Non occórre,* it is not necessary.
Básta, it is enough.	*Páre,* it seems.
Bisógna, it must.	*Piòve,* it rains.
Grándina, it hails.	*Lampéggia,* it lightens.

Tuòna, it thunders, and the like, which are conjugated with the third person singular of each tense; as,

Indicative. Present. *Bisógna*, it must *or* one must.

Imperfect. *Bisógnava*, it was needful.

Preterperfect-def. *Bisognò*, it was necessary.

Future. *Bisognerà*, it shall *or* will be needful.

Optative. *Che bisógni*, that it may be necessary.

Imperfect. *Che bisognásse*, that it might be needful.

Second Imperfect. *Bisognerèbbe*, it should be necessary.

Infinitive. *Bisognáre*, to be needful.

The particle *si*, which composes the second sort of impersonal verbs, is placed indifferently before or after the verbs; as *si dice* or *dicesi*, they say; *si áma* or *ámasi*, they love. In the like manner all the verbs active may become impersonal. They are conjugated with the third person singular and plural; as,

Present. *A'masi* or *si áma; si ámano* or *ámansi*, they love.

Imperfect. *Si amáva* or *amávasi; si amávano* or *amávansi*, they did love.

†‡† With respect to these verbs, observe, that when the noun that follows them is in the singular number, you must put the verb in the singular; if the noun be in the plural, you put the verb in the plural; example:

They praise the captain,	*si lòda il capitáno.*
They praise the captains,	*si lòdano i capitáni.*
They see a man,	*si véde un uòmo.*
They see men,	*si védono uòmini.*

₊ We must also take notice, when the particle *si* is put after a verb that is accented, the letter *s* is doubled, and the accent dropped; examples:

Fássi,	for	*si fa,*	they do.	
Dirássi,	for	*si dirà,*	they will say.	

The third sort of impersonal verbs are such as are conjugated with the pronouns personal, *mi, ti, gli* or *le, ci, vi, loro*, with the third person singular; example:

Indicative. Present. *Mi dispiáce*, I am sorry *or* displeased.

Ti dispiáce, thou art sorry.

Gli or *le dispiace*, he *or* she is sorry.

Ci dispiáce, we are sorry.
Vi dispiace, you are sorry.
Dispiace lóro, they are sorry.
Imperfect. *Mi dispiacéva,* I was sorry.
Preter-def. *Mi dispiácque,* I was sorry.
Future. *Mi dispiacerà,* I shall be sorry.
Optative. *Che mi dispiáccia,* that I may be sorry.
Imperfect. *Che mi dispiacésse,* that I were sorry.
Second Imperfect. *Mi dispiacerèbbe,* I should be sorry.

Conjugate after the same manner:

Mi accáde,	it happens to me.
Mi aggráda,	it agrees with me.
Mi avviène,	it happens to me.
Mi bisógna,	it behoves me.
Mi duòle,	it grieves me.
Mi occórre,	it happens to me.
Mi páre,	it seems to me.
Mi piáce,	it pleases me.
Mi rincrésce,	I am sorry.
Mi sovviène,	I remember.

Many of those impersonal verbs have the third person singular and plural; as,

My leg pains me, *la gámba mi duòle.*
My eyes are painful, *mi dòlgono gli òcchi.*
Your coat appears new to me, *il vòstro vestíto mi páre nuòvo.*
Your shoes seem to me too long, *le vòstre scárpe mi páiono tròppo lúnghe.*

How to express there is, there was.

There is, there was, are expressed by the help of the Italian particle *ci,* which answers to the French particle *y,* and is sometimes an adverb that denotes the place where we are; as,

Since I am here, I will dine here ; *giacchè sòn quì ci pranzerò.*

But, when naming a place where we are not, we must use *vi*; as, I have been in Holland, but I will never go there again ; *sòno státo in Olánda, ma non vi tornerò più.*

There is, however, this difference between the Italian *ci*, and the French *y;* that the French *y* is used in speaking of time, as *il y a un an*, it is a year since ; the Italian *ci* is not expressed ; as, *è un ánno* or *un anno fa; sóno dúe mesi*, or *due mési fa.* And so of all the tenses ; putting the verb *èssere*, to be, in the third person singular or plural, according to the number in which we express ourselves.

For the benefit of beginners I will conjugate the impersonal verb *c' è, c' èra*, &c. there is, there was, &c. through all its tenses, and point out its use in mentioning a place :

Conjugation of the Impersonal Verb èsser-ci *or* -vi.

Ci is changed into *vi* when you speak of different places ; but mentioning time, you must drop the *ci* and *vi*.

Singular.	Plural.
Ind. Pres. There is, *c' è*, or *v' è.*	There are, *ci sòno*, or *vi sono.*
Imperfect. There was, *c' èra* or *v' era.*	There were, *c' èrano* or *v' . . .*
Preter-def. There was, *ci fù.*	There were, *ci fúrono.*
Preterp. There has been, *c' è státo.*	There have been, *ci sono státi.*
Preterplup. There had been, *c' èra stato.*	The same, *c' èrano státi.*
Future. There shall be, *ci sarà.*	The same, *ci saránno.*
Imperat. Let there be, *ci sía* or *síaci.*	The same, *ci síano* or *siánci.*
Opt. That there may be, *che ci sía.*	The same, *che ci síano.*
Imperf. That there were, *che ci fòsse.*	The same, *che ci fòssero.*
Sec. Imp. There would be, *ci sarèbbe.*	The same, *ci sarèbbero.*

Preterperf. That there had been, *che ci* or *vi sía státo,* or *che ci siáno státi,* or *vi siano stati.*

Preterpluperf. If there had been, *se ci* or *vi fósse státo,* or *ci* or *vi fóssero státi.* That there had been, *che vi fósse státo,* or *che vi fóssero státi.* There would have been, *ci sarèbbe státo,* or *vi sarèbbero státi.*

Future. When there had *or* shall have been, *quando vi sarà státo,* or *quando vi saránno státi.*

Infinitive. To have been there, *èsservi státo.* Gerund. In having been there, *essèndovi státo.*

⁎ Note, in speaking of the feminine gender, we are to use *státa, státe,* instead of *státo, státi.*

⁎ Remember, that if after the adverb *ci* or *vi,* you find the verb *to have,* and the tenses of the verb *to have* are followed by a participle, as, *he has dined there,* then the tenses of the verb *to have* must be expressed by those of *avére,* and not by those of *èssere;* examples:

I have dined there,	*ci* or *vi ho pranzáto.*
Thou hast dined there,	*ci* or *vi hái pranzáto.*
He has lain there,	*ci* or *vi ha dormíto.*
We have read in it,	*ci* or *vi abbiámo lètto.*
You have said to it,	*ci* or *vi avéte détto.*
They have drunk there,	*ci* or *vi hanno bevúto.*

Observe the same rule throughout all the tenses except the participle *státo,* which is never joined with the tenses of the verb *avére;* example:

I have been there,	*ci* or *vi sòno státo* or *státa.*
Thou hast been there,	*ci* or *vi sèi státo* or *státa.*

And in like manner through all the tenses and persons.

⁎ Observe the particles *ci* and *vi* are sometimes omitted in the present tense; thus, we say, *è un uòmo,* instead of *ci è un uòmo; sono uòmini,* instead of *ci sóno uòmini.*

⁎ Learners of the Italian language are greatly at a loss how to render the following expressions, *there is some of it* or *of them; there is not of it ...; is there of it? is there not of it? there was of it; there was not of it,* &c. And as many find these expressions difficult, I will explain them at large for their greater ease, in the following conjugation:

Conjugation of the verb impersonal there is of it, when it marks the place through all its tenses.

There is of it *or* of them ... $\begin{Bmatrix} ce\ n'\ è \\ ve\ n'\ è \end{Bmatrix}$ or $\begin{Bmatrix} ce\ ne\ sóno \ldots \\ ve\ ne\ sono \ldots \end{Bmatrix}$

There is not of it...   *non ce n' è ; non ce ne sono ...*
Is there of it...?   *ce n' è? ce ne sono....?*
Is there not of it, &c.   *non ce n' è? non ce ne sono, &c.*

There was of it some,   *ve n' èra ; ve n' èrano.*
There was not of it, &c.   *non ve n' èra ; non ve n' èrano.*
Was there of it ?   *ve n' èra ? ve n' èrano ?*
Was there not of it ?   *non ve n' èra ? non ve n' èrano ?*

There was of it,   *ve ne fu ; ve ne fúrono.*
There was not of it,   *non ve ne fu ; non ve ne fúrono.*
Was there of it ?   *ve ne fu ? ve ne furono ?*
Was there not of it ?   *non ve ne fu ? non ve ne furono ?*

There shall be of it,   *ve ne sarà ; ve ne saránno.*
There shall not be of it,   *non ve ne sarà ; non ve ne saranno.*
Shall there be of it ?   *ve ne sarà ? ve ne saranno ?*
Shall there not be of it?   *non ve ne sarà? non ve ne saranno?*

That there may be of it, *che ve ne sía ; che ve ne siano.*
That there may not be of it, *che non ve ne sía ; che non ve ne síano.*
That there were of it, *che ve ne fósse ; che ve ne fóssero.*
That there were not of it, *che non ve ne fosse ; che non ve ne fóssero.*

There would be of it, *ve ne sarèbbe ; ve ne sarèbbero.*
There would not be of it, *non ve ne sarebbe ; non ve ne sarèbbero.*
Would there not be of it ? *non ve ne sarebbe ? non ve ne sarebbero ?*

If there had been of it, *se ve ne fósse stato* or *státa ; se ve ne fóssero státi* or *státe.*
If there had not been of it, *se non ve ne fósse stato ; se non ve ne fóssero stati.*

H 5

Had there been some *or* any of it? *ve ne sarèbbe státo?*
ve ne sarèbbero státi?
Had there not been of it . . . ? *non ve ne sarebbe stato . . . ?*
or *non ve ne sarèbbero státi . . . ?*

If there had been of it, *se ve ne fósse stato;* or *se ve ne*
fóssero stati.
If there had not been of it, *se non ve ne fósse stato; se*
non ve ne fóssero stati.

There would have been of it, *ve ne sarèbbe státo; ve ne*
sarèbbero stati.
There would not have been of it, *non ve ne sarebbe stato;*
non ve ne sarèbbero stati.

Would there have been of it? *ve ne sarebbe stato? ve ne*
sarebbero stati?
Would there not have been of it? *non ve ne sarèbbe*
státo? non ve ne sarèbbero státi?

There will have been of it, *ve ne sarà stato; ve ne sa-*
ránno stati?
There will not have been of it, *non ve ne sarà stato; non*
ve ne saránno stati.

Shall there have been of it? *ve ne sarà stato? ve ne*
saránno stati?
Shall there not have been of it? *non ve ne sarà stato?*
non ve ne saránno stati?

For there having been too much of it, *per èsservene stato*
tròppo.
In there having been too little of it, *essèndovene stato*
tròppo pòco.

⁎ But if you express yourself in the feminine
gender, you must say *státa, státe,* instead of *státo, státi.*

We must also render, there is of it *or* them, by *ce ne*
in speaking of a place where we are; and by *ve ne*
in mentioning a place where we are not; but it often

happens, and especially in speaking of time, that they leave out the *ce* entirely; example:

How many months is it? It is ten at least: *quánti mési sóno? sóno dièci alméno.*

Sometimes the phrase, there is of it *or* them, is expressed by *ne* only; as, how many months is it? ten of them are past; *quánti mési sóno? ne sóno passáti dièci.*

Sometimes the whole is expressed; as, how many months are there from this to new-year's day? there are ten of them: *quánti mési sono di qui all' ánno nuòvo? ce ne sono dièci.*

₊ When, after the pronouns conjunctive, *mi, ti, ci, vi,* me, thee, us, you, you find the particle *ci* followed by a verb, there is no occasion to express it:

Examples:

He will see me there, *mi vedrà :* he will give thee there, *ti darà.*

We shall see you there, *vi vedrémo :* you will write to us there, *ci scriveréte.*

CHAPTER V.

OF PARTICIPLES.

THE Participle (which ought to be called a supine) is a tense of the infinitive, which serves to form the preterperfects and preterpluperfects of all the verbs; as, *ho amáto, avéva amáto.*

Amáto, is a participle, and all the verbs in *are* form the participle in *ato :* as, *amáto, cantáto, parláto, andáto, dáto, confessáto, adoráto, studiáto,* &c.

Of all the verbs in *are,* the verb *fare* alone has two *tt's* in the participle, where it makes *fatto,* to distinguish it from *fato,* signifying *fate.*

Amato is likewise a noun-adjective; example: *uòmo amato, dònna amata, libri amati, lèttere amate.*

Some participles of the first conjugation are frequently abridged; as,

H 6

Accóncio		*acconciáto,*	fitted.
Adórno		*adornáto,*	adorned.
Asciútto		*asciuttáto,* or *asciugáto,*	dried.
Avvézzo		*avvezzáto,*	accustomed.
Cárico		*caricáto,*	loaded.
Désto		*destáto,*	awaked.
Férmo		*fermáto,*	stopped.
Gónfio		*gonfiáto,*	swelled.
Guásto		*guastato,*	spoiled.
Lácero		*lacerato,*	torn.
Mácero		*macerato,*	bruised.
Manifèsto		*manifestato,*	manifested.
Mózzo	for	*mozzato,*	cut off.
Nétto		*nettato,*	cleaned.
Págo		*pagato,*	paid.
Pésto		*pestato,*	pounded.
Prívo		*privato,*	deprived.
Scémo		*scemato,*	lessened.
Scóncio		*sconciato,*	disordered.
Sécco		*seccato,*	dried.
Stánco		*stancato,*	wearied.
Tócco		*toccato,*	touched.
Trónco		*troncato,*	cut off.
Tròvo		*trovato,*	found,
Vòlto		*voltato,*	turned.
Vòto		*votato,*	emptied.

And several others which the use of authors will point out.

The regular verbs ending in *ere,* form the participle in *uto;* as *credúto, ricevúto, temúto, godúto.*

The irregulars in *ere* have the participle in *so* or *to:* as, *prèndere, préso; rèndere, réso; piángere, piánto; púngere, pánto; lèggere, lètto; scrívere, scrútto.*

The verbs terminated in *íre,* in the infinitive, make their participles in *íto;* as, *sentíre, sentíto; finíre, finíto.*

Except *apparíre,* which makes *appárso; apríre, apèrto; comparíre, compárso; díre, détto; moríre, mòrto; offríre, offèrto; veníre, venúto.*

*** There are three sorts of participles, namely, active, passive and absolute.

The active participles are composed of the verb *avere;*

as, *ho amáto, avéva amato ; ha détto, hái detto ; ho credúto ; ho sentíto.*

The passive participles are preceded by the verb
èssere : as, *sòno amato, essèndo creduto,* &c.

The absolute participles are of the same nature as
those called *absolute* in Latin, and are composed of the
gerund of the two auxiliary verbs *having* and *being* ; as,
having loved, *avèndo amáto ;* being loved, *essèndo amáto ;*
being believed, *essèndo credúto.*

Having and *being* are often left out in Italian ; examples :

Having done that,	*fátto quéllo.*
Having said so,	*détto quésto.*
That being done,	*fátto quéllo.*
The sermon being done,	*finíta la prèdica.*

*** Observe, that the Italians have a peculiar way of
rendering the adverb *after,* by turning the expression ;
examples :

After he had done,	*fatto ch' èbbe.*
After he had spoken,	*parláto ch' ebbe.*
After he has written his letter,	*scritto che avrà la súa lèt-tera.*
After they had supped,	*cenáto ch' èbbero.*

See, in the Second Part, the Concord of Participles,
where will be found a full solution of the several difficulties relating to that part of speech.

CHAPTER VI.

OF ADVERBS.

THE adverb is that part of speech which gives more or
less force to a word. The adverb has the same effect
with the verb as the adjective with the substantive ; it
explains the accidents and circumstances of the action
of the verb.

There are many sorts ; as, adverbs of time, place,
quantity, &c.

Adverbs of time ; as, *at present, now, yesterday, to-
day, never, always, in the mean time.*

Adverbs of place ; as, *where, here, from whence, there, from hence, above, below, far, near.*

Adverbs of quantity ; as, *how much, how many, so much, much, little, too much.*

₊ Many adverbs are formed from adjectives, changing *o* into *aménte ;* as,

Sánto, santaménte,	holily.
Ricco, riccaménte,	richly.
Dòtto, dottaménte,	learnedly.
A'lto, altaménte,	highly.

From adjectives in *e* we likewise form adverbs, by adding *mente* to them ; as,

Costánte, costanteménte,	constantly.
Diligènte, diligenteménte,	diligently.
Prudènte, prudenteménte,	prudently.

₊ But if the adjectives happen to end in *le,* we must remove the *e,* and put *mente* in its stead.

Fedéle, fedelménte,	faithfully.
U'mile, umilménte,	humbly.
Tále, talménte,	such.

In order to assist the memory of learners, I have here collected a number of adverbs, which by frequent repetition may be easily retained, especially those terminating in *mente.*

A COLLECTION OF ADVERBS.

1.

Abbondanteménte, abundantly.
Con ragióne, meritaménte, justly
A cápo, at the end *or* at the head
A bríglia sciòlta, full speed
Assolutaménte, absolutely
A cavalcióni, a-straddle
A diròtte lágrime, with downright crying
Adèsso, óra, or, at this time
Adèsso adèsso, or' óra, presently

A piè zòppo, lamely
A pátti, upon condition
Con pátto che, upon condition that
Mal volentièri, against one's will
Da párte, da bánda, aside
Attualménte, actually
Appòsta, purposely
Con pensièro di, in order to
Addio, farewell
Mirabilménte, a maraviglia, admirably
Accortaménte, sagaceménte, cunningly
In ginocchióni, kneeling

Alla smascelláta, with a
    wide open mouth
Leggiadraménte, charm-
    ingly
Altróve, elsewhere
Così, so
Così sía so be it
Agevolménte, easily
Al copèrto, under shelter
All' oscúro, in the dark
In somma, alla fíne, in the
    end or in short
In frétta, in haste
A lúngo, at long run
Amichevolménte, amicably
A discreziòne, at discretion
Supíno, on one's back
Tacitamente, silently
In dispárte, apart
Per il drítto, the right way
Per il rovèscio, the wrong
    side outward
A gára, in emulation
A pròva, proof against
All' improvvíso, at unawares
Sènza sapúta, unknow-
    ingly
Sú sú, or vía vía, come
    away, away
Con tèmpo, con ágio, at lei-
    sure
Allóra, then
Anticamente, anciently
Quási, almost
Appúnto, giústo, just so
Posdimáni or dimán l' áltro,
    after to-morrow
Adèsso, óra, now
Alla rovèscia, against the
    grain
In diètro, backward

Malvolontièri, con rincres-
    ciménto, with regret
Cioè, to wit
Abbastánza, enough
Brancolóne, tentóne, grop-
    ing along
L' áltro ièri, ièri l' áltro, the
    day before yesterday
Prima di, before that
Al bálzo, at the rebound
Da cápo, at the beginning
In manièra alcúna, by no
    means
All' imprevista, or alla
    sprovvista, at unawares
Di sópra, above
Oggi, to-day
In véce, instead of
Prima, before
Quánto prima, as soon as
    possible
A'nche, ancóra, pure, also
Sì, così, as, so
Tánto, così, so much so
Gránde quánto, as great as
Súbito che, as soon as
Nel rèsto, moreover
Tánto, so much
Quánto, as much as
Altre vòlte, formerly
Altriménti, se non, otherwise
Altróve, somewhere else

2.

Laggiù, below there
Mólto, much
Assái più, mólto più, much
    more
Tanto più, so much more
Prèsto, quickly

Vie più prèsto, much sooner or quicker

Rigidaménte, aspraménte, rudely

Bestialménte, brutishly

3.

Or sù, vía, come away
Via dúnque, come along
Sta mattína, this morning
Sta nòtte, this night
Sta séra, quésta sera, this evening
Fin a tánto, till, on till
In tanto, in the mean time
Cèrto, sicúro, certainly
Básta, it is enough
Cioè, that is to say
Per ciò, that therefore
Caldamente, warmly
Cáro, mólto caro, dear, very dear
Chiaraménte, clearly
Quánto, how much
Quanto, quánta, quánti, quánte, how many
Cóme, siccóme, as, since
Come? how?
Di contínuo, continuaménte, continually
Correttaménte, correctly
Quésta vòlta, adèsso, now
Di primo láncio, all of a sudden
Animosamente, coraggiosa-mente, courageously
Sordidamente, sordidly
Crudelmente, cruelly
Di pòi, di quà innánzi, hereafter

Per l' addiètro, quì avánti, heretofore
Di sótto, quì sótto, here under
Di sópra, quì sopra, here-upon

4.

Súbito, di bèlla príma, at first
D'áltra párte, from another place
Pericolosaménte, danger-ously
Davvantággio, di più, over and above
A cáso, by chance
Tánto méno, so much the less
Tánto più che, so much the more that
Imperocchè, whereas
Sinceraménte, sincerely
Per tèmpo, a buòn' ora, in good time, early
Di quà a dièci ánni, in ten years
Di gran lúnga, by far
Su, in pièdi, up, up
Per tèma che, for fear that
Sin dai fondaménti, affatto, from top to bottom
Fuòri, abroad
Già, digià, already
Quindi, from hence
Dománi, dimani, to-morrow
Domattína, to-morrow morning
Nella medésima manièra, just so
Dall' úna e dall' áltra párte, on both sides
Di sálto, at one jump

In óltre, di più, oltracciò, moreover
Dópo since
Da iéri in quà, since yesterday
Fin da che tèmpo? fin da quando? since when
Da quel tèmpo in quà, since that time
Dacchè, dópo che, since
Di che sòrta? in che maniéra? after what manner?
Ultimaménte, lastly *or* lately
Dìetro, behind
In dìetro, backward
Fin' adèsso, till now
Súbito che, as soon as
Orámai, ormái, hereafter
Sótto, di sótto, under
Sópra, di sópra, upon
Di séguito, in continuance
Di quándo in quándo, from time to time
Avánti, innánzi, before
Per 'l avvenìre, henceforwards
A schièna d' ásino, sharply ridged
Dónde, from whence
Doppiaménte, falsaménte, doubly
Da párte a párte, through and through
Alméno, at least

5.

Sfacciatamente, impudently
Égualmente, equally
Ancóra, ánche, again, yet, already

Rotolóne, rolling along
Insième, together
Dipòi, dópo, afterwards
All' improvvíso, unawares
In sospésione, in dúbbio, in suspense
Intieraménte, affátto, entirely
Indárno, in vain
Intórno, circa, about
Capricciosaménte, perdutaménte, all' eccèsso, desperately
Spaventevolmente, dreadfully
Giustamente, justly
Stranamente, strangely
A pòsta, a bèlla pòsta, a bèllo stúdio, on purpose

6.

Facilmente, agevolmente, easily
Per mancánza di, for want of
Fissamente, steadfastly
Pazzamente, madly
Mólto, much, very
Liberamente, freely

7.

Via via, a vói, a voi, make way, out of the way
Grátis, gratis
Pòca, little
A cáso pensáto, wilfully

8.

Arditamente, boldly
Altamente, highly

Feliceménte, happily
Ièri, yesterday
Ièr séra, last night
Vergognosaménte, shame-
fully
Fuòri, out

9.

Mái, never
Quì, quà, here, there
Súbito, immediately
Appúnto, exactly
Sin, fin, insín, infín, until
Fín dóve? how far?

10.

Lì, là ; Non lontáno di là,
there; not far from thence
Vilménte, basely
Lontáno, lúngi, far
E' un pèzzo, it is a great
while

11.

Adèsso, óra, now
Mále, ill
Mio malgrádo, in spite of
me
Guái, woe be to
A'nche, ancóra, eziandío,
also
Nel medésimo tèmpo, at the
same time
Mèglio, better
Mediánte, provided that
Minóre, least

12.

Non, not

Nulladiméno, nondiméno,
nevertheless
Liberaménte, freely
Nè, neither ; *nè ánche,* nor
also
Nò, signór, nò, no, no, sir
Nonostánte, notwithstand-
ing

13.

Sì yes
Dóve, óve, where
Oltre, besides
Scopertamente, apertamente
openly

14.

Zitto! zitto! hush! not a
word
A oáso, by chance
A ménte, by heart
Di quà, on this side
Di là, on that side
Vèrbi grázia, per esèmpio,
for example
Però, however, therefore
Pòco, a little ; *ógni pòco,*
un tantíno, ever so little
Fórse, perhaps
Più, more
In quánt' a, as for
Quási, almost

15.

Quándo, when
In quánt' a me, as for me
Alle vòlte, sometimes
Alquánto, somewhat
Páce, pári, quits
Comúnque sia, however it
may be

16.

Di rado,	seldom
Scambievolménte,	reciprocally
In sómma,	in short
Niènte,	nothing

17.

Saviamente,	wisely
Sènza dúbbio, senz' altro,	without doubt
Secóndo,	according
Sossópra, alla rinfúsa, confusaménte,	topsy-turvy
Vèrso (la) séra,	towards the evening
Sta sera, quésta sera,	this evening
Abbastánza,	sufficiently

18.

Tánto,	so much
Ogni pòco, un tantíno,	ever so little

Adèsso, subito, or' óra,	presently
Or quésto, or quéllo,	sometimes one, and sometimes the other
Tárdi,	late
Tròppo,	too much
Prèsto, quick, soon ; *così prèsto!*	so soon !
Sèmpre,	always
Affátto,	altogether
Ad un trátto,	all of a sudden
Adágio!	softly ! gently !

19.

Prèsto,	quick
Ecco,	behold
Volentièri,	willingly
Veramente,	truly

20.

Ci, or *vi,*	here, to it, &c.

CHAPTER VII.

OF PREPOSITIONS([19]).

THE Preposition is a part of speech prefixed to the articles, nouns, pronouns and verbs, as has been mentioned in the introduction.

Every preposition requires some case after it, as you will observe in the following collection :

Gen. *Per rispetto di,* because of.

Per rispètto vostro, or *di voi,* on your account.

Per rispetto mio, or *di me,* on my account.

Dat. *In quánto a', all'* or *állo, alla,* with respect to.

D' intórno a. Gen. *All' intórno di,* round the.

Gen. *Acc. Dópo,* after.

Gen. *Diètro,* behind.

Gen. and Dat. *Di dietro,* behind.

---

[19] See EXERCISES, p. 83.

Gen. and Dat. *Alláto, vicíno di* or *a*, by the side of.

Gen. and Abl. *Di là del* or *dal*, on that side of.

Gen. and Abl. *Di quà del* or *dal*, on this side of.

Acc. *Avanti.* Gen. *Prima*, before.

Gen. *Prima di me*, before me.

    Avánti vói, prima di vói, before you.

Acc. *Con*, with.

Gen. Dat. *In mèzzo del, in mèzzo al*, in the middle of.

Gen. *Appiè délla*, at the feet of the.

    Apprèsso di, near to.

Gen. and Dat. *All' intórno del, intórno al*, round the.

    Da, in cása di, at.

Gen. and Abl. *Dal, dallo, in cása del*, at the.

    Dálla, in casa della, at the.

Gen. and Acc. *Cóntra del, contrà il*, against the.

    Contra me, contra di me, against me.

Acc. *In*, in.

    Nel, néllo, nélla, in the.

    Frà due giórni, in two days.

Abl. *Di quà dal*, on this side of the.

    Di là dal, on that side of the.

Dat. and Acc. *Déntro al* or *nel*, within the.

Gen. *Fuòri del*, without the.

Dat. and Acc. *Diètro al, diètro il*, behind the.

Gen. and Dat. *Sótto del, sotto al*, under the.

Gen. and Acc. *Sópra del, sopra il*, upon the.

    In, *before a noun, is expressed in Italian by* in.

Dat. *Di nascósto a suo pádre*, unknown to his father.

Acc. *Frà, trà*, between.

Gen. and Acc. *Vèrso di me* or *me*, towards me.

Acc. *Incírca*, round about, thereabout.

Acc. *Eccètto il*, except the.

Gen. *Fuòri del*, without the.

Gen. *A láto della mia casa*, close to my house ; or *accánto a casa mia*, Dat.

Gen. Dat. Acc. *Rasènte del, al, il muro*, close to the wall.

Dat. *Sin, fin, insin, infin*, until.

Gen. Abl. *Lontáno délla casa* or *dalla casa*, far from the house.

    Lontáno, lúngi, far.

Gen. Dat. Acc. *Lungo del, al, il fiúme*, along the river.

Acc. *Per*, by *or* for.

Gen. Dat. Acc. *Prèsso, vicíno*, near.

Gen. Acc. *Sènza, senza di, del* or *della*, without.

Secóndo il*, according to.

Gen. Acc. *Sótto la távola*, or *della*, under the table.

Sópra, upon *or* on.

Dat Acc. *Circa all' affáre, l' affare*, concerning the business.

Dat. *In quánto al*, concerning the.

Gen. and Acc. *Vèrso il, verso del*, towards the.

Gen. Dat. Acc. *Dirimpètto del, al, il*, over against the.

CHAPTER VIII.

OF CONJUNCTIONS([20]).

CONJUNCTIONS serve to connect phrases together: most of the words terminating in *che* and *que* are conjunctions; as, *benchè, ánche, adúnque*. There are others of a different sort, as you will observe in the following collection:

Con pátto che,	upon condition that	*In óltre*,	besides, over and above
A'nzi, al contrário,	on the contrary	*Di manièra che*,	so that
Acciò che, acciocchè,	to the end that	*In quánto*,	as
		E & ed,	and
Con tutto ciò,	notwithstanding all that	*Ma*,	but
Anche,	also	*Nientediméno,* *Nondiméno,* *Nulladiméno,*	nevertheless.
Benchè,	although	*Nè*,	neither *or* nor
Perchè, imperocchè,	for	*Nè ánch'io, nemmén'io*,	nor I either
Siccóme,	whereas		
Dúnque,	then	*Nemméno, neppúre*,	neither
Perciocchè,	forasmuch as	*Nonostánte che*,	notwithstanding that
Ancóra,	still yet		
Quantúnque,	although	*O, ovvéro, oppúre*,	or
In sómma,	at last	*Perchè*,	because

---

[20] See Exercises, on the Conjunctions, p. 77.

In caso che,	in case that	*Quand' ánche,*	though
Però,	therefore	*Benchè, sebbène, con tútto*	
Datochè,	suppose that	*che,*	although that
Purchè,	provided that	*Se,*	it
Piuttòsto che,	rather than	*Stante che,*	seeing that

CHAPTER IX.

OF INTERJECTIONS.

THE LAST PART OF SPEECH.

An Interjection is an expression of benevolence or passion, introduced among the other parts of speech.

Examples.

Aiúto! aiuto!	help! help!	*A vói! a voi!*	stand away!
Brávo! bravo!	well done!	*A'lto!*	halt!
Al fuòco!	fire! fire!	*Ahimè! Ohimè! áhi lásso!*	
All' ármi!	to arms!		alas!
Buòno! buono!	good!	*Zítto! zitto!*	hush! peace!
	good!	*Silènzio!*	silence!
A'nimo, corággio!	come,	*Via, via!*	away! away!
	cheer up!	*Ah! áhi!*	Ah!
Oh! uh! puh!	fie! fie!	*Oh!*	Oh!
Vergógna!	for shame!		

PART II.

THE Second Part contains Eight Treatises, extracted from the best authors, and particularly from those who have written on the purity of the Italian language.

TREATISE

FIRST TREATISE.

CHAPTER I.

OF ORTHOGRAPHY.

THE Italian Orthography has this advantage, that all the words are written as they are pronounced.

₊ Observe, as a general rule, that you must double the consonants at the beginning of compound words; as, *abbáttere, affannáre, appoggiáre, opprèsso, difficile, differire, offèndere, raccògliere, rassettáre, raddoppiáre.*

₊ They write *diffèndere*, and *difèndere*, but *difésa* ought to be written with a single *f.* See *Lod. Dólce, del raddoppiaménto delle consonánti.*

You must also double the *g*, when the vowels *io* and *ia*, which come after it, make but one syllable; as, *appòggio, lòggia, piòggia, Mággio, rággio;* a support, a lodge, rain, May, a ray. When the vowels *io* and *ia* constitute two syllables, or when the letter *i* is pronounced harder than in the preceding examples, you must not double the *g;* as *ágio,* easy; *privilègio,* privilege; *malvágio,* bad. See *Dólce, Buommatèi,* and *Bártoli.*

The letter *g* is also doubled in the infinitive of verbs, and in all their tenses, when they have a vowel before *gere;* as, *lèggere, règgere, fríggere;* but if there be a consonant before *g,* then *g* remains single; as, *fíngere, píngere, pòrgere.*

Those words which the English begin with a *j* consonant, that is, when it is followed by a vowel; as Jesus, just, judge, are written with a *g* by the Italians, in order to render their pronunciation more delicate; as, *Gesù, giústo, giúdice.*

Capéllo, with a single *p,* signifies hair.

Cappèllo, with a double *pp,* signifies a hat.

The different *tonic* accent placed on the *e* of these two words, shows that the former has a close sound, and the latter open ([21]).

Sol has two significations: when it is a substantive it signifies the sun; *il sol, del sol, al sol,* for *il sóle, del sóle, al sóle.*

Sol, when it is an adjective, signifies *alone,* or sometimes *only.*

Suòl has likewise two significations; when it is a noun, it signifies the earth; as, *il suòl* or *suòlo,* &c.

Suòl, a verb, signifies, he is used; as, *suòl veníre,* he is used to come.

Z is put single when preceded by a consonant; as, *speránza, licènza;* but it must be doubled between two vowels; as, *Bellézza, pèzzo, nòzze,* except *Lázaro, Fázio,* and a few other words.

---

[21] The Italians use only one accent, namely the *grave* (`), which is put only on the last vowel of a word, as *credè, lunedì, farò, virtù,* &c. and on some words to distingush them from others similarly spelt, but of a different meaning, as, *dì,* day; *dà,* he gives; *là,* there, &c. from *di,* of; *da,* from; *la,* the. See the N.B. at the end of p. 23, also p. 176.

The Italians do not double the letter *z*, when standing with three vowels, the first of which immediately following the *z* is an *i;* therefore it would be wrong to write *azzióne*, action, &c., but *azióne*, &c.

Piázza, a square, is spelled like a great many others of the like quality, with a double *z*.

The letter *x* of Latin words, often used in Italian before *c*, is changed into *c:* example, to excite, *eccitáre*, excellency, *eccellènza;* and when it does not happen to be before the *c*, it is sometimes changed into a double *s*, and sometimes into a single *s;* as, to exalt, *esaltáre;* graciously to hear, *esaudire*, &c.; the maxim, *la mássima;* Alexander, *Alessándro*, &c. The *x* is changed into a simple *s* when the vowel with which it forms a syllable is followed by a consonant, or another vowel which belongs to the same syllable; example: *exhaurire* in Latin is transformed into *esaurire* in Italian; but *axis* is transformed into *asse*, because the *i* which follows *x* is followed by the consonant *s*, which, together with the *i* and the *x*, forms but one syllable; *asis* is spelt axis.

A great many writers put the letter *z* before the vowel *i*, where the common orthography uses the letter *c;* for instance, instead of pronouncing and writing *Francése*, French; *pronunciáre*, to pronounce, &c. they write and pronounce *Franzése, pronunziáre;* but it is better to say *Francese*, and not *Franzese*.

The masculine relative plural *li* is written, for harmony's sake, with a *g* when followed by a vowel; example: I have some books, and I purchased them at Frankfort fair; *Ho dei libri, e gli ho compráti alla fièra di Francofòrte*.

It is better to write *chérico* than *chiérico; cerúsico* or *chirúrgo*, a surgeon, than *cirusico*.

The syllables *de* and *re*, in the beginning of English words, generally become *di* and *ri* in the beginning of Italian; as, to destroy, *distrúggere;* to renew, *rinnováre*, &c.

It was formerly the custom to write several adverbs and prepositions separately, which now make but one word; but most of them double the first consonant of the latter word, which is joined to the former, when this

I

ends by a vowel : for instance, *già che*, since, *giacchè ; in tanto, fra tanto*, in the meanwhile, *intánto, frattánto ; a ciò che, a fin che*, to the end that, *acciochè, affinchè ; si cóme*, as, *siccóme ; a dòsso al suo nemico*, upon his enemy, *addòsso al suo nemico ; óltra a ciò*, besides, *oltracciò : di nanzi al giúdice*, before the judge, *dinánzi al giúdice ; uòmo da bène*, an honest man, *uòmo dabbène.*

After is expressed by *dipòi* with the verbs, and by *dopo*, before the nouns.

It is true, nevertheless, is elegantly rendered in Italian by *égli è non per tanto véro.*

Non vi è scúse, signifies there is no room for excuse; and this is an ellipsis, instead of *non v' è luògo a scúse.*

We express *several* by *parécchi* for the masculine, and by *parrécchie* for the feminine ; example ; several masters of languages, *parécchi maèstri di língua* ; several women, *parécchie donne.*

For which, or *wherefore*, is expresed in Italian by *per lo che*, or *per la qual còsa*, or *perciò.*

Ne', with an apostrophe, signifies *in the* in the plural, when we are speaking of the masculine gender ; example : in the gardens, *ne'* or *néi giardini.*

As there is no future tense, no second preterimperfect in the Italian language that terminates in *arò* and *arèi*, except *sarò*, I shall be, and *sarèi*, I should be ; *starò*, I shall remain : *starèi*, I should remain ; *farò*, I will do ; *farèi*, I should do ; *darò*, I shall or will give ; *darèi*, I should or would give ; *saprò*, I shall or will know ; *saprèi*, I should know ; so we neither say nor write *amarò* and *amarèi*, &c., but *amerò* and *amerèi*. ·

The Italians usually place the particles *si, vi*, or the relative *ne*, and such like, after the persons of verbs marked with a grave accent ; but then they drop that grave accent, and repeat the consonant of those particles ; for instance, my brother will repent, *mio fratèllo pentirássi* ; I will give you an inkstand, *daròvvi un calamáio ; darònne uno*, I will give one of them.

The king has given a hundred thousand livres to the city of Paris, and he will give fifty to the town of Lyons.	*Il re ha dato cènto mìla lire alla città di Parigi, e daránne cinquánta a quélla di Lióne.*

CHAPTER II.

OF THE APOSTROPHE.

THE Apostrophe is a mark made like a comma, inserted between two letters, to denote the retrenchment of a vowel; as, *l' amóre, l' ánimo, l' onóre, l'uòmo.*

The Italians still observe the rule of old authors, never to make use of the apostrophe ,but when it renders the pronunciation more delicate; and not so frequently as those who have but a superficial knowledge of the language.

The apostrophe is generally placed after the articles, if they precede a word commencing with a vowel; as, *l' ánimo, dell' animo,* &c. (²²), *l' anima, dell' anima,* &c.

See what we have said concerning the apostrophe, treating of the articles, pp. 6 and 38.

We sometimes meet with *lo 'mpèro* for *l' impero; le 'nsídie* for *l' insidie;* but this ought rather to be avoided than imitated.

*** Sometimes there is an elision of the article *il,* by cutting off its first letter, which is quite the reverse of other elisions, by which we drop the vowel at the end of words; and when the article *il* happens to follow a word terminating in a vowel, the *i* of the article *il* is cut off, and the preceding word continues entire without any abbreviation; as, *sopra'l tétto,* for *sopra il tetto.*

E'l più garbáto, e'l più cortése, for *è il più,* &c.

Tutto'l móndo sa, for *tutto il mondo sa.*

Fra'l sì e'l nò, for *fra il sì e il no.*

Se'l capitáno dice che'l soldáto, &c. *se il ... che il,* &c.

N. B. Observe, in regard to this elision of the article *il,* that the best modern authors constantly make use of it; and the reason they allege is, that the *i* has a harsher sound than any of the other vowels.

Sometimes we make an elision of the article *lo,* even

---

²² The *tonic* accent, once indicated, will not be repeated on similar words which may immediately follow.

before words beginning with a consonant, and the two words coalesce into one ; as,

nol so,			*non lo so.*
sel créde,	} for {	*se lo crede.*
vel prométto,			*ve lo prometto.*

The apostrophe is also put after *mi, ti, ci, vi, di, si, lo* or *la, ne,* when they precede a vowel or the letter *h ;* as, *m'amáte, l'ascólto, l'intèndo, c'impórta, m'avéte, s'intènde, v'ingánna, l'incoraggisce, d'Antònio, n'arde, n'avrò, n'hái, n'hánno.*

Words abbreviated are written with an apostrophe, as, *de' signóri,* for *déi signori ; pie'* for *piède ; me'* poet. for *mèglio ; co'* for *cói* or *cólli ; un po'* for *un poco.*

CHAPTER III.

OF THE WORDS THAT MUST BE RETRENCHED.

THE last syllable of the subsequent six words, *úno, bèllo, gránde, sánto, quéllo, buòno,* must be retrenched when they precede a word beginning with a consonant ; example : *un giórno, bèl giardino, gran capitáno, san Piètro, quel páne, buon libro ;* and not *úno giórno, bèllo giardino, grande capitano,* &c.

Before masculine nouns, if the subsequent word commences with a vowel or an *h,* you only cut off the final vowel, and put an apostrophe when there are two consonants ; examples : *un amico, bell' aspètto, grand' ingégno, sant' Antònio, quell' uòmo, buòn aspètto.*

Before the feminine nouns beginning with a consonant *gránde* is the only one of those words that we abridge, both in the singular and plural ; as, *una casa, bèlla cámera, gran famiglia, sánta Maria, quélla signóra, bèlle case, gran ricchézze, sánte chièse, quélle virtù.*

The masculine plurals of the six preceding words are, *úni, bèlli, grándi* or *gran, sánti, quélli, buòni.*

The feminine plurals are, *úne, bèlle, grán* or *grandi, sánte, quélle, buòne,* without any other abbreviation than of *gran ;* and even this sometimes makes *grandi* with nouns commencing with a vowel ; as, *grandi ánime,* or *anime grandi.*

You may also retrench the final vowel of the words that have one of these four letters, *l, m, n, r,* for their penultima ; as,

Il carnevál passáto, quál signóre, instead of *carnevále* and *quále.*

Andiám prèsto, for *andiámo presto.*

Aman per l'onde i velóci delfini, instead of *ámano.*

Fiór grato, cuòr generóso, instead of *fióre* and *cuòre.*

N.B. When the retrenchment falls upon a word with two final consonants, you must put an apostrophe ; as, *crederánn' allóra,* instead of *crederanno allora ; vedémm' áltri venir,* for *vedemmo altri venir.* But in the modern orthography they write indifferently, *vedémmo áltri,* or *vedemm' altri,* and more generally *vedem altri,* with only one *m,* and without an apostrophe.

The words that have *m* or *n* for the penultima, are not so frequently retrenched as those that have *l* or *r*. If we should be directed by the opinion of the best authors, the following chapter would be sufficient for our purpose.

CHAPTER IV.

OF THE WORDS THAT MUST NOT BE RETRENCHED.

THE vowel which terminates a sentence, or which precedes a comma, or any other stop, must never be retrenched ; therefore we ought not to write, *Vo' Signoría, ha úna bélla man; chi è quel signór? quell' uòmo è gran;* but *V. S. ha una bella mano ; chi è quel signore? quell' uomo è grande ;* and so of the rest.

Neither must the words terminated in *a,* when they are before a consonant, be retrenched, except *óra, ancóra, finóra, allóra, talóra ;* for we may write, *or sú signóri, ancór non viène ;* but it would be wrong to write *úna buon cása, úna bel máno,* instead of *una buona casa, úna bèlla mano.*

Accented words must never be abbreviated ; such, for example, as *farò, dirò, martedì,* &c.

In not retrenching in the plural the words which have an *l* before the last letter, you are warranted by the authority of the best authors, therefore you must write *amábili persóne; fávole ben trováte; paròle scélte; nòbili cavalièri.* The singular number is more apt to admit of this abbreviation.

To write correctly, you must never abridge *Apòllo, affánno, tállo, dúro, ingánno, pégno, oscúro, sostégno, stráno, vèllo;* therefore you must not write *Apol, affan, tal, dur,* &c.

₌ The words beginning with an *s*, followed by a consonant, oblige the preceding word to terminate in a vowel; as, *bèllo stúdio, gránde státo, quéllo spírito, èssere státo;* and not *bel studio, gran stato, quel spirito, esser stato.*

₌ Observe, that if the preceding word cannot terminate in a vowel, that which commences with an *s*, followed by a consonant, takes an *i* before it; as, *per isdégno; in iscuòla,* instead of *per sdegno; in scuola.* See *Ferránte Longobárdi, Lod. Dólce,* and *Bentivòglio.*

N.B. In the beginning of a period, or when the sense is interrupted by a colon, or semicolon, we may omit the insertion of the vowel *i*.

We never retrench the *e* of *se*, signifying *if*, except it be followed by another *e;* for instance, we do not say *s'ámo lo stúdio,* if I love study, but *se amo lo studio.* On the contrary, we do not say, *se esercitásse l'árte,* if he exercised the art, but *s'esercitasse l'arte,* by reason that *esercitasse* begins with an *e;* example: I have seen my mother, and given her a gold snuff-box, *ho vedúto mia mádre, e le ho dáto una scátola d'òro :* or, he loves Anthony, *áma Antònio.* If we were to cut off the *e* from *le,* in the former sentence, we should not know whether this *l'* was in the accusative or dative, in the singular or plural; and if we were to retrench the final *o* from the word *ámo,* we should not be able to tell whether it was the first or third person of the present indicative, or the subjunctive, or the third person of the preter-definite. You must therefore write, without any elision of the vowel, *ho veduto mia madre, e le ho dato una scatola d'oro; amo Antonio,* and the rest in the same manner.

You must not retrench the *e* in *che,* when the following word begins with an *i*, for it is the *i* that ought rather to be retrenched : but when this *i* is the plural of the definite article, which does not admit of this elision, then you are to pronounce the *che* and *i* both together, as if it were only one word ; example : God grant the times may be good, and the winds be not very high next winter ; then, if my brother Anthony is well, and my cousin Harry is in town, I will go to Paris : *Dío vòglia che'l tèmpo sia buòno, e che i vènti non sieno gagliárdi'l vèrno pròssimo; allóra, se Antònio mio fratèllo starà bène, e s'Enríco mio cugíno sarà in città, andrò a Parígi.*

We never retrench the *i* from *ci*, us, before the vowels *a* and *o;* because it would render the pronunciation too harsh : hence we do not say, *il principe c' avéva promésso cènto scúdi*, the prince had promised us a hundred crowns, but *ci aveva; Vo' Signoria c' onóra*, you do us honour, but *V. S. ci onóra.*

It would be extremely proper, if, before words beginning with the letter *z* we were not to retrench the vowel, so as not to say, *buon zúcchero*, good sugar ; *gran zázzera*, a large head of hair : but *buòno zucchero, gránde zazzera.*

In Dante, Petrarch, Ariosto, Guarini, Tasso, Marini, and all the poets, we find several tenses of the verbs abridged. See further on this head in the Treatise of Poetic Licenses, where I have arranged them in alphabetical order.

SECOND TREATISE.

OF THE ITALIAN ACCENT.

THE accent, which is the very soul of pronunciation, is the stronger or weaker elevation of the voice on particular syllables, and the manner of pronouncing them, shorter or longer.

I intend to speak here only of the accent which the Italians make use of in writing.

The Italians, indeed, are acquainted with two accents, but they make use of one only, namely, the *grave*, which is figured by an oblique stroke from the left to the right, after this manner (`). It is put only in the last syllable of some words; as in, *annunziò che canterà Mercoledì.*

N. B. The other accent, called *acute*, is a contrary mark to that of the grave. The Italians never note it down; so that if we sometimes meet with it in books, as is now the case in this grammar, it is with a view of conveying thereby a just idea of the Italian accentuation, as well as the open and close sound of the vowels *e* and *o*. See the N. B. at the end of p. 23.

CHAPTER 1.

OF THE GRAVE ACCENT.

THE Italian nouns in *tà*, which in English terminate in *ty*, and in Latin in *tas*, are marked with a grave accent; as, *purità, castità, santità, maestà, gravità,* &c. These words form the plural in *tà* without any alteration.

But they do not place an accent on the *a* in *visita*, because it does not come from a Latin word in *tas*; neither are we to dwell upon the last syllable; and, moreover, it makes the plural *visite* and not *visita*.

The Italians also place a grave accent on nouns terminating in *u*; as, *virtù, servitù*, &c.

Monosyllables ending in *o* or *a*, according to some grammarians, are accented; as, *dò, dà; fò, fà; rè, sà; stò, stà*. But I should prefer the opinion of those who do not accent them, because a monosyllable ever preserves the same quantity, whether it be accented or not; so that the accent ought to be used only to distinguish one word from another; as, *dà*, he gives, from the indefinite article, *da*, from; *sè*, himself, from *se*, if, &c.

They likewise put the grave accent on the first and third person singular of the future tense; as *canterò, goderò, darò; canterà, goderà, darà*.

₊ Observe, that we may transpose the monosyllables which we happen to find before verbs accented on the last; and then we must double the first letter of the monosyllables and drop the accent of the verb; as, I have them, *hòlle*, for *le ho*; I will do it, *faròllo*, for *lo farò*; he showed me, *mostròmmi*, for *mi mostrò*; he heard me, *sentimmi*, for *mi sentì*.

This manner of transposition, after the tenses of accented verbs, is very common in poetry.

The verbs are marked with a grave accent in the third person singular of the preter-definite, whenever the first person terminates in two vowels: as, *amái, amò; credéi, credè; dormii, dormì*.

If the first person of the preter-definite does not terminate in two vowels, there is no accent on the third.

For which reason we put no accent on the last syllable of *vínse, árse, prése, dìède, féce, stètte*, which in the first person make *vínsi, ársi, prési, dìèdi, féci, stètti*.

N. B. The Italians put a grave accent on *dì*, a day; on *nè*, neither, nor; on *sè*, himself; on *è*, it is; and on *lì* and *là*, there; to show that these words are to be pronounced with greater emphasis, and with a somewhat longer pause; as also to distinguish the above-said *dì* from *di*, the genitive indefinite, *nè* from *ne* relative pron.; *lì*, there, from *li*, the relative masculine plural; examples: he does not give any either to you or to me, *non ne dà nè a voi, nè a me;* I promise three crowns, and I give them, *prométto tre scúdi, e li do:* and

on *là*, to distinguish it likewise from *la*, the relative feminine singular; as, the princess writes a letter, and causes it to be put in the post, *la principéssa scrive una léttera, e la fa métter alla pòsta.*

The grave accent is also put on *quì* and *quà*, here; on *costì* and *costà*, there; *giù*, below, down; *può*, he can; *più*, more; *così*, so or thus; *sì*, yes; because those words are to be sounded somewhat stronger, and, in some measure, with a greater pause; but on the other monosyllables they do not mark a grave accent, for it would be entirely superfluous, as they are always pronounced in the same manner.

We therefore do not accent *da*, from, the ablative indefinite: *a*, to; *ma*, but; *ne*, of it, of them or us; *re*, king; *o*, or; and others of the like nature; because no confusion or obscurity can arise from thence, as you will perceive by the following example: particularly with respect to *da* and *a*, the two monosyllables which seem to be somewhat equivocal, but by no means are so.

Alexander gives his word as an honest man, and he has no difficulty to give it to Peter and Paul, or to any other person.

Allessándro dà la súa paròla da galantuòmo, e non ha verúna difficoltà di dárla a Piètro ed a Páolo, o a chi si sia.

You see, therefore, very clearly, that in this example, the first *dà* is the verb, the second is the ablative indefinite; and that the first *ha* is in like manner a verb, being particularly written with an *h*, and that the other *a*'s are datives indefinite.

CHAPTER II.

OF THE PRONUNCIATION OF NOUNS.

WE have mentioned in the preceding chapter, that the Italians sometimes make use of the grave accent, and particularly in the examples above given; but as to what concerns the acute and grave accents indicating the close or open sound of the *e* and *o*, as well as the syl-

lable on which the stress lies, used in this book, these
have never been adopted in the Italian language ; because
without the greatest care of the writer, it would be impossible for the printer, though ever so exact, to mark it
wherever it might be wanting ; it would occasion such a
strange embarrassment and confusion in the letters, that
it would be scarcely possible to read them.   In order,
therefore, to illustrate this essential part of the Grammar,
I have formed a method, which to me appears very easy
and clear, and which may be of great use to such as are
desirous of learning this language, and even to the Italians themselves.   But, before I enter upon an explanation of the *particular rules* (p. 181), it will be necessary
to pay attention first to the *general ones* in the five following numbers.

No. I.

All nouns must be pronounced either short or long,
and their short or long sound depends entirely on their
penultima syllables, that is, the last but one : for all the
other syllables are to be pronounced steadily and uni-
formly, that is, without making use of any brevity, except these two nouns *aúgure*, an augur ; *claúsola*, a
clause ; which have the antepenultima (that is, the last
but two) short ; and some others mentioned in the exception of the letter *c*.

In order to know in what manner you are to sound
this penultima syllable, observe the penultima letter of
the noun you want to pronounce, and look for that
letter in the following arrangement, where you will see
the rule with its exceptions ; as, for example, if you
want to know whether the noun *rammarico* ought to be
pronounced short or long, you must look for the letter *c*
(p. 181), and its exceptions ; and if you do not find it
there, then you are to conform to the rule, which says,
all nouns that have the letter *c* for their penultima, are
pronounced short.

No. II.

Nouns of two syllables have no rule at all, because
they are subject to neither brevity nor length ; except

a very small number, which have an accent on the last
vowel, as will be observed in the following chapter.   I
shall give you here, as a general rule, all such nouns as
have two consonants before the final vowel, as *macilènte,
cangiaménto*, make the penultima long, of whatever
number of syllables they are; except a few, which you
will find at the letters *r* and *t*.

No. III.

Neither is there any need of a rule for nouns which
have a grave accent marked on the last vowel; it is
sufficient to know how to pronounce one of them properly; for example, *carità;* and you will be able to
pronounce *calamità, verità, virtù, bontà,* and all others of
the same kind, because you are to sound them all with
the same degree of quickness.

No. IV.

All feminine nouns follow the rule of the masculines,
from which they are derived.   All the plurals follow the
rule of their singulars, and compound nouns those of
their simples.

No. V.

There are some nouns which the Italians pronounce
as they please, that is, either long or short; and of these
I have mentioned some in the exceptions to the rules.
With regard to poetic nouns, we must be directed by the
measure of the verse; for poets have a license to abbre-
viate and lengthen a great many words. You pronounce
according to the custom of the country, when they
happen to be barbarous and foreign names, and all of
Hebrew and Greek derivations. Likewise the proper
names of persons, families, towns, provinces, &c. and
foreign or barbarous words, are generally pronounced
according to the custom of the place of their origin.

N. B. Before you proceed to the *particular rules,* see
first what has been said on the sound of the *e* and *o* at
p. 23.

PARTICULAR RULES,

Indicating the Long and Short Sounds of Nouns.

A.

Nouns having the letter *a* for the penultima are few among the Italian, and you must pronounce them long; as, *Archeláo, Niccoláo, Stanisláo,* &c.

B.

Nouns that have the letter *b* for their penultima, are also very few, and must be pronounced short; as, *A'rabo, Bárnaba, Cèlibe, I'ncubo, Súccubo.*

C.

All nouns whose penultima is the letter *c*, are short; as, *rammárico, rúbrica ;* the following excepted :

Alice.	*Felíce.*	*Orichícco.*
Amíco.	*Feníce.*	*Ortíca.*
Antíco,	*Feróce.*	*Paníco.*
Appendíce.	*Filúca* or *felúcca.*	*Pappafíco.*
Apríco.	*Lombríco.*	*Pendíce,*
Arcidúca.	*Lodovíco.*	*Perníce.*
Atróce.	*Lumáca.*	*Pudíco.*
Beatríce.	*Mammalúcco.*	*Rubríca,* a rubric.
Bereníce.	*Mantèca.*	*Sambúco.*
Bibliotèca.	*Marrúca.*	*Sommácco.*
Cadúco.	*Matríce.*	*Tameríce.*
Cervíce.	*Mendíco.*	*Triáca.*
Cloáca.	*Mollíca.*	*Velóce.*
Corníce.	*Moríce.*	*Verníce.*
Dappòco.	*Naríce.*	*Verrúca.*
Enríco.	*Nemíco.*	*Vescíca.*
Fatíca.	*Opáco.*	*Ubriáco.*

And all nouns terminated in *ace ;* as, *audáce. fornáce, spináce.* Likewise such as express female qualities, and end in *ice*, as *imperatríce, posseditríce, vendicatríce,* &c.

D.

Nouns which have the letter *d* for their penultima are short,

Except,

Alcíde.	*Disfída.*	*Palúde.*
Arrèdo.	*Erède.*	*Parentádo.*
Belgrádo.	*Eròde.*	*Parricída.*
Congèdo.	*Fratricída.*	*Rugiáda.*
Contádo.	*Ganimède.*	*Tancrédi.*
Contráda.	*Goffrédo.*	*Tolédo.*
Corrádo.	*Ignúdo.*	*Treppiède.*
Corrèdo, equipage.	*Lamprèda.*	*Zendádo.*
Cupído, Cupid.	*Mercéde.*	*Cittáde.*
Castòde.	*Nicomède.*	*Povertáde.*
Diomède.	*Omicída.*	*Virtúde.*

⎱ (²³)

E.

All nouns that have the letter *e* for their penultima are long,

Except,

Acúleo, Bòrea, Cesárea (title of majesty ; but when it signifies a city it is pronounced long) *Cerúleo, Coetáneo, Collatáneo, Empíreo, Etèreo, Línea, Mediterráneo, porpúreo, Tartárea, temporáneo.* Some pronounce the two names *Tesèo* and *Timotèo* long ; and they seem to be in the right. All nouns adjective derived from substantives are also short ; as, *fèrreo,* from *fèrro,* iron ; *marmòreo,* from *mármo,* marble ; *venèreo,* from *Vènere,* Venus. In all nouns of this termination, where the letter *u* alone forms their ante-penultima syllable, this letter is pronounced short as well as the syllable that follows ; as, *áureo, náusea,* &c.

F.

You are to pronounce all nouns short whose penultima is the letter *f;* except the three following, *Martúfo, Paráfo; Tartúfo,* which are long.

G.

You must pronounce all nouns short that have the letter *g* for their penultima,

Except,

Areopágo, Bottéga, Castigo, Collèga (*Congrèga*, though long, is sometimes pronounced short), *Dionígi, Federigo, Gonzága, Impiègo, Intrigo, Lattúga, Lettíga, Luígi, Lupágo, Orígo, Parígi, Pedagògo, Preságo* (several pronounce *pròroga* short), *Ripiègo, sanguisúga, selvágo, sinagòga, sossiègo* or *russiègo, tartarúga.*

I.

In some nouns where the letter *i* happens to be the penultima, it forms one syllable with the following letter, as they are pronounced jointly.

In others it is formed separately, forming a distinct syllable by itself.

The letter *i*, therefore, forms but one syllable with the subsequent vowel, in all nouns not contained in the following catalogue. It forms two syllables in the following nouns, and you are to pronounce them long; viz.

Agonia.	*Apoplessia.*	*Befania*, or *epifania*.
Albagia.	*Apostasia.*	
Amnistia.	*Aristocrazia.*	*Brio.*
Anagogia.	*Armonia.*	*Bugia.*
Analogia.	*Arpia.*	*Calpestio.*
Anania.	*Astrologia.*	*Carestia.*
Anarchia.	*Astronomia.*	*Castellania.*
Anatomia.	*Badia.*	*Codardia.*
Anfania.	*Balia,* power or	*Chiromanzia.*
Anfibologia.	authority.	*Chironia.*
Antologia.	*Balio* ([24]).	*Chirurgia.*
Antinomia.	*Baronia.*	*Compagnia.*
Antipatia.	*Bastia.*	*Cortesia.*
Apologia.	*Bigamia.*	*Chronologia.*

---

[24] This name is given in a part of Italy to the person who at Rome is called *cursóre*, a serjeant or bailiff; but *bálio* (short) means a foster-father.

Dio or Iddio.
Democrazia.
Diafania.
Desio.
Economia.
Elegia.
Elia.
Energia.
Eresia.
Etimologia.
Eucaristia.
Fantasia.
Fellonia.
Filologia.
Filosofia.
Fisonomia or fi-
  sionomia.
Fio.
Follia.
Frenesia.
Gagliardia.
Gelosia.
Genealogia.
Gengia.
Genia.
Geografia.
Geomanzia.
Geometria.
Gerarchia.
Geremia.
Golia.
Idrofobia.
Idrografia.
Idromanzia.
Idropisia.
Infingardia.
Ipocrisia.
Ironia.
Lebbrosia.
Leggio.
Latinie.

Liscia or Lescia,
  lye to wash with.
Litargia or letar-
  gia.
Liturgia.
Lombardia.
Lucia.
Magia.
Malacchia.
Malattia.
Malia.
Malvasia or Mal-
  vagia, Malmsey
  wine.
Malinconia,   or
  Maninconia.
Mattia.
Melanconia.
Melodia.
Mercanzia.
Messia.
Mio.
Monarchia.
Mormorio.
Natio.
Negromanzia.
Normandia.
Notomia.
Oblio.
Omilia or umilia.
Ortografia.
Paralisia.
Pavia.
Pazzia.
Pestio.
Peripezia.
Petralia.
Piccardia.
Pio, but émpio is
  pronounced
  short.

Piromanzia.
Poesia.
Prigionia.
Prosodia.
Pulizia.
Qualsisia.
Restio.
Ricadia.
Rio.
Ritrosia.
Romania.
Rosalia.
Saettia.
Sagrestia or sa-
  gristia.
Schiranzia   or
  scheranzia.
Schiavonia.
Scoppiettio.
Simonia.
Simpatia.
Sinfonia.
Sodomia.
Sofia.
Spia.
Stallio.
Stantio.
Tentinnio.
Teologia.
Tipografia.
Tirannia.
Tobia.
Traversia.
Turchia.
Vallacchia.
Vallonia.
Via.
Villania.
Zacchia.
Zio.
Zia.

We likewise give a long pronunciation to all those nouns which terminate in *ria;* as, *allegría, idolatría, osteria, mangeria,* &c.

Except feminine nouns derived from short masculines, only by changing the last vowel into *a;* as, *vittòrio, vittòria; fulminatòrio, fulminatòria;* because these are reducible to the rule of No. IV.

The following are also pronounced short.

A'dria.	*Fèria.*	*Mándria.*
Angúria.	*Fimbria.*	*Matèria.*
A'ria.	*Fúria.*	*Memòria.*
Artèria.	*Glòria.*	*Misèria.*
Baldòria.	*I'dria.*	*Mítria.*
Bòria.	*Indústria.*	*Penúria.*
Calábria.	*Ingiúria.*	*Píria.*
Cúria.	*I'stria.*	*Stíria.*
Dòria.	*Lussúria.*	*Stòria.*

Frádicio, múdicio, súdicio, which several Tuscans use instead of *frácido, múcido* and *súcido,* are nouns out of all rules; because, besides the conjunction of the two last vowels, they have the syllable *di* short.

In fine, all nouns that have for their penultima the letter *i,* forming one syllable with the final, as *desidèrio, propízio,* make the penultima long.

L.

Nouns that have the letter *l* for their penultima are short,

Except,

Acquamèle.	*Carmèlo.*	*Mezzúle.*
Aracèli.	*Caròla.*	*Michèle.*
Asílo.	*Cautèla.*	*Ossimèle.*
Batticúlo.	*Corruttèla.*	*Paralèllo.*
Bestiòla.	*Crudèle.*	*Parentèla.*
Cammèllo.	*Fedéle.*	*Paròla.*
Candéla.	*Idromèle.*	*Pistòla,* a pistol.
Capriòla.	*Loquèla.*	*Querèla.*

Raffaèle.	*Rosamèle.*	*Tordèla.*
Segála, (some	*Sequèla.*	*Vangèlo.*
pronounce it	*Soggólo.*	*Viòla.*
short).	*Strozzúle.*	*Urièle.*

And all nouns terminating in *ale ;* as, *canále, funerále, guanciále,* without reckoning *Annibale, Asdrúbale,* and *fónfale.*

You are likewise to pronounce all nouns long that before the final syllable have the letter *o* preceded by a vowel, here called accidental, which in verse is seldom used, but frequently in prose, though it is scarcely ever sounded; as, *figliuòlo, Romagnuòlo, vignajuòlo.* In like manner, nouns terminating in *ile ;* as, *Aprile, gentile, vedovile :* but of the latter there are fifteen short, viz.

Acquátile,	*Fèrtile.*	*Portátile.*
A'gile.	*Frágile.*	*Stèrile.*
Dòcile.	*Fútile.*	*Volátile.*
Difficile.	*Grácile.*	*U'mile.*
Fácile.	*Inútile.*	*U'tile.*

All adjectives in *bile,* which express possibility or impossibility of doing anything, are also short; as, *correggíbile, invincibile, suscettibile,* &c.

N. B. *Atrabile* is pronounced long; but all the other nouns in *ile,* as *amábile, nòbile, stábile,* &c. follow the rule of the letter *l.*

M.

Pronounce all nouns short which have the letter *m* for their penultima,

Except,

Abrámo.	*Guaime.*	*Problèma.*
Adámo.	*Idiòma.*	*Richiámo.*
Cinamòmo.	*Lattíme.*	*Soprannóme.*
Cognóme.	*Madáma.*	*Stratagèmma.*
Concíme.	*Opímo.*	*Sublime.*
Diadèma.	*Poèma.*	*Suprèmo.*
Estrèmo.		

Except, also, all nouns terminated in *ame* and *ume ;* as, *bestiáme, legnáme, costúme, legúme.*

N.

Pronounce all nouns long, whose penultima is the letter *n*,

Except

Abròtano.	Gránfano.	Pèttine.
Abrústino.	Garòfano.	Pástino, a dig-
A'cinò.	Gèmino.	ging up of the
Amázzone.	Gèrmine.	vineyard.
Antifona.	Gióvane, or gió-	Plátano.
A'rgine.	vine.	Plátina.
A'sino.	Gòmena.	Polèsine.
Cánone.	Intégina.	Polígono.
Cármine.	Lacedèmone.	Pròdano.
Cárpine.	Lámpana.	Ráfanv.
Còfano.	Lésina.	Rágano.
Cristòfano.	Líbano.	Rímini.
Dáino.	Limòsina, or ele-	Ròdano.
Diácono.	mòsina.	Sátana.
Diáfano.	Mácchina.	Stéfano.
Diògene.	Mácina.	Strággina.
E'bano.	Mángano.	Tèrmine.
E'glino.	Mòdena.	Tímpano.
E'lcino.	Ocèano.	Tráina.
Esámine.	O'rfano.	Trápano.
Fémmina.	O'rgano.	Túrbine.
Ferráina.	Orígano.	Vímine.
Fiórina.	Página.	Uòmini.
Fiòcine.	Pámpana.	Záino.
Fúlmine.	Pálina.	Zíngano.

You are likewise to pronounce all nouns short that terminate in *gine*; as *balordággine, orígine, piantággine;* and all those which end in *dine* in the singular; as, *róndine, disórdine, inquietúdine.*

O.

There are not more than four nouns, having the letter *o* for their penultima, in regard to which there

could be any doubt of their pronunciation: these are
A'loe, Síloe, Eròe, Nòe, some say *Nóè;* the two first
are pronounced with some rapidity, as if they had a
grave accent on the letter *e*, which indeed is used by
some: but the third is long.

P.

You are to pronounce all nouns short, that have the
letter *p* for their penultima;

Except

*Antipápa, archetipo, Cantalúpo, Ciclópo, dirúpo, Eu-
ròpa, Esòpo, Isòpo, Oroscòpo:* the following three are
better short than long, *Píropo, Pèlipo, Príapo.*

R.

Pronounce all nouns long whose penultima is the
letter *r,*

Except

A'lbero or *árbore.*	*Chiávari,* the	*Metèora.*
A'nitra or *ánatra*	name of a	*Nèttare.*
A'ncora, anchor.	country.	*Nèutro.*
A'nfora.	*Cláustro.*	*O'ngaro.*
A'rbitro.	*Còllera.*	*Páparo.*
A'saro.	*E'piro.*	*Pècora.*
Aúgure.	*Esámetro.*	*Pentámetro.*
Aústro.	*Fèretro.*	*Pésaro.*
Báratro.	*Fánfaro.*	*Piffero.*
Bárbaro.	*Fólgore.*	*Pitágora.*
Bávaro.	*Gámbero.*	*Pòrfiro.*
Bischero.	*Gáspero.*	*Pórpora*
Cánchero.	*Geòmetra.*	*Rèmora.*
Cánfora.	*I'caro.*	*Sátiro.*
Cántaro.	*Intèrprete.*	*Schèletro.*
Cáppero.	*Lázzaro.*	*Spálatro.*
Cáttedra.	*Lógoro.*	*Súghero.*
Cèlebre.	*Mártire.*	*Súperi.*
Cèrebro.	*Mártora.*	*Tártaro.*
Césare.	*Máschera.*	*Tènebre.*

Tórtora.	*Zácchera.*	*Zíngaro.*
U'ngaro.	*Zázzera.*	*Zúcchero.*

You are likewise to pronounce all nouns short, that terminate in *era, ere,* and *ero,* and have not the letter *i* before the antepenultima *e;* as *lèttere, Cèrere, número;* but we must except *austèro, chimèra, emisfèro, galèra, ingegnère, lusinghièro, lungatèra, menzognèro, messère, Omèro, pantèra, primavèra, sevèro, sincèro,* which conform to the rule: as do likewise almost all verbal nouns: as, *il piacére, il parére,* and some others, which are derived from the infinitives contained in the exception to the rule of the second number in the next chapter. And the abbreviated nouns preserve the same sound as they had before their abbreviation; for instance, we pronounce *altèro* long, because it is abridged from *altièro; intéro* from *intièro; magistèro* from *magistièro; monastèro* from *monastièro,* &c.

S.

All nouns are pronounced long which have the letter *s* for their penultima,

Except

Análisi.	*E'feso.*	*Paráfrasi.*
A'niso.	*E'nfasi.*	*Pláuso.*
Brindisi.	*E'stasi.*	*Sindèresi.*
Diágnosi.	*Gènesi.*	*Síntessi.*
Diògesi.	*Metamòrfosi.*	*Túnisi.*

T.

Pronounce those nouns long, having the letter *t* for their penultima,

Except

A'bito.	*A'gata,* a christian	*A'ndito.*
Accòlito.	name, and a pre-	*Anèlito.*
A'dito.	cious stone.	*Antídoto.*
A'lito.	*A'mbito.*	*Antístite.*

Apòstata.
Attònito.
Autòmata.
Còanito.
Còmito.
Cómpito, the work
    of a day, or a
    task.
Còmputo.
Crédito.
Cúbito.
Débito.
Decrèpito.
Dèdito.
Depòsito.
Disputa.
Dòmito.
E'mpito, for I'm-
    peto.
Epíteto.
Esáusto.
Esèrcito.
E'sito.
Esplícito.
Fégato.
Fòmite.

Fortúito.
Frèmito.
Gèmito ([25]).
Gènito.
Gómito.
Implícito.
I'nclito.
Intèrprete.
Intúito.
Ipòcrate.
Ipòcrito.
Ippòlito.
Lécito.
Líbito.
Lièvito.
Límite.
Mèrito.
Náscita.
Olocáusto.
O'spite.
Pálmite.
Pèrdita.
Plácido.
Prèmito.
Prèstito.
Pretèrito.

Propòsito.
Púlpito.
Recápito.
Recòndito.
Rèndita.
Sábato.
Séguito.
Sòccita.
Sòcrate.
Sòlito.
Sollécito.
Spírito.
Stímate, marks of
    wounds.
Stípite.
Strèpito.
Súbito.
Súddito.
Tácito.
Tránsito.
Trèmito.
Vègeto.
Véndita.
Vèneto.
Visita.
Vómito.

U.

Pronounce all nouns short, that have the vowel u for their penultima; example *árduo, perpètuo, residuo, assíduo,* &c.

Except

Altrúi, búe, dúe, dúo, and its compounds, as, *ambidúe, ventidúe, &c. colúi, costúi, cúi, lúi, súi, túi* for *tuòi.*

---

[25] When it is a noun adjective, it is pronounced almost always short; but when a supine, it is long.

V.

You are to pronounce those nouns short that have *v* for their penultima; examples: *còncavo, Gènova, tritavo, véscovo.*

Except

Bisávo, diciannòve, and the other numbers of the same termination; *Ginévra, incávo, soáve, ottávo,* and all the nouns terminating in *ivo* and *ava*; as *sostantivo, motívo, gengíva, invettíva.*

Z.

Pronounce all nouns long which have the letter *z* for their penultima, except the noun *pòlizza.*

CHAPTER III.

OF THE PRONUNCIATION OF VERBS AND ADVERBS

No. I.

DISSYLABLES, whether verbs or adverbs, with no accent on the last vowel, will have consequently the stress on the first syllable. See the preceding chapter, No. II, and with regard to words of two or more syllables, that have a grave accent on the last vowel, I refer to what has been said at Chapter II., No. III. p. 180.

No. II.

The infinitive of the verbs is terminated in *are, ere,* and *ire.* Those which terminate in *are* and *ire* are pronounced long, without any exception; and such as end in *ere* short, the following excepted: *avére, cadére, dissuadére, dolére, dovére, giacére, godére, parére, persuadére, piacére, potére, rimanére, sapére, sedére, solére, tacére, temére, tenére, valére, vedére, volére,* and all their compounds; as, *accadére, ottenére, provvedére,* &c. it being a general maxim, that the derivatives follow the rule of their primitives.

No. III.

All third persons plural are pronounced short, as, *ámano ; credévano, sentírono,* &c., except in the future tense, on account of the two consonants which precede the final vowel ; and short are to be said also the first person plural of all the preterimperfects subjunctive, as, *che amássimo,* that we might love ; *che leggéssimo,* that we might read, &c.

No. IV.

All other persons, of whatever tense or number, are made long, except those of some verbs of the first conjugation, which in the first person of the indicative, have the penultima short, and preserve this shortness in the other persons, not only of the indicative, but of the imperative and subjunctive moods ; for instance, *recápito,* the first person indicative of the verb *recapitáre,* has the syllable *pi* short : and the same quantity is preserved in *recápiti* and *recápita.* Further, this, and other like verbs, receive, by way of augmentation, in the third persons plural of the said moods, another syllable, which is sounded as short as the penultima ; for instance, *recápito, recápitano, recápitino ; dissímulo, dissímulano, dissímulino ;* and since there are several who mispronounce these third persons plural, I have thought fit to give a particular description of them in the two following numbers.

No. V.

In the first place, all verbs, whose infinitive terminates in *care,* without any other consonant before *c,* as *autenticáre, glorificáre, masticáre,* make the first person of the present indicative short, and of course, the other persons just now mentioned in the exception to the preceding number, except *affiocáre, arrocáre,* and such as you will find excepted in the following numbers.

2. All verbs, whose infinitive terminates in *oláre,* as, *immoláre, stimoláre, brancoláre.*

3. All verbs formed of nouns which have the penul-

tima syllable short; for example, *regoláre*, formed of
règola; generáre, of *gènero; sollecitáre*, of *sollécito.*
To the three foregoing numbers you must add the following verbs, which are contained therein, viz.

Affogáre.	*Imitáre.*	*Pulluláre.*
Agilare.	*Incorporare.*	*Rammemorare.*
Alterare.	*Insolferare.*	*Recitare.*
Anfanare.	*Interrogare.*	*Refrigerare.*
Annichilare.	*Investigare.*	*Ricuperare.*
Assiderare.	*Irritare.*	*Ruminare.*
Bucherare.	*Istigare.*	*Rumigare.*
Calcitrare.	*Iterare.*	*Scalpitare.*
Capitare.	*Litigare.*	*Schiccherare.*
Commemorare.	*Luminare.*	*Seguitare.*
Comprare.	*Meditare.*	*Seminare.*
Confederare.	*Moderare.*	*Sgomberare.*
Considerare.	*Mormorare.*	*Simulare.*
Contaminare.	*Munerare.*	*Smemorare.*
Corroborare.	*Navigare.*	*Spettorare.*
Decifrare.	*Necessitare.*	*Superare.*
Desinare.	*Nominare.*	*Suppeditare.*
Dissipare.	*Noverare.*	*Suscitare.*
Dominare.	*Occupare.*	*Tollerare.*
Dubitare.	*Palpitare.*	*Tumultuare.*
Eccettuare.	*Penetrare.*	*Ventilare.*
Felicitare.	*Precipitare.*	*Vigilare.*
Gratulare.	*Procrastinare.*	*Vituperare.*

To the above we may also add the verb *offríre*, belonging to the conjugation of verbs in *isco.* There are
some who pronounce the foregoing third person indifferently, short or long, in the verbs *migliorare, peggio-
ráre,* and *reputáre;* but they are pronounced short in
the verbs *concitáre, eccitáre, incitáre.*

No. VI.

From the whole we may conclude that infinitives of
two or three syllables, as, *fáre, cecáre,* with their compounds, as *disfáre, accecáre,* do not shorten the first
person indicative, nor the other persons, nor even the

infinitives derived from nouns whose penultima is long;
examples: *avventuráre*, derived from *ventúra*; *intricáre*,
from *intríco*; *minchionáre*, from *minchióne*; *contrastáre*,
from *contrásto*; *architettáre*, from *architétto*, &c. But
I am very sure that *persevèro*, I persevere, is oftener
pronounced short, though it comes from *sevèro*, which is
long; perhaps to distinguish it from the Latin verb
persevèro, which is sounded long.

No. VII.

With regard to the conjunctive pronouns, *mi*, *ti*, *si*,
&c. the four relatives, *lo*, *la*, *li*, *le*, and the particle *ne*, if
they happen to be at the end of infinitives terminated in
ere short, as, *scrívermi*, *rispónderti*, *vénderne*, and at the
end of the third person singular of the preterperfect
simple, marked with the grave accent, as also at the end
of the first and third person singular of the future; as,
rimproveròlli, *racconteròvvi*, *racconterássi*, &c.; there
arises from thence no change at all in the pronunciation,
though this union is productive of two consonants before
the final vowel; since the foregoing words, being placed
after the said persons, are always reduplicated, according
to what has been observed, p. 170, and as may be seen
in the above examples. If the said particles happen to
be united to other persons, as *parlátegli*, *temévami*, *in-
viándolo*, they cause the last verbal syllable, which is
the penultima of the word, to be pronounced short.

No. VIII.

When two of the said particles happen to be united
together, at the end of a person which without this
union is not pronounced short, as, *parláteg liene*, *inviás-
domene*, *portávameli*, then you shorten only the penultima syllable of the word, which is the first of the two
particles: but when they are joined together at the end
of infinitives, and of the persons marked at the beginning of No VII. you make no change, as I have already
observed, in the pronunciation; and the first of the two
particles, being the penultima of the word, is made

short; examples: *scrívermelo, véndergliene, rimprove-ròmmela, pentirássene,* &c.

No. IX.

With regard to adverbs, you must follow the rules and exceptions of the preceding chapter, especially as they are derived for the most part from nouns: for instance, *all' improvviso, un tantino,* see under the letter *s* for the former, and under *n* for the latter, and you will find that both of them have the penultima syllable long. As for such as have two consonants before their final vowel, as *allegraménte, incontanènte,* the rule mentioned in the preceding chapter, No. II., must be observed, and with respect to compounds, remember the rule, which says, that compounds follow the nature of their simples.

No. X.

Here I shall observe, that when the adverb *ècco* is joined to the conjunctive or relative particles, as *èccoci, èccoli, èccole,* the penultima syllable, thus united, is to be pronounced short; and it retains the same quantity when joined to the two aforesaid particles; for instance, *èccotene, èccovene, èccotelo:* you are moreover to observe, that the penultima, which is the first of the particles, is also pronounced short.

Excepted the adverb *altresì,* and the interjection *cáppita; Altróve, ancóra, assái dappòi, giammái, insième,* and *ovvéro,* have their penultima long.

In the two adverbs *adágio* and *pòscia,* the vowel *i* forms a syllable with the final vowels *o* and *a.*

THIRD TREATISE.
OF THE ITALIAN SYNTAX.

CHAPTER I.

OF THE DIVISION OF SYNTAX.

Syntax is a Greek word, by the Latins called *constructio;* and signifies the right placing and connecting of words in a sentence. It is divided into three parts; the first of order or arrangement, the second of concordance, the third of government. The syntax of order or arrangement, is the right disposition of words in a sentence. The syntax of concordance is, when the parts of speech agree with one another, as the substantive with the adjective, or the nominative with the verb. The syntax of government is, when one part of speech governs another; or, as some grammarians express it, when one part of speech is dependent on another.

The rules of syntax are much the same in Italian as in English; but for the sake of those who have not a grammatical knowledge of their own language, I shall lay down some general rules respecting Italian construction.

I. OF THE ORDER OF WORDS ([26]).

1. The nominative is that to which we attribute the action of the verb, and is always arranged in the first place; it is generally a noun, a pronoun, or an infinitive put for a noun; as, *Tommáso scrive,* Thomas writes; *io párlo,* I speak; *il dormíre gióva,* sleeping does one good.

2. When the action of the verb is attributed to many persons or things, these all belong to the nominative,

---

[26] See Bottarelli's Exercises on the Order of Words, p. 15.

and are ranged in the first place together with their conjunction; as, *Pietro e Páolo lèggono*, Peter and Paul read.

3. The adjectives belonging to the nominative substantive, to which the action of the verb is attributed, are put after the substantive, and before the verb; as, *gli scolári morigeráti e diligènti stúdiano*, mannerly and diligent scholars study.

4. If the nominative has an article, this article always takes the first place, that being its natural situation.

5. Sometimes a verb with its case stands for a nominative: as, *umána cosa è avére compassióne degli afflitti*, to have compassion on the afflicted is an act of humanity.

6. The nominative is sometimes understood; as, *ámo*, where you understand *io*; and so of the other persons of the verb.

7. After the nominative you put the verb; and if there is an adverb, it is to be placed immediately after the verbs, whose accidents and circumstances it explains; as, *Pietro áma ardenteménte la glòria*, Peter ardently loves glory.

8. The cases governed by the verb are put after it; they may be one or many, according to the nature of the action; as, *io ámo Pietro*, I love Peter; *io dóno un libro a Páolo*, I make a present of a book to Paul.

9. The preposition is always put before the case it governs: *vicíno a casa*, near home.

10. The relative is always placed after the antecedent; as, *Pietro, il quále stúdia*, Peter, who studies.

II. OF CONCORDANCE.

1. Adjectives agree with their substantives in gender, number and case; as, *un uòmo virtuóso*, a virtuous man; *sontuosi palazzi* (see note "), sumptuous palaces; *bella dónna*, or *una donna bella*, a handsome woman.

2. When two or more substantives singular come together, the adjective, or participle belonging to them must be put in the plural; as, *Perdiccóne, e'l padre, e la madre della Lisa, ed élla, altresì, contènti grandis-*

sima fèsta fécero; Perdiccone, and the father and mother of Lisa, and she, likewise, contented, made great rejoicings.

3. If the substantive happens to be one in the singular and the other in the plural, the adjective or participle may then agree with either; as, *essèndosi Dioneo, con gli áltri gióvani mésso a giuocáre a tavole;* Dioneo, with the other young men, having sat down to play at tables: *il re co' suòi compágni, rimontáti a cavállo, alla reále osteria sene tornáro;* the king and his companions, having mounted their horses again, returned to the royal ínn.

4. Every personal verb agrees with its nominative, expressed or understood, both in number and person.

5. If the nominative be a collective noun, the verb may be in the plural, though the nominative is in the singular; as, *il pòpolo comúne èrano ignoránti del véro Dío;* the common people were ignorant of the true God. But if in the collective noun, the multitude of the persons composing is not attended to as much as the whole; and if the action expressed by the verb cannot be done by many distributively, but only collectively, the verb must then agree with the number of the nominative; example: we must say, *il senáto decretò,* not *decretarono,* because a decree cannot be issued from the senators distributively, but by all together, forming only one moral body. But we may say, *il comune popolo erano ignoranti,* because ignorance is not exclusively attributed to the people, composing only one moral body, but to the individuals, each of which and all are ignorant.

6. When there happen to be two nominatives, one masculine and the other feminine, the preterite and participle of the verb agree with the masculine, if speaking of persons; but if anything else is meant, it may agree with the feminine; as, *convitáti le dònne e gli uòmini alle távole,* the men and women being invited to table; *ella avrèbbe così l' altra gamba, e l' altro piè fuòr mandáto,* she would have put out the other leg and the other foot.

7. The relative *quale,* with the article, agrees entirely with the antecedent; but without the article,

and denoting an absolute quality or likeness, it agrees with what follows : as, *quel cuòre il quále*, that heart which ; *séco pensándo quáli infra piccol tèrmine dovéan divenire*, thinking within himself what was shortly to become of them. Except *persóna*, which, though of the feminine gender, yet, when applied to a male, requires a masculine relative ; as, *alcúna persóna il* or *la quále*, any person who.

8. The question and answer always agree in every thing ; as, *cavalière, a qual dònna se' tu ? ed egli rispóse sòno alla regina*, what lady do you belong to, sir knight? and he answered, I belong to the queen.

III. OF THE DEPENDENCE OF THE PARTS OF SPEECH ON EACH OTHER.

1. THE nominative being the basis of the sentence, the verbs depend on it, as the other cases depend on the verb. The adjective depends on the substantive which supports it ; and the adverb on the verb whose accidents it explains.

2. The genitive depends on a substantive expressed or understood, by which it is governed.

3. The accusative depends either on a verb active, as *io ámo la virtù*, I love virtue : or on an infinitive, as *disse se in ciò avére erráto*, he owned himself to have been mistaken in that ; or on a preposition, as *vádo vèrso la chièsa*, I go towards the church.

4. The ablative depends on a preposition, by which it is governed : as *párto da Róma*, I go from Rome.

5. The dative and vocative have, strictly speaking, no dependence on the other parts. The dative is common, as it were, to all nouns and verbs. The vocative only points out the person to whom one speaks.

And so much for syntax in general. I proceed now to the construction of the several parts of speech.

CHAPTER II.

OF THE SYNTAX OF ARTICLES ([27]).

BEFORE we come to the Syntax of the Articles, remember that *lo, la, li, le, gli,* before the verb, and

---

[27] See Exercises on the Articles, p. 11.

K 4

the word *ècco*, are no longer articles, but pronouns relative.

Those who understand Latin will quickly perceive the difference, if they take notice, that every time they render *lo, la, li, le, gli*, by *illum, illam, illud;* or by *eum, eam, id; illos, illas, illa; eos, eas, ea;* they are relative pronouns.

The particles *in* and *to*, before the names of cities, are expressed by *in* and *a;* examples : in *or* at Rome, in *Róma;* to Rome, *a Roma*.

₊ The best authors often use the infinitives with the article *il* instead of substantives; as, singing rejoices me, *il cantáre mi rallégra*, instead of *il cánto mi rallegra*.

Note, the article *il* is put before the word *signór*, sir, or my lord, speaking of all qualities, dignities, and relations, for the masculine; examples : my lord the president, *il signór presidènte;* my lord duke, *il signor duca;* the gentlemen, *i signori;* of the gentlemen, *dei signori*.

We must omit the article in the singular before the possessive pronoun (or, to speak more properly, the possessive adjective) which precedes a noun of relation : as, *mio pádre mi ama*, my father loves me, instead of *il mio padre*, &c. But in the plural it must be expressed; thus say, *i mièi fratèlli*, instead of *mièi fratèlli*.

The same rule must be observed respecting the feminine article *la*, which is to be prefixed to *signóra*, speaking of *or* to the ladies; as, *la signóra principéssa*.

If the Italians express madam by *madáma*, they put the article *la* after it; as, madam the princess, *madama la principessa;* of madam the, &c. *di madama la*, &c.

₊ Sometimes the English particle *to*, before infinitives, is rendered in Italian by the article *il* or *lo;* example : it is easy to say, to see, to study; *è fácile il dìre, il vedére, lo studiáre :* with the latter we use the article *lo*, because *studiare* begins with an *s* followed by a consonant, called in Italian *s impura*.

We may also make use of the indefinite article *a;* as *è fácile a dire, a vedere, a studiare*, it is easy to say, to see, to study.

See further in the syntax of verbs, when it is proper

to express the articles *del, dello, della, delle, degli,* &c. after the verbs, and when not.

It is also to be observed, that the Italians frequently make use of the masculine articles plural *dei, ai, dai,* with the apostrophe, before possessive pronouns, and before all intermediate nouns ; for example :

De' mièi libri,	Of my books.
A' tuòi parènti,	To thy relations.
Da' suòi amíci,	From his friends.
La libertà de' pòpoli,	The liberty of the people.
E' permésso' a' viaggiatóri,	Travellers are permitted.
Si scríve da' paési lontáni,	They write from distant countries.

CHAPTER III.

OF THE SYNTAX OF NOUNS ([28]).

THE adjectives, as we have before observed, agree with their substantives in gender, number and case ; example, *uòmo virtuóso, dònna bellíssima, cása nuòva.*

The Italians sometimes use a noun adjective instead of a substantive ; as, *il cáldo del fuòco,* for *il calóre ; l' álto delle mura* for *l' altézza,* &c.

*** The comparatives govern a genitive ; and the particle *than,* which is after them, is expressed by *di,* or *del* or *dello,* &c. as you may see in the First Part.

We have taken notice in the chapter of Comparatives, p. 55, that the particle *than* is rendered by *che,* when it is before a noun adjective, a verb, or an adverb.

*** If the comparison is made between two substantives, *than* must also be rendered by *che ;* for example :

Virgil pleases me more than Ovid, *Virgilio mi piáce più che Ovídio.*

He is a better soldier than captain, *è migliór soldáto che capitáno.*

Rome would please me more than Paris, *mi piacerèbbe più Roma, che Parígi.*

---

[28] See Bottarelli's Exercises on the Syntax of Nouns, p. 15.

₀ When the comparison is made by *as much as,*
so as, they must all be rendered by *quánto;* for example :

The prince is not so powerful as the king, *il príncipe*
non è potènte quanto il re.

My book is as handsome as yours, *il mio líbro è bèllo*
quanto il vòstro.

You shall have as much of it as you please, *ne avrète*
quanto vorréte.

The poor are as much despised as the rich esteemed,
sóno vilipési i pòveri quanto sono stimáti i ricchi.

CHAPTER IV.

THE SYNTAX OF PRONOUNS.

I DO not intend to treat here of the personal pronouns ;
they have been sufficiently explained already in the first
part, from p. 62 to p. 65 ; to avoid any further repetition, I shall only give the following rule.

The English make use of the verb *to be,* put imper-
sonally through all its tenses, in the third person, before
the personal pronouns, *thou, he, she, we, you, they ; it is*
I, it is he, &c. In Italian, the verb *to be,* on this occasion, is not impersonal ; and they express, it is I, by *sóno*
io ; it is thou, *sèi tu ;* it is he, *è égli :* it is we, *siámo noi ;*
it is you, *siète voi :* it is she, *è élla ;* it is they, mas. *sóno*
églino or *sono éssi ;* it is they, fem. *sono élleno* or *sono*
ésse : and in like manner through all the tenses ; as, it
was I, *èra io ;* it was we, *eravámo noi, &c.*

₀ To express in Italian, *it is mine, it is thine, it is*
his, it is ours, it is yours, we must say in the singular
number,

	Masculine.		Feminine.
It is mine,	*è mio,*	or	*è mia.*
It is thine,	*è tuo,*		*è tua.*
It is his *or* hers,	*è suo,*		*è sua.*
It is ours,	*è nòstro,*		*è nostra.*
It is yours,	*è vòstro,*		*è vostra.*

In the plural we must say, *sóno mièi* or *mìe ; sóno*
tuòi or *túe ; sóno suòi* or *súe ; sóno nostri* or *nostre ;*
sono vostri or *vostre.*

Me, thee, him, to him, &c. are always expressed by the conjunctive pronouns *mi, ti, si, gli,* &c. when they are before or after a verb. See p. 65.

*** The conjunctive pronoun *gli* requires a particular remark, namely, that whenever it is found before the pronouns *lo, la, le* or *ne,* it takes an *e* at the end to join the following particle ; examples :

To give it to him, *per dárglielo,* and not *darglilo :* the vowels *i* and *e* ought to be pronounced as one syllable.

To give it to her, *per dárgliela.*

You shall return them to him, *gliéli renderéte.*

You shall ask him for some, *gliéne domanderéte.*

You shall speak to him of it, *gliene parleréte.*

*** When the conjunctive pronouns happen to meet with the particle *si,* they must be transposed, and *si* placed next to the verb ; examples :

They tell me, *mi si dice,* and not *si mi dice.*

They tell thee, *ti si dice,* and not *si ti.*

They tell him or her, *gli* or *le si dice.*

*** The pronouns conjunctive, *mi, ti, si, ci, vi,* change *i* into *e* when they are before *lo, la, le, gli,* or the particle, *ne ;* for example :

He returns it to me, *me lo rènde.*

The following words, *me some* or *of it, thee some* or *of it, him some* or *of it, us some, you some,* &c. are rendered in Italian by *me ne, te ne, se ne, gliéne, ce ne, ve ne,* as we have already observed in the chapter of conjunctive pronouns, p. 67.

Lóro, their, before a noun, is a pronoun possessive indeclinable ; as,

Their book,	*Il lóro líbro.*
Their room,	*La loro cámera.*
Their goods,	*I loro bèni.*
Their swords,	*Le loro spáde.*

When *lóro* is a possessive pronoun, put an article before it.

Lóro after a verb is a conjunctive pronoun ; as the master teaches them, *il maèstro inségna loro. Loro* is generally made to follow the verb, with whatever tense it be.

*** To render the expression in Italian more agreeable and polite, use the third person instead of the

x 6

second; thus, *you are in the right of it*, is expressed by *V. S. ha ragióne*, instead of *avéte ragione*, pronouncing *vo' signoría* or *vossignoría*, which is always marked by *V. S.* And to avoid the frequent repetition of *V. S.* they use in conversation, the pronoun *élla*, in the nominative.

Examples:

Nom.	*E'lla,*	or	*Vo' Signoría.*
Gen.	*di lèi,*		*di V. S.*
Dat.	*a lei,*		*a V. S.*
Acc.	*lei,*		*V. S.*
Abl.	*da lei,*		*da V. S.*

V. S. literally translated, means your lordship; but it is seldom used now.

In the plural it is *le signoríe lóro, delle signoríe loro, alle signoríe loro, dalle signoríe loro.*

₊ *That* is always expressed by *che*; for example: the book that I read, *il libro che lèggo*; what do you want? *che voléte? che vuòl' ella?* or *che vuòle V. S.?*

Chè often denotes *because*; especially when it follows the negative particle *non*; example: do not drink it, because it will hurt you, *non lo bevéte, chè vi farà male.*

₊ *Chi* is frequently made use of to express *he who*, and is more elegant than *quello che*; for example: *chi dice quésto, ha ragione*, he who says this, is in the right, for *quello che dice*, &c.

₊ The particle *it* is never expressed in Italian before the third person of the verb *to be*; for example:

It is well said,	*è bèn détto.*
It shall be well done,	*sarà ben fátto.*

The poets frequently make use of *áltri* for *altro*; example: *altri fu vágo di spiár tra le stélle, altri di seguir l' órme di fuggitíva fèra. altri d' atterrár órso,* Guarini, in the *Pastor Fido*.

CHAPTER V.

OF THE SYNTAX OF VERBS ([29]).

THE verbs, through every tense and mood (except the infinitive) ought, as we have already observed, to

---

[29] See Bottarelli's Exercises, on the Verbs, p. 40.

be preceded by a nominative case, either expressed or understood, with which they should agree in number and person. The nominative is expressed when we say, *io ámo, tu cánti, Piètro scríve;* understood, when they say, *cánto, andiámo, díco, rídono.*

The Italians, as well as the English, use the second person plural, though they address themselves but to a single person ; for example :

Fratèllo, avéte tòrto; Brother, you are in the wrong.

Pietro, avete ragióne; Peter, you are in the right.

And if we would speak in the third person, we must say, *V. S. (Vo' Signoría)* or *ella ha ragione.*

The verb active governs the accusative ; as, *stúdio la lezióne, áma la virtù.*

The verb passive requires an ablative after it ; as, the learned are esteemed by the ignorant ; *i dòtti sóno stimáti dagl' ignoránti.*

The verbs *to take away, to separate, to be distant from, to receive* and *obtain,* govern also an ablative and accusative ; as,

To take something from the hands ; *leváre quálche còsa dalle mani.*

To take from, is also translated in Italian by *prèndere a;* example : *mi présero il danáro,* or *présero al mio compágno quánto avea séco.*

To separate one from the other, *separáre l'un dall' altro.*

Get away from me, *scostátevi da me.*

I have received a letter from my father, *ho ricevúto una lèttera da mio pádre.*

I have obtained leave from the king, *ho ottenúto licènza dal re.*

*** The verbs *to come out, to depart, to come, to return,* govern a genitive and an ablative. The genitive, when the nouns have the definite article before them ; as I go out, *èsco;* I depart, *parto;* I come, *vèngo;* I return, *tórno;* from Paris, *di Parígi;* from France, *di Fráncia,* &c.

The ablative, when the nouns are preceded by the definite article ; as, I go, I depart, I come, I return from the garden, from the meadow, from the church ; *èsco, parto, vèngo, tórno, dal giardíno, dal prato, dalla chièsa,*

You must always put the particle *a* or *ad* after the verbs of motion ; as, *andáre, mandáre, inviáre, veníre,* when they precede an infinitive ; for example :

Let us go to see,	*andiámo a vedére.*
Send to look for,	*mandáte a cercáre.*
Come to ask for,	*veníte a domandáre.*

They do not say, *andiámo vedére, mandáte cercáre, veníte domandáre.* They make use of *ad* when the following verb begins with a vowel : as, let us go and give notice, *andiámo ad avvisáre,* &c.

After verbs, we must express *yes* and *no* by *di sì* and *di no;* and not by *che sì* and *che no;* for example :

I believe yes,	*crédo di sì.*
I believe not,	*credo di no.*
I say not,	*díco di no.*
I think not,	*pènso di no.*
I lay it is,	*scomméto di sì.*

Have you a mind to lay it is not ? *voléte scomméttere di no?*

I have observed in the first part, p. 90, that when we find the particle *if,* which in Italian is expressed by *se,* before the imperfect indicative, we must use the imperfect subjunctive in Italian ; examples : if I had, *se avéssi;* if we could, *se potéssimo;* and not *se avéva, se potevámo.*

This rule is not general, because we frequently are obliged to put the imperfect indicative after *se,* and not the imperfect subjunctive.

*** When we find in English *if* before a preterimperfect it is to be observed, that we speak either of a time past, or a time to come; as, *if I had riches, I was not master of them ; if I studied, it was to become learned:* in these two examples we speak of a time past; for which reason we must use the imperfect indicative, and say, *se avéva bèni, non n'èra padróne; se studiáva, èra per diventár dòtto.* But if we happened to speak of a future time, *if I studied, I should become learned: if I had riches, I would give something to the poor;* then we must make use of the imperfect subjunctive, and say, *se studiássi, diventerèi dòtto; se avéssi bèni, ne darèi ai pòveri;* because in the latter examples we speak by wish, and therefore we place the verbs in the optative ; and in the former we do not express ourselves either by wish or desire, but merely concerning a thing or time past.

₀ The English are apt to place the first imperfect of the subjunctive, where the Italians make use of the second ; for example :

He had done me a kindness ; the Italians will not say *m'avésse fatto un piacére*, but *m'avrèbbe fatto un piacere ;* becáuse one may say, *he would have done me a kindness.*

I had been in the wrong ; *avrèi avúto tòrto,* and not *avessi avuto torto ;* because one may say, *I should have been in the wrong.*

You had been blamed ; *saréste stato biasimáto,* and not *fóste stato biasimato ;* because *you had been* may be turned by *would have.*

N. B. That, to express in Italian *though that should be,* we must say, *quando ciò fósse,* and not *sarèbbe.* Because the phrase, *though that should be,* may be rendered by, *if that was ;* and as often as you can turn the second preterimperfect by the imperfect subjunctive, or the second preterpluperfect by the pluperfect subjunctive, you ought to do it ; and then those second preterimperfects are put in the subjunctive mood in Italian ; for example : *if I had been at Rome,* or *if I were at Rome, I should endeavour to live with the Romans.* Note. Here you may turn the phrase, and say, *if I were at Rome ;* in Italian you must say, *se fóssi stato a Róma, o se fossi a Roma, procurerèi di víver co' Románi.*

₀ The Italians use the future tense after the conjunction *if,* when they speak of a future action ; but the English, the present ; example ; to-morrow, if I have time, *dománi se avrò tèmpo,* and not *se ho ;* if he comes we shall see him, *se verrà lo vedrémo,* and not *se viène, lo vedremo.*

N.B. When they speak of visiting a person at his house, they use the verb *veníre* instead of *andáre ;* for example, I will go to-morrow to your house, *verrò da voi dománi.*

₀ When we forbid a person, to whom we say *thee* and *thou,* to do a thing, we ought to use the infinitive and not the imperative ; for example : do not thou speak, *non parlare ;* do not thou do that, *non far quésto ;* say thou nothing, *non dir niènte ;* do not thou stop, *non ti fermare.*

A conjunction between two verbs obliges the last to
be of the same number, person and tense as the first;
for example, the king wills and commands, *il re vuòle e
cománda;* I see and I know, *védo e conósco.*

---

*To know when to make use of the Subjunctive, read
attentively the following remarks.*   .

*** 1. The conjunction *che* generally requires the
subjunctive after it; for example: *bisógna che Piètro
cánti, créda, sènta, èsca,* &c.

2. Take notice, that *che* makes all the words to which
it is joined become conjunctions; as, *acciochè*, to the end
that; *prima che, avánti che,* before that; *benchè,* although; *dáto che, suppósto che,* suppose that; which
govern the subjunctive; for example: *acciochè, prima
che, benchè, suppósto che, io párli, io èsca,* &c.

*** 3. In order, therefore, to know when to put the
verb which comes after *che*, that, in the indicative, and,
when in the subjunctive, take particular notice of the
following examples : that I may speak, that I may love,
that I may sing.

Now these verbs, *speak, love, sing,* which are after
che, that, are in one sense in the indicative, and in another in the subjunctive mood.

The way, then, of not mistaking the one for the other
is, to suppose that the verb *fare,* to make, or to do,
stands in the place of the verb that follows *che.*

The verb *fare* makes, in the present of the indicative,
fo, fái, fa; facciámo, fáte, fánno.

The same verb *fare* makes, in the subjunctive, *fáccia,
faccia, faccia; facciámo, facciáte, fácciano.*

To know whether the above examples, *speak, love,
sing,* are in the indicative or subjunctive, put the verb
fare in their stead; example: *mio fratèllo vuòl ch'io
párli:* if, instead of the verb *parli,* you put the verb
fare, you will say, *mio fratello vuol ch'io fáccia;* the
verb *faccia* is in the subjunctive, consequently *parli*
will be in the same mood.

I shall give another example, in which the verb that
follows *che* will be in the indicative, and not in the sub-

junctive : *mio fratèllo créde ch'io párlo*. Instead of *parlo*, put the verb *fáre*; you will say, *mio fratello crede ch'io fo* : the verb *io fo* is in the indicative, therefore *párlo* must be in the indicative also ; and so of the rest of the verbs.

Hence, according to the first example, you will say, *mio fratello vuòl ch'io párli* ; and, according to the second, *mio fratèllo crede ch'io párlo* : *parlo* in the indicative, and *parli* in the subjunctive.

Observe, that to speak Italian correctly, you should make use of the subjunctive in both cases ; as, *vuòl ch'io párli*, and *créde ch'io parli*. The difference between these two examples is, that in the latter you may sometimes make use of the indicative, though not grammatically ; in the former you must always employ the subjunctive ; you therefore may say, *mio fratèllo crede che parli* or *parlo;* and *vuòl che párli*, and not *parlo*. In order rightly to know whether you are to make use of the indicative or of the subjunctive, attend to the following remarks :

*** 4. The verbs which signify *will, desire, command, permission, incertitude,* and *fear,* followed by the conjunction *che* or *se,* require the subjunctive after them ; for example : I will, I desire, I command, I permit, my brother to love, speak, see, go out, &c. *vòglio, desìdero, comándo, permétto, che mio fratèllo ámi, párli, véda, èsca,* &c. I fear he may not sing, he may not say, &c. *tèmo che non canti, che non dica,* &c.

When the verb expresses an operation of the mind, which consists in being certain of any thing, the verb which follows ought to be put in the indicative ; *so che sièle rèo,* I know you are guilty ; but we ought to say, *dubito se sia vero o no,* I doubt whether it be true or not, instead of *se è vero.*

*** 5. After the conjunction *although,* the English sometimes use the subjunctive ; as, *although he be an honest man, although he may do that.*

In Italian you must take care how you express *though* or *although;* if it is by *benchè*, you must put the subjunctive after it ; for example : though he is an honest man, *benchè sia galantuòmo;* though he does this, *benchè fáccia questo.*

†‡† But if you render *although* or *though* by *sebbène*, then you must not use the subjunctive, but the indicative; for example : though he is an honest man, *sebbèn è galantuòmo*, and not *sia;* though he does this, *sebbèn fa quèsto*, and not *fáccia.*

₊ 6. When you meet with two verbs, the former of which is preceded by the particle *non*, and the second by *che*, you must put the latter in the subjunctive; for example: I did not know you loved, *non sapéva che amáste;* I do not believe he studies, *non crédo che stúdi;* I do not think he walks, *non credo che cammini.*

₊ 7. When the pronoun *qual* precedes a verb, and you do not speak by an interrogation, you must put the following verb in the subjunctive; for example: not knowing what was the season proper for sowing, *non sapèndo qual fòsse la stagióne pròpria da semináre;* I do not see which is his intention, *non védo qual sia l'intenzióne súa;* I do not know which are your books, *non so quali síano i vòstri libri.*

But if we speak by interrogation, you must put the verb in the indicative; for example : which is yours? *qual' è 'l vòstro?*

₊ The articles *del, dello, della, degli,* &c. coming after a verb, are apt to perplex those who learn Italian : but to explain the matter,

₊ Observe, that the Italians often put the genitive after a verb active; for example: give me some *or* of the bread, *dátemi del pane;* eat some *or* of the pie, *mangiáte del pasticcio.* You observe by these examples, the genitive is put after a verb active; but observe at the same time, we are not speaking of a whole, but only of a part,'for *give me some pie, some bread, some wine, some meat,* denotes only a *bit*, or *some of the pie, bread, wine* or *meat.*

If we would speak of a whole, we must not express the articles *del, dello, della,* &c.; for example : I have eaten petty patties, *ho mangiáto pasticcétti;* I have seen men, *ho vedúto uòmini;* you owe me a hundred crowns; give me bread, wine and meat in payment, *mi dovéte cènto scúdi ; dátemi pane, vino e carne in pagaménto.*

In the last examples, the articles *del, dello, della,*

&c. are not expressed, because we speak of a sum, a quantity, a whole, that is not separated, and which has no regard or relation but to the person who speaks.

₊ Note also, that after the particle *si*, it is, or they, we must not express the articles *dél, déllo, délla*, &c. ; for example : they see men, *si védono uòmini;* they tell bad news, *si dicono cattíve nuòve.*

You must not express the articles *del, dello, della, degli,* &c. after the prepositions, as the French express *du, de la, de l', des;* for example : *avec des soldats* Fr., *con soldáti,* with soldiers; *pour des paysans* Fr., *per contadíni,* for peasants ; *dans des paniers* Fr., *in canèstri,* in baskets ; *sur des chevaux* Fr., *sópra caválli,* upon horses :

₊ But if the articles *del, dello, della,* signifying *concerning;* as, *they speak of your affairs,* that is to say, *concerning your affairs,* the article must then be expressed ; for example : they speak of you, *si parla di voi;* they treat of war, *si trátta della guèrra;* they talked of affairs of state, *si parláva dégli affári di stato.*

It is therefore true, that there are particular cases, in which the articles are not expressed ; nay, it is even elegant to omit them.

N.B. We may add to the above rule, that in general when the article is omitted in English, it is also omitted in Italian.

The verb impersonal *there is, there was, there will be,* has been explained at length, among the impersonal verbs, in the first part, p. 151.

CHAPTER VI.

OF THE SYNTAX OF PARTICIPLES ([30]).

Every participle in the Italian language ends in *to* or *so ;* as, *amáto, credúto, finíto, sólito, árso, préso, scéso, rimáso.*

The participles active that follow the verb *avére,* must end in *o ;* as,

---

[30] See Exercises, p. 68 and 71.

I have seen the king,	*ho vedúto il re,*
I have seen the queen,	*ho veduto la regina.*
I had loved books,	*avéva amáto i libri.*
I had carried the letters,	*aveva portáto le lèttere.*

We meet with authors who sometimes make the participles agree with the thing of which they are speaking; as, the sun had lost his rays, *il sole aveva perdúti i suòi ràggi.*

If the substantive is before the participle, they ought to agree together; examples : the books that I have composed, *i libri che ho compósti,* the letter that I have written, *la lèttera che ho scritta.* One may also say, *il sole aveva perduto i suòi raggi,* &c.; *i libri che ho compósto; la lettera che ho scritto.* But it is more advisable to follow the above rule.

*** If it be a verb neuter, the participle ought always to terminate in *o;* examples : the king has dined *il re ha pranzáto;* the queen has supped, *la regina ha cenáto;* the soldiers have trembled, *i soldáti hánno tremáto;* my sisters have slept, *le mie sorèlle hanno dormito;* your friends have laughed, *i vòstri amici hanno riso.*

When the active participle happens to precede an infinitive, it must be terminated in *o;* for example : *il giúdice gli ha fatto tagliáre la tèsta,* the judge has caused his head to be cut off; *mia sorella ha credúto partíre,* my sister had like to have gone.

The participles passive, which are joined to the tenses of the verb *èssere,* agree with the antecedent; that is to say, those participles must be put in the same gender and number as the preceding substantive; for example : the captain is praised, *il capitáno è lodáto;* virtue is esteemed, *la virtù è stimáta;* the idle will be blamed, *i pigri saránno biasimáti;* your jewels are sold, *le vòstre giòie sóno vendúte.*

*** Take notice, it is more elegant in Italian to use the tenses of the verb *veníre,* instead of those of the verb *èssere,* before a participle ; for example : he is esteemed, *viène stimato,* for *è stimato;* he shall be praised, *verrà lodato,* for *sarà lodato :* they shall be blamed, *verránno biasimáti,* for *saranno biasimati ;* and so of all the tenses, and all the persons.

We generally suppress the gerunds, *having* and *being,* before the participles; for example: having said so, *détto quésto;* the sermon being ended, *finíta la prèdica.*

*** In attempting to explain or translate an Italian book into English, we must remember that the participles frequently occur without any tenses of the verbs *avére* or *èssere* before them; as *il quále, intéso 'l diségno, maravigliátisi i cònsoli.* Then it is a sure sign that the gerunds *avèndo* or *essèndo* are suppressed: and to explain it properly, we must render it as if it were, *il quale avendo inteso 'l disegno; essèndosi maravigliáti i cònsoli.*

We must also observe, that although *avèndo* and *essèndo* are suppressed before the participles, we must not suppress the conjunctive pronouns, nor the monosyllables that ought to follow the gerunds *avendo* and *essendo,* but we should put them after the participles: for example, having seen it, *avèndolo vedúto:* in suppressing *avendo,* we must say, *vedútolo;* being aware of it, *essèndosene accòrto:* in suppressing *essendo,* we transpose *sene* after the participle, and say *accòrtosene.*

It is better to place the nominative after the gerund than before; as the king being a hunting, *essèndo 'l re alla cáccia;* the soldiers fighting valiantly, *combattèndo valorosaménte i soldati.*

If after the verb there is an accusative, or any other case, we must put the nominative before the verb; for instance, the soldiers being afraid of the enemy; in Italian we must say, *i soldati temèndo gl' inimíci:* and not *temendo i soldati gl' inimici.*

CHAPTER VII.

OF THE SYNTAX OF ADVERBS AND PREPOSITIONS.

At is expressed in Italian by *da,* or *in casa.*

When *at* is expressed by *da,* we put the pronouns personal after it; examples: at our house, *da nói;* at your house, *da vói;* at my house, *da me;* at thy house, *da te;* at his house, *da lúi;* at her house, *da lèi;* at their house, masc. *da lóro;* at their house, fem. *da ésse.*

₀ When *at* is expressed by *in casa*, instead of the personal pronoun, we must use the possessive pronouns ; as, at our house, *in casa nòstra ;* at your house, *in casa vòstra ;* at his or her house, *in casa sua ;* at thy house, *in casa tua ;* in their house, *in casa loro.*

₀ If after *at* there be an article or a possessive pronoun, you must render *at* by *dál, dállo, dálla, da', dái, dágli, dálle,* or else by *in cása,* with the articles of the genitive ; for example,

At the prince's,	{ *dal príncipe,* or *in cása del principe.*
At the scholar's,	{ *dallo scoláre,* or *in casa dello scolare.*
At the sister's,	{ *dalla sorèlla,* or *in casa della sorella.*
At the men's house,	{ *dagli uòmini,* or *in casa degli uomini.*
At my friend's,	{ *dal mio amico,* or *in casa del mio amico.*
At his relations,	{ *da' suòi parènti,* or *in casa de' suoi parenti.*
At the abbe's,	{ *dal signór abáte,* or *in casa del signor abate.*

The indefinite article *di* is not expressed after the adverbs of quantity, *how much, how many, much, little, as much as, more,* &c. ; but these adverbs are made to agree with the following noun, as if they were adjectives ; for example :

How much time,	*quánto tèmpo.*
How much meat,	*quanta carne.*
How many soldiers,	*quanti soldáti.*
A great deal of pleasure,	*mólto piacére.*
A great deal of pain,	*molta péna.*
A great many men,	*molti uòmini.*
A little time,	*pòco tèmpo.*
A little fever,	*poca fèbbre.*
So much patience,	*tánta paziènza.*
As much courage,	*tanto ánimo.*
A great many persons,	*mólte persóne.*
How many coaches,	*quánte carròzze*
I have no more hope,	*non ho più speránza.*

₊ *A great deal of*, is frequently expressed in Italian by *gran :* for example,

I have had a great deal of pain,	*ho avúto gran péna.*
A great deal of rain,	*gran piòggia.*
A great deal of time,	*gran tèmpo.*
A great deal of pleasure,	*gran piacére.*

₊ *A little of*, is rendered in Italian by *pòco di :* as, a little bread, *un poco di pane ;* a little of compassion, *un poco di pietà.*

Quì and *quà* signify, here. *Quà* is joined with verbs of motion ; example : *venite quà, passáte quà,* come here, pass here.

The Italians frequently use *costì* and *costà*, to point out the place where the person is, to whom we speak or write ; as *V. S. mi scriva di costì* or *di costà ;* See *Lodovico Dólce, nel capítolo dégli avvèrbj locáli :* yet I should prefer *costì* to *costà.* The best writers have often followed this rule.

₊ The Italians frequently use the adverb *oggi* to express *afternoon*, or *after dinner ;* for example : come and see me after dinner, *venite òggi a vedérmi, venite oggi da me.*

Important Remarks on the Particle si, *it is* or
they, &c. (³¹)

Si, used with a verb impersonal, signifies *it is*, or *they ;* examples : *si dìce,* it is said, *or* they say ; they speak, *si párla.*

They not is expressed by *non si :* as, *non si dìce,* they do not say ; *non si párla*, they do not speak.

We of it, they of it, is expressed by *se ne :* as, *se ne saprà quálche còsa,* they will know something of it.

They not of it, is expressed by *non se ne :* as *non se ne parla,* they do not speak of it.

₊ Note, learners are greatly at a loss how to express in Italian, *they us of it, they you of it, they him of it, they me of it, they thee of it,* &c. ; yet there is nothing more easy, if you but turn the phrase by the

---

(³¹) See Bottarelli's Exercises, p. 89.

tenses of the verb *èssere*, to be; for example, to render *they will speak to us of it*, we must turn it and say, *it will be spoken of to us, cene sarà parláto.*

They { will write to you of it,   *ve ne sarà scritto.*
      speak to him of it,   *gliéne vièn parláto.*
      write to us of it,   *ce ne viène scritto.*

They promise me some, *me ne sóno proméssi,* or *me ne vien promesso,* or *me ne vèngono promessi.*

By these last examples you find that it is more elegant to use the verb *venire* than the verb *èssere.*

Remember that the pronouns, *lo, la, li, le,* are not expressed after the particle *si;* for example : they say so, *si dice,* and not *si lo dice ;* it will be known, *si conoscerà,* or *si saprà ;* they are seen frequently together, *sóno vedúti spésso insième.* See at p. 211, what has been said concerning the articles *del, della, degli, delle, &c.*

Observe, nevertheless, that the best writers have often, and even with elegance, expressed these pronouns ; but at the present they are laid aside except by poets who use them sometimes to help the measure of their verse. Hence, we no longer say *e' si dice,* but simply *si dice; e' si conoscerà,* or *la si conoscerà,* but *si conoscerà.* Here are the letters, they will be read, *ècco le lèttere, si leggeránno.*

The conjunctive pronouns must be transposed whenever the particle *si* comes before them, as I have already observed, p. 203.

₊ Yet this rule for transposing the conjunctive pronouns, when the particle *si* comes before them, is not general ; for there are some phrases in which the conjunctive pronouns must by no means be expressed, but the phrase must be changed.

When the conjunctive pronouns are placed after the particle *si,* and there is neither a noun, nor a case after the verb that follows, you must then change the phrase without ever expressing the particle *si;* as, they ask for me, *sòno domandáto,* I am asked for; they seek you, *sièle cercáto,* you are sought for ; they will praise us, *sarémo lodáti,* we shall be praised.

But if there happen to be a case after the verb, as *they ask me for a crown,* you should express the conjunctive pronoun, and say, *mi si domànda uno scudo,* or *mi viène domandato uno scudo;* they ask some bread of you, *vi si dománda pane;* they will commend virtue to us, *ci sarà lodáta la virtù.*

*** If the conjunctive pronouns, that come after the particle *si*, be followed by a verb in the preterperfect definite, the phrase must be turned by the verb *èssere*, and you must put the preter-definite *fu* or *fúrono*, according as you are speaking in the singular or the plural; as, they gave me a book, *mi fu dato un libro;* they sent me letters, *mi fúrono mandate lèttere;* they wrote us a letter, *ci fu scritta una lettera.* Sometimes the phrase is turned thus, they sent us to Rome, *fúmmo mandati a Róma;* they blamed you, *fóste biasimáto,* or, speaking in the third person, *ella fu biasimata.*

When the third persons of the verb *avere*, to have, are preceded by the particle *si*, and after those third persons there follows a particle, you are to render the third persons of the verb *to have*, by those of the verb *essere*, to be; putting them in the same number with the thing mentioned; as, if they said so, *se si è détto quésto;* if they had read the letters, *se si fóssero lètte le lèttere.*

When they shall have taken the town, *quando la città sarà présa.*.

See, at page 149, the remarks on impersonal verbs, with the article *si*.

But when the tenses of the verb *to have* are preceded by the particle *si*, and there is no particle after the verb *to have*, we must use the tenses of the verb *avere*, instead of those of the verb *essere;* examples: they have some bread to eat, *si ha del pane,* or *pane da mangiáre;* they have servants to wait, *si hanno servitóri per servíre;* but it is much better to omit the particle *si* in both cases, and say *hanno.*

For the better explanation of the foregoing important remarks on the particle *si*, it will be proper, I apprehend, to add the following observations:

The first is, that this particle *si* must not be used with reciprocal verbs, but the phrase should be turned; otherwise you would have two *si's* joined together, which would be disagreeable. Thus you do not say, *si si sèrve delle creatúre per offènder Dío,* they make use of the creatures to offend God; but *úno si sèrve*, or *l' uòmo si serve*, &c.

The second is, that constant experience shows it to be extremely difficult for those who are beginning to learn Italian to express, *they me of it, they thee of it, they him of it, they us of it, they you of it, they them of it*, joined to a verb in the compound preterite. I shall therefore give here the indicative entire, which may serve as a general rule for all the other moods and tenses; therefore I shall say:

Indicative Present.

They write to me of it,	*me ne viène*, or *me n' è scritto*.
They write to thee of it,	*te ne viene*, or *te n' è scritto*.
They write to him of it,	*gliéne viene*, or *glien' è scritto*.
They write to us of it,	*ce ne viene*, or *ce n' è scritto*.
They write to you of it,	*ve ne viene*, or *ve n' è scritto*.
They write to them of it,	*ne viene*, or *n' è scritto loro*.

In the other tenses, I shall only put the first person singular, as it is easy to know the rest by means of the present indicative, which is conjugated entire.

Imperfect.

They wrote to me of it, *me ne veníva*, or *me n' èra scritto*, &c.

Preter-definite.

They wrote to me of it, *me ne vénne*, or *me ne fu scritto*, &c.

N. B. In the compound tenses we do not make use of the verb *veníre*, but of *èssere*. Thus,

Preterperfect.

They have written to me of it, *me n' è stato scritto*, &c.

Pluperfect.

They had written to me of it, *me n' èra stato scritto*, &c.

Future.

They will write to me of it, *me ne sarà scritto*, &c.

I shall insert here another indicative, to clear up the

difficulty of *mi si, ti si, gli si,* &c. they me, they thee, they him; and I will say thus,

Indicative Present.

They ask me, or I am asked for an Italian or French Grammar printed at London.	*Mi si dománda,* or *mi viène domandáta una grammática Italiána o Francése, stampáta in Lóndra.*
They ask thee, &c.	*Ti si dománda, &c.* or *ti viène domandáto or domandáta* (see note [33]).
They ask him, &c.	*Gli si domanda, &c.* or *gli viene domandato or domandata, &c.*
They ask us, &c.	*Ci si domanda, &c.* or *ci viene domandato or domandata, &c.*
They ask you, &c.	*Vi si domanda, &c.* or *vi viene domandato or domandata, &c.*
They ask them, &c.	*Si domanda lóro, &c.* or *viene domandato or domandata loro, &c.*

Imperfect.

They did ask me, *or they* were asking me, &c.	*Mi si domandáva* or *mi veníva domandáto or domandáta.*

Preter-definite.

They asked me, &c.	*Mi si domandò* or *mi vénne domandato or domandata.*

Preter-perfect.

They have asked me,	*M' è*	*stato domandato.* *stata domandata.*
	Mi s'è	*domandato or domandata.*

L 2

Pluperfect.

They had asked me, {
  M' èra {*stato domandáto.*
  stata domandata.}
  Mi s'era {*domandato* or *do-mandata.*}
}

Future.

They will ask me, {
  Mi si domanderà, or *mi verrà domandato* or *doman-data.*
}

*** Observe, that in using the verb *venire* instead of *èssere*, you do not express the particle *si*.

The prepositions govern some cases, as may be seen in the seventh chapter of the first part, where we treated of prepositions.

The Italians frequently use the particle *pure* only as an ornament of speech, as, *dite pure quél che vi piacerà,* say what (or) whatever you please.

It is customary for them to use *pur* or *pure* when the English repeat the verb in the imperative mood ; as, go, go then, *andáte pure;* give, give then, *date pure.*

Not is always rendered by *non;* example : *non dite niènte,* do not say anything (*or* say nothing).

In, before a noun, is expressed by *in;* example : *in Fráncia,* in France.

Some or *any,* before a verb, is expressed by *ne;* as, will you have some or any ? *ne voléte?*

In before the article *the* singular and plural, as also before pronouns possessive, is expressed by *nél, néllo, nélla, néi,* &c., as I have already remarked, page 42 ; example : in his book, *nel súo libro.*

However, *in* is generally expressed by *in;* as, in Paris, *in Parígi;* in me, *in me.*

*** Observe, that as often as *in* (or within) comes before numeral nouns to mark a time to come, it must be expressed by *trà* or *frà;* examples : in two hours, *frà due óre;* in three months, *frà tre mési.*

*** But if *in* precedes numeral nouns, without mark-ing the time, it must be expressed by *in;* examples :

in three bottles, *in tre bottiglie;* in a garden, *in un giardino.*

Very is expressed by *mólto,* &c.; examples :

He is very merry,   *è molto allégro.*

It is very hot,   *fa molto caldo.*

*** *A great deal of,* or *much,* is rendered by *gran* or *grande;* examples : there is a great deal of folly, *v'è gran pazzía;* he has a great deal of vivacity, *ha grande spírito.*

☞ *More,* or *more of,* is expressed by *maggióre* whenever you can turn *more* by *greater* or *more great;* examples : we must have more courage, *bisógna avere maggior corággio;* it may be turned thus, *we must have greater courage;* with more boldness, *con maggior ardire;* it may be turned, *with greater boldness.*

*** When *more* denotes a great number or quantity, it is expressed in Italian by *maggiór número di,* or *maggiór quantitâ di;* as, we must have more soldiers, more men, more wine ; *bisogna avere maggior número,* or *maggior quantità di soldáti, d'uòmini, di vino.*

*** When *more than* happens to precede a word of time, you may put *più* at the end or at the beginning of the phrase ; examples : it is more than ten years, *sóno dièci anni e più;* it is more than an hour, *è un' óra e più;* you may likewise say *sono più di dièci anni, è più d'un' óra.*

*** The conjunctive *so,* before adjectives and adverbs, is rendered in Italian by *così* or *sì,* with a grave accent : examples : so great, *così grande; così tardi;* or, *sì grande, sì tardi: sì fatto,* masc. *sì fatta,* fem. signifies *such* : they likewise use *così;* as *cóme, siccóme.*

FOURTH TREATISE.

REMARKS ON SOME VERBS AND PREPOSITIONS,
which have different significations.

THE following Phrases contain great part of the Italian Idioms, which constitute the chief elegance and beauty of that language.

Different significations of Andáre.

We may use the verb *andáre*, through all its tenses, to express all the actions of the verbs of motion, by putting the same verbs of motion in the gerund, and the verb *andáre* in the tense and person that the verb of motion ought to be in ; as,

He runs, instead of *corre, va corrèndo.*

They take a walk, *spasséggiano* or *vanno spasseggiándo.*

He will tell every where, *andrà dicèndo da per tutto.*

They must run, *bisógna che vádano corrèndo.*

Make use of the verb *Andáre,* through all the tenses, for the following phrases.

Andár d>ètro, signifies to follow, to press, or to solicit a [person
.. *male,* to perish
.. *vía,* to go away
.. *in èstasi,* to be in an ecstacy
.. *in còllera,* to put one's self in a passion [reason
.. *cercándo il pélo nell' uòvo,* to censure without
.. *a galla,* to float upon the water
.. *in pace,* to go in peace

Andar in mal' òra,	to perish, to be ruined
.. *avánti,*	to go before
.. *alla lúnga,*	to be tedious
.. *alle córte,*	to make haste
.. *innánzi,*	to advance, improve
.. *attórno,*	to go about
.. *altièro,*	to be proud, or stately [thing
.. *dìetro ad una còsa,*	to stand trifling with any
.. *colla pèggio,*	to be worse
.. *in semènza,*	to run to seed
.. *per la ménte,*	to come into one's mind
.. *di mal in pèggio,*	to go on from bad to worse
A lúngo andare,	at the long run
Ci va della vita,	life is at stake
Andar mal in arnése,	to be ill dressed
.. *a gámbe leváte,*	to squander
.. *a cavállo,*	to ride on horseback
.. *a dilètto,*	to go to be merry
.. *a dipòrto,*	to go sporting
.. *a sollázzo,*	to go merry-making
.. *a spásso,*	to go to take a walk
.. *a giróne,*	to ramble about
.. *a fílo,*	to march in order
.. *a láto,*	to go aside
.. *all' árca,*	to put in pawn
.. *alla búsca,*	to go a plundering
.. *alla mázza,*	to go to the slaughter
.. *all' oscuro,*	to walk in ignorance
.. *a mónte,*	to prove vain
.. *a ónde,*	to go waving
.. *a pélo,*	to succeed in one's wishes
.. *a ruba,*	to go a stealing
.. *a ruòta,*	to go a wheeling, or to hover
.. *a sacco,*	to be plundered
.. *a secónda,*	to go down the tide
.. *a scòsse,*	to go a reeling
.. *a sinistra,*	to miscarry by the way
.. *a sòldo,*	to go for a soldier
.. *a sparvière,*	to go a fowling
.. *a vanga*	to thrive well

Andar a véla,	to sail
.. *a vèrso,*	to succeed well
.. *a zónzo,*	to lie rolling, as a ship
.. *a bándo,*	to be published by proclamation
.. *barcolóne*	to go staggering
.. *carpóne,*	to go crawling
.. *col calzáre di piómbo,*	to go cautiously
.. *con le bèlle,*	to go handsomely to work [the stake
.. *cóme la bíscia all' incánto,*	to go as a bear to
.. *con la pièna,*	to be on the strongest side
.. *di palo in frásca,*	to leap from bough to bough
.. *di buòne gámbe,*	to set willingly about a thing
.. *dicèndo,*	to publish *or* report
.. *fallíto il pensièro,*	to fail in one's purpose
.. *gattolóne,*	to go groping
.. *gròsso,*	to look big
.. *in béstia,*	to fall into a passion
.. *in busca,*	to go a seeking
.. *in cérca,*	to search up and down
.. *in córso,*	to go a cruising
.. *in fáscio,*	
.. *in còsa materiále,* }	to go to work
.. *in negòzio,*	
.. *in ròlta,*	to be routed
.. *in síncope,*	to fall into a swoon
.. *in súcchio,*	to have one's mouth water
.. *in tráccia,*	to go a tracing
.. *in vòlta,*	to go ranging about
.. *alla rónda,*	to walk the rounds
.. *per il mondo,*	to travel up and down the world
.. *per la pésta,*	to follow the vulgar fashion
.. *per la piána,*	to go the straightforward way
.. *per filo,*	to be forced to do a thing
.. *piággia a piággia,*	to sail close to the shore
.. *ramingo,*	to be wandering
.. *rattenúto,*	to go warily to work
.. *spanto,*	to be extravagantly dressed
.. *sópra le parò!e,*	to believe fair words
.. *strétto,*	to go about a thing sparingly
.. *tapinándo,*	to go a begging
.. *tentóne,*	to grope about

Andar a vuòto,	to miss one's aim
.. *sene préso alle grída,*	to believe every idle report
Quésto non mi va,	that does not please me

Different significations of Dare.

Dáre,	signifies, to give, to fight, to strike
.. *d'òcchio,*	to cast one's eyes on [one
.. *addòsso ad úno,*	to throw one's self upon any
.. *a gámbe,*	to run away
.. *nélla réte,*	to fall into the snare
.. *le carte,*	to deal or give the cards
.. *ánimo,*	to give courage, or encourage
.. *si'l cuòre,* or *l'ánimo,*	to have courage
.. *féde,*	to believe
.. *ad intèndere,*	to make one believe
.. *del tu,*	to thee-and-thou one
.. *in nulla,*	not to succeed
.. *si l'ácqua a' pièdi,*	to praise one's self
.. *in luce,*	to publish
.. *si a fare,*	to set about a thing
.. *si pensièro*	to take care for
.. *del signóre,*	to call one a gentleman
.. *del furfánte,*	to call one a rogue
.. *paròla,*	to promise
.. *ne' ladri,*	to fall into the hands of thieves
.. *la búrla ad úno,*	to laugh at a person
.. *lèva,*	to provoke
.. *in prèstito,*	to lend
.. *fuòco,*	to set on fire
.. *sicurtà,*	to give bail
.. *in istravagánze,*	to talk nonsense
.. *nel mátto,*	to play the madman
.. *la quádra,*	to criticise
.. *la cáccia,*	to put to flight
.. *princípio* or *fine,*	to begin *or* to end
.. *cónto,*	to give an account
.. *si allo stúdio,*	to apply one's self to study [shadow
.. *calci al vènto, e pugni all' ária,*	to fight with one's

L 5

[one's self

Dar-si la záppa su'l piède, e la mazza in cápo, to wrong
   .. si bel tèmpo,   to divert one's self

[every one's business

   .. di bócca da per tutto,   to concern one's self with
   .. da parláre,   to make people speak
   .. da beccáre,   to feed poultry
   .. a credènza,   to sell upon credit
   .. addiètro,   to give back
   .. ádito,   to give access to
   .. alla máno,   to bribe
   .. all' árme,   to cry out for help
   .. a pigióne,   to let out for rent
   .. a ruba,   to give up to plunder
   .. assúnto,   to give charge of
   .. a táglio,   to strike with the edge
   .. a travèrso,   to hit across
   .. a vedére,   to give one to understand

[vain hopes

   .. baggiáne, or gonfiáre alcúno,   to puff one up with
   .. baldánza,   to embolden
   .. bando,   to banish by proclamation
   .. bastonáte,   to beat with a stick
   .. briga,   to trouble one
   .. cagióne,   to give cause
   .. campo,   to give liberty
   .. capo,   to come to the end of the matter
   .. capo mano,   to go beyond reason in a business
   .. caròte,   to make one believe any thing
   .. che pensáre,   to give cause of suspicion
   .. compiménto,   to finish
   .. credènza,   to give credit to
   .. cròllo,   to shake
   .. da bére,   to give drink
   .. da dormire,   to give one a night's lodging
   .. da mangiáre,   to give one some food
   .. da rídere,   to give cause of laughter
   .. de' calci,   to kick
   .. delle bòtte,   to beat
   .. delle calcágna,   to spur one, to kick
   .. delle coltelláte,   to stab with a knife
   .. delle mani,   to strike with one's hands

Dáre delle púgna,	to cuff
.. *déntro,*	to fall to
.. *di bròcca,*	to hit the nail on the head
.. *di còzzo,*	to butt as sheep do
.. *di gráppo,*	to snatch at
.. *di máno,*	to lay hold of
.. *di mira,*	to take aim at
.. *da parlár di sè,*	to give occasion to be talked of
.. *di pénna,*	to cancel a writing
.. *di pètto,*	to hit with one's breast
.. *di piátto,*	to strike flat
.. *di píglio,*	to catch hold suddenly of
.. *di punta,*	to hit with a thrust
.. *di stoccáta,*	to give a thrust
.. *fastídio,*	to molest
.. *finòcchio,*	to give fair words
.. *fóndo,*	to sink
.. *fondo alla 'ròba,*	to waste one's property
.. *fórma,*	to shape
.. *il battésimo,*	to baptize
.. *il buòn anno,*	to wish a happy new year
.. *il buon giórno,*	to bid one good-morrow
.. *il buon viággio,*	to wish one a good journey
.. *il buon arrivo,*	to bid one welcome
.. *il cane,*	to watch one
.. *il compìto,*	to give an end to
.. *il cuòre ad una còsa,*	to apply one's self to a thing
.. *il dòsso,*	to turn one's back
.. *il mòtto,*	to pass one's word
.. *il passo,*	to give free passage
.. *il viso,*	to turn one's eyes on any thing
.. *in prestánza,*	to lend
.. *indúgio,*	to put off time
.. *in sèrbo,*	to give in keeping
.. *in su la vóce,*	to bid one speak lower
.. *in tèrra,*	to run a-ground
.. *in úno,*	to meet with one by chance
.. *la bála, dar la bèrta,*	to mock one
.. *la ben venúta,*	to bid one welcome
.. *buòna mano,*	to give for drink
.. *la còrda,*	to give the strappado, to be troublesome
.. *la fava,*	to give one's consent

L 6

Dáre la mála pásqua,	to vex one sadly
.. *l' allòdola,* ⎫	
.. *la quádra,* ⎬	to coax, to flatter, to give fair words
.. *la sòia,* ⎭	
.. *la mala ventúra,*	to wish a man ill luck
.. *la mano,*	to give a helping hand
.. *la mano,*	to marry
.. *passo,*	to despatch
Dar-si spasso,	to amuse one's self
Dare l' anèllo,	to marry
.. *la palma,*	to yield the victory
.. *la paríglia,*	to give as good as he brings
.. *la spínta,*	to push one
.. *la pòsta,*	to appoint the time or place
.. *la salda,*	to stiffen or starch
.. *la strétta a qualcúno,*	to overreach one
.. *la tratta,*	to give leave to export goods
.. *la vóce,*	to raise a report
.. *la vòlta,*	to turn as milk does, to overturn
.. *la vòlta al canto,*	to lose one's wits
.. *le calcágna,*	to run away
.. *le mòsse,*	to give a racer a start
.. *la spálle,*	to take to one's heels
.. *le prése,*	to let one take his choice
.. *l' último cròllo,*	to fall down dead
.. *martèllo,*	to make one jealous or suspicious
.. *mènda,*	to find fault
.. *mòdo,*	to help or support one
.. *nel berságlio,*	to hit the mark
.. *nell' idròpico,*	to fall into a dropsy
.. *nelle mani,*	to fall into the hands
.. *nelle scattáte,*	to fall into bad company
.. *nel vino,*	to find out the design of a thing
.. *nóia,*	to tire one
.. *nóme,*	to spread a report
.. *nórma,*	to prescribe a rule
.. *òglio,*	to soothe one
.. *ómbra,*	to give suspicion
.. *òpera,*	to endeavour at a thing
.. *parte,*	to share or acquaint
.. *passáto,*	to omit
.. *pasto,*	to feed one

SOME VERBS AND PREPOSITIONS.

Dáre per Dío,	to give for God's sake
.. ricápito,	to deliver safely
.. sèsto,	to put in order
.. spálla,	to abet
.. stènto,	to give cause of sorrow
.. un carpíno,	to beat one soundly
.. vista,	to seem to do a thing
.. vita,	to give time or life
.. una finta,	to make a feint
.. una gira vòlta,	to take a turn
.. un' occhiáta,	to cast an eye on
.. un grifóne,	to strike one in the mouth
.. un pax tecum,	to stun one with a blow
.. -la vinta,	to yield the victory
.. -si a,	to apply one's self to
.. si a che si sía,	to be for anything
.. si a quálche còsa,	to give one's self up to anything
.. si a crédere,	to believe
.. si a dilètti,	to give one's self up to pleasure
.. si ad intèndere,	to flatter one's self
.. si ad úno,	to give one's self up to one
.. si attórno,	to go the round
.. si briga, nóia, fastídio,	to trouble one's self
.. s' in prèda,	to yield one's self as a prey
.. s' in úno,	to refer one's self to one
.. si maraviglia,	to wonder at
.. si martèllo,	to vex one's self
.. si pace,	to live quietly
.. si vanto,	to brag, to boast

Different significations of Fáre.

Far ánimo,	to give courage
Farsi ánimo,	to take courage
Far a propòsito,	to do on purpose
Fatto a propòsito,	to be proper or fit
Far mótto,	to make a sign
.. del bravo,	to act the braggart
.. scélta,	to choose
.. pómpa,	to boast
.. il muso,	to pout at one
.. danári,	to make money

Far gènte, or *soldati,*	to raise soldiers
Il far della luna,	the new moon,
Al far del giórno,	at the break of day
Su 'l far délla nòtte,	towards the evening
Far di mestièri,	to be necessary
.. *guadágni,*	to win
.. *due vòlte l' ánno,*	to bear fruit twice a year
Farsi innánzi,	to come forward
.. *si in quà,*	to approach or advance
.. *si in là,*	to go back
.. *si in dìetro,*	to retire
Far bríndisi,	to toast a health
.. *capolíno,*	to deceive or ensnare
.. *la spía,*	to be spying
.. *pace,*	to agree
Fate pace,	agree among yourselves
Far a bottíno,	to share alike
.. *a capèlli,*	to pull one another by the hair
.. *accogliènza,*	to show kindness to one
.. *a compásso,*	to work by the compass
.. *a concorrènza,*	to strive, to vie
.. *acquísto,*	to gain
.. *crédere,*	to make one believe
.. *a gara,*	to strive for the victory
.. *agguáti,*	to lay ambushes
.. *a púgni,*	to box
.. *all' amóre,*	to make love
.. *alle coltelláte,*	to fight with knives
.. *alle púgna,*	to box
.. *alto,*	to halt
.. *a mano,*	to come to blows
.. *a malincuòre,*	to do against one's will
.. *a metà,*	to do by halves
.. *a pennèllo,*	to do a thing exactly
.. *apprèsto,*	to make preparation
.. *a regátta,*	to struggle, or scramble
.. *a fársela,*	to take one's revenge
.. *arròsto,*	to roast meat
.. *sapére,*	to make one know
.. *a sassi,*	to fight with stones
.. *tacére,*	to make one be silent
.. *avánzo,*	to strive

ar baco baco,	to play at bo peep
. *bando,*	to proclaim
. *bèffe,*	to flout at
. *bellìn bellìno,*	to soothe or fawn upon
.. *bisógno,*	to be needful
.. *bròglio,*	to make a hurly-burly
.. *buòna riuscíta,*	to come to a good effect
.. *buona vicinánza,*	to keep fair with one's neighbours
.. *buon fiánco,*	to be merry and jovial
.. *buon partíto,*	to make a good offer
.. *cantáre,*	to make one yield
.. *cappelláccio,*	to beat a man with his own weapons
.. *capo,*	to grow to a head
.. *capo ad úno,*	to have recourse to one for help
.. *capo in un luògo,*	to meet in some appointed place
.. *casèlle,*	to pump a man of his secrets
.. *caso,*	to make account of, or esteem
.. *cérca,*	to seek after
.. *cérchio,*	to make a ring
.. *cervèllo,*	to call his wits together
	[mugger
.. *che che si sia alla mácchia,*	to do things in hugger-
.. *cipíglio,*	to look frowningly
.. *colazióne,*	to breakfast
.. *collezióne,*	to make a collection
.. *compársa,*	to make a show
.. *cómpra,*	to buy a bargain
.. *come lo sparvière,*	to live from hand to mouth
.. *congiúra,*	to conspire
.. *consèrva,*	to lay up in store
.. *cónto,*	to reckon
.. *còpia,*	to make a copy
.. *cordóglio,*	to lament
.. *cortéggio,*	to fawn upon one
.. *còse di fuòco,*	to do wonderful things
.. *cuòre,*	to encourage
.. *da céna,*	to get supper ready
.. *del grande,*	to take state upon one
.. *del cappèllo,*	to pull off one's hat
.. *di méno,*	to do without
.. *divièto,*	to prohibit
.. *d' òcchio,*	to wink upon one

Far dòsso di buffòne,	[the world says to do a thing and not care what
.. *d' úna láncia un fuso,*	[pence to bring a noble to nine
.. *due chiòdi in una calda,*	[stone to kill two birds with one
.. *fáccia,*	to set a good face on things
.. *fagòtto,*	to pack up and begone
.. *filáre uno,*	to make one do anything
.. *fòrte,*	to strengthen
.. *frétta,*	to make haste
.. *frónte,*	to face
.. *gabbo,*	to flout at
.. *gala,*	to be gay and merry
.. *gallòrio,*	to show signs of joy
.. *gènte,*	to raise men
.. *giornáta,*	to fight a battle
.. *grázia,*	to do a favour
.. *gréppo,*	to make mouths as a child
.. *grida,*	to cry out
.. *grúzzolo,*	to hoard up money
.. *ostería,*	to set up an inn
.. *i fatti suòi,*	to mind one's own business
.. *il balórdo,*	to play the simpleton
.. *il bèllo in piázza,*	[streets to show one's fine clothes in the
.. *il buòn prò,*	to do one good when one eats
.. *il cómpito,*	to end one's task
.. *il diávolo,*	to play the devil
.. *il gáttone,*	to pretend not to see or know
.. *il Giórgio,*	to strut in fine clothes
.. *il latino a cavállo,*	to be put hard to it
.. *il rómbo,*	to make a rumbling noise
.. *il santo,*	to play the hypocrite
.. *il vèrno,*	to pass away the winter
.. *il séme,*	to come to perfection
.. *istánza,*	to be urgent with one
Farla ad úno,	to play any one a trick
Far la busca,	to scramble for
.. *la fèsta ad uno,*	to kill one
.. *la fischiáta,*	to make a whistling noise
.. *la gatta mòrta,*	to play at bo-peep

Far la ninfa,	to mince it
.. *la nòtte,*	to pass the night
.. *la rónda,*	to walk the round
.. *la scárpa,*	to cut a purse
.. *la scopèrta,*	to keep a watch
.. *la scòrta,*	to be a guide
.. *le carte,*	to deal at cards
.. *le paròle,*	to speak at large
.. *la lèpre vècchia,*	to avoid a danger that's seen
.. *le spálle gòbbe,*	to shrug up one's shoulders
.. *la sica,*	to flirt at one
.. *le spése,*	to bear one's charges
.. *le stimáte,*	to esteem one greatly
.. *leváta,*	to raise men
.. *le vòlte del leóne,*	to continue walking in one place
.. *lo spasimáto,*	to over-play the lover
.. *lo spaventácchio,*	to brag much
.. *luògo,* or *piázza,*	to give place
.. *mala riuscíta,*	to have ill luck
.. *mala vicinánza,*	to be a bad neighbour
.. *mal d' òcchio,*	to have sore eyes
.. *mal prò,*	to do one no good
.. *máschera,*	to be masked
.. *mercáto,*	to cheapen
.. *mercè,*	to show mercy
.. *merènda,*	to eat one's luncheon
.. *mòtto,*	to give notice of
.. *motto ad úno,*	to salute or send word
.. *natále,*	to keep Christmas
.. *òcchio,*	to wink at
.. *ogni possíbile,*	to do one's utmost
.. *òpera,*	to do the same
.. *orécchio di mercánte,*	to pretend not to hear
.. *paragóne,*	to compare together
.. *partíto,*	to make a match or bargain
.. *passággio,*	to pass over slightly
.. *passáta,*	to get easily through a business
.. *pasto,*	to eat a meal
.. *patto,*	to make a bargain
.. *pedúccio,*	to soothe one
.. *punto,*	to make an end
.. *punto falso,*	to make a false thrust

Far pòpolo,	to make one amongst the rest
.. *prèzzo,*	to make much of
.. *prèstito,*	to lend
.. *prò,*	to do good
.. *questióne,*	to question
.. *rabbúffo,*	to chide
.. *ragióne,*	to do right or pledge one
.. *ricredènte,*	to make one change his opinion
.. *richámo,*	to appeal unto
.. *ròba,*	to heap up riches
.. *ruòta,*	to wheel or hover about
.. *sacco,*	to hoard up
.. *saccománo,*	to sack or ravage
.. *salvo,*	to give a volley of shot
.. *sángue,*	to bleed
.. *sapére,*	to let one know
.. *scala,*	to come to a landing place
.. *scomméssa,*	to lay a wager
.. *scónto,*	to make an abatement
.. *-sela,*	to go away
.. *sembiánte* or *vísta,*	to make a show of
.. *sfòggi,*	to make a fine show
.. *sicurtà,*	to be bound
.. *spálla,*	to back one
.. *stáre,*	to over-reach one
.. *stár fòrte,*	to over-reach one cunningly
.. *stare a ségno,*	to keep one under
.. *stare a stecchétto,*	to force one to his obedience
.. *tantára,*	to be gay and merry together
.. *tavoláccio,*	to prepare for good cheer
.. *tempóne,*	to live a merry life
.. *tèsta,*	to make head
.. *trébbio,*	to live merrily in good company
.. *il tríbolo,*	to cry for money
	[bottom
.. *tutte le uòva in un panière,*	to venture all in one
.. *valére,*	to cause to prevail
.. *vedúta, vísta, fìnta,*	to make a show
.. *vedúta,*	to make one believe what is not
.. *véla,*	to sail
.. *vélo,*	to make resistance
.. *vézzi,*	to caress

Far una bravàta,	to make a bravado
.. *un cavallétto ad úno,*	to cheat one
.. *una trincàta,*	to make a merry drinking
.. *una giòstra ad uno,*	to put a jest upon one
.. *una prèdica ad uno,*	to admonish one fairly
.. *un farfallóne,*	to make some mistake
.. *uno sfrégio ad uno,*	to mark one in the face
.. *un manichétto,*	to point at one in scorn
.. *un marróne,*	to commit a great error
.. *un passeròtto,*	to do a thing hand over head
.. *un pènzolo,*	to be hanged by the neck
.. *úno smácco ad uno,*	to affront one
.. *uno stáglio,*	to fix
.. *un tiro,*	to shoot or play a prank
.. *vuotáre la sèlla,*	to supplant a man
.. *uòva,*	to lay eggs

Different significations of Stare.

We use the verb *stáre* to mark an action of repose, by putting the verb which follows in the gerund or infinitive, with *a* or *ad*.

Sta studiándo, or *sta a studiáre,*	he studies
Stanno scrivèndo, or *stánno a scrívere,*	they write [together
Staréte leggèndo, or *a lèggere insième,*	you will read

Stáre has several other significations ; as,

Star in pièdi,	to stand upright
.. *bène o male,*	to be well or ill
.. *su,* to rise ; *státe su,*	rise
.. *giù,* to sit down ; *state giù,*	sit down
.. *a sentire,* to listen ; *sto a sentire,*	I listen
.. *a sedére,*	to be sitting
State a sedere,	sit down
Sta bène,	it is well, it is very well
Star per uscíre,	to be just going out
.. *bene a cavállo,*	to sit well on horseback
.. *in casa,*	to stay at home
.. *lèsto,*	to be upon one's guard
.. *su le burle,*	to jest, or banter

Star saldo,	to hold out stoutly
.. *per cadére,*	to be ready to fall
.. *per moríre,*	to be like to die
.. *in dúbbio,*	to be in doubt
.. *a vedére,*	to expect the issue
.. *con le mani in cíntola,*	to stand idly
.. *su le súe,*	to look grave
Questo vi sta bène,	that becomes you well
Questo non mi sta bene,	that does not become me
Star a bada,	to linger or expect
.. *a bottéga,*	to mind one's shop
.. *a crèpa cuòre,*	to live at heart's grief
.. *ad alcúno,*	to be at any man's turn
.. *ad ascoltáre,*	to hear
.. *in diságio,*	to be uneasy
.. *a dormíre,*	to lie sleeping
.. *a dozzína,*	to board
.. *a fare,*	to be doing
.. *a frónte,*	to out-face
.. *a gálla,*	to float
.. *a giacére,*	to be lying down
.. *al détto,*	to rely on a person's word
.. *alla pòsta,*	to watch for an opportunity
.. *all' érta,*	to look heedfully about
.. *alle vedétte,*	to stand centinel on a tower
.. *allégro,*	to live or be merry
.. *al móndo,*	to live in the world
.. *a locánda,*	to live in a hired room
.. *al parágone,*	to bear the touchstone
.. *a martèllo,*	to live in anxiety
.. *in perícolo,*	to be in danger
.. *a pètto,*	to be opposite
.. *a pigióne,*	to live in a rented house
.. *appoggiáto,*	to lean upon
.. *apprèsso,*	to stand or dwell near
.. *a ségno,*	to stand near the mark
.. *in speránza,*	to live in hopes
.. *aspettándo,*	to expect
.. *a stènto,*	to live in distress
.. *attórno,*	to stand about
.. *a tu per tu,*	to be free and easy

'tar ad úno,	to depend upon one
.. bène a casa,	to be well at home
.. buòna pèzza,	to stand a good while
.. caldo,	to lie warm
.. chéto,	to be hushed
.. con áltri,	to live with others
.. del débito,	to answer for a debtor
: di buòna vòglia,	to be merry
.. di mala voglia,	to be sad
.. di sópra,	to lie over
.. di sótto,	to lie under
.. frésco,	to be badly off
.. in agguáto,	to lie in wait
.. in biláncia,	to stand in doubt
.. innánzi,	to stand before
.. in ármi,	to be in arms
.. in cervèllo,	to have a care, or to be weary
.. in lètto,	to be a-bed
.. in orécchio,	to hearken
.. in pendènte,	to be in suspense
.. in rischio,	to be in danger
.. in sè,	to be positive
.. in sentóre,	to listen with suspicion
.. in sospètto,	to be suspected
.. in su 'l puntíglio,	to stand upon punctilios
.. in villa,	to live in the country
.. in zurlo,	to stand in a maze
.. lontáno,	to live far
.. per,	to stand for, to be about
.. sópra di sè,	to presume too much on one's self
.. sano,	to be in health
.. su 'l avvíso,	to be prepared
.. su 'l duro,	to be obstinate
.. su 'l ritróso,	to be coy
.. su 'l tiráto,	to stand upon strict points
.. tra sì e' l no,	to be in suspense
.. vicíno,	to be neighbours
.. vigilánte,	to be watchful
.. zitto,	to be silent
.. sulla cáccia,	to be very fond of hunting

Different significations of Avére.

Aver dell' uòmo da bène,	to appear as an honest man
.. *del mirácolo,*	to look as a miracle
.. *caro, avér a caro,*	to be well pleased
.. *a bène,*	to approve of
.. *per bene,*	to like or consent
.. *per male,*	to disapprove of
.. *a male,*	to dislike
.. *a cuòre,*	to have at heart
.. *il cápo altróve,*	to think of other things
.. *da fare,*	to be busy
.. *in prègio, in istíma,*	to esteem
.. *in òdio,*	to hate
.. *per costúme,*	to be wont
.. signifies to believe ;	[believe him ignorant as, *l'ho per ignoránte,* I
.. *il vízio nelle òssa,*	to be very vicious
.. *a capitále,*	to esteem much
.. *a cura,*	to be entrusted with
.. *da dare,*	to have to give
.. *a dispètto,*	to have in despite
.. *a dispiacére,*	to be displeased with
.. *fastídio,*	to loath
.. *ágio,*	to be at ease
.. *a grado,*	to like
.. *alle mani,*	to have in hand
.. *a mani,*	to have ready at hand
.. *a ménte,*	to remember well
.. *ánimo,*	to have courage or a mind to
.. *a nóia,*	to dislike
.. *a pètto,*	to have at heart
.. *ardíre,*	to dare
.. *a schèrno,*	to scorn
.. *a schífo,*	to loath
.. *a vile,*	to hold very cheap
.. *bèl tèmpo,*	to live a merry life
.. *buòna vóce,*	to be well spoken of
.. *che si sia per un pèzzo di pane,*	[for a trifle to have a thing
.. *cimière ad ógni elmétto,*	to be ready for any thing

Aver da tornáre,	to be about to return
.. *del tóndo,*	to have little sense
.. *dèstro,*	to have fit occasion
.. *di che,*	to have wherewith
.. *dièiro,*	to contemn
.. *di grázia,*	to take it as a favour
.. *fáccia,*	to dare
Non aver faccia,	to blush for shame
Aver faiíca,	to have trouble
.. *fède in,*	to confide in
.. *fréddo ai pièdi,*	to be in great want
.. *frétta,*	to be in haste
.. *fumo,*	to be proud
.. *góla,*	to have a longing desire
.. *il capo a' grilli,*	to have one's wits wool-gathering
.. *cavèlle a oriuòli,*	to be fickle
.. *grand' opinióne,*	to presume much on one's self
.. *d' uòpo,*	to have need
.. *il cervèllo che vóli,*	to have a roving head
.. *il cimúrro,*	to have a whim in one's head
.. *il súo pièno,*	to have one's full allowance
.. *il tòrto,*	to be in the wrong
.. *in consègna,*	to have in trust
.. *in cónto,*	to have esteem of
.. *in guárdia,*	to keep
.. *in negligènza,*	to be careless
.. *in órdine,*	to have in readiness
.. *sulle dita,*	to have at one's finger's ends
.. *la palla in mano,*	to have the law in one's own [hands
.. *l'asso nel ventríglio,*	to have an itching for gaming
.. *língua,*	to have notice of a thing
.. *l'òcchio al pennéllo,*	to mind one's business
.. *l'osso del poltróne,*	to have a bone in one's leg
.. *le campáne gròsse,*	to be deaf
.. *le mani ad úno,*	to hold one fast at his pleasure
.. *le travéggole,*	to take one thing for another
.. *luògo,*	to be expedient
.. *mala gatta da peláre,*	to have an ill crow to pluck
.. *mala vóce,*	to be ill spoken of
.. *male campáne,*	to be deaf

Aver mangiáto nóci,	to have the absent ill spoken of
.. *martèllo,*	to be passionately jealous of
.. *mèzzo* or *mòdo,*	to be able, or have means
.. *nell' idèa,*	to bear in mind
.. *òbbligo,*	to be obliged
.. *òcchio,*	to have a fair outside
.. *occhio d' áquila,*	to have a sharp look
.. *odóre,*	to have an idea of a thing
.. *ómbra,*	to be suspicious of
.. *paúra,*	to be afraid
.. *pensière,*	to be full of care, or thoughtful
.. *per iscusáto,*	· to excuse one
.. *piède,*	to get footing
.. *poco sale in zucca,*	to have but little sense
.. *ragióne da véndere,*	to have reason to spare
.. *sdégno,*	to disdain
.. *sónno,*	to be sleepy
	[crime
.. *la códa taccáta di mal pélo,*	to be tainted with some
	[end
.. *sulla púnta della lìngua,*	to have at one's tongue's
	[stake
.. *tutto 'l súo in su'l tavolière,*	to have one's all at

Different significations of Èssere.

'*Esser per fare,*	to be just going to do
.. *da quálche, còsa,*	to be good for something
.. *da pòco,*	to have but little sense
.. *da niènte,*	to be good for nothing
.. *a cavállo,*	to be out of trouble or pain
	[able
Non èsser da tanto,	not to be capable of, not to be
Esser di giovaménto,	to help, to assist
.. *di buòna náscita,*	to come of a good family
	[condition
.. *per la mala vía,*	to be ruined, to be in a bad
.. *per la fratte,*	to be undone or ruined
.. *fuòr di Bológna,*	to be ignorant

Esser a ferri,	to lie close together
.. *a grado,*	to be acceptable
.. *a mal partíto,*	to be in a bad taking
.. *a parte,*	to be partaker of
.. *in questióne,*	to squabble
.. *bèn vedúto,*	to be kindly entertained
.. *d'avvíso,*	to deem
.. *bène in gambe,*	to be strong and lusty
.. *bríllo,*	to be tipsy
.. *danno,*	to be pitied
.. *di pòca levàta,*	to be of small worth
.. *di tèsta,*	to be hairbrained
.. *fòrza,*	to be constrained
.. *in détto,*	to have good luck at play
.. *in assètto,*	to be prepared
.. *in détto,*	to be agreed
.. *in disgrázia,*	to be in disgrace
.. *in èssere,*	to be in state, quality, and condition
.. *in faccènde,*	to be busy
.. *in fióri,*	to be in one's prime
.. *in fortúna,*	to be lucky
.. *in pièga,*	to be pending
.. *in predicaménto,*	to be in consideration
.. *largo di bócca,*	to be a great talker
... *luògo,*	to be convenient
.. *mala língua,*	to sow distrust among friends
.. *mal vedúto,*	to be unwelcome
.. *pace,*	to be quits at play
.. *tenúto,*	to be holden to
.. *una còppa d'òro,*	to be one in a thousand

Different significations of Sapére.

Sapére,	signifies to know or perceive
.. *a ménte,*	to know by heart
.. *a ména díto,*	to have at one's finger's ends
.. *male,*	to displease, to smell ill
Quésto mi sa male,	that displeases me,
Sapér di buòno, sapér buono,	to smell well
.. *di cattívo,*	to smell ill
.. *di muffa,* or *di múcido,*	to have a mouldy smell

M

Sapér di niènte,　to have no smell, to smell of nothing
　.. *tròppo di pòvero,*　　　　　　　　to appear poor
　　　　　　　　　　　　　　　　　　　　　　　[sharp
　.. *trovár il pelo nell' uòvo,*　　to be cunning, to be
Ti so dire　　　　　　　　　　　　I can tell thee
Sapér di lèttere,　　　to have a smattering of learning
　.. *di múschio,*　　　　　　to taste or smell of musk
　.. *di sécco,*　　　　　　　　to smell of the cask
　.. *mèglio,*　　　　　　　　to take in better part
　.. *per prática,*　　　　　　　　to know by rote
　.. *grádo di checchessía,*　to be pleased with any thing

Different significations of Tenére.

Tenére da úno,　　　　　　　　　to be of one's side
　.. *a bada,*　　　　　　　　　　to amuse one
　.. *in contrário,*　　　to be of a contrary opinion
　.. *per galantuòmo,*　　　　to believe one honest
Lo tèngo per matto,　　　　I take him to be mad
Tenére le lágrime,　　　　　to forbear weeping
Tenére le risa,　　　　　　to forbear laughing
Non ho potúto téner le risa,　I could not forbear laughing
Tenér alla tráccia,　　　　　　　　to pursue
　　　　　　　　　　　　　　　　　　　[a person
　.. *cónto ad úno,*　　to make an account of, to esteem
　.. *-la per sè,*　　　to keep a thing to one's self
Tenétela per voi,　　　　　　keep it for yourself
Tenér a ménte,　　　　　　　to call to mind
　.. *la favèlla ad úno,*　to hinder one from speaking
　.. *a battéssimo,*　　　　　　to stand godfather
　.. *mano al furto,*　　　to be accessory to a theft
　　　　　　　　　　　　　　　　　　[servants
　.. *carròzza e servitóri,*　　to keep a carriage and
Tièni quésto,　　take this (in the imperative)
Téner il sacco,　　　　　　　to hold the bag
Tenére la battúta,　　　to beat time in music
　.. *l'invíto,*　　　to accept what is proposed
　.. *a dièta,*　　　　　to keep low in diet
　.. *a cimènto,*　　　　　to hold to a trial
　.. *a stènto,*　　　　　　to keep in pain
　.. *còrte bandíta,*　　　to keep open house

Tenér dozzína,	to keep a boarding house
.. *a báda,*	to hold in suspense
.. *il bordóne,*	to be still in one's mind
.. *férmo,*	to keep one's word
.. *in bòcca,*	to keep a secret
.. *le pòste,*	to hold stakes
.. *mano,*	to lend a hand
.. *ménte,*	to heed
.. *mercáto,*	to bargain
.. *ragióne,*	to judge according to law
.. *parlaménto,*	to hold a parley
.. *in sospéso,*	to hold in suspense
.. *per fède,*	to take upon trust
.. *trattáto,*	to hold correspondence with

Different significations of Volére.

Volére	signifies to believe ; as
Vògliono alcúni,	some believe
Volérla con úno,	to have a spite against one
Volér bène	to love
.. *male,*	to hate
.. *piuttòsto,*	to have rather
Le cose vògliono èssere così,	things must be so
Si vuòle,	they will, or will have
Volér dire,	to mean
.. *mèglio,*	to have rather
.. *la báia,*	to affect mocking
.. *la gátta,*	to pick a quarrel with one
.. *male a mòrte,*	to hate deadly
Volésse pur Dio !	oh ! would to God !

Different significations of Veníre.

	[faint
Venír méno, venír manco,	to fall into weakness or
.. *in súcchio,*	to have one's mouth water
.. *in sòrte,*	to fall to one's lot
.. *sótto il nóme,*	to go by the name of

Venír stimáto	to be esteemed
.. *biasimáto,*	to be blamed
.. *alle strétte,*	to come to a conclusion
Non mi vièn bène,	it does not please me
Quésto vi vien bene,	that becomes you well
Quánti ve ne vengono?	how many must you have?
Me ne vengono dúe,	I must have two of them
Mi viène vòglia,	I have a mind
Venír addòsso,	to fall upon
.. *al di sópra,*	to have the upper hand
.. *alle prése,*	to come to close fight
.. *alle brutte,*	to come to foul words
.. *a battáglia,*	to fight a battle
.. *a bène,*	to come to good
.. *a dire,*	to import or mean
.. *alle mani,*	to come to blows
.. *détto,*	to be said
.. *pósti gli òcchi,*	to fix one's eyes on
.. *fallíto,*	to miss one's aim or purpose
.. *scontráto,*	to meet withal
.. *a táglio,*	to suit well
.. *trováto,*	to happen to find

Of the Particles ci *and* vi.

Ci signifies *us*; he speaks to us, *ci parla*, &c. *Vi* signifies *you*; he speaks to you, *vi parla*; he gives you, *vi da.*

Ci and *vi* are adverbs of place; as,

Ci siámo, we are here, there, *or* at it.

Vi andrémo, we will go there.

Ci and *vi* are conjunctive pronouns, when they signify *us* and *you*; and when *ci* and *vi* signify *there*, *at it*, &c. they are adverbs of place.

Different significations of che.

Che signifies *that, who, whom, that he, that she, that they, which, what?*

Che signifies *what?* mas. what man is that? *che uòmo è? Che?* what? fem. what house? *che casa?*

Che? what? plural mas. what books have they? *che libri hanno?*

Che, plural fem. what lessons? *che lezióni?*

Chè signifies *because; chè la dònna nel desiár è bèn di noi più frale*, because a woman is much more weak in her desires than we are. Guaríni, *nel Pastór Fído.*

Che signifies *so that* or *in that manner.* I will do it, so that, or in that manner, that you shall be contented, *farò che saréte contènto.*

Different significations of vía.

Vía signifies *the way;* example: by the way of Paris, *per la vía di Parígi.*

Vía is put after the verbs *andáre, passáre, condúrre, fuggire, gettáre,* and then these verbs have more force and elegance; as,

Andár vía,	to go away.
Va' vía,	get thee away.
Passa vía, furfánte!	get thee gone, scoundrel!
Condúr vía,	to turn away.
Fuggíre vía,	to run away.
Gettáte vía quésto,	throw this away.

Vía or *víe* signifies *much:* as, much more learned, *víe più dòtto.*

Vía signifies *come;* as, come, come, gentlemen, do not fear, *vía, vía, signóri, non teméte.*

Vía is sometimes taken for *vòlta;* example: *tre vía tre, fan (fanno) nòve*, three times three make nine; *quáttro vía quattro fan sédici*, four times four make sixteen.

Vía signifies the means; as, by the means of the passages in the holy fathers, *per vía de' tèsti de' santi padri.*

Different significations of da.

Da is oftentimes the ablative of the indefinite article, and signifies in English *from;* example: *ho ricevúto da Piètro,* I have received from Peter.

Da' with an apostrophe is the ablative of the definite article, and signifies *from the,* or *by the;* example: *è stimáto da' Francési,* he is esteemed by the French.

Dà signifies *he gives;* examples: *mi dà buòna speránza,* he gives me good hopes, &c.

Da signifies *upon the faith;* example: *da galant' uòmo,* upon the faith of an honest man.

Da signifies *like;* examples: *ha trattáto da galant' uòmo,* he has acted like an honest man. *V. S. parla da amico,* you speak like a friend.

Da signifies *of,* or *to put;* example: *una scátola da tabácco,* a snuff-box, or a box to put snuff in.

Da signifies *about;* example: *sarà stato quì da cinquánt' ánni,* he will have been here fifty years.

Da signifies *from:* examples, from Rome to Paris, *da Rôma a Parigi. Da che vi vidi,* since I saw you.

Da before infinitives signifies *to be;* example: it is easy to be seen, *è fácile da vedére.*

Different significations of per.

Per signifies *for;* example: for me, *per me.*

Per signifies *through,* or *all over;* example: through or all over the city, *per tutta la città.*

Per signifies *during;* as, during a year, *per un anno.*

Per signifies *to fetch,* and *seek after;* example: go and fetch it, *andáte per ésso;* go for a physician, *andáte per un mèdico.*

Per signifies *how;* example: how good soever it be, *per buòno che sía.*

Per signifies *each* or *every;* example: one in each hand, *uno per mano.*

Per signifies *just* or *ready to;* example: he is just going away, he is ready to go, *sta per partíre.*

Per signifies every one; example: every one, *un per úno.*

Per signifies *depending on;* example: it does not depend on me, *non rèsta per me.* It signifies, *as far as;* example: as far as I see, *per quel che védo.*

Per signifies *as for;* example: as for me, *io, per me.*

Per ánche signifies *not yet;* example: I have not seen him yet, *non l'ho per ánche vedúto.*

Different significations of si, ne, *and* pur *or* pure.

Though the following particles *si, ne, pur* or *pure,* are not prepositions, yet their vast extent and signification in Italian has induced me to insert the different acceptations of them here, for the greater ease and advantage of the learner.

Si

Signifies *it is, they, men, the world, yes, so, so as, as much, as well, until, nevertheless, himself,* &c. Examples:

Si díce,	it is said.
Si áma, or *si ámano.*	they love.
Si dirà,	the world, *or* people will say.
Sì, signóre,	yes, sir.
Cavalière sì avventuráto non fu mái,	never was there so fortunate a gentleman.
Sì per il mio; quanto per il vòstro interèsse,	as well for my interest as yours.
Sì la móglie come il maríto,	as well the wife as the husband.
Sì vi ámo, perchè...	nevertheless I love you, because...
Egli si ricordò....	he *or* she remembered....

⁎ Note, that when *si* is accented, it is always an adverb.

Ne

Signifies *nor, neither, in the, with, hence, thence, away, at it, of it, us, from us, none, any, some, thereof, else,* &c.

M 4

Examples :

Nè quésto, nè quéllo vi concèdo,	I grant you neither this nor that.
Spasseggiándo ne' campi,	walking in the fields.
M' incontrái ne' mièi amíci,	I met with my friends.
Váttene pe' fatti tuòi,	get thee hence about thy business.
Egli sene viène alla vòlta nòstra,	he is coming towards us.
Egli ne ha tòlto il nòstro ripòso,	he has taken our rest from us.
Io me ne vado,	I am going away.
Se ne ride,	he laughs at it.
Se ne laménta,	he complains of it.
Egli ci diède il buòn dì,	he bade us good morrow.
Io non ne ho,	I have none.
Se ne avéssi,	if I had any
Ve ne farèi parte,	I would give you some.
Voi ne potréte dispórre,	you may dispose of it.

Note, that when *ne* is accented, it is always an adverb.

Pur or *pure*

Is a particle of great use and elegance in the Italian language, and signifies in English, *yet, although, moreover, besides, notwithstanding all conditions, in the end, when all is said and done, so much as, not only, in case, surely, even, at least, needs* or *of force:* as it would be tedious to give examples of all the different significations of this extensive particle. I shall only mention the following phrases :

Examples :

Pur adèsso,	even now.
Pur óra,	just now.
Pur mò,	at this instant.
Pur allóra,	even then.
Pur assái,	too, too much.
Pur paròle?	what; nothing but words?
Pur pure,	yet, for all that.

°•° Note, that the following particles, *dì, è egli, sib-*

ben, nè già, pur me, che, il, have often no signification at all, but are used as expletives by way of embellishing the discourse. See the Eighth Treatise, Chapter I., of Expletives.

FIFTH TREATISE.

Of COMPOSITION, *and Rules for Writing and Speaking Italian, contained in a few Themes* (").

AFTER we have learned the auxiliary verbs, and the three conjugations, we may begin to translate English into Italian, and observe the rules of concordance : and, if we think proper, we may compose the following themes, upon the principles of the Italian language, without looking at the Italian that is put after the English, except it be to compare it with the translation.

The first is upon the *articles.*
The second upon the verb *avére.*
The third upon the verb *èssere.*
The fourth upon the pronouns, *mi, ti, ci, vi, gli.*
The fifth upon the particle *si.*
The sixth upon *there is, there was, there will be, there has been.*
The seventh upon the articles, *of the, of,* &c.

Be careful in composing these themes, as they contain a great many niceties in the Italian tongue. I have put them in Italian, word for word, to render them the more easy. The words marked with a number shows that there are some rules to be observed, as appears by the page which follows the Italian theme.

" The student is also recommended to consult Bottarelli's Exercises upon the various parts of Italian speech, and referring to the rules of this grammar.

M 5

THEME.

On the Articles.

My brother's fancy and desire for the study of the Italian language, are the cause that the passion he had for hunting, gaming, and musical instruments, is at present much abated; if he had believed the advice you gave him in the president's garden, when he spoke to us of the wit of that gentleman, who was much esteemed by the king, he would then have begun to have studied the principles of it, he would at present have known part of the difficulties, and would have made a great many journeys with the nephew of a great prince, who would have had him.

1   2   3

La vòglia, e 'l desidèrio di mio fratèllo, per lo stúdio

4

della lingua Italiána, sóno cagióne, che gli ardóri che

5 6 7

avéva per la cáccia, i giuòchi e gli struménti da música,

8   9

sóno adèsso mólto moderáti; se avésse credúto ai consigli

10   11   12 13

che gli daváte nel giardíno del signór presidènte, quando

14 15 16

ci paláva dell' ingégno di quel gentiluòmo ch' èra tanto

17   18 19

stimáto dal re, avrèbbe allóra cominciáto a studiárne i

20   21

princípj, saprèbbe adèsso una parte delle difficoltà, ed

22 23 24

avrèbbe fatto mólti viággi col nipóte d' un gran príncipe

25

che lo voléva séco.

This theme and those which follow are translated word for word.

The number 1. shows that *l'* is in the place of *il*; see page 171.

Number 2. teaches that we must say *di mio*, and not *del mio ;* see page 69.

3. *lo,* and not *il,* p. 36.
4. *gli,* and not *gl',* p. 38.
5. *i* is better than *li,* p. 38.
6. *giuòchi,* and not *giuoci,* p. 49.
7. *gli,* and not *li,* p. 38.
8. *se avesse,* and not *se aveva,* p. 90.
9. *agli avvisi,* and not *gl' avvisi,* p. 38.
10. *gli,* and not *lui,* p. 64.
11. *nel,* and not *in il,* p. 41.
12. *del,* and not *dello,* p. 36.
13. *signór presidènte,* and not *signore,* p. 173.
14. *ci,* and not *noi,* p. 66.
15. *dell',* and not *del,* p. 38.
16. *quel,* and not *quello,* p. 56.
17. *dal,* in the ablative, p. 95.
18. *studiárne,* and not *ne studiare,* p. 67.
19. *i* for *li,* p. 37.
20. *princìpj,* and not *princìpi,* p. 50.
21. *difficoltà,* and not *difficoltè,* p. 44.
22. *viàggi,* and not *viaggii* or *viaggj,* p. 50.
23. *col,* and not *con il,* p. 43.
24. *gran,* and not *grande,* p. 56.
25. *lo,* and not *il,* p. 73.

THEME.

In which all the tenses of the Verb Avére *are inserted.*

I have the curiosity to know whether you have done the business I had recommended to you ?

If I had had time, I would have done it; but not having had it, I have not been able to do it.

You would have had it if you had been willing, and if you had not played so much.

I have quitted play altogether, to have my mind at rest.

I shall therefore have some hopes that you will work for me.

It is reasonable that I take care of your affairs, since you take care of mine.

Have some of mine, and I will have some of yours.

1   •   2

Ho la curiosità di sapére se avéte fatto l'affáre che
   3

v' avévo raccommandáto ?

    4   5   6

Se avéssi avúto tèmpo, l' avrèi fatto, ma non avèndolo
       7

avuto, non l' ho potúto fare.

                 8

L' avréste avúto, se avéste volúto, e se non avéste giuocáto tanto.

                 9

Ho lasciáto il giuòco affátto, per avére lo spírito in ripòso.

   10

Avrò dúnque qualche speránza, che lavoreréte per me.

             11   12

'*E ragionévole ch' abbia cura de' vòstri affari, giacchè*
   13

voi n' avete de' mièi.

         14   15

Abbiátene de' mièi, e n' avrò de' vòstri.

---

1. *curiosità*, with an accent, p. 176.
2. *l' affáre*, and not *lo affare*, p. 36.
3. *v'avévo*, for *vi avevo*, p. 172.
4. *avéssi*, and not *avevo*, p. 90.
5. *l' avrèi*, for *lo avrei*, p. 172.
6. *avèndolo*, and not *lo avendo*, p. 41.
7. *l' ho*, for *lo ho*, p. 172.
8. *avéste*, and not *avevate*, p. 90, 91.
9. *avére*, without an *h*, p. 29.
10. *avrò*, with an accent, p. 177.
11. *ch' ábbia*, and not *che abbia*, p. 172.
12. *de'* is better than *delli*, p. 37, 172.
13. *n' avete*, instead of *ne avete*, p. 172.
14. *de'* is better than *delli*, p. 37, 172.
15. *n' avrò*, for *ne' avrò*, p. 172.

THEME.

On the Tenses of the Verb Èssere.

I am much pleased in being received as tutor to those gentlemen who have been in the country where you have been.

You have reason to be pleased, for they are very generous gentlemen.

I should be yet more glad if they had not been in Italy, because I should have made that journey with them.

It seems that you were there for some months last year.

I should have been there, it is true, if my brother had been here, when those gentlemen were with you in the army; but not being here, I was obliged to stay at Paris.

₊ Before you compose this theme, remember that the verb *èssere* is formed or conjugated by itself; and that you must never put any tense of the verb *avére* before the participle *státo:* for we say, *sòno stato, siámo státi,* and not *ho stato, abbiámo stati.*

You must use *státo* in speaking of a single person only, by *you;* example: you have been my friend, *siète stato mio amico,* and not *siète stati.*

        1   2

Sòno mólto contènto d'èssere stato ricevúto per precet-

              3

tóre di que' signóri, che sóno stati nel paése dove siète stato.

                   4   5

Avéte ragióne d' èssere contènto, perchè sóno gentiluò-
mini mólto generósi.

           6

Sarèi ancóra più contènto, se non fòssero stati in Itá-

         7   8

lia, perchè avrèi fatto quel viággio con lóro.

       9   10

Mi pare che vi fóste per alcúni mési l' anno passáto.

11

Vi sarèi andáto, è véro, se mío fratèllo fôsse stato quì,
12
quando quéi signori èrano con voi all' armáta; ma non
13
essèndoci, fúi obbligáto di restár in Parígi.

---

1. *èssere stato,* and not *avere stato,* p. 84.
2. *essere stato,* and not *esser stato,* p. 174.
3. *nel,* and not *in il,* p. 42
4. We do not express *they,* p. 205, 206.
5. *uomo,* in the plural *uòmini,* p. 48.
6. *se,* before the imperfect, p. 90.
7. *quel* and not *quello,* p. 172.
8. *con loro,* and not *col loro,* because *loro* is a pronoun conjunctive, p. 203.
9. *vi,* and not *ci,* p. 151.
10. *alcúni,* and not *qualche,* p. 75.
11. *se mío,* and not *se il mío,* p. 69.
12. *quei,* or *quelli,* p. 70.
13. *essèndoci,* and not *ci essendo,* p. 67.

THEME.

On the Pronouns conjunctive, mi, ti, ci, vi, gli, le.

You had promised me that you would send us the book which we had asked of you, and you have not sent it to us.

I had promised it to you, it is true, I remember it; but you should have sent to ask it of me, and I would have sent it to you.

Do not put yourself to any more trouble about it. I know that my sister has one of them : here is my servant. I will bid him go to her house to ask it of her.

Go directly to my sister's, do not stay any where; you will tell her, that I beg her to lend me her manuscript : that I will send it her back in an hour ; you will give my service to my brother-in-law ; and if you see any roses in his garden, you will ask him for some of them.

1   2   3   4   5
M' avevále promésso che c'invieréste il libro che v' ave-
                6   7
vámo domandáto, e non ce l' avéte mandáto.

8   9 10 .
Ve l' avévo promésso, è véro, me ne ricòrdo; ma biso-
                11   12   13
gnáva mandár a domandármelo, e ve l' avrèi inviáto.

                14   15   16
Non ve ne pigliáte più fastídio: so che mia sorèlla n'ha
17   18   19
úno: ècco il mio servitóre; gli dirò d' andár da lèi per
                20
domandárglielo.

                                                21
Va' quanto prima da mia sorèlla, non ti fermár in
                22   23   24
nessún luògo; le dirái che la prègo di prestármi 'l súo
                25   26
manoscrítto, che le rimanderò fra un' óra: farái i mièi
                                                27   28
compliménti a mio cognáto, e se vedrái or védi ròse nel
                29   30
suo giardino, gliéne domanderái alcúne.

1. *m'aveváte,* in the plural, p. 205.
2. *m'avevate,* for *mi avevate,* p. 172.
3. *promesso,* and not *promisso,* or *promettuto,* p. 138.
4. *c',* and not *ci,* p. 66.
5. *vi avevámo,* or *v'avevamo,* p. 65.
6. *ce l' avete,* or *celo avete,* p. 172.
7. *ce l' avéte,* and not *celo avete,* p. 65.
8. *ve l' avévo,* and not *vi l' avevo,* p. 65.
9. *me ne,* and not *mi ne,* p. 66.
10. of it, before a verb is expressed by *me ne,* p. 65.
11. *mandáre a,* p. 205.
12. *domandármelo,* p. 66.
13. *ve 'l avrei,* p. 65.
14. *ve ne,* p. 65.
15. *mia sorèlla,* and not *la mia,* p. 67.
16. *n'ha,* and not *ne ha'* with an apostrophe, p. 168.
17. *uno,* and not *un,* p. 172.

18. *gli,* and not *lui,* p. 64.
19. *d' andár,* with an abbreviation, pp. 172, 173.
20. *domandárglielo,* and not *lui lo,* p. 64.
21. *non ti fermar,* and not *non ti ferma,* p. 207.
22. *le dirái,* and not *la dirai,* p. 64.
23. *prestármi,* and not *mi prestar,* p. 67.
24. *il suo,* and not *suo,* p. 68.
25. *le,* and not *lui,* p. 64.
26. *i mièi,* and not *miei,* p. 68.
27. *se vedrai,* or *se vedi,* p. 88.
28. *nel,* and not *in,* p. 42.
29. *gliene,* and not *le ne,* p. 67.
30. *alcune,* and not *qualche,* p. 75.

*** We advise the learner to go over this, and the three following themes, more than once.

THEME.

Containing all the difficulties of the Particle si, *it is,
they, we, &c.*

It is said that you do not know whether we have received the letters which we expected the last post; and that in case we have not received them, or do not receive them to-day, they will send fifty men into the forest, where it is thought they have robbed the courier, because they knew we had given him letters of great consequence; and it is not doubted but they are enemies that have detained him, because we have had certain advice that they have some of our letters in their hands. We have sent a spy to inform himself of what they say, and we promise him two hundred crowns if we can have any tidings of them.

I do not put the number which refers you to the rules upon these two last themes, because to make this, it will be sufficient to read the page, 247.

*Si dice che non sapéte se sóno state ricevúte le lèttere
(or se si sono ricevute le lettere), che s' aspettávano
l' ordinário passáto, e che in caso che non síano state rice-*

vute, o che non si ricévano òggi, manderánno cinquánta uòmini nella sélva, óve si crede che sia stato svaligiáto 'l corrière, perchè si sa che gli èrano state (or gli s' erano) consegnate lèttere di gran conseguènza; e come non si ha dúbbio che siano i nemici, che l'hanno ritenúte, giacchè si hanno avvìsi cèrti, che sono státe viste alcúne delle nòstre lettere nelle loro mani; si è inviáta una spia per informársi segretaménte di quanto (or di quel che si passa or rather di quanto si dice), e gli si prométtono dugènto scúdi, se se ne potrà avér nuòva (or se potránno averne nuove).

THEME.

On the Phrases there be, there is, there was, &c.

Before you compose this theme, refer to the pages 150, 151.

Remember also that you must express *there is of it* or *them, there was of it* or *them*, by *ce n' è*, or *ce ne sóno, ce ne fu* or *ve ne fúrono*, and not by *ci ne, vi ne*. See pp. 153, 154.

There is a man in the street, who says, that yesterday there was a riot opposite the palace, where there were three men killed; and he swears that if he had been present, there would have been a great many more, because he has heard there have been two of his friends wounded, and that two women, and three children have also been maimed. They talk likewise of several merchants whom the passengers report to have been cruelly beaten; and that of the ten soldiers who are in prison, four of them will be hanged, and the six others are condemned to the galleys.

V' è (or c' è) un uòmo nella strada, che dice che vi fu ièri un gran rumóre dirimpètto al palázzo, óve fúrono uccísi tre uòmini; e giúra che, se vi fósse stato, ve ne sarèbbero stati mólti più; perciocchè ha sapúto che v'èrano stati feríti due amíci suòi, e che due dònne e tre fanciúlli vi sóno stati storpiáti. Si parla anche di molti mercanti, che i viandánti dicono èssere stati atroceménte battúti, e che di dièci soldáti che sono in prigióne, ve ne saránno quattro impiccáti, e che gli altri sèi sono condannáti alla galèra.

Observe, that according to the rule in p. 150, one might leave out *v'* or *c'* of the first line, and only put *è un uòmo nella strada.*

THEME.

To learn when to express, and when to omit, in Italian, the Articles the, of the, of; &c.

See pages 210, 211, &c., where you will find all the difficulties explained.

There are men and women that look on the pictures, who say that they are paintings much esteemed by all the connoisseurs, and the ignorant themselves.

Do not come here with persons of your country, to talk of the affairs of your brother.

You will have time to write letters to all your friends.

We must separate them from the rest, and give nothing to them but bread and water.

I received yesterday news of the prince, and of madam the princess.

I have received a hundred crowns from the prince, and fifty from the princess.

Talk to me of philosophy, and of the affairs of the times.

He labours for ungrateful people, that give pain and sorrow to all their relations.

You will be praised by the soldiers, but you will be blamed by the captains, and the chief officers of the army.

You have had a great deal of pain, and little profit.

We have eaten for dinner partridges, quails, and young pigeons.

1. Give us some bread, some wine and some meat.
2. Give us bread, wine and meat.

Your brothers are arrived from the Indies: they have brought pearls, diamonds and a great many other goods, in deal boxes, upon horses and camels.

*_** I have put the phrase *give us bread, wine, and* *meat*, twice, that you may consider when to express, and when to omit, the article *of the*.

A translation according to the Rules.

ʻEcco uòmini e dònne, che considerano i quadri, e che dicono, che sóno pittúre mólto stimáte da tutti i dòtti, e dagl' ignoránti stessi.

Non veníte quà con persóne del vòstro paése, per parlár dégli affari di vòstro fratèllo.

Avréte tèmpo per iscrivere lèttere a tutt' i vòstri amíci.

Bisógna separárli dagli altri, e non dar lóro che pane ed ácqua.

Ricevéi ièri nuòve del signór príncipe, e della signóra principéssa.

Ho ricevúto cènto scudi dal príncipe, e cinquánta dalla principéssa.

Parlátemi della filosofía, e dégli affári del tèmpo.

Lavóra per ingráti, che danno péna e fastídio a tutt' i lóro parènti.

Saréte lodáto dai soldáti, ma saréte biasimáto dai capitáni, e dai principáli dell' armáta.

Avete avúto grand' incòmodo, e pòco profitto.

Abbiámo mangiáto a pranzo perníci, quáglie e piccioncini.

1. Dáteci del pane, del vino e della carne.
2. Dáteci pane, vino e carne.

I vòstri fratèlli sóno arriváti dalle Indie; hanno portato pèrle, diamánti e molte altre mercanzíe in iscátole di abéte, sópra caválli e cammèlli.

SIXTH TREATISE.

OF POETICAL LICENSES, AND THE SYNONYMOUS NAMES OF THE HEATHEN GODS.

The principal difficulties of the Italian poetry consist in the poetical licenses, and in the different synonyma; which shall constitute the two chapters of this treatise.

CHAPTER I.

OF POETICAL LICENSES.

Poetical licenses are certain diminutions or augmentations at the end of words, which frequently occur in poetry; as,

álma	for	*ánima*	the soul
áltri		*áltro*	one, and some
andáro		*andárono*	they went
andár'		*andárono*	they went
andiánne		*andiámocene*	let us go away
amáro		*amárono*	they loved
augèi		*augèlli*	birds
appo		*apprèsso*	near to
baciánne		*baciámoci*	let us kiss
béa		*béva*	let him drink
beéa		*bevéva*	he was drinking
bée		*béve*	he drinks
bèi		*bèlli*	fair, beautiful
cággio		*cádo*	I fall
caggiámo		*cadiámo*	we fall
capéi		*capélli*	hairs
cavái		*caválli*	horses
cadéo		*cadde*	he fell
cèle		*cèla*	he, or she hides *or* conceals
cèlan		*cèlano*	they hide

ce l' hán		ce l' hánno	they are angry with
chère		chiède	he demands [us
china		chináta	a bending down
chíno		chináto	bent down
coltèi		coltèlli	knives
còr		cògliere	to gather
corrém		coglierémo	we shall gather
costáro		costárono	they did cost
costár'		costárono	they did cost
crederia		crederèbbe	he should or would
de' or dèe		dève	he owes [believe
dèggio		dèvo	I owe
dèggi or dèi		dèvi	thou owest
dèggia		dèbba	he may owe
deggiámo		dobbiámo	we may owe
dèggiano		dèbbano	they may owe
deggiáte		dóbbiate	you may owe
dèggio		dèbbo	I owe
degg'io ?		dèbb' io?	do I owe?
dèggiono		dèbbono	they owe
dènno	for	dèbbono	they owe
dèo		dèbbo or dèvo	I owe
dèono		dèvono	they owe
die'		diède	he gave
dièro		dièdero	they gave
dier', dièron		dièdero	they gave
dièronsi		si dièdero	they gave or applied themselves to
dicestù		dicésti tu	saidst thou
dísser		dissero	they said
dómo		dománo	tamed
éi, e'		égli	he
empío		empì	he filled
face		fa	he does or makes
facéan		facévano	they were making
fè		fede	faith
fè'		fece	he did or made
féa		facéva	he was doing
féi		fèci	I did or made
félli		li fece	he made them
fèmmo		facèmmo	we made

fĕnne		*ne fĕce*	he made some, *or of*
férno		*fĕcero*	they made [them
fĕo		*fĕce*	he made
féro		*fĕcero*	they made
fĕra		*ferísca*	strike
fére		*ferísce*	he strikes
féron		*fĕcero*	they did *or* made
férono		*fĕcero*	they did *or* made
fĕste		*facéste*	you did *or* made
fĭa		*sarà*	he shall be
fĭan		*saránno*	they shall be
fĭe		*sarà*	he shall be
fĭeno		*saránno*	they shall be
fĭ		*sii*	be thou
fòra		*sarèbbe*	he should be
fòran		*sarèbbero*	they should be
fóssino		*fóssero*	they might be
fra'		*fráte*	a brother
fúe		*fu*	he was
fur'		*fúrono*	they were
fúro	for	*fúrono*	they were
gía		*andáva*	he was going
giro or *gir'*		*andárono*	they went
gíte		*andáte*	go you
gíva		*andáva*	he was going
hággio		*ho*	I have
halle		*le ha*	he has them
halmi		*me l' ha*	he has it to me
han		*hánno*	they have
avèi		*avrèi*	I should have
avía		*avrèbbe*	he should have
avian		*avrèbbero*	they should have
have		*ha*	he has
avía		*avéva*	he had
avría		*avrèbbe*	he should have
havvi		*vi ha*	there is
hòlle		*le ho*	I have to her
hònne		*ne ho*	I have some of it
i'		*io*	I
ir		*andáre*	to go
íte		*andáte*	go ye

ivan		*andávano*	they were going
là've		*là dove*	there where
len		*gliéne*	to him of it
lodáro		*lodárono*	they praised
lodár		*lodárono*	they praised
me'		*mèglio*	better
men		*me ne*	me some of it
men		*méno*	less
morio		*morì*	he died
nè 'l		*nè il*	neither the
nòsco,		*con nói*	with us
pága		*pagáta*	contented
págo		*pagáto*	contented
par		*pare*	it seems
por		*pórre*	to put
piè		*piède*	a foot
pònno		*pòssono*	they can
puòte		*può*	he can
potría		*potrèbbe*	he could
que'		*quélli*	those
ritòr	for	*ritògliere*	to retake
sallo		*lo sa*	he knows it
salsi		*salii*	I went up
salse		*salì*	he went up
salti?		*ti sa?*	dost thou find?
salti buòno?		*ti sa buòno?*	dost thou like?
se'		*sèi*	thou art
sèggio		*sèggo* or *sièdo*	I sit down
sèggiono		*sèggono*	they sit down
sel		*sé lo*	to himself of it
sì		*così*	so, as much,
sède		*sième*	he sits
sèdon		*sèggono*	they sit
sien		*síano*	they be
sollaváro		*sollevárono*	they raised up
sollevár		*sollevarono*	they raised up
spène, speme		*speránza*	hope
spírto		*spírito*	a spirit
sta		*quésta*	this
ste'		*stètte*	he stood *or* dwelt
stel		*stèlo*	the stalk *or* stem

sulla		sópra la	upon the
tái		tali	such
terrállo		lo terrà	he will hold it
tièllo, tiènlo		tièni lo	hold it thou
tòmmi		tòglimi	take me away
tòr		tògliere	to take away
trónche		troncáte	cut off, f. pl.
trónco		troncáto	cut off, m. sing.
u'		óve	where
valso		valúto	worth
vanne		váttene	go away, be off
ve'		védi	see thou
véggio		védo or véggo	I see
véggiono	for	védono	they see
vèglio		vècchio	an old man
vélle		védile	see thou them, fem.
vélli		védili	see thou them, mas.
vélli		èccoli	there they are
véllo		èccolo	there he is
ven		ve ne	you some of it
vèr		vèrso	towards
vo'		vòglio	I will
vólto		voltàto	turned
vòsco		con voi	with you
usciano		uscívano	they were going out
uscio		uscì	he went out
usciro		uscírono	they went out

₊ Observe, that the third person plural of the pre-terperfect definite terminating in *árono*, as, *legárono*, *amárono*, *scolorárono*, *negárono*, are generally to have their poetical terminations in *áro*; thus they say, *legáro*, *amáro*, *scoloráro*, *negáro*. See *Petrárca*, *Tasso*, *Guarini*, and all the other poets.

The poets generally retrench an *l* from the articles *dello*, *della*, *delli*, *delle*; *alli*, *alle*, &c. and from *nella*, *nelli*, *nelle*; *colla*, *colle*, hence they put, *de lo*, *de la*, *de li*, &c. *ne la*, *ne li*, *ne le*; *co la*, *co le*, &c.; example: *de la futúra cáccia*.

They use sometimes *il* before verbs instead of *lo*; as, *il védo* for *lo védo*; *il dicèa* for *lo dicéva*.

Remember also, that the poets more frequently use the verbs in *gio*, than those in *do*, when they have two terminations; thus they write *véggio* oftener than *védo*; *veggèndo*, more usually than *vedèndo*.

CHAPTER II.

OF THE DIFFERENT SYNONYMA OF THE HEATHEN GODS AND GODDESSES.

THE poets make use of different Synonyma to express the names of the Heathen Gods and Goddesses, which I have inserted in this Chapter, in their alphabetical order.

They use as Synonyma for

APÒLLO,

Fèbo.—Il divìn músico.
Il bióndo Dìo, che in Tesságlia s' adóra
L' orácolo di Dèlfo
Il rettóre del Parnáso
Il Dìo d' Elicóna.

BACCO,

Il giovinétto Dìo che 'l Gange adóra
Il Dìo nutríto dalle Ninfe di Nisa
Il Dìo due vòlte nato.

CICLÒPI,

I tre fratèlli d'un sol òcchio in frónte
I gigánti di Vulcáno
I fabbri di Vulcano.

CIÈLO,

Etérea mòle.—Régione stelláta
La magióne degli Dèi.

CÉRERE,

Inventrìce delle prime biáde
Madre di Proserpìna.—Dea d' Elèusi.

N

CIBÈLE,

La Dèa Dindimèna
La Dèa Berecènzia
La móglie di Satúrno
Rèa.

CUPÍDO,

L'amóre.—Il vincitór degli Dèi
L'aláto Dío.—L'arcièro volánte
Il faretráto Arcièro.—Il núdo Arcièro
Il vagabóndo aláto
Il nudo pargolétto
Garzón sóvra l' etáde astúto
Vago figlio di Ciprígna, di Citerèa, di Vènere
Fanciúl bendáto e nudo.

DIÁNA.

Cínzia.—La Luna.—La sorèlla di Fèbo.
Dèlia.—La Dèa delle sélve, de' mónti.

ÈOLO,

Dío de' vènti.

FLÒRA,

Dèa de' Fióri.—Dèa amica di Giunóne.

GIÁNO,

Amíco di Satúrno.—Il Dío bifrónte
Il Dío che pòrta due chiávi.

GIÒVE,

Rettóre delle stélle
Prímo figlio di Satúrno
Il gran motóre.—L'altitonánte.

GIUNÓNE,

La móglie di Giòve.—La Dèa Lucína
La Dea gelósa.—La regína degli Dèi
L' orgogliósa Diva.

INFÈRNO,

Bólgia ardènte
Báratro puzzolènte.—Avèrno.—Néro spèco.

LUCÍFERO STÉLLA,

Forièra del giórno
Stélla núnzia del giórno.

LÚNA,

Diána; Cinzia; E'cate
Regina della nòtte.

MÁRE,

Pèlago; Ocèano; Règgia Cristallina
Régno úmido.—Il padre de' fiúmi.

MÁRTE,

Dio della guèrra.

MERCÚRIO,

Mésso, intèrprete degli Dèi
Inventór della lòtta.—Il divín Citarista
Il Dio de' ladróni.—Cillínio.

MINÈRVA,

Pállade. La Dèa di Samo
La Dea che Atène adóra
Inventríce delle prime ulíve.

NETTÚNO,

Il regnatór canúto de' flutti
Il gran rettóre delle ácque
Il fréddo ed úmido Maríto di Tèti.

PÁLLADE,

Quella che sènza madre dal gran Giòve nácque
Bellóna; Minèrva. Dèa della guèrra
Dea che trovò l' úso dell' òlio e della lana
Inventríce delle prime ulíve.

PLUTÓNE,

Dio delle tènebre.—Dio dell' oscúro régno
L'autóre della sepoltúra
Il prímo che onorò con esèquie i mòrti.

PROSÈRPINA,

La fíglia di Cèrere.—La móglie di Plutóne
La regína delle gròtte Tartáree
Dèa del cupo fóndo.

SATÚRNO,

Il tèmpo.—Il Dio del tèmpo
L'aláto vècchio, or veglío ; il vècchio edáce.

SÓLE,

Il príncipe delle óre. Il gran monárca de' tèmpi
Il luminóso auríga ; Apòllo
Fèbo ; il Fratèllo di Diána
Il pianéta etèrno.

TÈRRA,

La madre comúne de' mortáli
L'antica madre.—Il suòlo.

TÈTI,

Regína de' flutti.—La dèa del mare.

VÉNERE,

Citerèa ; Ciprína or Ciprígna ; Verticòrdia
La Dèa Ericína
Figlia del máre.—Dea di Pafo
Dèa che per Adóne ardéva
Dea d' Amatúnta
Dea or dònna del tèrzo giro.
Leggiádro onór dell' ácque.

VÙLCÁNO,

Zòppo Dío. Fábbro adústo. Il divin artísta
Il genitór d'amóre in Lènno.

SEVENTH TREATISE.

ITALIAN, like all other languages, has its corruptions. Even in the capital of Tuscany, where it is generally spoken with elegance and purity, the careless and illiterate not only fall into the error of eating a moiety of their words, but pronounce others in a guttural and slovenly manner. It is not surprising, therefore, that foreigners should sometimes have preferred the broad but hard accent of the Romans, to the soft and liquid speech of the Florentines. Hence, perhaps, has originated the singular aphorism, *Lingua Toscana in bocca Romana.* There can be little doubt, however, that either a Roman or a Tuscan may have a correct pronunciation, if he has bestowed some attention to get clear of national prejudices and mistakes.

Among the various errors they commit in Rome in their speech, we will notice one only, very common there, and which a foreigner should guard against, and that is of making the first person plural of the preterperfect-definite end in *ssimmo* instead of *mmo;* viz. *amássimo, credéssimo, sentíssimo,* &c., for *amámmo, credémmo, sentímmo,* we loved, we believed, we felt.

Neither must we say, *amaréssimo, crederéssimo,* and the like, to express we should love, we should believe; but *amerémmo, crederémmo,* and the same with regard to all verbs in the second imperfect.

Avoid saying, likewise, as the Florentines frequently do, *voi dicévi, voi amávi, voi credévi, voi andávi,* and the like, instead of *voi diceváte, voi amaváte, voi credeváte, voi andaváte,* because the termination in *vi* is never used but with *tu* in the singular; as, *tu amávi, tu dicévi.*

For the same reason you must not say, *voi amásti, voi credésti, voi vedésti,* but *voi amáste, voi credéste, voi vedéste.*

Neither must you say, as those of Lucca do, *io*

dirébbi, io farébbi, io sarébbi, to express *I should say,
I should do, I should be,* instead of *io dirèi, io farèi, io
sarèi.*

You must mind also not to say, as all Italians in
general sometimes do, *ámono, cántono, bállono,* in the
third person plural of verbs of the first conjugation,
when all terminate in *ano;* therefore write and speak
ámano, cántano, bállano: because there are none but
the verbs in *ere* and in *ire,* that end in *ono* in the third
person plural of the indicative.

To express *we read, we remain, we say, we go out,*
you must say, *leggiámo, rimaniámo, diciámo, usciámo;*
and not *legghiámo, rimanghiámo, dichiámo, eschiámo,* and
that for two incontestable reasons:

First, because there are none but verbs terminated
in the infinitive in *care* and *gare,* as *cercáre, pagáre,*
&c., that take an *h* in the tenses and persons where
the letter *c* or *g* precedes an *e* or an *i,* as I have said
before. So that the verbs in *ere* and *ire* are not included in this rule.

Secondly, because *leghiámo* comes from *legáre,* signifying *to tie,* and so of the rest.

Now concerning the first person singular of the imperfect indicative of all verbs, see first what has simply
and justly been said at note 13, p. 75. But in regard
to this article, one might implicitly follow the rule which
commonly prevails, that is, to terminate it with *a* and
not with *o,* and that we should say *era* and not *ero,
amava* and not *amavo.* For my part, I think quite
the contrary, and am convinced that the words *era,
avéva, amava,* &c. are more suitable to the vulgar than
to polite persons and people of education, because I
cannot comprehend how those who ought naturally to
surpass others so much in knowledge, should attempt
to defend a rule in many respects repugnant to
good sense. Besides, I have three reasons for being of
this opinion. The first is, that in all verbs, and in
what sense soever, I never could find that the third
person was used instead of the first. The second is,
that this change is productive of ambiguity in discourse,
which ought always to be avoided. The third and last

reason, which to me appears altogether definite in regard to those who pay so great a deference to the authority of writers of the first order is, that since we often meet with both terminations in their works, and it will not be granted us, that either of them is owing to the mistakes of printers, this is a demonstration, that these writers looked upon both the one and the other termination as equally good, since they could not make use of *amávo*, which some moderns absolutely proscribe, without thinking of *amáva*, which they would surely have adopted had they thought it more elegant than the other. The best argument, however, in favour of the latter termination is, that it may deserve the preference in phrases where a great number of words terminating in *o* might be disagreeable to the ear; but even then it will be proper to make use of the pronoun personal, in order to avoid the ambiguity I have mentioned.

EIGHTH TREATISE

OF EXPLETIVE COMPOUND WORDS, CAPITALS AND PUNCTUATION.

CHAPTER I.

OF EXPLETIVES.

EXPLETIVES are certain particles which, though not absolutely necessary for the grammatical construction, add great strength and elegance to discourse.

There are three sorts of Expletives. First, those which give energy to speech, so as to represent the thing, as it were, to your sight. Secondly, those which add grace and ornament. Thirdly, those which the Italians call *accompágna nómi*, and *accompágna vèrbi;* and are certain particles added to nouns or verbs, redundant indeed in sense, but peculiar to the Italian idiom.

I. Of the first sort are the following : *ècco*, behold or see now, in the beginning of a sentence ; as, *ècco, io non so dir,* . . . behold, I cannot tell . . .

Bène, well, is used in the beginning of a sentence before an interrogation ; *bène, che fái tu quì?* well, what dost thou here? or in answering in the affirmative, *bene, io lo farò*, well, I will do it : sometimes the particle *sì* is added to it ; *disse Calandrino, sì bene*, Calandrino said, yes, indeed : sometimes *ora* or *or* is prefixed to it, as, *or bene, cóme farémo?* well, what shall we do?

Pur is equivalent to the English word *indeed*, and adds evidence and clearness : *la còsa andò pur così*, the thing went so indeed ; when it is prefixed to a particle of time, it signifies *exactly: perciocchè pur allóra, n' èrano smontáti i signóri*, because the gentlemen had then exactly dismounted.

Già has also sometimes the force of *indeed: ora fóssero éssi pur già dispósti a venire*, now if they were really disposed to come ; sometimes the particle *mái* is added to it, and then it signifies *never: non usáva giammái*, he never used.

Mái either prefixed to or put after *sèmpre*, gives it great force : *io sempre mai farò ciò*, I will always do this; *che si giáce mai sempre in ghiáccio*, that is always covered with ice.

Mica and *punto* strengthen negatives : *non mica d' uòmo di pòco affare*, a man of no small consequence ; *il re non è punto mòrto, ma vivo*, the king is not dead, but alive.

Tutto gives strength : *la gentíl gióvane tutta tímida*, the genteel young woman quite afraid.

Via, joined to verbs, increases their force, *via a casa del prète ne portárono*, they carried us away to the priest's house.

II. Of the second sort of Expletives are the following :

Egli is sometimes used for ornament, without regard to gender or number : *égli è il véro*, it is true ; *égli è óra di desináre a casa*, it is dinner time at home.

Ella is therefore used as an ornamental expletive : *cominciò a dire élla non andrà sempre così*, she began to say, it shall not go always so.

Esso is used in both genders and numbers, with the particle *con* before some pronouns, and even without the pronouns : *élla voléva con ésso lúi digiunáre*, she was willing to fast with him ; *rise con ésso lei*, he laughed with her ; *cominciò a cantare con ésso loro*, he began to sing with them ; *che vènga a desináre con ésso nói*, let him come and dine with us.

Ora is used in resuming or continuing a discourse, in the same manner as *now* in English : *óra io ve l'ho udíto dire mille vòlte*, now, I heard you say it a thousand times.

Si has a particular beauty as an expletive : *óltre a quéllo ch' égli fu òttimo filòsofo, si fu egli leggiadríssimo e costumáto*, for besides his being an excellent philosopher, he was, moreover, very courteous and mannerly.

N 5

Di is used in a manner peculiar to the Italian language; *nè di giorno nè di nòtte*, both day and night.

Non is often used as an expletive: *aspettáte finchè non l'ábbia ricevuto*, wait till I have received it. This is worth observing, because we find thereby that in Italian *non* does not always imply a negative.

Altriménti is also used merely as an ornament: *sènza sapér altriménti che égli si fòsse*, without knowing who he was.

III. Of the third sort are the following words:

Uno and *una*, not as numeral nouns, but as particles whose office it is to accompany nouns, without adding any thing to the signification, for which reason the Italians call them *accompagnanómi*: *io crédo che gran nóia sia ad una bèlla e delicáta dònna avér per maríto un mentecátto*, I believe it is very disagreeable for a fine sensible woman to have a fool for a husband.

Alcúno is sometimes used instead of *uno*; *èrano legáti in alcún luògo púbblico*, they were tied in a public place.

The particles that accompany verbs without adding any thing to the signification, are *mi*, *ti*, *ci*, *vi*, *si*, and *ne*.

Mi: *io mi crédo, che le dònne sièn tutte a dormíre*, I believe the women are all asleep. Sometimes the particle *ne* is added to it; but then we say *me*, and not *mi*: *sommene venúto*, I am come.

Ci: *La donna e Pirro dicévano, noi ci seggiámo*, the woman and Pyrrhus said, Let us sit down. With relative pronoun it makes *ce*; *e pòscia cel godrémo quì*, and afterwards we will enjoy it here. *Vogliámcene noi andáre ancóra?* shall we go yet?

Ti: *Che tu cón nói ti rimánga per quésta sera*, stay with us this evening. Before the pronoun relative they say *te*: *tu te ne pentirái*, thou wilt repent it.

Vi: *Io non so se voi conoscéste il cavalière*, I know not whether you were acquainted with the gentleman. With *ne* they say *ve*: *voi potréte tornárvene a casa*; you may go home.

Si: *Del palágio s' uscì, e fuggíssi a casa súa*, he went out of the palace, and ran home. With a relative pronoun it becomes *se* : *se gli mangiò*, he ate them ; *féce vista di bérsela*, he pretended to drink it.

Ne : *Chetaménte* n' *andà*, he went away quietly ; *andiánne là*, let us go there.

CHAPTER II.

OF COMPOUND WORDS.

THE Italians, for the sake of elegance and strength of expression, have often recourse to compound words ; concerning which it is impossible to give any general rule ; the surest way is to make use of those which are established by custom ; as,

Ognúno,	every one.
Gentiluòmo,	a gentleman.
Sottovóce,	whispering.
Sottománo,	underhand,
Nondiméno, nulladiméno,	nevertheless,
Trentòtto,	thirty-eight,
Quarantacínque,	forty-five,
Sottosópra,	topsy-turvy.

We shall make only those remarks on this subject, which may be of use to the learner.

When the first of the compound words ends with a vowel and the second begins with a consonant, the Italians are accustomed to pronounce them with greater emphasis, and therefore they repeat the first consonant of the second word, as, *dello, colassù, laggiù, appiè*, &c. we except from this rule the verb *raddirizzáre*.

The first of the compound words sometimes loses the last vowel whatever consonant it precedes ; and the first consonant of the second word is repeated, as, *sottèrra, sèggiola, soppánno, sossópra*, &c.

When one of the compound words is a pronoun, and the last syllable of the word is accented, the consonant of the particle is repeated, unless it happens to be followed by another consonant : for example, we say *dímmi*, tell me ; *diròtti*, I will tell thee ; *diròglí*, I will tell him.

CHAPTER III.

OF CAPITALS.

IN regard to Capital Letters, the following rules are established by the Italians :

1. Proper names always begin with a capital.

2. Names of nations taken substantively begin with a capital; as, *i Francési fécero guèrra*, the French made war; but taken adjectively they require a small letter, and so they write *un mercánte inglese*, *un militare fiancése.*

3. The expressing of a genus or species requires a capital, hence they write *l' Uomo è la più nòbile delle inferióri creatúre*, Man is the noblest of the inferior creatures; *il Cavállo è útile alla guèrra*, the Horse is useful for war; but the capital is dropped when they are applied to individuals; *quest' è un buòn uòmo*, this is a good man; *ecco un bèl cavállo*, there is a fine horse.

4. Those appellatives which are used instead of proper names, require a capital; hence they write *il Padre, il Mèdico, il Maèstro*, the Father, the Physician, the Master, when speaking of some particular person.

OF PUNCTUATION.

The use of stops or points is to distinguish words and sentences, so as to express the sense with clearness. The Italians have five stops or pauses.

1. The *punto férmo*, called in English full stop (.), is used at the end of a period, to show that the sentence is completely finished.

2. The *mèzzo punto*, viz. colon (:), is the pause made between two members of a period, that is, when the sense is complete, but the sentence not ended.

3. The *punto e vírgola*, semicolon (;), denotes that short pause which is made in the subdivision of the members or parts of a sentence.

4. The *point of interrogation* (?) or the point of admiration (!).

5. The *virgola*, comma (,), is the shortest pause of resting in speech, being used chiefly to distinguish nouns, verbs and adverbs, as also the parts of a shorter sentence.

The use of these stops is much the same among the Italians as the English; if the former have any particularity, it is in regard to the *virgole*, concerning which we shall make the following remarks:

Whenever a word or a preposition is inserted in a period, of which it does not form a part, it is put between commas: as, *facciám dúnque a cotésto módo; ma con quésto, védi, che tu non parta da me*, let us proceed in this manner; but with this condition, *take care*, that you do not leave me.

The conjunction *e*, and the disjunctions *o* or *ne*, require a comma before them; yet when these particles are repeated, and the first stands as an expletive, it ought to have no comma before it.

The relatives *che* and *quale*, require a comma before them, as they suppose some kind of pause, though very small; but when *che* signifies *what*, it requires no comma, as *attènto a vedére* che *di lui avvenisse*, attentive to see what became of him; *avvèngane che può*, let what will happen.

When conjunctions and adverbial expressions are repeated, and correspond to one another, the first does not require a comma, *èra Cimóne, sì per la súa fórma, che per la nobiltà e ricchezza del pádre, quási nòto a ciascúno del paése*, Cymon was known almost to every man in the country, as well on account of his person, as for the nobility and wealth of his father.

THE END OF THE SECOND PART.

PART III.

CONTAINING,

A Vocabulary of Words most used in discourse.—A Collection of Verbs. — Familiar Dialogues. — Italian Phrases, in which the delicacy of that language consists.—Several little Stories, Jests, Sentences of divers Authors, and a Collection of the choicest Italian Proverbs.—An Introduction to Italian Poetry.—Fine Thoughts from the Italian Poets.—Different Inscriptions and Titles used in Italian Letters, and Letters of Business and Compliment.

A VOCABULARY OF WORDS

MOST USED IN DISCOURSE.

OF THE HEAVENS AND THE ELEMENTS.

Dio, Iddio	God	*l' infèrno*	hell
Gesù Cristo	Jesus Christ	*il móndo*	the world
lo Spírito Santo	the Holy Ghost	*il fuòco*	the fire
		l' ária	the air
la Trinità	the Trinity	*la tèrra*	the earth
gli ángeli	the angels	*il mare*	the sea
un profèta	a prophet	*l' acqua*	the water
il cièlo([33])	heaven	*il sóle*	the sun
il cielo	the sky	*la luna*	the moon
il paradíso	paradise	*le stélle*	the stars

[33] See, as to the accents used on the words of this Vocabulary, Dialogues, Stories, &c., the second N. B. at p. 23.

i rággi	the rays	*il gèlo*	the frost
le núvole	the clouds	*il ghiáccio*	the ice
il vènto	the wind	*la rugiáda*	the dew
la piòggia	the rain	*la nébbia*	a fog or mist
il tuòno	the thunder	*il terremòto,*	the earth-
il lampo	the lightning	*il tremuòto*	quake
la grándine	the hail	*un dilúvio*	a deluge or
il fúlmine	the thunder-		flood
	bolt	*il caldo*	the heat
la néve	the snow	*il fréddo*	the cold

OF THE TIME AND SEASONS.

Il giórno	the day	*un mése*	a month
la nòtte	the night	*un anno*	a year
il mèzzo giórno	mid-day	*un minúto*	a minute
		un istánte	an instant
la mèzza nòtte	midnight	*un momènto*	a moment
		la primavèra	the spring
la mattina	the morning	*l' estáte, fem.*	the summer
la séra	the evening	*l'autúnno*	autumn
òggi	to-day	*l'invèrno*	the winter
ièri	yesterday	*una fèsta*	a holiday
dománi	to-morrow	*un giòrno di*	a working-
ièr l' altro	the day be-	*la vóro*	day
	fore yes-	*il levár del*	the sun-
	terday	*sóle*	rising
domán l' altro	the day after to-morrow	*il tramontár del sole*	the sun- setting
úna settimána	a week	*l' alba*	the dawn

THE DAYS OF THE WEEK.

Lunedì	Monday	*Venerdì*	Friday
Martedì	Tuesday	*Sábato*	Saturday
Mercoledì	Wednesday	*Doménica*	Sunday
Giovedì	Thursday		

THE MONTHS.

Gennáio	January	*Lúglio*	July
Febbráio	February	*Agósto*	August
Marzo	March	*Settèmbre*	September
Aprile	April	*Ottóbre*	October
Mággio	May	*Novèmbre*	November
Giúgno	June	*Dicèmbre*	December

THE HOLIDAYS OF THE YEAR.

Il capo d' anno	New year's day	*il giórno di Pásqua*	Easter-day
l'Epifania	Twelfth-day	*la Pentecòste*	Whitsuntide
la Quarésima	Lent	*il giorno de' Mòrti*	All-souls day
la Doménica delle palme	Palm-Sunday	*il Natále*	Christmas-day
la settimána santa	Passion-week	*la vigília*	the eve
il Venerdì santo	Good-Friday	*la mietitúra*	the harvest
		la vendémmia	the vintage

OF ECCLESIASTICAL DIGNITIES.

Il papa	the pope	*un canònico*	a canon
un cardinále	a cardinal	*un prète*	a priest
un arcivéscovo	an archbishop	*un capelláno*	a chaplain
un véscovo	a bishop	*un elemosinière*	an almoner
un núnzio	a nuncio		
un preláto	a prelate	*un curáto*	a curate
un rettóre	a rector	*un predicatóre*	a preacher
un vicário	a vicar		
un decáno	a dean	*un sagrestáno*	a sexton
		un chérico	a clerk

NAMES OF SOME ARTICLES OF FOOD.

Pane	bread	*un pasticcio*	a pie
ácqua	water	*una minèstra*	a soup
vino	wine	*un bròdo*	a basin of broth
birra	beer		
carne	meat *or* flesh	*un' insaláta*	a salad
pésce	fish	*una salsa*	the sauce
allésso	boiled meat	*delle frutta*	fruit
arròsto	roast meat	*del cácio*	cheese

THE COVERING OF THE TABLE.

La távola	the table	*le smoccola-tóie*	the snuffers
úna sèdia	a chair		
la továglia	the table-cloth	*un bacíle*	a basin
		un bicchière	a glass
un tovagli-uòlo	a napkin	*un fiásco*	a flask
		úna bottíglia	a bottle
un coltèllo	a knife	*una tazza*	a cup
una for-chétta	a fork	*una sotto-còppa*	a saucer
un cucchiáio	a spoon	*un' asciuga-máni*	a towel
un tóndo	a plate		
un piátto	a dish	*un servízio*	a service, or course
una salièra	a salt-seller		
una zucche-rièra	a sugar-dish	*un panière*	a basket
		una pínta	a pint
un candelière	a candle-stick	*un boccále*	a jug
una candéla	a candle	*un cavasú-ghero*	a corkscrew

WHAT IS EATEN AT TABLE AS BOILED MEAT.

Bue, manzo	beef	*agnèllo*	lamb
castráto	mutton	*una gallina*	a hen
vitèllo	veal	*un pollástro*	a fowl

FOR THE FIRST COURSE.

Un guazzétto	a ragout	*mortadella di Bológna*	Bologna sausage
una fricassèa	a fricassee	*salame di Firènze*	Florence sausage
uno stufáto	stewed meat	*del fégato*	liver
un' animèlla di vitèllo	sweet bread	*delle radíci*	radishes
una torta	a tart	*popóne*	a melon
dei pasticcétti	petty patties	*un cocómero*	a water-melon
del prosciútto	some ham		
delle salsicce	sausages		

WHAT IS ROASTED.

Un cappóne	a capon	*una lèpre*	a hare
pollástri	pullets	*un coniglio*	a rabbit
picción i	pigeons	*un cèrvo*	a stag
le beccácce	woodcocks	*un maiále*	a pig
le pernici	partridges	*un porchétto*	a pig
i tordi	thrushes	*un cinghiále*	a wild boar
le lòdole	larks	*un cosciòtto di castrato*	a leg of mutton
le quáglie	quails	*un lombo di vitèllo*	a loin of veal
i fagiáni	pheasants		
un gallináccio or *un tacchíno* }	a turkey	*una spallétta di castráto*	a shoulder of mutton
un' òca	a goose	*una braciuòla*	a steak
un pápero	a gosling	*del selvaggiúme*	game
un' ánitra	a duck		

TO SEASON MEAT WITH.

Del sale	salt	*della cannèlla*	cinnamon
del pépe	pepper	*dei cápperi*	capers
dell' òlio	oil	*dei fúnghi*	mushrooms
dell' acéto	vinegar	*dei tartúfi*	truffles
dell' agrèsto	verjuice	*delle cipólle*	onions
della mostárda	mustard	*delle cipollétte*	young onions
dei garòfani	cloves		

dell' áglio	garlick	*del prezzé-*	parsley
del lardo	bacon	*molo*	
dei limóni	lemons	*della salvia*	sage

FOR A SALAD.

Dell' èrbe	herbs	*de' sèdani*	celery
dell' indívia	endive	*del cerfòglio*	chervil
della lattúga	lettuce	*del crescióne*	cresses

FOR FISH DAYS.

Del burro	butter	*dei gámberi*	shrimps
del latte	milk	*delle òstriche*	oysters
delle uòva af-	poached eggs	*del salmóne*	salmon
fogáte		*del merlúzzo*	cod-fish
delle frittèlle	fritters	*delle acciúghe*	anchovies
una frittáta	an omelet	*dei pisèlli*	peas
dei gámberi	crawfish	*delle fave*	beans
un lúccio	a pike	*degli spináci*	spinage
una tròta	a trout	*dei carciòfi*	artichokes
una sògliola	a sole	*degli spáragi*	asparagus
un' anguílla	an eel	*dei cávoli*	cabbages
una tinca	a tench	*dei bròccoli*	sprouts
uno storióne	a sturgeon	*del cávol-*	cauliflowers
un' aringa	a herring	*fiore*	
una locústa	a lobster	*del finòcchio*	fennel

FOR THE DESSERT.

Delle méle	apples	*dei fichi*	figs
delle pére	pears	*delle susíne*	plumbs
delle pèsche	peaches	*dell' úva*	grapes
delle albi-	apricots	*delle nóci*	nuts
còcche		*delle noc-*	filberts
delle cirìège	cherries	*ciuòle*	
dell' uvaspina	gooseberries	*delle ca-*	chesnuts
dei lampóni	raspberries	*stágne*	
delle mòre	mulberries	*delle mán-*	almonds
delle frávole	strawberries	*dorle*	

delle nèspole	medlars	*delle aránce*	oranges
delle mela-gráne	pomegra-nates	*delle ulíve*	olives

DEGREES OF KINDRED.

Il padre	the father	*il gènero*	the son-in-law
la madre	the mother		
il nònno (*l'avo*)	the grand-father	*la nuòra*	the daughter-in-law
la nònna	the grand-mother	*il nipotíno*	the grand-son
		la nipotina	the grand-daughter
il bisávo	the great-grandfather	*i genitóri*	the parents
la bisava	the great-grandmother	*lo spòso*	the spouse, *masc.*
il fíglio	the son	*la sposa*	the spouse, *fem.*
la figlia	the daughter		
il fratèllo	the brother	*i gemèlli*	the twin-brothers
la sorèlla	the sister		
il primogè-nito *il maggióre*	the eldest son	*il figliòccio*	the god-son
		la figlioccia	the god-daughter
il cadètto *il minóre*	the youngest son	*il compáre*	the god-father
lo zio	the uncle	*la comáre*	the god-mother
la zía	the aunt		
il nipóte	the nephew	*la bália*	the nurse
la nipote	the niece	*un parènte*	a relative
il cugíno	the cousin	*un maríto*	a husband
la cugina	the female cousin	*una móglie*	a wife
		un védovo	a widower
il cognáto	the brother-in-law	*úna védova*	a widow
		un erède	an heir
la cognata	the sister-in-law	*úna erede*	an heiress
		un pupíllo	a ward
il suòcero	the father-in-law	*úna pupilla*	a female ward
		un tutóre	a guardian
la suocera	the mother-in-law		

OF THE CONDITIONS OF MAN AND WOMAN.

Un uòmo	a man	*una zitèlla*	a maid
úna dònna	a woman	*il padróne*	the master
un vècchio	an old man	*la padrona*	the mistress
una vecchia	an old woman	*il servitóre*	the man servant
un gióvane	a young man		
una giovane	a young girl	*la sèrva*	the female servant
un bambíno	an infant		
una bambína	an infant	*il cittadíno*	the citizen
un ragázzo	a boy	*un conta-dino*	a peasant
un ragazzíno	a little boy		
una fanciul-lina	a little girl	*un forestièro*	a stranger.

WHAT IS NECESSARY FOR DRESSING ONESELF.

Un vestíto } *un ábito* }	a coat	*úna camícia*	a shirt
un cappèllo	a hat	*una camiciòla*	an undershirt
una parrúcca	a wig	*una sottovèste*	a waistcoat
una cravátta	a cravat	*una mánica*	a sleeve
un ferraiuòlo	a cloak	*i manichíni*	the ruffles
le calzétte	socks	*una berrétta*	a cap
calze	stockings	*una vèsta da cámera*	a morning gown
le scárpe	the shoes	*una tasca*	a pocket
gli scarpíni	the pumps	*i calzóni*	trousers
le pianèlle	the slippers	*le mutánde*	drawers

WITH CLOTHES, WE MUST HAVE

Dei nastri	ribbons	*un oriuòlo*	a watch
dei merlétti	lace	*un manicòtto*	a muff
dei bottóni	buttons	*delle fíbbie*	buckles
gli ucchièlli	button-holes	*delle legácce*	garters
della frángia	fringe	*un anèllo*	a ring
dei guánti	gloves	*un pèttine*	a comb
un fazzolétto	a handkerchief	*una tabac-chièra*	a snuff-box

FOR THE LADIES.

Una cúffia	a head-dress	*le mósche*	patches
úna sottána	a petticoat	*ácque odoróse*	scent waters
il busto	the stays	*della pólvere*	powder
il grembiále	the apron	*una scátola*	a box
una máschera	a mask	*le giòie*	jewels
un vélo	a veil	*un gioièllo*	a jewel
gli orecchíni	ear-rings	*un diamánte*	a diamond
i ricci	the curls	*uno smeráldo*	an emerald
un ventáglio	a fan	*un rubíno*	a ruby
una stécca	a busk	*una pèrla*	a pearl
gli smanígli	bracelets	*un záffiro*	a sapphire
la tuelètta	the toilet	*un astúccio*	a case
gli spilli	pins	*della téla*	linen
un torsèllo	a pincushion	*una rócca*	a distaff
le fòrbici	the scissors	*il fuso*	the spindle
un ditále	a thimble	*la séta*	silk
un ágo	a needle	*la lana*	wool
il rèfe	thread	*dell' ámido*	starch
il liscio	paint	*del sapóne*	soap

OF THE PARTS OF THE BODY.

La tèsta	the head	*la língua*	the tongue
il viso	the face	*le labbra*	the lips
la frònte	the forehead	*il paláto*	the palate
gli òcchi	the eyes	*i pizzi*	the whiskers
le cíglia	the eyebrows	*i baffi*	the musta-
le palpèbre	the eye-lids		chios
la pupilla	the eye-ball	*il ménto*	the chin
le orécchie	the ears	*il còllo*	the neck
i capélli	the hair	*la góla*	the throat
le tèmpia	the temples	*le spálle*	the shoulders
le guánce	the cheeks	*le bráccia*	the arms
il naso	the nose	*il gómito*	the elbow
le naríci	the nostrils	*il pugno*	the fist
la barba	the beard	*la mano*	the hand
la bócca	the mouth	*il dito*	the finger
i dènti	the teeth	*il pòllice*	the thumb

le únghie	the nails	il cervèllo	the brain
lo stòmaco	the stomach	il sángue	the blood
il séno	the bosom	le véne	the veins
le còste	the ribs	le artèrie	the arteries
le ginòcchia	the knees	i nèrvi	the nerves
la gamba	the leg	i múscoli	the muscles
la pólpa della gamba	the calf of the leg	la pèlle	the skin
la nóce del piède	the ancle bone	il cuòre	the heart
il còllo del piede	the instep	il fégato	the liver
		i polmóni	the lungs
il piede	the foot	la tósse	the cough
il calcágno	the heel	il catárro	the rheum
il portaménto	the demean-our	il fiáto	the breath
		la vóce	the voice
la grassézza	the fatness	la paròla	the speech
la magrézza	the leanness	un sospiro	a sigh
la statúra	the stature	la vista	the sight
l'andatúra	the gait	l'udíto	the hearing
il gèsto	the gesture	l' odoráto	the smell
		il gusto	the taste
		il tatto	the feeling

FOR STUDY.

La libreria	the library	un sigíllo	a seal
il gabinétto	the closet	una lèttera	a letter
un líbro	a book	un bigliétto	a note
la carta	the paper	la scrittúra	the writing
un fòglio	a leaf	il taccuíno	the pocket-book
úna página	a page		
una pénna	a pen	la cartapè-cora	parchment
l'inchiòstro	ink		
un calamáio	an ink-stand	il pennèllo	the brush
un temperino	a pen-knife	il lápis	the pencil
lo spago	packthread	una lezióne	a lesson
la pólvere	sand	una tradu-zióne	a translation
il polveríno	the sand-box		
la ceralácca	the sealing-wax	un tèma	a theme

INSTRUMENTS OF MUSIC, &c.

Un violíno	a violin	*un liúto*	a lute
una viòla	a bass-viol	*un' arpa*	a harp
ur còrno	a horn	*un órgano*	an organ
un fláuto	a flute	*una trómba*	a trumpet
uno zúfolo	a flageolet	*un tambúro*	a drum
una zam-	a bagpipe	*un piffero*	a fife
pógna		*un' orchèstra*	an orchestra
un òboe	a hautboy	*una banda'*	a band
una chitárra	a guitar	*il basso*	the bass
un cémbalo	a harpsichord	*il sopráno*	the treble
un pianforte	a piano-forte	*il tenóre*	the tenor

OF A HOUSE AND ITS PARTS.

La cása	the house	*la riméssa*	the coach-house
la pòrta	the door		
il portóne	the gate	*la cantina*	the cellar
una stanza	a room	*le scale*	the stairs
la cámera	the bed-room	*una scala*	a ladder
un lètto	a bed	*il primo*	the first floor,
una sala	a drawing-room	*piáno, &c.*	&c.
		il terrázzo	the terrace
la sala da pranzo	the dining-room	*la soffitta*	the garret
		il tétto	the roof
la sala ter-réna	the parlour	*i tégoli*	the tiles
		le grondáie	the gutters
l' anticámera	the anti-chamber	*la fontána*	the fountain
		il giardíno	the garden
un salóne	a hall	*il muro*	the wall
il gabinétto	the closet	*il cammíno*	the chimney
la finèstra	the window	*i mattóni*	the bricks
le invetriáte	the panes of glass	*il fórno*	the oven
		una trave	a beam
la cucína	the kitchen	*i travicèlli*	the joists
la dispènsa	the pantry	*le távole*	the planks
il cortíle	the yard	*la pigióne*	the rent
il pózzo	the well	*il gèsso*	the plastering
la stalla	the stable	*la calcína*	the lime

il marmo	the marble	il polláio	the hen-house
la piètra	the stone		
la colombáia	the pigeon-house	il luògo cò-modo	the water-closet

---

THE FURNITURE OF A ROOM.

La tappez-zeria	the tapestry	i quadri	the pictures
		la cornìce	the frame
lo spècchio	the looking-glass	un orològio	a clock
		le sèdie	the chairs
il lètto	the bed	úna poltróna	an arm-chair
le lenzuòla	the sheets	la távola	the table
le materásse	the mat-tresses	il tappéto	the carpet
		il sofà	the sofa
la cóltrice	the feather-bed	la credènza	the cupboard
		una cassa	a chest
il saccóne	the straw-bed	una scátola	a box
		l'indoratúra	the gilding
il capezzále	the bolster	la scultúra	the carving or sculpture
le cortíne	the curtain		
la copèrta	the counter-pane	l'intagliatúra	carving on wood
il guanciále	the pillow	úna figúra	a figure
la spónda del lètto	the bed side	una státua	a statue
		una colónna	a pillar
una pittúra	a painting	un piedistállo	a pedestal

WHAT WE FIND ABOUT THE CHIMNEY.

La porcel-lána	the China wàre	úna fascina	a faggot
		il soffiétto	the bellows
un' urna	an urn	la palétta	the shovel
un vaso	a vase, a vessel	le mòlle	the tongs
		l'attizzatóre	the poker
il fuòco	the fire	gli zolfanèlli	the matches
il carbóne	coals	l'acciaríno	the steel
la cénere	ashes	la piètra fo-cáia	the flint
il focoláre	the earth		

o

l' ésca	the tinder	*il fumo*	the smoke
la fiámma	the flame	*la fulíggine*	the soot
il parafuòco	the screen	*il parabráce*	the fender

WHAT WE FIND IN THE KITCHEN.

Lo spiède	the spit	*una forchétta*	a fork
il girarròsto	the jack	*uno scalda-*	a chafing-
il ramíno	the kettle	*vivánde*	dish
una padèlla	a frying-pan	*lo scaldalètto*	the warming-
un treppiède	a trivet		pan
una gratèlla	a gridiron	*un uncíno*	a hook
una bròcca	a pitcher	*una grat-*	a grater
una sécchia	a pail	*túggia*	
una fune	a rope	*una tortièra*	a pudding-
un catíno	an earthen		pan
	pan	*un mortáro*	a mortar
una pignát-		*un pestèllo*	a pestle
ta }	a pot	*una scópa*	a broom
una péntola		*un cèncio*	a rag
un cucchiáio	a spoon	*uno strofi-*	a duster
una méstola	a ladle	*náccio*	

WHAT WE FIND IN THE CELLAR.

Una bótte	a butt	*vin vècchio*	old wine
un baríle	a barrel	*vin nuòvo*	new wine
un imbúto	a funnel	*vin rósso*	red wine
un cérchio	a hoop	*vin biánco*	white wine
la fèccia	the dregs	*vin dólce*	sweet wine
del vino	wine	*víno aspro*	sour wine
della birra	beer	*acéto*	vinegar
del sidro	cider	*mósto*	must

WHAT IS FOUND ABOUT A DOOR.

La chiáve	the key	*il saliscéndi*	the latch
la serratúra	the lock	*il chiavistèllo*	the bolt
il catenáccio	the bolt	*il battitóio*	the knocker

la campa-nèlla	the bell	*la sòglia*	the threshold
la stanga	the bar	*gli arpioni* *i cárdini* }	the hinges

WHAT WE FIND IN THE STABLE.

Del fièno	hay	*la frusta*	the whip
della biáda	oats	*le cínghie*	the girths
della páglia	straw	*le staffe*	the stirrups
una rastrel-lièra	a rack	*gli spróni*	the spurs
		il cavicchio	the peg
una mangia-tóia	a manger	*l' arcióne*	the saddle-bow
la sémola	the bran	*una cavézza*	a halter
il pèttine	the comb	*il mózzo di stalla*	the groom
la stríglia	the curry-comb	*i caválli*	the horses
un váglio	a sieve	*la carròzza*	the coach
la briglia	the bridle	*i muli*	the mules
la sèlla	the saddle	*il calèsso*	the chariot
il petto-rále	the breast-plate	*un carro*	a waggon
		un carrétto	a cart

WHAT IS FOUND IN THE GARDEN, THE FLOWERS, AND THE TREES.

Una spal-lièra	a row of wall-trees	*un ciriègio*	a cherry-tree
		un susíno	a plum-tree
una pèrgola	an arbour	*un albicòcco*	an apricot-tree
una ròsa	a rose		
un gelsomíno	a jessamin	*un pèsco*	a peach-tree
dei garòfani	pinks	*un mándorlo*	an almond-tree
del giránio	geraniums		
dei tulipáni	tulips	*un mòro*	a mulberry-tree
dei gigli	lilies		
delle viòle	violets	*un fico*	a fig-tree
delle gion-chíglie	jonquils	*un ulívo*	an olive-tree
		il láuro	the laurel-tree
un mélo	an apple-tree		
un péro	a pear-tree	*l'abéte*	the fir-tree

la quèrcia	the oak	*l'édera*	ivy
il fàggio	the beech-tree	*un ramo*	a branch
		un viále	an avenue
l'ólmo	the elm	*un boschétto*	a little wood
l'aráncio	the orange-tree	*l' ómbra*	the shade
		il frésco	the cool
un rosáio	a rose-bush	*una fontána*	a fountain
un mirto	a myrtle	*un cespúglio*	a bush
il semenzáio	the nursery	*la verzúra*	verdure
la vite	the vine	*un mazzo di fióri*	a nosegay
la vigna	the vineyard		

TEMPORAL DIGNITIES.

Un imperatóre	an emperor	*il marchése*	the marquess
una imperatríce	an empress	*la marchésa*	the marchioness
un re	a king	*il cónte*	the earl
una regína	a queen	*la contéssa*	the countess
ib delfino	the dauphin	*il viscónte*	the viscount
la delfina	the dauphiness	*la viscontéssa*	the viscountess
il príncipe	the prince	*il baróne*	the baron
la principéssa	the princess	*la baronéssa*	the baroness
il grandúca	the grand-duke	*un baronétto*	a baronet
la granduchéssa	the grand-duchess	*un cavalière*	a knight
l' arcidúca	the arch-duke	*il governatóre*	the governor
l' arciduchéssa	the arch-duchess	*la governatrice*	the governor's lady
il dúca	the duke	*l' ambasciatóre*	the ambassador
la duchéssa	the duchess	*un inviáto*	an envoy
		un residènte	a resident
		un agènte	an agent
		un cónsole	a consul

OFFICES AND OFFICERS OF JUSTICE.

Il cancellière	the chancellor	il procuratóre	the attorney
il guarda sigilli	the keeper of the seals	il procuratór fiscále	the attorney-general
il segretário di stato	the secretary of state	un sostitúto	a deputy
l' intendènte	the surveyor	un notáro	a notary
il tesorière	the treasurer	un segretário	a secretary
il presidènte	the president	un sollecitatóre	a solicitor
il consiglière	the councillor	uno scriváno	a clerk
il giúdice	the judge	un copista	a hackney-writer
il magistráto	the magistrate	l' uscière	the usher
il podestà	the mayor	il cursóre	the sergeant
uno schiavíno	an alderman	un carcerière	a jailor
l' avvocáto	the advocate	un litigánte	a pleader
		un prigionière	a prisoner

OFFICERS OF WAR.

Il generále	the general	il cornétta	the cornet
l' ammiráglio	the admiral	l' alfière	the ensign
il luogotenènte generále	the lieutenant-general	il sergènte	the sergeant
		il caporále	the corporal
un maresciállo di campo	a major-general	un quartiermástro	a quartermaster
un brigadière	a brigadier	un commissário	a commissary
il colonnèllo	the colonel	un cavalière	a horse-man
il tenènte colonnello	the lieutenant colonel	un fante	a foot-soldier
		il cavalleggièro	the light-horseman
il maggióre	the major	un dragóne	a dragoon
l' aiutánte maggiore	the adjutant	un moschettière	a musqueteer
il capitáno	the captain	la banda	the band
il tenènte	the lieutenant	un trombétta	a trumpeter
		un tamburíno	a drummer
		il piffero	the fifer

la sentinèlla	the sentinel	*un minatóre*	a miner
la rónda	the round	*i volontárj*	volunteers
la pattúglia	the patrole	*i fanti perdúti*	the forlorn hope
un guastatóre	a pioneer		
un cannonière	a gunner	*un ingegnère*	an engineer

THE ARMY.

Un' armáta	an army	*la prima fila, &c.*	the first rank, &c.
una flòtta	a fleet		
una squadra	a squadron	*il bagáglio*	the baggage
la van- guárdia	the van- guard	*i cannóni*	the guns
		le tènde	the tents
la retro- guárdia	the rear- guard	*il padi- glióne*	the pavilion
il còrpo di ri- sèrva	the body of reserve	*un reggi- ménto*	a regiment
una línea	a line	*una compa- gnía*	a company
la cavallería	the cavalry		
la fantería	the infantry	*una guarni- gióne*	a garrison
uno squadróne	a squadron		
un batta- glióne	a battalion	*una brigáta*	a division

THE FORTIFICATIONS.

U'na città	a city	*le trincière*	the trenches
la cittadèlla	the citadel	*una mina*	a mine
un fòrte	a fort	*una contra- mina*	a counter- mine
una fortézza	a fortress		
un castèllo	a castle	*una tórre*	a tower
le mura	the walls	*un parapètto*	a parapet
il fòsso	the ditch	*il terrapièno*	the rampart
una palizzáta	a palisado	*una piatta- fórma*	a platform
la cortína	the curtain		
la mèzza luna	the half- moon	*un cavalière*	a cavalier
		un bastióne	a bastion
la casamátta	the casement	*le munizióni*	provisions
un fortíno	a small fort	*le munizioni*	ammunition

un assèdio	a siege	i soccórsi	succours
un assálto	a storm	una sortíta	a sally
le capitolazióni	the capìtulations		

TRADES AND PROFESSIONS.

Un autóre	an author	un incisóre	a copperplate engraver
un editóre	an editor		
un traduttóre	a translator	un intagliatóre	a carver
un libráio	a bookseller		
uno stampatóre	a printer	un pittóre	a painter
un legatór di libri	a bookbinder	un ricamatóre	an embroiderer
un mèdico	a physician	un falegnáme	a carpenter
un chirúrgo	a surgeon	un muratóre	a mason
uno speziále	an apothecary	un magnáno	a locksmith
		un mugnáio	a miller
un barbière	a barber	una lavandáia	a washerwoman
un fornáio	a baker		
un pasticcière	a pastrycook	un orologiáro	a watchmaker
un rosticcière	a cook that roasts	un gioiellière	a jeweller
		un argentière	a silversmith
un macelláro	a butcher	un oréfice	a goldsmith
un locandière	an innkeeper	un tapezzière	an upholsterer
un mercánte	a merchant		
un negoziánte		un vetráio	a glazier
		un rigattière	a broker
un sartóre	a tailor	un guantáio	a glover
un calzoláro	a shoemaker	un commediánte	a player
un ciabattino	a cobbler		
un cappelláio	a hat-maker	un suonatóre	a musician
		un coltelláio	a cutler
un merciáio	a mercer, haberdasher	una modista	a milliner
		un facchíno	a porter
un selláio	a sadler	uno spazzacammíno	a sweeper
un maniscálco	a farrier		

OFFICERS OF THE HOUSE.

Un lacchè	a running footman	*il coppière*	the cup-bearer
uno staffière	a footman	*il cantinière*	the butler
un servitóre	a man-servant	*il credenzière*	the cupboard-keeper
il cocchière	the coachman	*il pággio*	the page
il palafre- nière	the groom	*il maèstro di casa*	the steward
la sèrva	the maid-servant	*il segretário*	the secretary
		il cappelláno	the chaplain
la camerièra	the chamber-maid	*l' inlendènte*	the intendant
		il cuòco	the cook
il camerière	the valet	*il giardinière*	the gardener
i portantíni	the chairmen	*il padróne*	the master
il portináio	the porter	*la padróna*	the mistress
lo scalco	the carver	*il sovráno*	the sovereign

QUALITIES, DEFECTS, IMPERFECTIONS, DISEASES, &c. OF MAN.

Un òrbo	a one-eyed man	*un briccóne*	a rascal
		un furfánte	a rogue
un guèrcio	a squint-eyed man	*un mago*	a magician
		uno stregóne	a sorcerer
un cièco	a blind man	*una strèga*	a witch
un gòbbo	a hunch-backed man	*un cattívo*	a wicked fellow
uno zòppo	a lame man	*la malattía*	sickness
uno storpiálo	a cripple	*un ammaláte*	a sick person
un mancíno	a left-handed man	*la fèbbre*	fever
		la terzána	the tertian ague
un mónco	a one-handed man	*la quartána*	the quartan ague
un sórdo	a deaf man		
un muto	a dumb man	*il trèmito*	the cold fit
un tartáglia	a stammerer	*úna fertía*	a wound
un calvo	a bald man	*una contu- sióne*	a contusion
un nano	a dwarf		
un ladro	a thief	*la gótta*	the gout

la còlica	the colic	*una cadúta*	a fall [ear
la rosolìa	the measles	*uno schiáffo*	a box on the
il vaiuòlo	the small-pox	*un púgno*	a cuff
		un cálcio	a kick
un raffred-dóre	a cold	*una stoccáta*	a thrust with a sword
il reumatismo	the rheuma-tism	*una pistolet-táta*	a pistol-shot
la tósse	the cough	*un' archibu-sáta*	a gun-shot
la rógna	the itch		
il pizzicóre	the itching	*uno sveni-ménto*	a swooning
un apostèma	an im-posthume	*un accidènte*	an accident
una sgraffia-túra	a scratch	*una disgrázia*	a misfortune
		la mòrte	death

OF BIRDS.

Un' áquila	an eagle	*una pássera*	a sparrow, *fem.*
un ucèllo	a bird		
un accellíno	a little bird	*un pappa-gállo*	a parrot
un cardellíno	a goldfinch		
un canaríno	a canary-bird	*un mèrlo*	a blackbird
un lucheríno	a goldfinch	*una gazza*	a magpye
una róndine	a swallow	*una ghian-dáia*	a jay
un usignuòlo	a nightingale		
uno stórno	a starling	*una tortorèlla*	a turtle dove
un fringuèllo	a chaffinch	*un allòdola*	a lark
un passeròtto	a sparrow	*uno struzzo*	an ostrich

OF QUADRUPEDS.

Un cane	a dog	*una capra*	a goat
una cagna	a she dog	*un pòrco*	a pig
un cagnolíno	a little dog	*una tròia*	a sow
un gatto,	a cat	*una vólpe*	a fox
una gatta	a she cat	*un lupo*	a wolf
un sórcio	a mouse	*un tòro*	a bull
un tòpo,	a rat	*una vacca*	a cow
una scímmia	a monkey	*un vitèllo*	a calf
una pècora	a sheep	*un mulo*	a mule

o 5

una mula	a mule, *fem.*	*un leopárdo*	a leopard
un cavállo	a horse	*una tigre*	a tiger
una caválla	a mare	*un leóne*	a lion
un ásino	an ass	*un orso*	a bear
un cammèllo	a camel	*un elefánte*	an elephant

OF REPTILES AND INSECTS.

Un ròspo	a toad	*úna zanzára*	a gnat
una rana	a frog	*una tignuòla*	a moth
una lucèrtola	a lizard	*un brúco*	a caterpillar
una lumáca	a slug snail	*un vérme*	a worm
una chiòcciola	a shell snail	*un pidócchio*	a louse
uno scorpióne	a scorpion	*una pulce*	a flea
un ragno	a spider	*una címice*	a bug
un serpènte	a serpent	*una formíca*	an ant
una farfálla	a butterfly	*una tar-*	a tortoise
una mòsca	a fly	*taruga*	

WHAT ONE SEES IN THE COUNTRY.

La strada	the road	*la biáda*	oats
la strada maèstra	the high-way	*una vigna*	a vine
		un giardíno	a garden
una pianúra	a plain	*un viále*	an alley, or walk
una valle	a valley		
una montágna	a mountain	*un castèllo*	a castle
		un campaníle	a steeple
un pòggio		*un prato*	a meadow
un còlle	a hill	*un lago*	a lake
una collína		*uno stágno*	a pond
un bòsco	a wood	*uno scòglio*	a rock
una forèsta	a forest	*un fòsso*	a ditch
una sièpe	a hedge	*un ruscèllo*	a brook
un cespúglio	a bush	*un fiúme*	a river
un álbero	a tree	*un pónte*	a bridge
un ramo	a branch	*una barca*	a bark
il grano	corn	*una palúde*	a marsh
il formènto	wheat	*una lagúna*	a slough
l' òrzo	barley	*un villággio*	a village
il fièno	hay	*un bórgo*	a suburb

WHAT WE SEE IN A CITY.

una città	a city, a town	*il convènto*	the convent
la piázza d' árme	the place of arms	*lo spedále*	the hospital
la dogána	the custom-house	*il palázzo*	the palace
		la casa	the house
il mercáto	the market	*la prigióne*	the prison
la fièra	the fair	*la stráda, la via*	the street
la bottéga	the shop	*una piázza*	a square
la chièsa	the church	*il pónte*	the bridge
la cappèlla	the chapel	*la pòrta*	the gate
		una fontána	a fountain

THE SEVERAL GAMES.

La pallaccòrda	tennis	*alle bòcce*	at bowls
il biliárdo	billiards	*al volánte*	at shuttle-cock
a' dadi	at dice	*al beccaláglio*	at blind-man's buff
álle carte	at cards	*all' òca*	at the game of goose
all' ómbre	at ombre	*quadrigliáti*	quadrille
alla bassétta	at basset	*tavolière*	draught-board
agli scácchi	at chess	*a dama*	at draughts
alle trichetráche	at trick-track	*scacchière*	chess-board
alle piastrèlle	at quoits		

COLOURS.

Biánco	white	*colór páglia*	straw-colour
néro	black	*cremesino*	crimson
rósso	red	*scarlatto*	scarlet
vérde	green	*colór carnicino*	pink
giállo	yellow	*pórpora*	purple
turchino	blue	*azzúrro*	sky-blue
bígio	grey	*colór lilla*	lilac
pavonázzo	violet colour	*arancióne*	orange
incarnáto	carnation	*colór bruno*	brown
olivástro	olive-colour		

o 6

OF METALS, &c.

L'òro	gold	la calamíta	a loadstone
l' argènto	silver	la latta	tin
il fèrro	iron	lo zólfo	brimstone
il piómbo	lead	il verde-	verdigris
l' ottóne	brass	ráme	
l' acciáio	steel	il vétro	glass
il rame	copper	il vitriòlo	vitriol
lo stágno	pewter	l' allúme	alum
l' argènto vivo	quicksilver	il cristállo	crystal

OF NATIONS.

Italiáno	an Italian	Ungherése	a Hungarian
Tedésco	a German	Danése	a Dane
Portoghése	a Portuguese	Maltése	a Maltese
Inglése	an English-man	Turco	a Turk
		Fiamíngo	a Fleming
Irlandése	an Irishman	Lorenése	a Lorrainer
Scozzése	a Scotchman	Tártaro	a Tartar
Olandése	a Dutchman	Europèo	a European
Russo	a Russian	Asiático	an Asiatic
Svizzero	a Swiss	Africáno	an African
Piemontése	a Piedmont-ese	Indiáno	Indian
		Americáno	an American
Francése	a Frenchman	Chinése	a Chinese
Spagnuòlo	a Spaniard	Giapponése	a Japanese
Svedése	a Swede	Egiziáno	an Egyptian
Pollácco	a Polander	Lapponése	a Laplander

KINGDOMS, CAPITAL CITIES.

Spágna	Spain	Madrid	Madrid
Fráncia	France	Parigi	Paris
Inghiltèrra	England	Lóndra	London
Scòzia	Scotland	Edinbúrgo	Edinburgh
Irlánda	Ireland	Dublíno	Dublin
Boèmia	Bohemia	Praga	Prague
Norvègia	Norway	Bergen	Bergen

Prússia	Prussia	*Berlíno*	Berlin
Polònia	Poland	*Varsávia*	Warsaw
Rússia	Russia	*Pietrobúrgo*	Petersburgh
		Mosca	Moscow
Danimárca	Denmark	*Copenaghen*	Copenhagen
Svèzia	Sweden	*Stockolmo*	Stockholm
Turchía	Turkey	*Costantinò-poli*	Constanti-nople
Ungheria	Hungary	*Presburgo*	Presburg
Nápoli	Naples	*Nápoli*	Naples
Sicília	Sicily	*Palèrmo*	Palermo
Toscána	Tuscany	*Firènze*	Florence
Piemónte	Piedmont	*Toríno*	Turin

A COLLECTION OF VERBS,

MOST NECESSARY TO BE FIRST LEARNT.

FOR STUDY.

Studiare	to study	*scancelláre*	to blot out
imparare	to learn	*tradúrre*	to translate
imparar a ménte	to learn by heart	*cominciare*	to begin
		continuare	to go on
lèggere	to read	*finire*	to make an end
scrivere	to write		
sottoscrívere	to sign or subscribe	*ripètere*	to repeat
		fare	to do, to make
piegáre	to fold up	*sapére*	to know
sigilláre	to seal	*potére*	to be able
far la sopra-scrítta	to put the su-perscrip-tion	*volére*	to be willing
		ricordársi	to remember
		dimenticáre	to forget
corrèggere	to correct	*comparare*	to compare

TO SPEAK.

Pronunziáre	to pronounce	*dire*	to say
accentuare	to accent	*ciarláre*	to prattle
proferíre	to utter	*cicalare*	to chat

gridáre	to cry out	*serràr la*	to shut it
sgridáre	to scold	*bócca*	
aprire la	to open one's	*tacére*	to be silent
bócca	mouth	*chiamáre*	to call
		rispóndere	to answer

TO DRINK AND EAT.

Masticáre	to chew	*far colazióne*	to breakfast
inghiottire	to swallow	*merendare*	to lunch
tagliare	to cut	*pranzare*	
provare, gu-	to taste	*desinare* }	to dine
stare		*cenare*	to sup
sciacquare	to rinse	*avér fame*	to be hungry
bére	to drink	*aver séte*	to be thirsty
mangiare	to eat	*aver appetito*	to have an
digiunare	to fast		appetite

TO GO TO SLEEP.

Andár a lètto	to go to bed	*addormentársi*	to fall asleep
or *coricarsi*		*sognare*	to dream
dormíre	to sleep	*russare*	to snore
vegliáre	to watch	*svegliarsi*	to wake
riposare	to rest	*levarsi*	to rise

TO DRESS ONE'S SELF.

Vestirsi	to dress one's self	*méttersi la*	to powder
		pólvere	one's head
spogliársi	to undress one's self	*farsi i ricci*	to curl one's hair.
calzarsi	to put on one's shoes	*méttersi 'l*	to put on
		cappèllo	one's hat
levarsi le	to pull off	*abbottonarsi*	to button
scarpe	one's shoes		one's self
pettinarsi	to comb one's	*appuntare*	to pin
[*cápo*	head [head	*affibbiársi*	to lace one's
acconciarsi 'l	to dress one's		self

THE ORDINARY ACTIONS OF MEN.

Rídere	to laugh	*asciugare*	to dry or wipe
piángere	to weep		
sospiráre	to sigh	*tremare*	to tremble
starnutíre	to sneeze	*gonfiare*	to swell
sbadigliare	to gape	*tossíre*	to cough
soffiare	to blow	*èssere infred-*	to have a cold
físchiare	to whistle	*dáto*	
ascoltare	to hearken	*guardáre*	to look
odorare	to smell	*pizzicare*	to pinch
sputare	to spit	*grattare*	to scratch
soffiarsi 'l naso	to blow one's nose	*solleticare*	to tickle

ACTIONS OF LOVE AND HATRED.

Amáre	to love	*negare*	to deny
accarezzáre	to caress	*proibíre*	to forbid
lusingare	to flatter	*strappaz-zare*	to use ill
far carézze	to show a kindness	*báttere*	to beat
abbracciare	to embrace	*odiare*	to hate
baciare	to kiss	*scacciare*	to drive away
salutare	to salute	*mandár via*	to send away
insegnare	to teach	*perdonare*	to pardon
nudrire	to nourish	*disputare*	to dispute
corrèggere	to correct	*contrastare*	to quarrel
punire	to punish	*litigare*	to plead
castigare	to chastise	*protèggere*	to protect
frustare	to whip	*abbando-nare*	to forsake
lodare	to praise		
biasimare	to blame	*benedire*	to bless
dare, concè-dere	to give, to grant	*maledire*	to curse
		abborríre	to abhor

FOR DIVERSION OR EXERCISE.

Cantáre	to sing	*balláre*	to dance
córrere	to run	*saltare*	to jump

giuocáre	to play	*pèrdere*	to lose
sonare la chi-	to play on	*scomméttere*	to lay a wager
tárra	the guitar	*risicare*	to venture
sonare 'l vio-	to play on	*èsser pace*	to be quits
líno	the violin	*scartare*	to lay out
sonar il fláuto	to play the	*mescolare*	to shuffle
	flute	*alzare*	to lift up
tirár di spada	to fence	*divertírsi*	to divert
cavalcare	to ride on		one's self
	horseback	*scherzare*	to joke
giuocar pal-	to play at	*burlarsi*	to laugh at
laccòrda	tennis	*motteggiare*	to make one
giuocar alle	to play at		laugh
carte	cards	*star in pièdi*	to stand up
giuocar a	to play at	*inchinársi*	to .stoop
picchétto	picquet		downward
giuocar a'	to play at	*girare*	to turn
dadi	dice	*fermarsi*	to stop
víncere	to win		

FOR BUYING.

Domandáre	to ask the	*vénder caro*	to sell dear
il prèzzo	price	*vender vílio*	to sell cheap
quanto vale?	how much is	*prestare*	to lend
	it worth?	*pigliár in*	to borrow
quanto còsta?	what does it	*prèstito*	
	cost?	*impegnare*	to pawn
stiracchiare	to haggle	*disimpegnare*	to take out of
misurare	to measure		pawn
comprare	to buy	*dare*	to give
pagare	to pay	*ingannare*	to cheat
offríre	to bid or offer		

FOR THE CHURCH.

Andár in	to go to	*predicare*	to preach
chièsa	church	*ornare*	to adorn
pregár Iddio	to pray to	*battezzare*	to baptize
	God	*confermare*	to confirm
comunicársi	to receive the	*sonare le*	to ring the
	sacrament	*campáne*	bells

seppellíre	to bury	*inginocchi-*	to kneel
sotterrare	to inter	*arsi*	
cantare	to sing	*rizzarsi*	to rise

FOR THE ACTIONS OF MOTION.

Andáre	to go	*giúngere*	to arrive
veníre	to come	*andar all' in-*	to go to meet
tornáre	to return	*contro*	
fermársi	to stop or stay	*entrare*	to go *or* come in
camminare	to walk	*uscíre*	to go *or* come out
córrere	to run		
seguitare	to follow	*salire*	to go *or* come up
fuggire	to fly		
scappare	to escape	*scéndere*	to go *or* come down
partire	to depart		
avvicinarsi	to approach	*sedére*	to sit down
voltarsi	to turn	*spasseggiare*	to take a walk
cadére	to fall down		
sdrucciolare	to slide	*andare a*	to go a walk- ing
farsi male	to hurt one's self	*spasso*	
ferire	to wound	*affrettarsi*	to make haste

MANUAL ACTIONS.

Lavoráre	to work	*presentáre*	to present
toccare	to touch	*donare*	to give
maneggiare	to handle	*regalare*	to make a present
legare	to tie *or* bind		
sciòrre	to untie	*ricévere*	to receive
attaccare	to tie	*stríngere*	to tie fast
staccare	to detach	*tenére*	to hold
allentare	to let loose	*rómpere*	to break
tògliere	to take away	*nascóndere*	to hide
prèndere	to take	*comprire*	to cover
rubare	to steal	*scoprire*	to discover
raccògliere	to gather up	*sporcare*	to dirty
strappare	to tear	*pulíre*	to clean

stropicciare	to rub	*solleticare*	to tickle
tastare	to feel	*sgraffiare*	to scratch
pizzicare	to pinch	*scorticare*	to flay

ACTIONS OF THE MEMORY AND IMAGINATION.

Ricordársi	to remember	*giudicare*	to adjudge
dimenticársi	to forget	*conchiúdere*	to conclude
pensáre	to think	*risòlvere*	to resolve
crédere	to believe	*fingere*	to feign
dubitare	to doubt	*intestarsi*	to be conceited of
sospettare	to suspect		
osservare	to observe	*ostinarsi*	to be obstinate
avvertire	to take care		
conóscere *sapére* }	to know	*ingannarsi*	to mistake
		èsser gelóso	to be jealous
immaginarsi	to imagine	*imbrogliarsi*	to embroil one's self
bramare	to wish		
sperare	to hope	*avér sulla punta delle dita*	to have it at one's finger's end
temére	to fear		
assicurare	to assure		

FOR ARTS AND TRADES.

Dipíngere	to paint or draw	*smaltare*	to enamel
		indorare	to gild
incídere	to engrave	*inargentare*	to silver over
intagliare	to carve	*incassare*	to inlay
disegnáre	to design	*inverniciare*	to varnish
abbozzare	to draw a sketch	*stampare*	to print
		lavorare	to work
ricamare	to embroider	*guarnire*	to trim

FOR THE ARMY.

Recrutare	to recruit	*marciare*	to march
sonar il tambúro	to beat the drum	*accamparsi*	to encamp
		allogiare	to lodge
sonáre la tromba	to sound the trumpet	*montar a cavállo*	to get on horseback

smontare	to alight	far saltár la mina	to spring a mine
dar battáglia	to give battle	sparare	to fire
riportare la vittòria	to gain the victory	capitolare	to capitulate
scompigliare	to put in disorder	réndersi a patti	to surrender on terms
sconfíggere	to rout	apríre la trincièra	to open the trenches
saccheggiare	to sack		
dare 'l guásto	to lay waste	sonar la raccòlta	to sound a retreat
stríngere	to blockade		
assediare	to besiege	incalzare il nemíco	to pursue the enemy
dar un assálto	to storm	feríre	to wound
prènder d' assálto	to take by storm	uccídere	to kill
		trucidare	to slay

SHORT AND FAMILIAR PHRASES,

IN ITALIAN AND ENGLISH.

I.

I beg of you?	Vi prègo ([34])?
Give me.	Dátemi.
Do not give me.	Non mi date.
Bring me.	Portátemi.
Do not bring me.	Non mi portáte.
Some toast.	Del pane arrostíto.
Some rolls.	Dei panétti.
Some butter.	Del burro.
Some milk.	Del latte.
Some cream.	Della crèma.
Some tea and coffee.	Del tè, e del caffè.
Some chocolate.	Della cioccoláta.
Some water.	Dell' ácqua.
Some wine.	Del vino.
Some beer.	Della birra.

[34] See, as to the accents, the second N.B. at p. 23 and note 22.

Some meat.	*Della carne.*
My hat.	*Il mio cappèllo.*
My cane.	*Il mio bastóne.*
My shoes.	*Le mie scarpe.*
His boots.	*I suòi stiváli.*
My books.	*I mièi libri.*
Yes, sir.	*Sì, signóre.*
No, madam.	*No, signóra.*
Good morning.	*Buòn giórno.*
Good evening.	*Buòna séra.*

II.

I am not ready.	*Non son prónto.*
After you.	*Dópo di voi.*
It is true.	*E' véro.*
It is so.	*Così è.*
Here I am.	*E'ccomi.*
Here we are.	*E'ccoci.*
Here she is.	*E'ccola.*
Here he is.	*E ccolo.*
Believe me.	*Credétemi.*
Do not believe me.	*Non mi credéte.*
Lend me.	*Prestátemi.*
Some money.	*Del danáro.*
Do me.	*Fátemi.*
This favour.	*Quésto favóre.*
This pleasure.	*Questo piacére.*
Permit me.	*Permettétemi.*
Where are you going?	*Dóve andáte ?*
Where do you come from?	*Di dove venìte ?*
I am going home.	*Vado a casa.*
I come from church.	*Vèngo di chièsa.*
I am going.	*Me ne vado.*
Come (or go) up stairs.	*Salite.*
Go down.	*Andáte giù.*
Come up.	*Venite su.*
Wait for me here.	*Aspettátemi qui.*
Come here.	*Venite quà.*
Come (or go) down.	*Scendéte.*

III.

How do you do?	*Cóme state?*
Well, I thank you.	*Bène, grázie.*
Not very well.	*Non tròppo bene.*
What ails you?	*Che còsa avéte?*
I have a cold.	*Sòno infreddáto.*
I have a head-ache.	*Mi duóle il capo.*
I have a pain in my heart.	*Mi sènto male.*
That makes me ill.	*Quésto mi fa náusea.*
I have the tooth-ache.	*Ho dolór di dènti.*
How long since?	*Da quándo in quà?*
Since this morning.	*Da quésta mattína.*
Since yesterday.	*Da ièri in quà.*
I have a sore throat.	*Ha male alla góla.*
You must keep in bed.	*Bisógna star in lètto.*
And your sister?	*E vòstra sorèlla?*
She has a head-ache.	*Ha mal di tèsta.*
She has the gout.	*Ha la gótta.*
I am sorry for it.	*Me ne dispiáce.*
She is better.	*Sta mèglio.*
I am very glad of it.	*Me ne rallégro.*
Is she at home?	*E' ella in casa?*
I think not.	*Crédo di no.*
I think so.	*Credo di sì.*

IV.

I thank you.	*Vi ringrázio.*
Your most humble servant.	*Servitore umilissimo.*
I am yours.	*Padrón mio.*
Your servant.	*Sèrva vòstra.*
Without compliments.	*Sènza cerìmònie.*
Sit down.	*Accomodátevi.*
You are very polite.	*Sièle mólto civile.*
You are very obliging.	*Siete molto compito*
Go and play.	*Andáte a divertírvi.*
Come, come.	*Via, via.*
Presently.	*Or óra.*
O how tiresome you are.	*Sèi pur noióso, 2d per. t*
You are very naughty.	*Sièle mólto cattivo.*

Leave me in peace.	*Lásciami in pace.*
Let me alone.	*Lasciátemi stare.*
Don't stun me.	*Non mi stordíre.*
Don't plague me.	*Non mi stordíte.*
Go about your business.	*Andáte a spasso.*
I come from there.	*Ne vèngo.*
Go away then.	*Andáte via dunque.*
O ! thank God.	*Oh ! sía ringraziáto Iddio.*

V.

Have you dined ?	*Avéte pranzáto ?*
Not yet.	*Non ancóra.*
At what o'clock do you sup ?	*A che óra cenáte ?*
At nine o'clock.	*Alle nòve della séra.*
I dine at five.	*Io désino alle cínque.*
And I at half-past four.	*Ed io alle quattro e mèzzo.*
It is a convenient hour.	*E' un' óra còmoda.*
Prepare breakfast.	*Preparáte la colazióne.*
Eat something.	*Mangiáte qualche còsa.*
I have no appetite left.	*Non ho più appetíto.*
I am very thirsty.	*Ho gran séte.*
Drink a glass of water.	*Bevéte un bicchièr d' ácqua.*
Have you breakfasted ?	*Avéte fatto colazióne ?*
It is too soon.	*E' tròppo prèsto.*
You are still sleepy.	*Sièle ancóra addormentáto.*
Rise up quickly.	*Levátevi súbito.*
Do not take the trouble.	*Non v' incomodáte.*
Shut the door.	*Chiudéte la porta.*
Open the window.	*Aprite la finèstra.*
It is open.	*E' apèrta.*
Shut it then.	*Serrátela dunque.*
You are in the right.	*Avéte ragióne.*
He is in the wrong.	*Egli ha tòrto.*
Make haste.	*Spicciátevi.*
Go to bed.	*Andáte a lètto.*

VI.

| What is it o'clock ? | *Che óra è ?* |
| Tell me what it is o'clock. | *Dítemi che ora è.* |

Do you know what o'clock it is?	*Sapéte che ora è?*
I do not know exactly.	*Non lo so precisaménte.*
Look at your watch.	*Guardáte al vòstro oriuòl*
It is almost one o'clock.	*E' quási un' óra.*
It has struck one.	*E' un' ora sonáta.*
It is a quarter past one.	*E' un' ora e un quárto.*
It is almost two.	*Son quási le dúe.*
It is half-past two.	*Sóno le due e mèzzo.*
It has just struck two.	*Son le due sonáte.*
It is three quarters past two.	*Son le due e tre quarti.*
It is not three o'clock yet.	*Non sono ancóra le tre.*
What weather is it?	*Che tèmpo fa?*
It is fine.	*Fa bèl tempo.*
It is bad weather.	*Fa cattívo tempo.*
It is gloomy weather.	*Fa un tempo tristo.*
The wind is changed.	*E' cambiáto il vènto.*
It will rain.	*Vuòl piòvere.*
See the sun appears.	*Ecco che èsce il sóle.*
Let us go and take a walk.	*Andiámo a spasso.*

VII.

Hear me.	*Ascoltátemi.*
Hear him.	*Ascoltátelo.*
Hear her.	*Ascoltátela.*
Look at them.	*Guardáteli.*
Tell him, her.	*Ditegli* m. *ditele* f.
Show it me.	*Mostrátemelo.*
Let him know it.	*Fáteglielo sapére.*
Tell it him (or her).	*Diteglielo* (m. *or* f.)
Do not look for it.	*Non lo cercáte.*
Do not speak to him.	*Non gli* (m.) *parláte.*
Tell her nothing.	*Non le* (f.) *dite nièute.*
Remember.	*Ricordátevi.*
Do you remember?	*Vi ricordáte voi?*
Take care of yourself.	*Badáte a voi.*
Stop.	*Fermátevi.*
Dress yourself.	*Vestítevi.*
Help me.	*Aiutátemi.*
Go away.	*Andátevene.*

I repent it.	*Me ne pènto.*
Thou shalt go.	*Tu te n' andrái.*
He will be angry at it.	*Egli se ne sdegnerà.*
He will speak to us about it.	*Egli ce ne parlerà.*
He gave him two of them.	*Gliéne diède dúe.*
He wrote it to him.	*Gliélo scrísse.*
He sent for them for him.	*Glieli fèce veníre.*

VIII.

What are you doing?	*Che state facèndo?*
I am writing some letters.	*Sto scrivèndo delle lèttere.*
Have you been at the play?	*Sièto stato al teátro?*
I have not been there.	*Non vi sòno stato.*
What did they perform yesterday?	*Che si rappresentò ièri?*
Look at the bill.	*Guardáte al cartèllo.*
Do you like tragedy?	*Vi piácciono le tragèdie?*
No, I like comedy.	*No, mi piácciono le commèdie.*
Do you like operas?	*Vi piácciono le Opere in música?*
O yes, very much.	*Oh, sì, moltíssimo.*
Did you amuse yourself well?	*Vi sièto bèn divertíto?*
Who is the first singer?	*Chi è il primo uòmo?*
And the first actress?	*E la prima dònna?*
What parts did they play?	*Che parte facévano?*
Who is the first violin?	*Chi è il primo violíno.*
He plays well on the flute.	*Suòna bène il fláuto.*
He plays like a professor.	*Lo suòna da maèstro.*
Have you heard Persiani?	*Ha élla sentito la Persiáni?*
What do you think of Grisi?	*E cóme le piáce la Grisi?*

IX.

Where do you dine to-day?	*Dóve pranzáte òggi?*
I dine out.	*Pranzo fuòri.*
With much pleasure.	*Con mólto piacére.*
There are so many things.	*Vi sóno tante còse.*
There were so many people.	*V' èra tanta gènte.*
My father will be there.	*Vi sarà mio padre.*

My friend is not there.	*Il mio amíco non v' è.*
Send him word.	*Fáteglielo dire.*
I think he is gone out.	*Crédo che sia ito fuòri.*
I shall go to your house.	*Verrò da voi.*
If I had known it yesterday.	*Se lo sapéva ièri.*
If you knew that....	*Se sapéste che....*
I would if I could.	*Vorrèi se potéssi.*
I could if I would.	*Potrèi s' io voléssi.*
You need not tell it me.	*Non occórre che me lo diciáte.*
I cannot help it.	*Non saprèi che farci.*
You must stay at home.	*Bisógna restáre in casa.*
I will tell you the same.	*Vi dirò lo stesso.*
I was going to write.	*Stavo per iscrívere.*
I have just been eating.	*Ho già mangiáto.*
Who does this belong to?	*Di chi è quésto?*
It is mine, it is his, &c.	*E' mio, è súo, &c.*
It is our turn to speak.	*Tocc' a nói a parláre.*
It is my turn to deal.	*Tocc' a me a far le carte.*

X.

You are more clever than I.	*Voi sièle più bravo di me.*
Do not be sorry for it.	*Non ve ne dispiáccia.*
I am rather poor than rich.	*Son piuttòsto pòvero che rícco.*
It is better to laugh than to cry.	*E' mèglio rídere che piángere.*
It is better late than never.	*E' mèglio tardi che mái.*
M. is taller than he.	*M. è maggiór di lúi.*
He is very clever.	*Ha mólto ingègno.*
Every body says so.	*Ognún lo dice.*
They were near fifty.	*Erano da cinquánta in circa.*
Stay with me.	*Restáte méco.*
Tell him from me.	*Dítegli da parte mía.*
Let us have a game.	*Giuochiámo una partíta.*
Cut a part.	*Tagliátene una parte.*
He is of a very strong party.	*Egli è d'un partíto fortíssimo.*
Draw near the fire.	*Avvicinátevi al fuòco.*

P

They say so.	Così dicono.
One says what one thinks.	Si dice quel che si pènsa.
They do not say so.	Non si dice questo.
Speaking of you.	Parlàndo di voi.
I think I see her.	Parmi di vedérla.
It seems to me so natural.	Mi par tanto naturále.
He did all that was bid him.	Féce quanto gli fu détto.
I saw my parents.	Véddi i mièi genitóri.
I saw them this morning.	Gli ho vedúti stamattina.
I wanted to tell them	Volévo dir loro. . . .
You know as much about it as I.	Ne sapéte quanto me.
You speak as I do.	Voi parláte cóme me.
I know it as well as you.	Io lo so al par di voi.
The prince is not so powerful as the king.	Non è tanto poténte il príncipe, quanto il re.
How does Mr. N—— do ?	Cóme sta il Signór N. ?
He is just gone out.	E' uscíto di casa in quésto moménto.
As for Mr. N——, he is not well.	In quanto al Signór N. non istà bène.
Yesterday he was perfectly well.	Ièri stáva a maravíglia.

FAMILIAR DIALOGUES.

DIALOGUE I.

In meeting an Acquaintance.	Nell' incontro d'una Conoscènza.
Good morrow, sir.	Buòn giórno, signóre.
Good night, sir.	Buòna séra, signore.
How do you do, sir ?	Cóme sta ?
Well; not very well; so so.	Bène ; non tròppo bene ; così così.
Very well to serve you.	Benissimo per servírla.
I am glad to see you in good health.	Ho gran gusto di vedérla in buòna salúte.
I am obliged to you, sir.	Le sòno obbligáto, signóre.

I thank you.	La ringrázio.
How does your brother do?	Cóme sta súo fratèllo.
He is well, I thank you.	Sta bène, grazie.
He will be glad to see you.	Avrà gusto di vedérla.
I shall have no time to see him to-day.	Non avrò tèmpo di vedérlo òggi.
Be pleased to sit down.	S' accòmodi, la prègo.
Give a chair to the gentleman.	Date una sèdia al signóre.
There's no occasion.	Non è necessário.
I must go to pay a visit in the neighbourhood.	Bisógna che vada a far una visita qui vicíno.
You are in great haste.	Ella ha gran fretta.
I will be back presently.	Tornerò súbito.
I am your servant.	Sèrvo súo.
Your most humble servant.	Umilíssimo servo?
Your servant.	Sèrva súa, fem.
Your most humble servant.	Umilíssima serva.

DIALOGUE II.

To make a Visit in the Morning.	Per far una Visita la Mattína.
Where is your master?	Dov' è il tuo padróne?
Is he asleep still?	Dòrme ancóra?
No, sir, he is awake.	Signór no, è svegliáto.
Is he up?	E' égli alzáto?
No, sir, he is in bed.	Signór no, sta ancóra a lètto.
What a shame it is to be in bed at this time of day!	Che vergógna di star a lètto a quest' óra!
I went to bed so late last night, I could not rise early this morning.	Andái ièri a letto tanto tardi, che non ho potúto levármi a buòn' óra.
What did you do after supper?	Che si fèce qui dopo céna?
We danced, we sang, we laughed, we played.	Si ballò, si cantò, si rise, si giuocò.
At what game?	A che giuòco?
We played at piquet with the knight.	Giuocámmo a picchétto col signór cavalière.

P 2

What did the rest do?	*Che fécero gli altri?*
They played at chess.	*Giuocárono a scacchi.*
How grieved am I, I did not know it.	*Quanto mi dispiáce di non avérlo sapúto.*
Who won? who lost?	*Chi ha vinto? Chi ha perdúto?*
I won ten pistoles.	*Ho guadagnáto dièci dóppie.*
Till what hour did you play?	*Fin a che óra avéte giuocáto?*
Till two in the morning.	*Fin alle dúe dopo mezzanòtte.*
At what o'clock did you go to bed?	*A che óra sièle andato a lètto?*
At three, or half an hour after three.	*Alle tre, o alle tre e mèzzo.*
I don't wonder at your rising so late.	*Non mi maraviglio che vi leviáte così tardi.*
What's o'clock?	*Che ora è?*
What do you think it is?	*Che ora credéte che sia?*
Scarcely eight, I believe yet.	*Crédo che non síano ancora le òtto.*
How! eight! it has struck ten!	*Cóme, le otto! son sonáte le dièci!*
Then I must rise with all speed.	*Bisógna dúnque che mi lèvi súbito.*

DIALOGUE III.

To dress one's self.	*Per vestírsi.*
Who is there?	*Chi è di là?*
What do you want, sir?	*Che cománda, signóre?*
Be quick, make a fire, dress me.	*Su su, prèsto, fate fuòco, vestítemi.*
There is a fire, sir, since seven o'clock.	*Il fuòco è accéso, signore, fin dalle sette.*
Give me my shirt.	*Dátemi la mia camícia.*
It is here, sir.	*E'ccola, signóre.*
'Tis not warm, 'tis quite cold.	*Non è calda, è ancóra frédda.*

If you please, sir, I'll warm it.	*Se vuòle, la scalderò.*
No, no; bring me my silk stockings.	*No, no; portátemi le mie calzétte di séta.*
They are torn.	*Sóno rótte.*
Darn them a little, or get them mended.	*Dáteci un punto, o fátele rimendare.*
I have given them to the stocking-mender.	*Le ho date alla calzettáia.*
You have done right.	*Avéte fatto bène.*
Where are my slippers?	*Dóve sóno le mie pianèlle?*
Where is my night-gown?	*Dov' è la mia vèsta da cámera?*
Comb my hair.	*Pettinátemi.*
Take another comb.	*Pigliáte un altro pèttine.*
Give me a handkerchief.	*Dátemi un fazzolétto.*
There is a clean one, sir.	*E ccone úno pulíto, signore.*
Give me that which is in my pocket.	*Dátemi quello ch' è nélla mia tasca.*
I gave it to the washer-woman; it was dirty.	*L' ho dato alla lavandáia; èra súdicio.*
Has she brought my linen?	*Ha ella portáto la mia biancheria?*
Yes, sir, there wants nothing.	*Signór sí, non ci manca niènte.*
What clothes will you wear to-day?	*Che vestíto si vuòl métter òggi?*
Those I wore yesterday.	*Quello ch' avéva ièri.*
The tailor will bring your cloth suit presently.	*Il sartóre dève portár prèsto quello di panno.*
Somebody knocks, see who it is.	*E' stato picchiáto, vedéte chi è.*
Who is it?	*Chi è?*
It is the tailor.	*E' 'l sarto.*
Let him come in.	*Fátelo entráre.*

DIALOGUE IV.

The Gentleman, and the Tailor.	*Il Gentiluòmo, ed il Sartóre.*
Do you bring my suit of clothes ?	*Portáte forse il mío vestiário ?*
Yes, sir, here it is.	*Sì, signóre, èccolo quì.*
You make me always wait a great while.	*Mi fate sempre aspettár mólto.*
I could not come sooner.	*Non ho potúto venir più prèsto.*
It was not finished.	*Non èra finíto.*
The lining was not sewed.	*La fòdera non èra cucíta.*
Will you be pleased to try it on, sir?	*Vuòle provárselo ?*
Let's see whether it be well made.	*Vediámo s' è bèn fatto.*
I believe it will please you.	*Crédo che Vo' Signoría ne sarà contènta.*
It seems to me to be very long.	*Mi pare mólto lungo.*
They wear them long now.	*Si pòrtano lunghi adèsso.*
Button me.	*Abbottonátemi.*
It is too close.	*Mi strínge tròppo.*
To fit properly it ought to be close.	*Per èsser ben fatto, bisógna che sia giústo.*
Are not the sleeves too wide?	*Le mániche non sóno tròppo larghe ?*
No, sir, they fit very well.	*Signór no, stanno beníssimo.*
This coat becomes you extremely well.	*Quest' ábito le sta beníssimo.*
It is too narrow.	*E' tròppo strétto.*
Pardon me, sir, it fits very well.	*Le chièggo scusa, le sta anzi bène.*
How do you like my trimming?	*Che dite della mía guarnitúra ?*
'Tis very fine and rich.	*E' bellíssima e ricchíssima.*
What did these ribbons cost a-yard ?	*Quanto còstano al bráccio questi nastri ?*
I paid a crown.	*Li ho pagáti uno scudo.*

That's not too much, 'tis cheap.	Non è tròppo, non son cari.
Where is the rest of my cloth?	Dov' è 'l rèsto del mio panno?
There is not a bit left.	Non v' è niènte affátto d'avánzo.
Have you made your bill?	Avéte fatto 'l vòstro cónto?
No, sir, I had not time.	Signór no, non ho avúto 'l tèmpo.
Bring it to-morrow, I will pay you.	Portátelo dománi, e vi pagherò.

DIALOGUE V.

To go to Breakfast.	Per far Colazióne.
Bring us something for breakfast.	Portáteci quálche còsa da far colazióne.
Yes, sir, here is tea and coffee.	Signór sì; ècco tè e caffè.
Do you choose some bread and butter?	Vuol' ella che pòrti pane e butirro.
Yes, bring it; we will cut some slices of it.	Sì, portátene; ne taglierémo due fette.
Bring some cold meat, and some eggs.	Portáte della carne frédda, e delle uòva.
Set the ham on the table.	Mettéte del prosciútto in távola.
Lay a napkin on the table.	Mettéte una salviétta sópra la tavola.
Give us plates, knives and forks.	Dáteci tóndi, coltèlli e forchétte.
Give the gentleman a chair.	Date una sèdia al signóre.
Sit down, sir; sit by the fire.	Sègga, signóre; si métta vicíno al fuòco.
I am not cold, I am very well here.	Non ho fréddo, sto beníssimo quì.
Let us see whether the tea is good.	Vediámo se 'l tè è buòno.
Give me that cup.	Dátemi quélla tazza.
Taste that coffee, pray.	Di grázia, asśággi questo caffè.

How do you like it? what say you to it?	*Che gliéne pare? che ne dice?*
It is not bad, it is very good.	*Non è cattivo, è squisito.*
Here is the toast, take away this plate.	*Ecco il pan arrostito, leváte questo piátto.*
Eat some toast.	*Mangi del pan arrostito.*
I have eaten some, it is very good.	*Ne ho mangiáto, è buoníssimo.*
Give me some more coffee, sir.	*Mi dia dell' altro caffè.*
Sir, I thank you.	*La ringrázio, signóre.*
You do not eat.	*Ella non mángia.*
I have eaten so much, I shall not be able to eat any dinner.	*Ho mangiáto tanto, che non potrò pranzáre.*
You only jest, you have eaten nothing at all.	*Ella burla, non ha mangiáto affátto.*
I have eaten very heartily both of the bread and butter, and toast.	*Ho mangiato beníssimo del pane e burro, e del pan arrosto.*

DIALOGUE VI.

At Dinner.	*A Pránzo.*
At what o'clock do you dine?	*A che óra pranza élla?*
Dinner is generally on table at seven.	*Generalménte il pranzo è in távola alle sette.*
I think that hour is fitter for supper than dinner.	*Mi par che a quell' óra sia piuttòsto tèmpo da céna che da pranzo.*
Yes, it is true; but it is a very convenient hour for gentlemen and merchants.	*Sì, è vero: ma è un' ora molto còmoda pei Signóri ed i negoziánti.*
Shall you have much company to-day?	*Vi sarà mólta gènte òggi a pranzo?*
No, there will be only you, my wife, the doctor, and I.	*No, non vi sarà altri che lèi, mia móglie, il mèdico ed io.*

Have you always a doctor to dine with you?

Suol' èlla pranzar sèmpre in compagnía d' un mèdico?

No, sir; it is only through friendship.

No, signóre; è solaménte per amicízia.

I have more appetite to-day than usual.

O'ggi mi sènto appetíto più del sòlito.

Well, we are going to have dinner served up immediately.

Ebbène, óra farémo portár in távola.

Francis, lay the cloth.

Francésco, apparecchiáte.

Put on a cleaner cloth.

Mettéte una továglia più pulíta.

Rinse the glasses well.

Sciacquáte bène i bicchièri.

Do not forget the napkins too.

Non dimenticate le salviétte.

Where are the silver salts?

Dóve son le salière d' argènto.

Dust that sideboard: don't you see that it is quite covered with dust?

Ripulíte quella credènza: non vedéte ch' è tutta copèrta di pólvere?

Make haste, tell the cook to send up the dinner as soon as it is ready.

Prèsto dite al cuòco che lo mandi in távola súbito che sarà prónto.

First, put the chairs round the table.

Mettéte prima le sèdie intórno alla tavola.

Ladies and gentlemen, dinner is on table.

Signóri, il pranzo è in távola.

Please to sit next to the lady.

Favorísca sedére quì accánto alla Signóra.

Much obliged to you.

Grázie infiníte.

Do you like rice soup with fowl broth?

Le piáce la minèstra di riso còtto nel bròdo di póllo?

Yes; but I like it much better in the Venetian way, with parmesan cheese.

Sì; ma mi piace molto più alla Veneziána col cácio parmigiáno.

I will give you a slice of this boiled beef, which seems very tender.

Le darò una fétta di questo lésso, che mi par molto tènero.

P 5

I do not think it is done enough.

Non mi par còtto abbastánza.

But, my dear friend, when meat is too much done, it loses its flavour; it becomes like tow.

Ma, caro amíco, quando la carne è tròppo còtta, non ha più gusto, divénta stóppa.

No matter, I will eat some roast beef.

Non impòrta, mangerò del manzo arròsto.

There is also some fried fish, if you do not like meat.

V' è anche del pésce fritto, se la carne non le piáce.

Favour me rather with some of that pigeon pie.

Mi favorísca piuttòsto di quel pastíccio di picciόni.

Immediately ; here is some salad too.

Súbito : ècco qui anche dell' insaláta.

Oh ! what a fine lettuce !

Oh che bèlla lattúga.

Will you have an anchovy in it ?

Vuòle méttervi un' acciúga ?

Willingly : your oil is excellent ; where do you get it.

Volontièri : il suo òlio è eccellènte : dóve lo fa prèndere ?

An Italian merchant, a friend of mine, furnishes it to me in small boxes of thirty bottles each.

Me lo fornísce per cassétte di trénta fiaschétti, uno spedizionière Italiáno mio amíco.

To make a good salad, it is absolutely necessary to have oil of the best quality, and vinegar made from wine, as I perceive your's is.

Per fare una buòna insaláta è indispensábile che l' òlio sia della migliόr qualità, e che l' acéto sia di vino, cóme m' avvédo che è 'l suo.

But, sir, you do not drink.

Ma, ella non béve.

O ! yes, I had forgot it ; I will take a glass of wine with all my heart.

Oh ! sì, me n' èro scordáto ; beverò volontièri un bicchièr di vino.

Will you have red, or white ?

Vuòl élla del rósso, o del biánco ?

I will first take a glass of beer.

Prenderò prima un bicchièr di birra.

Help yourself as you please.

Si sèrva cóme le aggráda.

Your health, sir!	*Beverò alla sua salúte: evviva!*
Thank you, sir.	*Evviva, grázie.*
What do you think of it? what do you say to this wine?	*Che gliéne pare? còsa dice di questo vino?*
It is not bad: on the contrary, it is excellent.	*Non è cattivo: è anzi squisito.*
Taste now a glass of this other.	*Assággi adèsso un bicchièr di quest' altro.*
Oh! this is delicious, and it is much older than the other.	*O! questo sì ch' è una delizia, ed è molto più vècchio dell' altrò.*
It is so: I have had this more than ten years in my cellar.	*E' vero: son più di dièci anni che l' ho in cantína.*
It cannot be denied that Port is a very good wine.	*Non si può negáre che il vin d'Opòrto non sia un gran buòn vino.*
Now we will have on table a fine roasted bird, which I do not know how to name in Italian.	*Or óra porteránno in távola un bèll' uccèllo arròsto, che non sapréi come chiamáre in Italiáno.*
In Tuscany it is called *tacchino*, and in other parts of Italy *gallinaccio* or *pollo d' India*.	*In Toscana si chiama tacchíno, ed in altre parti d' Italia gallináccio.*
Help yourself, for I know that you carve very well.	*Si sèrva da sè, perchè so che ella trincia a maraviglia.*
No, indeed; I am not expert at it.	*No, davvéro: io non ci ho tròppo buòna mano.*
Will you give me leave to assist you?	*Mi permette di servìrla.*
If you please; but I beg of you to attend to the lady first.	*Mi farà grázia: ma la súpplico di servir prima la signóra.*
Shall I help you to a bit of the breast?	*Vuòl che le dìa un pèzzo di pètto.*
I beg your pardon, if you	*Scusi, poichè vuòl favo-*

will favour me, I will beg of you to cut me a wing.

With pleasure : I will also give you a little of the stuffing.

You will oblige me ; but give me also a little of the gravy.

James, a spoon ; don't you see that we have no pepper.

Change these plates, and bring the second course.

Bring the fruit.

Here are some fine cherries.

They are beautiful ; I would rather eat some of those strawberries, and raspberries.

Take some of these currants, some gooseberries, and one of these fine peaches.

At this season apples are no longer good.

That is a winter fruit.

Oranges, however, are always good when juicy.

In England fruit is not so plentiful as in Italy.

Pray do not bring it to my memory ; for, when I think on those figs, those grapes, and, above all, the water-melons, my mouth waters.

Well, let us not think any

rírmi, la pregherò di tagliármi un' ala.

Con piacére : le darò anche un pòco del ripièno.

Mi farà piacére : ma mi dia anche un po' d' intínto.

Giácomo, un cucchiáio; non vedéte che non abbiámo pépe.

Cambiáte questi piátti, e portate il secóndo servízio.

Portate in távola le frutta.

Ecco quì delle bèlle ciriège.

Son bellíssime ; mangerò piuttòsto quattro di quelle frávole, e di quei lampóni.

Prènda anche del ribes, dell' uva spina, ed una di queste bèlle pèsche.

Le méle in questa stagióne non sóno più buòne.

E' un frutto d' invèrno.

Le aráncie, per altro, son sèmpre buòne tutto l' anno quando son sugóse.

In Inghiltèrra le frutta non sóno così abbondánti cóme in Itália.

Per caritá, non me ne rinfréschi la memòria; chè quando pènso a quéi fichi e a quell' uva, e soprattútto ai cocómeri, mi viène l' acquolina in bócca.

Via, non ci pènsiamo più,

more about it; let us go and take a turn in the garden.

andiámo a far una passeggiáta nel giardíno.

DIALOGUE VII.

To speak Italian.

Per parlar Italiáno.

How goes on your Italian?
Come va l' Italiano?

Are you much improved in it now?
Vi ha ella fatti già mólti progrèssi?

Not much; I know scarcely any thing.
Non tròppo; non so quasi niènte.

It is said, however, you speak it very well.
Si dice, però, che parla benìssimo.

I wish it were true. Those that say so are much mistaken.
Volésse il cielo, che fósse véro! Quéi che lo dícono s'ingánnano mólto.

I assure you I was told so.
L' assicúro che così m' è stato détto.

I can say a few words which I have learnt by heart.
Pòsso dire alcúne paròle che so a ménte.

And so much as is necessary to begin to speak.
E' quanto basta per cominciár a parláre.

The beginning is not all, you must make an end.
Il cominciáre non è il tutto, bisógna finíre.

Be always speaking, whether well or ill.
Parli sèmpre, bène o male.

I am afraid of making mistakes.
Tèmo di far erróri.

Never fear; the Italian language is not difficult.
Non tèma, signóre; la língua Italiána non è difficile.

I know it, and that it possesses many graces.
Lo so, e so che ha mólta leggiadría.

It is true; and especially from the mouth of a lady.
E' véro, e particolarménte nella bócca delle Signóre.

How happy should I be if I were master of it.
O quanto sarèi contènto se la sapéssi.

Application is the only way of learning it.
Per imparárla bisógna studiáre.

How long have you been learning?	*Quant' è che ella la stúdia?*
Scarcely a month yet.	*Non è ancóra un mése.*
What books do you use?	*Di che libri si sèrve?*
I have Veneroni's Italian and English Grammar; and Rosteri's in Italian and French.	*Ho la grammática Italiána ed Inglése di Veneróni; e quélla di Rosteri in Italiáno e Francése.*
What Dictionaries?	*Che Dizionárj?*
Alberti in Italian and French; Baretti's Italian and English; and also Graglia's Small Dictionary. I then also use Bottarelli's Exercises.	*Quéllo di Albèrti in Italiáno e Francése; quello di Baretti in Italiáno ed Inglése; ed anche il piccolo Dizionário di Graglia. Mi sèrvo poi dégli Esercizj di Bottarèlli.*
What authors do you read?	*Che autóri lègge?*
At present I read Goldoni's Select Comedies, Soave's Moral Tales, and Metastasio.	*Adèsso lèggo le Commèdie Scélte di Goldóni; le Novèlle Moráli di Soáve, e Metastásio.*
What is your master's name?	*Cóme si chiáma 'l suo maèstro?*
His name is ——.	*Si chiáma ——.*
I have known him a great while.	*E' un pèzzo che lo conósco.*
He has taught several friends of mine.	*Ha insegnáto a mólti de' mièi amíci.*
Does he not tell you that you must constantly speak Italian.	*Non le dice che bisógna parlár sèmpre Italiáno?*
Yes, he often tells me so.	*Signor sì, me lo dice spésso.*
Why do you not talk, then?	*Perchè dúnque non parla?*
Whom will you have me talk with?	*Con chi vuòl ch'io parli?*
With those that will talk to you.	*Con quéi che le parleránno.*
I wish to talk, but dare not.	*Vorrèi parláre, ma non ardisco.*
You must not be afraid; you must be bold.	*Non bisógna temére; bisógna èsser ardíto.*

DIALOGUE VIII.

Of the Weather.	*Del Tèmpo.*
What sort of weather is it?	*Che tèmpo fa?*
It is fine weather.	*Fa bèl tempo.*
It is bad weather.	*Fa cattivo tempo.*
Is it cold? is it hot?	*Fa fréddo? fa caldo?*
Is it not cold? is it not hot?	*Non fa egli freddo? non fa caldo?*
Does it rain? does it not rain?	*Piòve? non piòve?*
I do not believe it.	*Non lo crédo.*
The wind is changed.	*Il vènto è cambiáto.*
We shall have rain.	*Avrémo della piòggia.*
It will not rain to-day.	*Non pioverà òggi.*
It rains, it pours.	*Piòve, dilúvia.*
It thunders. It hails. It snows.	*Tuòna. Grándina. Névica.*
It lightens.	*Lampéggia.*
It is very hot.	*Fa mólto caldo.*
Did it freeze last night?	*Ha geláto sta nòtte?*
No, sir, but it freezes now.	*Signór no, ma gèla adèsso.*
It appears to me to be a great fog.	*Mi par che fáccia una gran nébbia.*
You are not mistaken, it is true.	*Non s'ingánna, è véro.*
You have caught a violent cold.	*Ella è molto infreddáta.*
I have had it this fortnight.	*Sóno quíndici giórni che sòno infreddáto.*
'Tis the fruit of the season.	*Sóno frutti della stagióne.*
What's o'clock.	*Che óra è?*
'Tis early, 'tis not late.	*E' di buòn' óra, non è tardi.*
Is it breakfast time?	*E' tèmpo di far colazióne?*
'Twill be dinner-time immediately.	*Sarà prèsto tèmpo di desináre.*
What shall we do after dinner?	*Che farémo dópo pranzo?*
We'll take a walk.	*Andrémo a spasso.*

Let us take a turn now.	*Andiámo a far un giro adèsso.*
We must not go out by this weather.	*Non bisógna uscír con questo tèmpo.*

DIALOGUE IX.

Of the Charms of a young Lady.	*Delle Bellézze d'una Signorína.*
There's a beautiful young lady.	*Ecco una bèlla signorína.*
She is finely shaped.	*E' bèn fatta.*
She is charming, she is pretty.	*E' leggiádra, è vezzósa.*
Do you know her?	*La conoscéte?*
I do not know her.	*Non la conósco.*
She has fine eyes.	*Ha di bègli òcchi.*
I never saw a better shape.	*Non ho mái vedúto un più bèl personále.*
She has an easy carriage.	*E' disinvòlta.*
She has a noble mien.	*Ha un aspètto nòbile.*
The shape of her face is well proportioned.	*Il contórno del suo viso è bèn fatto.*
Her cheeks are plump and delicate.	*Le sue guánce sóno pienòtte e delicáte.*
Her mouth is little and red.	*La sua bócca è piccola e vermíglia.*
Her nose is well made.	*Il naso è ben fatto.*
Have you taken notice of her complexion?	*Avéte osserváto la sua carnagióne?*
It is a fair and lively complexion.	*E' una carnagióne biánca e viváce.*
What white hands she has!	*Che bèlle mani che ha!*
The white and vermilion of her cheeks shame the lilies and the roses.	*Il biánco e vermíglio del suo viso fanno, sènz' altro, tòrto ai gigli ed alle ròse.*
She has teeth as white as snow.	*Ha i dènti biánchi cóme la néve.*
It may be said that she's a fair beauty.	*Si può dire ch' è una bèlla biondína.*

She is the finest brown woman one can see.	E' la più bèlla brunétta che si pòssa vedére.
She has a noble gait.	Cammína con bèl garbo.
She has a sprightly countenance.	Ha una fisonomía spiritósa.
She has exquisite features.	Ha fattézze vaghe.
She is greatly extolled for her beauty.	E' molto pregiáta per la súa bellézza.
They say her wit is equal to her beauty.	Si díce che sía altrettánto spiritósa che bèlla.
Then she is an epitome of all perfections.	E' dunque un compèndio di tutte le perfezióni.

DIALOGUE X.

To inquire after News.	Per domandár quel che si dice di Nuòvo.
What news is stirring?	Che si díce di nuòvo?
Do you know any?	Sapéte niènte di nuovo?
I have heard none.	Non ho intéso dir niènte.
What is the talk of the town?	Di che si parla?
There's no talk of any thing.	Non si parla di niente.
Have you heard no talk of war?	Avéte sentíto dire che avrémo la guèrra?
I have not heard any thing of it.	Non ne ho intéso parláre.
There's a talk however of a siege.	Si parla però d'un assèdio.
It was reported so, but it is not true.	Si dicéva, ma non è véro.
On the contrary, there's a talk of peace.	Al contrário, si parla di pace.
Do you think we shall have peace?	Credéte che avrémo la pace?
I believe so.	Crédo di sì.
What say they at court?	Che si díce a córte?
They talk of a secret expedition.	Si parla d' una spedizióne segréta.

When do they think the king will set out?	*Quando si créde che partirà il re?*
'Tis not known. They do not say when.	*Non si sa. Non si dice quando.*
Where do they say he'll go?	*Dóve si dice che andrà?*
Some say into Flanders, others into Germany.	*Chi dice in Fiándra, chi in Germánia.*
And what says the Gazette?	*E la Gazzétta, che dice?*
I have not read it.	*Non l' ho létta.*
Is what is reported of Mr. —— true?	*Sarèbbe vero quel che si dice del Sig. ——?*
What of him?	*Che se ne dice?*
They say he's mortally wounded.	*Si dice che sía mortalmente feríto.*
I should be sorry for that; he's a worthy man.	*Mi dispiacerèbbe, perchè è un galantuòmo.*
Who wounded him?	*Chi l' ha feríto?*
Mr. —— in a duel.	*Il Signór —— in un duèllo.*
Is it known why?	*Si sa perchè?*
The report is, a quarrel at the Opera.	*Córre vóce che sía per una dispúta avuta all' Opera.*
I do not believe it. Nor I neither.	*Non lo crédo. Nemmen' io.*
However, we shall soon know the truth.	*Comúnque sía, si saprà prèsto il véro.*
Is the newspaper come in?	*E' arriváta la gazzétta?*
Does it mention the duel?	*Parla del duèllo?*
No, not a word about it.	*No, non ne fa paròla.*
Then let us hope there is no truth in the report.	*Dúnque speriámo che sía un falso rappòrto.*

DIALOGUE XI.

To inquire after one.	*Per domandáre d' uno.*
Who is that gentleman that spoke to you a little while ago?	*Chi è quel signóre che vi parláva pòco fa?*
He is a German.	*E' un Tedésco.*

I took him for an Englishman.

Lo credéva Inglése.

He came from Saxony.

E' della parte di Sassònia.

He speaks French very well.

Parla beníssimo Francése.

He speaks French like the French themselves.

Parla Francése côme un Francese stesso.

The Spaniards take him for a Spaniard, the English for an Englishman.

Gli Spagnuòli lo prèndono per uno Spagnuòlo, e gl' Inglési per un Inglese.

It is difficult to be conversant in so many different languages.

E' pur difficile d'èsser prático in tante língue così differènti.

He has been a long time in those countries.

E' stato un pèzzo in quéi paési.

Have you known him for any time?

E' un pezzo che lo conoscéte?

About two years.

Sóno due anni incirca.

He has a noble air, he has a good mien.

Ha un aspètto nòbile, ha una ciéra da galantuòmo.

He is a genteel person.

E' di bèlla presènza.

He is neither too tall, nor too short.

Non è nè tròppo grande, nè troppo píccolo.

He is handsome, he is well shaped.

E' bèn fatto, ed ha un bel portaménto.

He plays upon the flute, the guitar, and several other instruments.

Suòna 'l flàuto, la chitárra, e molti altri struménti.

I should be very glad to know him.

Avrèi a caro di conóscerlo.

I will bring you acquainted with him.

Ve ne procurerò la conoscènza.

Where does he live?

Dove sta di casa?

He lives just by.

Sta costì vicíno.

When will you have us go and wait on him?

Quando voléte che andiámo a riverírlo?

Whenever you please, for he is my intimate friend.

Quando vi piacerà, perchè è amico mio intrínseco.

It shall be when you have leisure.

Sarà quando avréte tèmpo.

We'll go to-morrow morning.	*V' andrémo domattina.*
I shall be obliged to you.	*Ve ne sarò obbligáto.*

DIALOGUE XII.

To write.	*Per iscrívere.*
Give me a sheet of paper, a pen, and a little ink.	*Dátemi un fòglio di carta, una penna, ed un pòco d' inchiòstro.*
Step into my closet; you'll find on the table whatever you want.	*Entráte nel mio gabbinétto; troveréte sopra la távola quanto vi farà di bisógno.*
There are no pens.	*Non vi sóno pénne.*
There are a great many in the ink-stand.	*Ve ne sono mólte nel calamáio.*
They are good for nothing.	*Non vágliono niènte.*
There are some others.	*E`ccone delle altre.*
They are not made.	*Non sóno temperáte.*
Where is your penknife?	*Dov' è 'l vòstro temperíno?*
Can you make pens?	*Sapéte temperár le pénne?*
I make them my own way.	*Le tèmpero a mòdo mio.*
This is not bad.	*Questa non è cattiva.*
While I finish this letter, do me the favour to make a packet of the rest.	*Méntre finisco questa lèttera, favorítemi di far un piègo di quélle altre.*
What seal will you have me put to it?	*Che sigíllo voléte che ci métta?*
Seal it with my cipher, or coat of arms.	*Sigillátelo cólla mia cifra, ovvéro colle mie armi.*
What wax shall I put to it?	*Che céralacca ci metterò?*
Put either red or black, no matter which.	*Mettétevi la róssa o la néra, non impòrta.*
Have you put the date?	*Avéte mésso la data?*
I believe I have, but I have not signed it.	*Crédo di sì, ma non ho sottoscrítto.*
What day of the month is this?	*Quanti n' abbiámo del mése?*

The eighth, the tenth, fifteenth, twentieth. — *Siámo òggi agli òtto, ai dièci, ai quíndici, ai vénti.*

Put the direction. — *Mettéteci la soprascrítta.*

Where is the powder? — *Dov' è la pólvere?*

You never have either powder or sand. — *Non avéte mai nè polvere, nè réna.*

There is some in the sand-box. — *Ve n' è nel polveríno.*

There's your servant; will you let him carry the letters to the post-house? — *Ecco l' vòstro sèrvo; volète che pòrti le lèttere alla pòsta?*

Carry my letters to the post-office, and don't forget to pay the postage. — *Portáte le míe lettere alla posta, e non vi dimenti-cáte di pagárne il pòrto.*

I have no money. — *Non ho quattríni, signóre.*

Hold your hand, there's a pistole. — *Tenéte, quest' è una dóppia.*

Go quickly, and return as soon as possible. — *Andáte prèsto, e tornáte quanto prima.*

DIALOGUE XIII.

To buy. — *Per compráre.*

What do you want, sir? — *Che brama, signóre, che cérca?*

What would you please to have? — *Còsa cománda, signóre?*

I want a good fine cloth to make me a suit of clothes. — *Vorrèi un panno che fosse bèllo e buòno da farmi un vestíto.*

Be pleased to walk in, sir; you'll see the finest in London. — *Vo' Signoría éntri, vedrà quì i più bèi panni di Lóndra.*

Show me the best you have. — *Mostrátemi 'l miglióre che avéte.*

There's a very fine one, and what's worn at present. — *E'ccone uno bellissimo, e cóme si usa adèsso.*

'Tis a good cloth, but I do not like the colour. — *E' buòno, ma 'l colór non mi piáce.*

There's another lighter piece. — *E'ccone un' altra pèzza più chiára.*

I like that colour well, but the cloth is not strong; 'tis too thin.

Il colóre mi piáce, ma il panno non è fòrte abbastánza; è tròppo sottile.

Look at this piece, sir; you'll not find the like any where else.

Véda V. S. quésta pèzza; non ne troverà così bèlla altróve.

What do you ask for it an ell?

Quanto lo vendéte il bráccio?

Without exacting, 'tis worth thirty shillings.

Sènza díre a V. S. un sòldo di più, vale trénta scellíni.

Sir, I am not used to stand haggling: pray tell me your lowest price.

Signóre io non sóno avvézzo a stiracchiáre; dítemi, di grázia, l' último prèzzo.

I have told you, sir, 'tis worth that.

Gliel' ho detto; questo è il prèzzo ristrétto.

'Tis too dear; I'll give you twenty-five.

E` tròppo caro; ve ne darò venticínque.

I can't bate a farthing.

Non v'è un sòldo da leváre.

You shall not have what you ask.

Non avréte quanto avéte domandáto.

You asked me the lowest price, and I have told you.

V. S. m'ha domandáto l' último prèzzo, ed io gliel' ho détto.

Come, come, cut off two ells of it.

Via, vía, tagliátene dúe bráccia.

I protest, on the word of an honest man, I don't get a crown by you.

Le giúro da galantuòmo, che non guadágno uno scúdo con lèi.

There are four guineas, give me the change.

E`cco quattro ghinèe, dátemi 'l rèsto.

Be pleased, sir, to let me have another; this is too light, it wants weight.

La prègo a darmi un' áltra ghinèa, che questa è leggièra, non è di péso.

Here's another.

E`ccone un' altra.

I thank you, Sir.

Grazie, Signore.

DIALOGUE XIV.

To play.	*Per giuocáre.*
Let us play a game at picquet.	*Giuochiámo una partíta a picchétto.*
What will you play for?	*A quanto voléte giuocáre?*
Let us play for half-a-crown to pass away the time.	*Giuochiámo mèzza coróna per passatèmpo.*
Give us cards.	*Dáteci delle carte.*
Let us see who shall deal.	*Vediámo a chi toccherà a fare.*
You are to deal; I am to deal.	*Tócca a vói; tócca a me.*
Shuffle the cards; all the court cards are together.	*Mescoláte le carte; tutte le figúre sóno insième.*
They are shuffled enough.	*Sóno mescoláte abbastánza.*
Cut, sir.	*Alzáte, signóre.*
Have you all your cards?	*Avéte le vòstre carte?*
I believe I have.	*Crédo di sì.*
How many do you take?	*Quante ne pigliáte?*
I take all. I leave one.	*Píglio tutto. Ne láscio una.*
I have a bad game.	*Ho un cattívo giuòco.*
Deal again.	*A mónte.*
Not this time.	*Signór no, per quésta vòlta.*
Have you laid out?	*Avéte scartáto?*
No, sir, my game puzzles me.	*Signor no, il mio giuòco, m' imbarrázza.*
You must have good cards; for I have nothing.	*Dovéte avér bèl giuòco, poichè io non ho niènte.*
Tell your point.	*Contáte 'l vòstro punto.*
Fifty, sixty.	*Cinquánta, sessánta.*
It is not good; it is good.	*Non vale: è buòno.*
A quint major, a quint to a king, a small quint, fourth to the queen, a tierce to a knave.	*Quinta maggióre, quinta al re, quinta bassa, quarta alla dama, tèrza al fante.*
I have as much.	*Ne ho altrettánto.*
Fourteen by kings, three aces, three queens.	*Quattórdici di re, tre assi, tre dame.*
Play.	*Giuocáte.*

Hearts, spades, clubs, diamonds.	*Cuòri, picche, fióri, quadri.*
The ace, the king, the queen, the knave, the ten, the nine, the eight, the seven.	*L' asso, il re, la dama, il fante, il dièci, il nòve, l' òtto, il sètte.*
I have lost; you made a pique, a re-pique.	*Ho perdúto; avéte fatto un picco, ripicco.*
You have won.	*Avete vinto.*
You owe me half-a-crown.	*Mi dovéte mezza coróna.*
You owed it me, pardon me.	*Scusátemi, me la doveváte.*
We are quits, or even, then.	*Siámo pace* or *pari, dunque.*

DIALOGUE XV.

For a Journey.	*Per un Viággio.*
How many miles is it from this place to N.?	*Quante miglia vi sóno, da quì a N.?*
It is eight miles.	*Vi sóno òtto míglia.*
We shall not be able to get thither to-day, it is too late.	*Non vi potrémo arrivár òggi, è tròppo tardi.*
It is not more than twelve o'clock, you have time enough yet.	*Non è più di mèazo giórno, vi arriveréte ancór di buòn' óra.*
Is the road good?	*E bèlla la strada?*
So, so; there are woods and rivers to pass.	*Non tròppo; vi sóno bòschi, e fiúmi da passáre.*
Is there any danger upon that road?	*V'è perícolo per quella strada?*
There is no talk of it; it is a highway, where you meet people every moment.	*Non se ne parla; è una strada maèstra, dóve si tròva gènte ad ógni moménto.*
Do they not say there are robbers in the woods?	*Non si dice che vi síano ladri nei bòschi.*
There is nothing to be feared, either by day or night.	*Non v' è nulla da temére, nè di giórno, nè di nòtte.*
Which way must one take?	*Che strada bisógna pigli-* [áre?

When you come near the hill, you must turn to the right.

Quando saréte vicíni alla collína, piglieréte a man dritta.

It is not necessary to ascend a hill then?

Non bisognerà dunque salír la collína?

No, sir, there is only a little hill in the wood.

Signór, no, non v'è che un picciol còlle nel bòsco.

Is the way difficult through the wood?

E' difficile la strada nel bòsco?

You cannot lose your way.

Non potéte smarrírvi.

As soon as you are out of the wood, remember to keep to the left hand?

Quando saréte fuòri del bòsco, ricordátevi di pigliár a mano manca.

I thank you, sir, and am much obliged to you.

Vi ringrázio, signore, e vi rèsto mólto obbligáto.

Come, come, gentlemen, let us take horse.

Via, via, signóri, montiámo a cavállo.

Where's the marquis?

Dov' è 'l signor marchése?

He's gone before.

E' andato innánzi.

He will wait for you just out of town.

V' aspetterà fuòri della città.

What do we stay for now? come, come, let's begone, let's have done.

Che aspettiámo? partiámo, andiámo via, finiámola.

Farewell, gentlemen, farewell.

Addío, signóri, state bène.

I wish you a good journey.

V' áuguro un felíce viággio.

DIALOGUE XVI.

For Supper and Lodging.

Della Céna, e dell'Allòggio.

So! we are arrived at the inn.

E'ccoci giúnti all' albèrgo.

Let us alight, gentlemen.

Smontiámo, signóri.

Take these gentlemen's horses, and take care of them.

Pigliáte i caválli di quésti signori, ed abbiátene cura.

Now let's see what you will give us for supper.

Orsù, vediámo che ci daréte da céna.

A capon, a half dozen pi-

Un cappóne, una mèzza

Q

geons, a salad, six quails, and a dozen of larks.

dozzína di picción, un' insaláta, sèi quáglie, ed una dozzína di lòdole.

Will you have nothing else?

Non vógliono altro lor signori?

That's enough, give us some good cheese and some fruit.

Quésto basta, dáteci del buòn formággio e delle frutta.

Let me alone, I'll please you, I warrant ye.

Láscino far a me, saránno contènti.

Light the gentlemen.

Fate lume a questi signori.

Let us have our supper as soon as possible.

Fáteci cénar quanto prima.

Before you have pulled your boots off, supper shall be upon the table.

Prima che si siano caváti gli stiváli, la céna sarà in órdine.

Let our portmanteaus and carpet bags be carried up stairs.

Si pòrtino sopra le nòstre valígie, e le nostre sacche da nòtte.

Pull off my boots, and then go and see whether they have given the horses any hay.

Cavátemi gli stiváli, e poi andréte a vedér se hanno dato del fièno ai caválli.

You shall conduct them to the river, and take care they give them some oats.

Li condurréte al fiúme, ed avréte cura che sia loro data la biáda.

I'll take care of every thing: do not trouble yourself.

Avrò cura di tutto: non si pigli fastídio.

Gentlemen, supper is ready, it is upon the table.

Signori, la céna è in órdine, è in távola.

We'll come presently.

Adèsso, adèsso, veniámo.

Give us water for our hands.

Dáteci dell' ácqua per le mani.

Let us go to supper, gentlemen, that we may go to bed in good time.

Andiámo a cenáre, signori; acciochè possiámo andár a lètto di buòn' óra.

Give us some drink.

Dáteci da bére.

Health to you, gentlemen.

Alla loro salúte, signori.

Is the wine good?

E' buòno 'l víno?

It is not bad.	Non è cattivo.
The capon is not done enough.	Il cappóne non è còtto abbastánza.
Give us some oranges, with a little sugar.	Dáteci delle aráncie, con un pòco di zúcchero.
Why don't you eat of this roast beef.	Perchè non mangiáte di quésto rosbíffe.
I have eaten one pigeon and three larks.	Ho mangiáto un piccióne e tre lòdole.
Go call for a chafing dish, and some pepper.	Andáte a domandár uno scaldavivánde e del pepe.
Tell the landlord we wish to speak with him.	Dite all' òste che vogliámo parlárgli.

DIALOGUE XVII.

To settle with the Landlord.	Per far i Cónti coll' Oste.
A good evening, gentlemen, are you satisfied with your supper?	Buòna séra, signóri, sóno contènti della céna?
We are, and we will satisfy you too.	Siámo contènti, e vogliámo che lo siáte voi pure.
What's the charge?	Quanto è il cónto?
The charge is not great.	La spésa non è grande.
See what you must have for us, our men, and our horses.	Vedéte quanto vi viène, per noi, per i nostri servitóri, e per i nòstri caválli.
Reckon yourselves, and you will find it comes to seven crowns.	Fácciano il cónto loro stéssi, e vedránno che sóno sètte scudi.
Methinks you ask too much.	Mi pare che domandiáte tròppo.
On the contrary, I am very reasonable.	Anzi, sono discretíssimo.
How much do you make us pay for the wine?	Quanto ci fate pagár per il vino?
Three shillings a bottle.	Tre scellíni la bottíglia.
Bring us another, and tomorrow morning we will	Portátene un' altra, e vi darémo domattína òtto

Q 2

pay you eight crowns, with breakfast included.

scúdi, facèndo però colazióne.

Methinks the gentleman is not well.

Pare che 'l signóre non istia bène.

I am very well, but weary and fatigued.

Sto bène, ma sòno uggióso e stánco.

Get your bed warmed, and go to bed.

Si fáccia scaldáre il lètto, e vada a dormire.

Bid my man come and undress me.

Dite al mio servitóre che vènga a spogliármi.

He waits for you in your chamber.

E' in cámera che l'aspètta.

Good night, gentlemen, I wish you merry.

Buòna nòtte, signóri, stiano allegraménte.

Do you want any thing?

Avéte bisógno di quálche cosa?

Nothing at all but rest.

Niènte altro che ripòso.

Order them to give us clean sheets and dry.

Dáte órdine che si dian lenzuòla pulite e asciutte.

Do not be afraid.

Non ábbia paúra.

Let us be called to-morrow very early.

Fáteci svegliáre dománi a buòn' óra.

I will not fail. Farewell, gentlemen; good night.

Saránno servíti. Buòna nòtte, Signori, stiano bène.

DIALOGUE XVIII.

To mount on Horseback.

Per montár a Cavállo.

This horse, I think, looks very bad.

Questo cávállo mi pare cattívo.

Give me another horse, I will not have that.

Dátamene un altro, non lo vòglio questo.

He cannot go.

Non può cammináre.

He is broken-winded; he is foundered.

E' bólso, è rattrappíto.

Are you not ashamed to give me such a hack as this?

Non avéte vergógna di darmi una rózza di quella sòrte?

He has no shoes; he's pricked in his foot.

E' sferráto; è inchiodáto.

You must lead him to the farrier's.

Bisógna condúrlo dal manescálco.

He is lame, he is maimed; he is blind.

Zòppica, è stroppiáto; è cièco.

This saddle will gall me.

Quésta sèlla mi farà male.

The stirrups are too long, too short.

Le staffe sóno tròppo lunghe, troppo córte.

Let them out, then; shorten them.

Allungáte le staffe; tiráte su le stáffe.

The girths are rotten.

Le cigne sóno imporrate.

What a wretched bridle is here!

Che cattiva briglia!

Give me my whip.

Dátemi la mia frusta.

Tie on my portmanteau, my cloak.

Attaccáte la valígia, il mantèllo.

Are your pistols loaded?

Sóno cáriche le sue pistòle?

I forgot to buy powder and ball.

Mi sòno dimencáto di comprár della pólvere, e delle palle.

Let us put on, let us get on faster.

Sproniámo, andiámo più prèsto.

I never saw a viler beast.

Non ho mái veduto una peggiór béstia.

He will neither go forward nor backward.

Non vuòl andar nè innánzi, nè indiètro.

Let go the bridle a little.

Rallentátegli la briglia.

Hold the reins shorter.

Tenete le rèdini più córte.

Spur him stoutly, make him go on.

Spronáte con vigóre, fátelo andár innánzi.

I may spur, but it is of no use.

Pòsso bène spronáre, non ne posso venír a capo.

Alight, I will make him go.

Scendéte, che lo farò bèn andáre.

Take care he don't kick you.

Badáte che non vi tiri un cálcio.

He kicks, then, I find.

Tira cálci dunque, a quel che sènto.

See if I have not tamed him.

Vedéte se l'ho sapúto domáre.

DIALOGUE XIX.

To visit a sick Person.	*Per visitár un Ammaláto.*
How have you passed the night?	*Cóme avéte passáta la nòtte?*
Very badly, I have not slept at all.	*Malaménte, non ho dormíto niènte.*
I have had a fever all night.	*Ho avúto la fèbbre tutta la notte.*
I have pains all over my body.	*Sènto dolóri per tutta la vita.*
You must be let blood.	*Bisógna farvi cavár sángue:*
I have been bled twice.	*M'è stato caváto sangue due vòlte.*
Where does your apothecary live?	*Dóve sta il vostro speziále?*
What physician attends you?	*Che mèdico viène a visitárvi?*
Go bid the surgeon come and dress me.	*Andáte a dir al cerúsico che vènga a medicármi.*
We do not know what health is, till we are ill.	*Non si sa còsa sia salúte, che quando si sta male.*
You must have a good heart; it will be nothing.	*Bisógna farsi ánimo, non sarà niènte.*
My wound pains me extremely.	*Sènto un gran dolóre alla mia piaga.*
How much physic have you taken?	*Quante medicíne avete prése?*
I am tired of physic.	*Sòno stufo di medicíne.*
I am fearful of being delirious.	*Tèmo di dar in delírio.*
Drink some toast and water.	*Bevéte dell' acqua panáta.*
Take nothing but broth.	*Non pigliate altro che bròdi.*
The doctor has ordered me some whey.	*Il mèdico m'ha ordináto il sièro.*
I am not able to move.	*Non mi pòsso muòvere.*
Give me a pillow.	*Dátemi un guançiále.*
Put my bolster right.	*Accommodátemi il capezzále.*
Draw the curtains.	*Tiráte le cortíne.*

Every thing I take seems bitter to me.

Tutto ciò che prèndo mi par amáro.

It is a long sickness.

Questa è una malattìa lunga.

How tired I am of lying in bed!

Quanto sòno stanco di star in lètto!

How happy are you in the enjoyment of health!

Beáto voi, che state bène!

DIALOGUE XX.
On Civility.

Della Civiltà.

I am happy, sir, to meet you here, I intended to wait upon you.

Gòdo, signóre, di trovárla, giacchè contava di venire in questo moménto da lei.

You do me too much honour, far beyond any thing I can possibly merit.

V. S. mi fa tròppa grázia, ed un onóre che non mèrito.

But what is your pleasure, sir? lay your commands on me.

Ma che cománda, signóre? in che pòsso servírla?

All I wanted, sir, was to assure you of my most humble respects;

Altro non voléva, padrón mio, se non assicurárla de' mièi umilìssimi rispètti;

And at the same time to beg a favour of you, which was, to recommend me to your mother's protection.

E pregarla nel medésimo tèmpo d'un favore, qual sarèbbe quello di raccomandármi alla protezióne della sua signóra madre.

You may rest assured that my mother and myself are entirely at your service.

Ella può vivér sicúra che tanto mia madre, quant' io viviámo dipendènti da' suòi cénni.

I may therefore expect your mother and you will, on this occasion, favour me with your interest?

Dunque pòsso speráre che ella e la sua signora madre mi favoriránno, in quest' occasióne, della loro efficacìssima interposizióne?

Make not the least doubt of that; and believe me, that both my mother and myself will receive a particular pleasure in serving you.

Non ne dúbiti punto, signor mio, e créda pure che mia madre ed io, ci farémo un sensibilíssimo piacére di servírla.

By these noble expressions I am enabled to form a judgment of your generosity:

Conósco in vèro dalle nòbili súe espressióni, quanto generósa sía:

And from your cordial professions of friendship, I perceive, that you are the worthy offspring of so worthy a mother.

E bèn m'accòrgo, da' suòi cordiáli sentiménti, essèr V. S. dégno figlio della degníssima súa genitríce.

No more compliments, sir, I beg; the events will afford you a sufficient proof of the sincerity of our friendship.

Non più compliménti, signore; gli effètti le daránno pròve sicúre della nòstra servitù.

I will be silent now; but when I have obtained the favour, I shall wait upon you with my thanks.

Tacerò adèsso; ma, ottenúto che avrò il favore, verrò da lei per ringraziárla.

Do me the favour to pay my respects to your mother.

Mi favorísca di riveríre distintissimaménte per parte mía la sua signóra madre.

DIALOGUE XXI.

Of the Seasons, Weather, &c.

Delle Stagióni, del Tèmpo, &c.

Spring is of all seasons the most agreeable.

La Primavèra è la più grata di tutte le stagióni.

Then every thing in nature smiles.

Tutto ride allóra nella natúra.

The country looks like a vast garden.

La campágna è cóme un gran giardíno.

The meadows resemble a large green carpet.

I prati somigliano ad un gran tappéto vérde.

The weather is mild and serene.	Il tèmpo è mólto dólce e seréno.
The air is temperate.	L'ária è temperáta.
The trees are full of leaves.	Gli álberi sóno copèrti di fôglie.
The melody of the birds enraptures me.	Il canto degli uccèlli m'innamóra.
The weather is neither too hot, nor too cold.	Il tèmpo non è nè tròppo caldo, nè troppo fréddo.
It is very healthy.	E' mólto sano.
All living creatures are then cheerful.	Tutti gli animáli allóra sono pièni di vivacità.
Nature seems to revive.	La natúra par che rinásca.
We have no spring this year.	Quest' anno non abbiámo primavèra.
The spring is backward.	La primavera è tarda.
It is like winter.	E' un piccol' invèrno.
I am fond of the country in summer-time, and of the town in winter.	Amo la campágna nell' estáte, e la città nell' invèrno.
We have a very hot Summer.	Abbiámo una State bèn calda.
The heat makes me both dull and idle.	Il calóre mi rènde pesánte e pigro.
The harvest will be very plentiful.	La raccòlta sarà molto abbondánte.
It would be still more fertile, if we had a little rain.	Lo sarébbe ancór più, se avéssimo un poco di piòggia.
There is a great plenty of fruit.	V' è úna grande abbondánza di frutta.
We want a little rain.	Abbiámo bisógno d'un po' di piòggia.
Rain would be very beneficial.	La pioggia ci farèbbe molto bène.
They begin to cut down the corn.	Si comíncia a segare il grano.
Summer is gone.	L'estáte è passáta.
Summer did not last long.	L'estáte non ha duráto molto.

Autumn has taken its place.	L'Autúnno ha préso il suo luògo.
Autumn is the season of fruits.	L'autúnno è la stagióne dei frutti.
Wine will be good this year.	Il vino sarà buòno quest' anno.
We shall drink good wine.	Beverémo buon vino.
The vines are very fine.	Le vigne sóno bellíssime.
They are loaded with large grapes.	Sóno cáriche di gròsse uve.
The days are very much shortened.	I giórni sóno mólto accorciáti.
We shall soon use candle at five o'clock.	Accenderémo quanto prima la candéla a cinque óre.
The mornings are cold.	Le mattináte sóno frédde.
We shall soon be obliged to make a fire.	Sarémo bèn tòsto costrétti d' avére del fuòco.
Winter comes on.	L'Invèrno viène.
Winter draws near.	L'inverno s'appròssima.
The mornings are short.	Le mattináte sóno córte.
The evenings are long.	Le seráte sono lúnghe.
The trees are divested of their leaves.	Gli álberi sono spogliáti delle loro fòglie.
Nature appears benumbed.	La natúra sémbra intorpidíta.
Winter does not please me.	L'invèrno non mi piáce.
It pleases nobody.	Non piace a nessúno.
Nevertheless it is pleasing to walk in the sun.	Nulladiméno il paseggiáre al sóle fa piacére.
It is soon night.	Fa prèsto nòtte.
The days are very short.	I giórni sóno mólti córti.
We have scarcely eight hours' daylight.	Abbiámo appéna òtto óre di giórno.
Twilight does not make its appearance before seven o'clock in the morning.	Il crepúsculo non comíncia mái ad apparíre avanti le sètte óre della mattina.
They light candles at five in the afternoon.	Alle cínque óre pomeridiáne s' accèndono le candéle.
It is not daylight the	Il giórno non ritórna a com-

next day before eight o'clock. — *parire avanti le òtto ore del giorno dopo.*

The days are somewhat lengthened. — *I giorni sono alquánto allungáti.*

That foretells the return of Spring. — *Quésto ci annúnzia il ritorno délla Primavèra.*

Its return will exhilarate Nature. — *Il suo ritorno rallegrerà la Natúra.*

DIALOGUE XXII.

Short and Idiomatic Phrases. — *Frasi Córte ed Idiomátiche.*

Whence do you come? — *D'onde viène èlla?*

I come from the city, where I met your brother. — *Vèngo dalla città, óve incontrái súo fratèllo.*

Whither are you going? — *Dóve va?*

Whither do you run so fast? — *O've córre così in frétta?*

Which way do you go? — *Da che parte va?*

Which way do you take? — *Che via prènde?*

Can I go with you? — *Pòsso io andár con lèi?*

Stay a little, I will go with you. — *Aspètti, che 'l accompagnerò.*

Will you wait for me ten minutes? — *Vorrèbbe aspettármi dièci minúti?*

I shall be ready in less than ten minutes. — *Sarò prònto in méno di dièci minúti.*

Tell me where you are going. — *Mi dica óve va.*

I am going into the country. — *Vado in campágna.*

Come up into my room, I have something to tell you. — *Salga nella mìa stanza, ho quálche còsa da dirle.*

Come in, and sit down. — *E'ntri e sègga.*

Do not you stir from thence. — *Non si muòva di là.*

Stay there. — *Stìa là.*

Now, you may go out. — *Può uscìre adèsso.*

Come down with me. — *Scénda méco.*

Q 6

Adieu, I wish you a happy journey.	*Addio, le áuguro un buòn viággio.*
But, stop, come hither.	*Ma, aspètti, vènga quì.*
Wait a little.	*Aspètti un pòco.*
Stop, that I may speak to you.	*Si férmi, ch'io le parli.*
Do not go so fast.	*Non vada così prèsto.*
You go too fast.	*Ella va tròppo presto.*
What do you stop me for?	*Pèrche mi férma élla?*
Do not touch me.	*Non mi tócchi.*
You make me lose my time.	*Mi fa pèrder il mio tèmpo.*
My time is too precious for me to mispend it.	*Il mio tèmpo è tròppo prezióso per pèrderlo così.*
Leave that alone.	*Lo lasci stare.*
Don't touch that.	*Non lo tócchi.*
Touch nothing.	*Non tócchi niènte.*
Why do you recommend me that, sir, or madam?	*Perchè mi raccománda ella quésto?*
Because I recommend it to every body.	*Perchè lo raccomándo a tutti.*
I am well here.	*Sto bène quì.*
I find myself very well here.	*Mi tròvo molto bene quì.*
The door is shut.	*La pòrta è chiúsa.*
Who has shut the door?	*Chi ha chiuso la porta?*
I can't open it.	*Non pòsso aprírla.*
I can't turn the key.	*Non posso voltár la chiáve.*
The lock is not good.	*La serratúra non è buòna.*
Open the door.	*Apra la pòrta?*
It is open.	*E' apèrta.*
Shut the door.	*Chiúda la porta.*
It is shut.	*E' chiúsa.*
Open the window.	*Apra la finèstra.*
Shut the window.	*Sèrri la finestra.*
What do you look for?	*Che cérca ella?*
What have you lost?	*Che ha pèrso?*
If you have lost any thing, I have not found it.	*Se ha perso quálche còsa, io non l'ho trováta.*
I never find any thing.	*Non tròvo mái niènte.*
Speak loud.	*Parli fòrte.*

Speak distinctly.	*Parli distintaménte.*
Open your mouth.	*Apra la bócca.*
You speak too low.	*Ella parla tròppo piáno.*
Do not be bashful.	*Non sia tímido.*
To whom do you speak?	*A chi parla élla?*
Do you speak to me?	*Parla a me?*
Say, is it to me that you are speaking?	*Dica, è a me ch' élla parla?*
Speak to me, then.	*Mi parli, dúnque.*
Speak to him, speak to her.	*Gli parli, le parli.*
Do you speak French?	*Parla ella Francése?*
I speak it a little.	*Lo parlo un pòco.*
What do you say?	*Che dice?*
Do you say any thing?	*Dice élla quálche còsa?*
I say nothing.	*Non dico nulla.*
What have you said?	*Che ha ella détto?*
I have said nothing.	*Non ho detto niènte?*
I don't believe it.	*Non lo crédo.*
What does he say?	*Che dice égli?*
He says nothing.	*Non dice nulla.*
I thought he had spoken.	*Credéva che avésse parláto.*
What has he told you?	*Che le ha detto?*
Has he told you nothing?	*Non le ha detto niènte?*
What does she say?	*Che dice essa?*
What has she told you?	*Che le ha éssa detto?*
She said nothing to me.	*Essa non m'ha detto niènte.*
Don't tell her that.	*Non le dica questo.*
I won't tell it her.	*Non glielo dirò.*
Don't tell it to them.	*Non lo dica lóro.*
What are you doing?	*Che fa élla?*
I am doing nothing.	*Non fo nulla.*
What have you done?	*Che ha fatto?*
I have done nothing.	*Non ho fatto niènte.*
Have you done your work?	*Ha ella fatto il suo lavóro?*
No; I have been idle.	*No, sòno stato pigro.*
Shall you soon have done?	*Avrà ella finíto prèsto?*
Yes, in half an hour.	*Sì, in una mèzz' óra.*
Have you not done?	*Non ha ella finíto?*
I thought you had done.	*Credévo che avésse finito.*
You go very slow.	*Va molto adágio.*
Has he nothing to do?	*Non ha égli niènte da fare?*

Has he no business?	*Non ha egli alcúna occupazióne?*
How does he spend his time?	*Cóme passa egli 'l suo tèmpo?*
What is her amusement?	*In che si divèrte?*
Is she fond of music?	*Ama essa la música?*
Does she write? does she read?	*Scríve? Lègge?*
Does she go to the play?	*Va éssa al teátro?*
What do you ask?	*Che dománda élla?*
Do you ask for any thing?	*Dománda ella qualche còsa?*
Say what you ask.	*Dica ciò che dománda.*
If you want any thing, speak.	*Se ha bisógno di qualche cosa, parli.*
Answer me.	*Mi rispónda.*
Why do you not answer me?	*Perchè non mi rispónde?*
Are you afraid, or do you scorn to answer me?	*Tème, o sdégna ella di rispóndermi?*
If you do not answer me, I'll speak to you no more.	*Se non mi rispónde, non le parlerò più.*

DIALOGUE XXIII.

On Italy.	Sull' Itália.
Courage, Miss, we now are at the top of the highest of these hills.	*Corággio, signóra, siámo già alla cima della più alta di quéste colline.*
I assure you I can go no further; my breath fails me: this ascent is too steep.	*Le assicúro che non ne pòsso più; mi manca il fiáto; quésta salíta è un po' tròppo érta.*
Now that we are arrived, we may rest ourselves.	*Ora che siámo arriváte, possiámo riposárci.*
Yes, let us rest, for I need it much.	*Sì, riposiámoci pure, chè ne ho gran bisógno.*
What do you think? Did I not tell you that we should enjoy a beautiful sight?	*Còsa le pare? non le ho detto che si sarèbbe godúta una bèlla vedúta?*

O yes; I admire it much. What a fine landscape all around!

You, who have travelled in Italy, I suppose, must have found some charming prospects in that country.—How long is it since you came from thence?

It is almost three years.

Have you been always in the same place?

No: I have travelled continually, from town to town.

What do you think of that climate?

Charming! The country is so well cultivated, that it seems a collection of gardens.

I am told, however, that there are some lands which lie uncultivated.

Very true. The Italians have attended more to the embellishment of their cities, than to the cultivation of the country.

Without doubt there are very beautiful works of architecture?

Yes, all master-pieces: but neglected fields in some parts of Italy, reproach the inhabitants with their indolence.

By which road did you enter Italy?

Oh sì; l'ammíro mólto. Che bèl paése tutt' all' intórno!

Ella, che ha viaggiáto in Itália, avrà, mi figúro, vedúto di bèi punti di vista in quel paése.— Quanto tèmpo è ch' élla ne manca?

Son quási tre anni adèsso.

E' stata sèmpre néllo stésso luògo.

No: ho viaggiáto continuaménte, óra in una città, ed óra in un' altra.

Che le pare di quel clima?

Stupèndo! Le campágne son così bèn coltiváte che páion tanti giardíni.

Mi si dice per altro che vi síano alcúni terréni incòlti.

Veríssimo. Hanno gl' Italiáni attéso più all' abbelliménto delle città, che alla coltúra delle campágne.

Vi saránno bellíssime òpere d' architettúra, m'immágino?

Sì, tutti capi d'òpera: ma le neglètte campágne d' una parte d' Italia rimpròverano ágli abitánti la lóro indolènza.

Da qual parte è ella entráta in Italia?

By the road of Venice, a city which is exactly like an immense fleet, resting quietly on the midst of the waters, and to which there is no approaching but by boats or ships.—In this respect, Venice is a unique city.

In that town are there neither horses, nor carriages?

None at all. The carriages for the Venetians are the gondolas; and the gondoliers are generally very eloquent; and their repartees are full of the most pleasing attic salt.

Did you stay much at Venice?

Only five months, which is the time the carnival lasts, during which one goes always masked, with the greatest liberty, to all sorts of diversions.

Which is the principal square in Venice?

St. Mark's square, on the east side of which stands St. Mark's Church.

Have you been at Bologna?

Yes, madam; but first I passed through Ferrara, which in its walls will show you a fine and extensive solitude, almost

Dalla parte di Venèzia, città la quale è appúnto cóme una vasta flòtta, che si ripòsa tranquillaménte sulle ácque, ed a cui non si a; pròda che per mèzzo di barche o navi.—Su quésto punto, Venèzia è única.

In quésta città non vi saránno dunque nè caválli, nè carròzze?

Niènte affátto. Le carròzze dei Veneziáni son le góndole; e i gondolièri son uòmini per lo più mólto eloquènti; e i loro concèlti son pièni di sali argutíssimi.

E' stato molto tèmpo in Venèzia?

Cínque mési solaménte; quanto ivi dura il carnevále, in cúi si va sèmpre in máschera con la maggiór libertà ad ógni sòrta di divertiménti.

Qual è la piázza principále di Venèzia?

La piazza di San Marco; dall' lato orientále vi è la Chièsa di San Marco.

E' stata mai a Bológna?

Sì, signóra; ma son passáta prima per la città di Ferrára, che nel suo recínto le farà vedére una bella e vasta solitúdine, silen-

as much so as the monument of Ariosto, who rests there.

I have heard that at Bologna there is a greater abundance of provisions than in any other place in Italy.

It is true, and for that reason it is named the *Fat*. There the sciences are familiar also to the fair sex; and the conversation of the inhabitants is very entertaining.

What road did you take on quitting Bologna?

That of Rimini, along the sea-coast of the Adriatic, as far as Ancona, and from thence to Loretto, a pilgrimage once famous for the concourse of strangers, and the superb treasures with which its church was enriched.

I should be very glad to hear now something of Rome too.

On returning from Loretto, crossing the Apennines and a great number of small towns, we at last arrive at Rome, formerly the queen and capital of the world.

To see all the curiosities of that famous city, I have heard that it was neces-

ziósa quasi quanto la tómba dell' Ariòsto, che ivi ripòsa.

Ho sentíto dire che in Bológna vi è più abbondánza di víceri, che in qualúnque altra parte d'Itália.

E' véro, e per quésto vien denomináta la Grassa. Quivi le sciènze son familiári anche al·bèl sèsso; e la conversazióne degli abitánti rallégra moltíssimo.

Che strada ha ella préso partèndo di Bológna?

Quélla di Rimini, lungo la riva del mare Adriático, fino ad Ancóna, e quindi a Loréto, pellegrinággio famóso una vòlta, pel concórso dei forestièri, e pei supèrbi tesòri, de' quali èra arricchíto il suo tèmpio.

Sarèbbemi mólto caro sentir ora quálche còsa di Róma.

Partèndo da Loréto, attraversándo gli Apennini e una moltitúdine di piccole città, si arriva finalménte a Roma, anticaménte regina e capitále del móndo.

Per vedére tutte le rarità di quésta famósa città, ho sentíto dire che bisógna

sary to employ a Cicero-
ne: what does that mean?

It signifies, perhaps, speak-
er; because such per-
sons accompany stran-
gers every where, in-
forming and explaining
to them all that is to be
seen.

What was Rome, when
the French took from it
all that was most pre-
cious?

Exactly what it was before.
The churches, the pa-
laces, the public squares,
the pyramids, the obe-
lisks, the columns, the
galleries, the fronts, the
theatres, the fountains,
the prospects, the gar-
dens, all will show you
the grandeur of a city,
which always was, and
always will be, above
others, universally ad-
mired.

Are the modern Romans as
warlike as the ancient?

Certainly not: but in the
quarter of the town called
Trastevere, we observe
even now countenances
resembling the ancient
busts.

I have heard much about
the famous Appian way;
does it still exist?

Yes, madam, but not in

---

*far uso di un Ciceróne:
còsa vuòl égli dire?*

*Ciceróne, vorrà dir parla-
tóre, perchè questi tali
accompágnano i fore-
stièri da per tutto, infor-
mándoli, e spiegándo loro
quanto v' è da vedére.*

*Come trovávasi Roma, al-
lorchè i Francési le tol-
sero quanto v' éra di più
prezióso?*

*Precisamente com' èra pri-
ma. Le chièse, i palázzi,
le piázze púbbliche, le
pirámidi, gli obelischi, le
colónne, le gallerie, le
facciáte, i teátri, le fon-
táne, le vedute, i giardini,
tutto le indicherà la grandézza d' una città che è
stata sèmpre, e sarà con
preferènza universale am-
miráta.*

*Sóno i nuòvi Románi gènte
bellicósa quanto gli an-
tichi?*

*No sicuraménte: ma nel
quartiére detto Trasté-
vere ossérvansi anche al
dì d'òggi fisonomie simili
agli antichi bústi.*

*Ho sentito tanto parláre
della famósa via A'ppia;
sussiste ancóra?*

Sì, signóra, ma non già nel

the same state it was at the time of the ancient Romans.

Do you remember at what time that famous road was made?

It was in the year of Rome four hundred and forty-. one, by order of Appius Claudius, the Censor, and it was one of the finest works of Roman magnificence. It leads from Rome to Brundusium, at the furthest end of Italy, towards the east.

Doubtless you have travelled as far as Naples, one of the finest cities of Italy, as they tell me.

Yes, madam. And exactly by that famous Appian road we arrive at that fine Parthenope, where rest the ashes of Virgil, upon which is seen a laurel growing, which cannot be better placed.

Were you not afraid of living in a city where they often feel earthquakes, and where fire descends from the mountains?

No, my dear; it is not so terrible as it is said; nay, Mount Vesuvius on one side, and the Elysian fields on the other, offer

medésimo stato, in cui èra al tèmpo degli antíchi Románi.

Si ricòrda ella a qual tèmpo fu costruíta questa famósa strada?

Fu nell' anno di Róma quattrocènto quarantuno, per órdine del Censóre A'ppio Cláudio, e fu uno de' più bèi lavóri della Romána magnificènza. Conducéva éssa da Roma fino a Bríndisi all' estremità dell' Itália vèrso levánte.

Mi figúro ch' ella ábbia viaggiáto fino a Nápoli, città delle più bèlle d'Itália, a quelche mi dícono?

Sì, signóra. Ed appúnto per quésta famósa via Appia si arríva a quélla bella Partènope, óve ripòsano le céneri di Virgílio, sulle quali védesi germogliáre un láuro, che non può èsser mèglio collocáto.

Non ha avúto paúra di restáre in una città dóve si sèntono spesso tremuòti, e dove scénde giù fuòco dalle montágne?

No, cara; non è tanto terríbile quanto si díce; anzi il Mónte Vesúvio da un lato, e i Campi Elisj dall' altro, presèn-

prospects which are very delightful.

Did you ever see any eruption of this Vesuvius?

Yes, I have seen it once in a great rage, and then I saw it throw out torrents of fire, which majestically spread over the country.

They say, that the Neapolitans are lively and witty, but too much inclined to pleasure and idleness, to be what they might be.

Very true, and certainly Naples might be an incomparable city, if one did not meet a crowd of plebeians, otherwise called Lazzaroni, who look like wretches and thieves, and often are neither.

But in speaking of Rome and Naples, we have left behind us Florence, and the other cities of Tuscany which are so celebrated.

We may easily go back and travel three hundred miles (for that is the distance between Naples and Florence,) with the same facility that we have travelled the others.

Tell me then something of Florence, which is

tano dei punti di vista singolaríssimi.

Ha ella mai vedúto nessúna eruzióne di quésto Vesúvio?

Sì, l' ho vedúto una vòlta in gran furóre, e vidi allóra rigurgitáre dal suo séno torrènti di fuòco che maestosaménte si spandévan per le campágne.

Si dice che i Napoletáni son viváci e spiritósi, ma tròppo inclináti ai piacéri ed alla pigrízia, per èsser quel che potrèbbon èssere.

Veríssimo, e certaménte sarèbbe Nápoli un' impareggiábile città, se non vi s' incontrásse una fòlla di plebèi, altrimenti détti Lazzaróni, che hanno ária di ribáldi e di malandríni, sènza èsser sovènte nè l'un, nè l' altro.

Ma col parlar di Roma e di Nápoli abbiámo lasciáto indiètro Firènze, e le altre città della Toscána, tanto rinnomáte.

Possiámo facilménte tornár indiètro e far anche trecènto míglia (che tante ve ne sóno da Nápoli a Firènze) con la medésima facilità che abbiámo fatto le altre.

Mi dica dúnque qualche còsa di Firenze, che vièn

acknowledged as the mother of the fine arts, and then I will not trouble you any more.

riguardata cóme madre delle bèlle arti, e pòi non le darò più incòmodo.

On the contrary, you give me pleasure. Florence is not very large, but it is noble and beautifully adorned; every where are seen traces of the grandeur and the good taste of the Medicis.

Anzi mi dà piacére. Firènze non è mólto grande, ma è gentíle e vagaménte adórna: quívi scòrgonsi da per tutto le tràcce della splendidézza e del buòn gusto dei Mèdici.

I would say a little more about this beautiful city; but now being obliged to leave you, I will enter more into particulars at our next meeting.

Vorrèi dirle di più intórno a questa bèlla città; ma dovèndo ritirármi, le ne dirò qualche còs' altro più con còmodo quando ci rivedrémo.

You will give me much pleasure..

Mi farà gráxia.

A COLLECTION OF ITALIAN IDIOMS,

WHICH CONSTITUTE THE PECULIAR DELICACY OF THAT LANGUAGE ([35]).

TO PRAY OR EXHORT.

Dear sir, do me that favour. | *Caro signóre, mi fáccia quésto favóre.*
Pray! I conjure you. | *Deh! la scongiúro.*
I pray you. | *Deh! la prègo.*
I beseech you. | *In cortesía.*
Do me the favour. | *Favorísca.*

[35] This Collection, which contains the true Idioms, or modes of speaking, with the turns of the Italian Phrases, divided according to their respective subjects, will be found useful.

TO EXPRESS CIVILITY.

Your servant, sir.	*Servitór súo, signóre.*
At your service.	*Per obbedìrla.*
I thank you.	*La ringrázio.*
You may depend upon me.	*Fáccia capitále della mia persóna.*
See if it is in my power to serve you.	*Véda, signore, se son capáce di servírla.*
Command me.	*Mi comándi.*
Do what you please with your servant.	*Dispónga d'un súo servitóre.*
I wait for your commands.	*Aspètto i suòi comándi.*
Since you will have it so.	*Poich' élla così vuòle.*
You are the master.	*Ella è padróne.*
I am infinitely obliged to you.	*Le rèsto infinitaménte obbligáto.*
I will not be guilty of that fault.	*Non farò questo mancaménto.*
Away with these titles and ceremonies.	*Lasciámo quésti titoli e queste cerimònie.*
It is my duty to serve you.	*E' un dovére di servírla.*
You are very obliging.	*Ella è mólto cortése.*
I know not how to make a proper return for so many favours.	*Non saprèi cóme contraccambiáre tante bontà.*

TO COMPLAIN, HOPE OR DESPAIR.

How unfortunate am I, if that be !	*Guái a me, se questo è !*
Poor miserable creatures that we are !	*Poverétti nói !*
How unfortunate I am !	*Me infelíce, disgraziáto me !*
Ah cruel fortune !	*Ahi sòrte avvèrsa !*
To what are we reduced !	*A che siám ridótti !*
We are undone; we are ruined !	*Siámo perduti ; rovináti !*
There only wanted that !	*Ci mancáva anche questo !*
We are at last come to it.	*Ci siám pur giúnti.*

That was the cause of my grief.	E'cco ciò che cagionáva il mio dolóre.
There is what completes our ruin.	E'cco l' última nòstra rovina.
That is the misfortune.	Questo è 'l male.
It is really a pity.	E' veraménte un peccáto.
O the poor child or fellow!	O pòverino!
I am the most unfortunate of men!	Sòn il re dei disgraziáti!
What is to be done? what shall I do? what shall we do?	Che s'ha da fare? che farò? che farémo?
We must have patience.	Bisógna avér paziènza.
We must conform ourselves to the will of God.	Bisógna riméttersi alla volontà di Dío.
Nothing further can be done.	Non si può far altro.
I hope that God, ... I hope that heaven ...	Spèro in Dio, ... spero nel Cièlo ...
We must swallow that.	Fòrza è che ce la beviámo.
We must die, sooner or later.	Ad ògni mòdo bisógna morire un giórno.

TO EXPRESS AFFIRMATION, CONSENT, BELIEF OR REFUSAL.

However, it is true.	E' pur véro.
It is but too true.	E' pur tròppo vero.
To tell you the truth.	A dirvi 'l vero.
Indeed it is so.	In fatti, così è.
There's no doubt of it.	Non v' è dúbbio alcúno.
I bet it is.	Scommétto di sì.
I bet it is not.	Scommetto di no.
I think so, I think not.	Crédo di sì, credo di no.
Not to tell an untruth.	Salvo 'l vero.
Nobody would say so ridiculous a thing.	Niúno dirèbbe úna stravagánza símile.
Say likewise that the snow is not white.	Dite anche che la néve non è biánca.
I can tell you it is a very fine one.	Vi so dire ch' élla è bellissima.

I would lay a wager.	*Scommetterèi quálche còsa.*
O you jest, sir.	*Oh ella burla, signóre.*
I speak in earnest.	*Parlo sul sèrio.*
You have guessed rightly.	*L' avéte indovináta.*
I believe you, one may believe you.	*La crédo, le si può crédere.*
Let it be then, let it be so.	*Sìa dúnque, così sìa.*
You shall be satisfied.	*Ella resterà soddisfatta.*
Softly, not so fast.	*Adágio, adagio, non tanto prèsto.*
Nor that either.	*Nè manco questo.*
I would not give you a fig.	*Non ti darèi un fico.*
Yes, truly.	*Sì davvéro.*
They are trifles.	*Sóno inèzie.*
Do not make me giddy or deaf.	*Non mi stordire,* 2d sing.
Get thee to bed.	*Va' a lètto.*

TO DENY.

I say not.	*Dico di no.*
It is not true.	*Non è véro.*
It is not so, it is so.	*Quésto no, questo sì.*
Positively I will not.	*Non vòglio in nessún mòdo.*
I jested.	*Io burláva.*
I did it only by way of jest.	*Lo facéva per ischérzo.*

TO CONSULT.

What is to be done?	*Che s'ha da fare?*
What course shall we take?	*Che partito piglierémo?*
Let's do so and so.	*Facciámo così e così.*
Let's do one thing.	*Facciamo una còsa.*
It will be better that.	*Sarà mèglio che.*
Stay a little.	*Aspettáte.*
It would be better that.	*Sarèbbe meglio che.*
Let me do.	*Lasciáte far a me.*
I had rather.	*Vorrèi piuttòsto.*
Were I in your place.	*Se fossi in voi.*

TO WISH WELL TO A PERSON.

Heaven preserve you.	*Il Cièlo vi guárdi.*
I wish you every thing that's good.	*Vi auguro ógni bène.*
God assist you.	*Iddio v' aiúti.*
God forgive you.	*Iddio vi perdóni.*
God be with you.	*Andáte con Dío.*
May you be happy.	*Siate felíce.*
I wish you true content.	*Vi áuguro ógni maggiór contentézza.*
God grant you all the prosperity you desire.	*Dio vi concèda ógni prosperità desiderábile.*
Till I see you again.	*A rivedérci.*
I am your most humble servant.	*Servitór suo umilíssimo.*
You are welcome.	*Bèn venúto.*
Well met.	*Ben trováto.*
Much good may it do you.	*Buòn pro vi-fáccia.*

TO ASSERT SOLEMNLY.

Upon my faith.	*In fede mia.*
In my conscience.	*Sulla cosciènza mia.*
Upon my life.	*Per la vita mia.*
Upon my honour.	*Sull'onor mio.*
Upon my word.	*Sulla mia paròla.*
I swear, as I am a gentleman.	*Ve lo giúro da cavalière.*
As I am an honest man.	*Da galantuòmo.*
As I am a man of honour.	*Da uòmo onoráto.*
By Jupiter (*Gióve*)!	*Per Bacco* (Bacchus).

TO THREATEN OR INSULT.

I will give you a Roland for your Oliver.	*Ti renderò pan per focáccia.*
Let me alone, I will see whether	*Láscia far a me, ch' io saprò se....*
You shall pay it me.	*Tu mela pagherái,* 2d sing.

R

I vow you shall repent it.	*Giuro al cièlo che te ne fa-* *rò pentíre.*
I will give it you, go.	*Te la darò, va'.*
If you put me in a pas- sion.	*Se tu mi fai andár in còl-* *lera.*
If I put myself in a pas- sion.	*Se mi comíncia a fumáre.*
Do not awake a sleeping lion.	*Non destáre 'l can che* *dòrme.*
Softly, softly.	*Pián, piáno.*
Woe be to thee.	*Guái a te.*
Thou shalt not escape me.	*Tu non mi scapperái.*
Hold your tongue, don't speak.	*Non più paròle, taci.*
'Tis enough, 'tis sufficient.	*Basta, basta.*
Thou art undone.	*Sèi mòrto, va'!*
In spite of thee.	*A túo márcio dispètto.*

TO ADMIRE.

O God! Good God!	*Dio mio! Dio buòno!*
O Heavens!	*Oh Cièlo!*
Is it possible!	*Possibile!*
Who ever saw the like!	*Chi vide mái tanto!*
Who would have thought, believed, said!	*Chi l' avrèbbe pensáto, cre-* *dúto, détto!*
See now a little!	*Guardáte un pòco!*
I was wondering.	*Io mi maravigliávo.*
O strange!	*Che maraviglia!*
I don't wonder.	*Non mi maraviglio.*
How can that be?	*Com' è possibile?*
So goes the world?	*Così va 'l mondo.*

TO EXPRESS JOY OR DISPLEASURE.

What a pleasure!	*O che gusto!*
What joy!	*O che allegrézza!*
How pleased I am!	*Qual' è il mio contènto!*
O how happy am I!	*O me felice!*
O happy day!	*O giorno felice!*

What happiness!	*O che fortúna !*
O how happy are you!	*Beáto voi ! or beáto lei !*
I am sorry for it.	*Me ne rincrésce.*
That touches my very soul.	*Mi dispiáce fin all' ánima.*
It pierces me to the heart.	*Mi trafigge 'l cuòre.*

TO REPROACH.

Is this the way to deal with gentlemen?	*Così si tratta co' galantuòmini.*
Ought not you to be ashamed?	*Non ve ne vergognáte ?*
To affront me thus!	*Far a me questo affrónto !*
To such a man as I am.	*Ad un parì mio.*
To me, is it not?	*A me, eh ?*
Do you deal thus?	*A questo mòdo si tratta ?*
So, is it not?	*Così, eh ?*
What a fine way of proceeding!	*Che bel mòdo di procèdere !*
You ought not to treat me thus.	*Non dovréste trattarmi così.*
Do you think that is well?	*Vi par che stia bène?*
We shall see immediately?	*Adèsso si vedrà.*
What the deuce has he done?	*Che diámine ha egli fatto ?*
What, obstinate still?	*Ancóra ostináto ?*

TO CALL.

Hark.	*Ascólta, ascoltáte.*
Listen.	*Udite.*
Where are you?	*Dove sèi ? dove siète.*
Hark ye.	*Sentite úna paròla.*
Hear you.	*Sentite, udite.*
Hark ye a little.	*Sentite un pòco.*
A word.	*Una parola.*
I will speak but two words to you.	*Due parole solaménte.*
Stay you.	*Fermátevi.*

R 2

TO EXPRESS UNEASINESS, TROUBLE OR SORROW.

I am sorry.	*Mi dispiáce, mi rincrésce.*
Leave me alone.	*Lásciami stare.*
Prithee get thee gone.	*Va' vía, ti prègo.*
Do not stun me.	*Non mi rómpere 'l capo.*
Away, away, I beg of thee.	*Via vía, ti prègo.*
Get you out of my sight.	*Levátevimi d' innánzi.*
Get you gone from hence.	*Levátevi di quà.*
Go, mind your own business.	*Andáte pei fatti vòstri.*
Do not split my ears.	*Non m' intronár le orécchia.*
How tiresome you are!	*O quanto sèi noióso!*
You have told it me a hundred times already.	*Me l' hai giá detto cènto vòlte.*

TO EXCITE COURAGE.

Cheer up, sirs.	*A'nimo, signori.*
Come on, gentlemen, come on.	*Su su, signori.*
Come, let's set to work.	*Su su, all' òpera.*
Let's give over.	*Finiámola.*

TO ASK.

What news?	*Che si dice di nuòvo?*
What's that?	*Che c' è?*
Where are you going?	*Dóve si va: dove andáte?*
Whence come you?	*Dónde si viène?*
What means that?	*Che vuòl dire questo?*
To what purpose?	*A che sèrve?*
What do you think?	*Che vi pare?*
To what end?	*A che propòsito? a che fine?*
Why do you make such a stir?	*A che tante stòrie, perchè tante smòrfie?*
Tell me, may one know?	*Dítemi se si può sapére?*
Tell me, may one ask you?	*Dítemi s' è lécito di domandárvelo?*
Who has been so bold?	*Chi ha avúto cotánto ardíre.*

TO FORBID.

Let that alone.	*Lasciáte lo* or *la stáre.*
Do not touch.	*Non toccáte.*
Say not a word.	*Non dir niénte,* 2d sing.
Do not stir from hence.	*Non ti partír di quà.*
In the name of heaven, do not do it.	*Non lo fáre, in nome del Cièlo.*
Have a care.	*Guardátevi bène.*
.Take care.	*Avvertíte.*
I forbid it.	*Lo proibísco.*

IDIOMS, &c. OF DIFFICULT TRANSLATION,

EVEN WITH THE HELP OF A DICTIONARY.

To make an appointment with a person.	*Dar convégno ad uno,* obs.
To have somebody in one's power.	*Averlo in pugno.*
He liked the proposal.	*La cosa gli entrò.*
He came to live with me as a servant.	*Si allogò meco per servitóre.*
He is a mischievous person.	*E' un commétti male.*
He does not go there with a good grace.	*Non ci va di buòn grado.*
To propose deliberating upon an affair.	*Intavoláre un affáre,* or *métterlo in campo.*
To look tenderly.	*Far l' occhiolíno.*
To play the fop.	*Far lo zerbíno.*
To play the prude.	*Far la modèsta.*
To new cast a work.	*Rifáre un libro di piánta.*
To owe some one a spite.	*Star gròsso con uno.*
At all hazards.	*A qualùnque còsto.*
To look big.	*Stare sul grande.*
His table was like a king's.	*La sua távola èra méssa alle reále.*
With a firm look.	*Con vólto férmo.*
At the worst.	*Alla più trista.*

R 3

To leave somebody pleased.	*Lasciár uno a bócca dólce.*
Made with exactness.	*Fatto a pennèllo.*
In spite of wind and tide.	*A dispètto di mare e vènto.*
Keeping always on the left.	*Tenèndosi sèmpre alla sinistra.*
It was unlucky for us.	*Piglióccene male,* obs.
He has lost his reputation.	*Ha perdúto la sua riputazióne.*
To impose upon somebody.	*Gettár della pólvere negli òcchi.*
She is not handsome, but she is engaging.	*Non è bèlla, ma è avvenènte.*
To drive some one mad.	*Fare uscíre uno dai gángheri.*
To rack one's brains.	*Lambiccársi il cervèllo.*
To make idle schemes.	*Far dei lunárj.*
To cry bitterly.	*Piángere amaraménte.*
I think you will suit him.	*Crédo che faréte per lui.*
Dinner is served up.	*Il pranzo è in távola.*
We diverted ourselves very well.	*Ci siámo bèn ben divertíti.*
My honour is at stake.	*Si tratta del mio onóre.*
He drew his sword.	*Snudò la spada.*
We must come to blows.	*Bisógna veníre álle mani.*
He is near fifty.	*Egli è sui cinquánta.*
Let us see how he sets about it.	*Vediámo come vi si prènde.*
I am out of the scrape.	*Sòno fuòri d' impáccio.*
He is a sad fellow.	*E' un cattívo soggètto.*
Make a fair copy.	*Mettételo a pulíto.*
It will be the worst that can happen to me.	*Gli è il pèggio che mi pòssa toccáre.*
At the worst, I risk nothing.	*Al pèggio andáre non ríschio nulla.*
I will hold out.	*Mi terrò férmo.*
Go and clean my room.	*Andáte a pulír la mia stanza.*
To find it difficult to live.	*Stentáre a vívere.*
To play the devil.	*Fare il diávolo.*
It is good for nothing.	*Non val niènte affátto.*

He ran away as fast as he could.	*Si salvò a sciòlte gambe.*
He suspects my intention.	*Dúbita del mio disègno.*
He looks like an honest man.	*Ha ciéra di galantuòmo.*
It did not stop there.	*La còsa non finì così.*
We spoke of you.	*Si parlò di voi.*
I shall be much obliged to you.	*Ve ne sarò molto tenúto,* or *ve ne saprò grado.*
She has no pretensions to learning.	*Ella non se la pretende in sapére.*
He never gives over speaking.	*Non la finísce mai.*
This gown fits you well.	*Cotésta vèste vi sta bène.*
She is a woman of quality.	*E' úna signóra di rango.*
A gentleman.	*Un uòmo di garbo.*
It was very near.	*C' è mancáto pòco.*
What do you ask for this?	*Còsa pretendéte di questo?*
Let it be as it will.	*Comúnque síasi.*
Face to face.	*A quattr' òcchi.*
His head is giddy.	*Gli gira il capo.*
It is a pun.	*E' un bistíccio.*
He is going to meet him.	*Va ad incontrárlo.*
I guessed his meaning.	*Indovinái che cosa voleva dire.*
He began to write.	*Si mise a scrívere.*
He whispered to me.	*Mi disse all' orécchio.*
This is one of your tricks.	*Questa è una delle vostre.*
To drink a good draught.	*Fare una gran bevúta.*
In a moment.	*In un istánte.*
At once.	*Ad un tratto.*
Without doubt.	*Sènza fallo.*
When the time is over.	*Dopo il fatto.*
Once more.	*Ancóra una vòlta.*
To get out of the scrape.	*Cavársi d' impáccio.*
He delivered me from prison.	*Mi ha liberáto di prigióne.*
He draws no profit from it.	*Non ne ricáva útile.*
To draw a bill of exchange.	*Far tratta.*
He fired a shot.	*Sparò un' archibugiáta.*

He pointed at me.	*Mi accennò.*
There is a villain.	*Ecco un avánzo di forca.*
He pumped him.	*Gli cavò di bócca il se-gréto.*
He was born lucky.	*E' nato vestíto.*
He looks with an ill eye upon me.	*Mi guárda di mal' òcchio.*
He spoke at random.	*Egli parláva a caso.*
Without coming to vio-lence.	*Sènza venire a fatti.*
It is just what I want.	*Gli è appúnto quel che mi ci vuòle.*
It was in vain for me to tell him.	*Ebbi un bel dirgli.*
He lives by his wits.	*E' úno scroccóne.*
To-morrow is a fast-day.	*Dománi è giórno di di-giúno.*
They are sleight of hand tricks.	*Son giuòchi di mano.*
He writes a good hand.	*Ha un buòn caráttere.*
He put his hands upon him.	*Gli póse le mani addòsso.*
To treat with severity.	*Trattár severaménte.*
He has a great wish to do some mischief.	*Gli pizzicano le mani.*
I made a mistake.	*Ho préso un equívoco.*
He has spent all his pro-perty.	*Ha consumáto tutto il suo.*
It is a good league off.	*E' una buòna léga di quì.*
Do you think it good?	*Vi sémbra buòno?*
Make him come up.	*Fátelo venir su.*
He becomes always more idle.	*Divénta sèmpre più pol-tróne.*
He is equal to him in rank.	*Va del pari con lui.*
I think it is true.	*Lo crédo véro.*
To conduct one's self well.	*Regolársi bène.*
He will not yield to him.	*Non gliéla cederà.*
She is perfectly well made.	*E' fatta a pennèllo.*
He put the garrison to the sword.	*Mise la guarnigióne a fil di spada.*
On the way.	*Strada facèndo.*

Do not take it ill.	*Non lo prendéte a male.*
He took that seriously.	*La prése sul sèrio.*
You take my words ill.	*Interpretáte male le mie paròle.*
He has been made a doctor.	*Ha préso la láurea.*
He knows how to take things as they come.	*Sa pigliár il móndo come viène.*
Mind it well.	*Badáteci bène.*
Take care of yourself.	*Abbiátevene cura.*
Take care of him.	*Guardátevi bene da lui.*
He was lucky in having been warned.	*Buòn per lui d'èssere stato avvertíto.*
He took leave.	*Prése comiáto.*
He dismissed him.	*Lo licenziò.*
He is much interested in it.	*Vi s'interèssa mólto.*
Come, decide.	*Vía, decidéte.*
The business is settled.	*L' affáre è finíto.*
He flatters him shamefully.	*Lo ádula sfacciataménte.*
As rich as they are.	*Ricchi cóme sóno.*
Come, friend, give me your hand.	*A'nimo, amico, dátemi la mano.*
I whispered to him.	*Gli dissi sótto vóce.*
Gently, if you please.	*Adágio, in grázia.*
No, I won't give it up.	*No, non vo' darla vinta.*
It is ready money.	*Egli è òro lampánte.*
He is rather tipsy.	*E' un po' brillo.*
They ran after him.	*Gli si misero dIètro.*
This sets him off a little.	*Questo lo rimétte un pòco.*
My late father.	*Il defúnto mio padre.*
Persons of quality.	*Le persóne di rango.*
He is a military man.	*E' un militáre.*
His hair is well dressed.	*E' ben pettináto.*
He has three rooms on a floor.	*Ha tre stanze per piáno.*
Is the cloth laid?	*E' apparecchiáto?*
He is clever in every thing.	*E' bravo in tutto.*
The business goes on well.	*L' affáre è bèn incamminálo.*

R 5

Let him say what he will, I do not believe it.

Dica pur quel che vuòle, non ne crédo niènte.

They think only of mischief.

Non pènsano che a far del male.

A COLLECTION OF ITALIAN PROVERBS.

A PROVERB is a child of experience.

Il provèrbio è figlio dell' esperiènza.

Well begun is half done.

Chi bèn princípia è alla metà dell' opra.

A house built, and a vine planted, are never sold for what they cost.

Casa fatta, vigna pósta, non si pága quánto còsta.

To expect and not to come; to lie in bed and not to sleep; to serve and not to please, are three things enough to kill one.

Aspettáre e non veníre; star in lètto e non dormíre: ben servíre e non gradíre, son tre còse da moríre.

There is no one happy in this world, but he that dies in his cradle.

Nel móndo non è felice, se non colui che muòre in fasce.

To travel post requires the purse of a prince, and the strength of a porter.

La pòsta è úna spésa da principe, ed un mestiere da facchíno.

It is better going alone, than in bad company.

E' mèglio andár sólo, che mal accompagnáto.

Misfortunes and pleasures never come single.

Le sciagúre e le allegrézze non vèngono mai sóle.

Fine to fine is not good to make a lining.

Duro con duro, non fa buòn muro.

Love and greatness will not associate.

Amór e signoría non vòglion compagnía, or amore e maestà non vanno insième.

A good stomach needs no sauce.

Buòn appetíto non vuòl salsa.

We think no more of vows when the danger is past.

Passáto 'l perícolo, gabbáto 'l santo.

Old sin, new penance.

Peccáto vècchio, penitènza nuòva.

The beast once dead, the venom dies also.

Mòrta la béstia, mòrto 'l veléno.

Fair words are very powerful, and cost nothing.

Un bèl parláre di bócca assái vále, pòco còsta.

A hundred pounds of sorrow will not pay an ounce of debt.

Cènt' ore di malinconía non págano un quattríno di débito, or cènto pensièri non págano un débito.

He who goes to bed without his supper, will toss and tumble all night.

Chi va a lètto sènza céna, tutta la nòtte si diména.

Ravens never pluck out each other's eyes.

Còrvi con corvi non si cávan mái gli òcchi.

Tell me your company, and I shall know what you do.

Dimmi con chi vai, saprò quel che fai, or ti dirò chi sei.

He has fallen out of the frying-pan into the fire.

E' cadúto dalla padèlla sulla brace.

Every bird likes his own nest.

Ad ógni uccèllo, il suo nido è bèllo.

A barking dog never bites.

Can che abbáia non mòrde.

Do not wake a sleeping lion.

Non destáre il can che dòrme.

He who is fonder of you than usual, either has cheated you, or designs it.

Chi ti fa carézze più che suòle, o t'ha ingannáto, o ingannár ti vuòle.

To ask a landlord if his wine is good.

Domandár all' òste se ha buòn vino.

Good wine needs no bush.

Il buòn vino non ha bisógno di frasca.

It is better one's foot slip than one's tongue.

E' mèglio sdrucciolár co' pièdi che cólla lingua.

He who buys land, buys trouble.

Chi cómpra tèrra, compra guèrra.

He who cheats is often cheated.

Chi cérca d'ingannár, rèsta ingannáto.

Fair words and foul play,

Bèlle paròle, e cattivi fatti,

cheat both the young and the old.

ingánnano savj e matti.

There are no roses without thorns.

Non si può avér la ròsa, sènza le spine.

With artifice and deceit they live half the year;

Con arte e con ingánno, si vive mèzzo l' anno;

With deceit and artifice they live the other half.

Con ingánno e con arte, si vive l' altra parte.

He who serves the public obliges nobody.

Chi sèrve al comúne, non sèrve a nessúno.

A good friend is worth a hundred relations.

E' mèglio un buòn amico, che cènto parènti.

Fevers in autumn are long or mortal.

Fèbbre autunnále è lunga o mortále.

To sell bladders for lanterns.

Vénder lúcciole per lantèrne.

Every country has its fashions.

Tal paése, tale usánza.

To mind two things at once.

Aver un òcchio alla péntola, e 'l altro alla gatta.

To be on both sides.

Dar un cólpo alla bótte, ed un altro al cérchio.

To have two strings to one's bow.

Tenér il piède in più staffe.

To cheat two at once.

Pigliár due colómbi ad una fava.

We must love the dog for the sake of its master.

Bisógna portár rispètto al cane, per amór del padróne.

We must hide nothing from our physician and our lawyer.

Al mèdico ed all' avvocáto non tenére 'l vér celáto.

Short reckonings make long friends.

Patti chiári, amíci cari.

Eggs of an hour, bread of a day, wine of a year, and a friend of thirty.

Uòvo d' un' óra, pane d' un dì, vino d' un anno, amíco di trénta.

Bread that sees, wine that sparkles, cheese that weeps.

Pan che véda, vin che salti, formággio che piánga.

A salad ought to be well

Insaláta bèn saláta, pòco

salted, to have a little vinegar, and plenty of oil.

It is better to be a bird in a field than in a cage.

A bird in the hand is worth two in the bush.

A bad agreement is better than a good law-suit.

He gains enough who relinquishes useless hope.

Poverty has neither relations nor friends.

It is better to be friends at a distance than enemies near home.

If you would be revenged of your enemy, govern well yourself.

He is a fool who gives a quail unto a sparrow-hawk in keeping.

A solitary man is either a brute or an angel.

Men meet, when mountains cannot.

Do not judge by laws or writ, before thou hearest both parties.

To the wise few words are sufficient.

---

acetáta, e bene oliáta.

E' mèglio èsser uccèllo di frasca che di gábbia.

E' meglio un uòvo òggi, che una gallína dománi.

E' mèglio un cattivo accòrdo, che una buòna lite.

Assai guadágna chi vana speránza pèrde.

Povertà non ha nè parènti, nè amíci.

E' meglio èsser amíci da lontáno, che nemíci da vicíno.

Vuòi far vendétta del tuo nemíco, govèrnati bène.

Stolto è chi dà la quáglia in guárdia allo sparvière.

L' uòmo solitário è, o béstia o ángelo.

Gli uòmini s' incóntrano, e le montágne nò.

Non giudicár dalle léggi nè dalle carte, se non ascólti l' una e l' altra parte.

A buòno intenditór pòche paròle.

A COLLECTION OF DIVERTING STORIES, &c.

Paríni (²⁶) ammaláto.

Essèndo Paríni ammaláto, vénnero due mèdici a visitárlo; dicéva l'úno: E' duòpo dar tuòno alla fibra; l' altro conviène scemárle tuòno; ed égli, costóro ad ogni mòdo mi vòglion far moríre in música.

Lo stésso Paríni nel Município di Miláno.

Essèndo Paríni mèmbro del Município di Milano, acreménte un giórno perseguitáva coll' indágine cèrti tali, che avéano rubáto a nóme dello stésso Município, e trovándovisi, chi con ismoderáto garríto cercava di travòlgere la verità, l'argúto Piètro Vèrri disse a Parini, *Il ladro alla fine siète voi, che qui rubáte il soggètto d'una bèlla sátira.*

Leone X.

Michelángelo nel quadro del Giudízio Universále, che tròvasi nella cappèlla Sistina nel palazzo del Vaticáno, fra le altre figúre rappresentáte nell' infèrno, aveva messo un certo cardinale che non èra uno dei suòi amici, e l' avéa dipinto sì al naturále, che ognúno potéa facilménte riconóscerlo. Il cardinále trovándosene offèso, andò súbito dal Papa a domandár giustízia dell' affrónto, pretendèndo che la sua figúra fosse immediataménte tòlta via dal quadro; ma il Papa gli rispose, " Voi sapéte fin dove giúnge il mio potére; posso liberár dal purgatòrio, ma non dall' infèrno."

Di Papa Giúlio Secóndo.

Un nòbile Románo, amíco intrínseco di Papa Giúlio Secóndo, gli disse che si lagnávano mólto che sua santità attendésse con tròppo calóre alla guèrra cóntro i Fran-

---

²⁶ One of the most celebrated of modern Italian poets.

cési : giacchè Iddío gli avéva dato le chiávi della sua chièsa, per serráre le pòrte della discòrdia, ed apríre quelle della riconciliazióne. Il Papa rispóse al nòbile : Quei tali che dícono símili còse, non sanno forse che san Piètro e san Páolo sóno stati compágni, ed ambidúe príncipi della chièsa. I predecessóri mièi si sóno servíti delle chiávi di san Pietro, adèsso io vòglio adoperáre la spada di san Paolo. Il nòbile replicò : Vòstra santità sa però che Cristo, disse a Pietro : Rimétti la tua spada nel fòdero. E' véro, soggiúnse 'l Papa, ma ricordátevi che Cristo non lo disse prima, ma dópo che Pietro èbbe ferito.

La genealogía di due presuntuósi.

Due presuntuósi di bassa estrazióne èransi arrichíti nella mercatúra. Volèndo mettér su carròzza, trattávasi di creáre gli stèmmi, e messa ìn campo la questióne della loro genealogía, non sapèndo essi che la sciènza del Blasóne èbbe origine non più remòta della prima guèrra di Palestína, dicévansi l' un e l' altro : La mia nobilità risale a 500 anni e più.—Ma la mia a 800 e più.—Ma cosa dico 500 anni ! dal diluvio !—Ma cosa dico 880 anni ! da Adamo !—Credo anzi che la nobiltà di voi altri due, rispóse un tèrzo, fosse ben ancór più antica d'Adámo, perchè infátti prima di lui fúron creáte le bèstie.

Menecráte Médico.

Venèndo fatto al Mèdico Menecráte di guaríre cèrte infermità disperáte, ed essèndo per ciò appelláto Giòve, con gran fasto facéva uso égli stesso di questo nome, e osáto avèndo di scrívere ad Agesiláo in questa manièra : Menecráte Giove al re Agesiláo salúte. Agesiláo gli riscrísse in quest' altra : Il re Agesiláo a Menecráte sanità.

Sòcrate.

Socrate percòsso nella púbblica piazza da un cálcio d'un mascalzóne, e stimoláto a dimandárne soddi-

sfazióne, rispóse di non potérlo fare, perchè i calci dell'
ásino non èrano stati mai chiamáti in giudízio.

Marc' Antònio e Bottón da Cesèna.

Avèndo maèstro Marc' Antònio compósto una lun-
ghíssima commèdia, e di varj atti, Botton da Cesena gli
disse: A far la vòstra commèdia bisogneránno per lo
apparáto quanti légni sóni in Ischiavonía: Rispóse
Maestro Marc' Antònio: E per l'apparáto della tua
tragèdia basterán tre solaménte.

Il Predicatóre di pòca Memòria.

Un Predicatóre dovèndo fare il panegírico di S. Luca,
súbito che fu in púlpito, perdè talménte la memòria,
che non potè dir altro che il tèsto del suo discórso,
Lucas medicus salutat vos, Luca mèdico vi salúta.   Ri-
petè tante vòlte queste paròle, sènza potérsi ricordár d'
altra còsa, che gli uditóri stanchi, s' alzárono tutti, e
nell' andársene, uno di loro disse al Predicatóre: Padre
mio, salutátelo anche da parte nòstra.

Il Missionário.

Un giórno predicáva in una parròcchia di Madríd un
cèlebre Missionário; tutti gli uditóri piangévano, méno
uno; della qual còsa maravigliátosi il predicatóre, a
quello si rivòlse dicèndogli, e perchè non piángi tu?
Padre, rispóse: Io non dèvo piángere; questa non è la
mia parròcchia.

Umanità d' un Leóne.

Vèrso la fine del sècolo decimosèttimo, fuggì dal
parco del Grandúca di Toscána un leóne.   Ognuno può

figurarsi quale potesse èssere stato lo spavènto di quelli
che s'intoppávano in questa fièra. Una donna col suo
bambíno al còllo, imbattèndosi in esso, atterrita da tal
sorpresa, si láscia cader il figlio dalle mani; il leone
l' agguanta súbito pei panni, e se lo porta via. La
madre disperata, tòsto gli corre apprèsso, e raggiúnto che
l' ebbe, gèttasi davanti tutta ansante colle bráccia apèrte
e gli occhi spauríti: Rèndimi, grida, rendimi il figlio.
Il leone che gia aveva sospéso il passo, la guarda un
istante, e come se venerasse in lei l' amor di madre,
depóne dolcemente la prèda, sènza la mènoma offesa, e
riprènde la sua fuga.

Astúzia d' un Sacerdòte Egiziáno.

I Caldèi si elèssero per Iddío il fuòco, e dicévano
tutti gli altri Dèi èssere di nessún valóre apprèsso di
lui, ed i Sacerdòti portándo quello per i paési circonvi-
cíni, voléano che gli altri Dei gli dèssero tribúto, o
veníssero seco in pròva, laónde tutti perdévano; perciocchè essèndo i simulácri d'òro, d'argento, di brónzo,
di légno o d'altro, venívano dal fuòco consumáti e
guasti; talchè lo Dío déi Caldèi èra il più ricco per le
mólte offèrte, che gli èrano fatte, ed il più potènte per
le mólte vittòrie avúte che altro Dío che fòsse in quéi
tèmpi. Ultimaménte portándo il loro Dío, se ne andárono i Caldei in Egítto per far la guèrra ágli Dei del
paése. La qual còsa considerándo un Sacerdòte del
Tèmpio di Canòpo, e che egli èra in perícolo di pèrdere
l'offèrte, le ricchézze e la riputazióne, s'immaginò una
bèlla astúzia per difèndersi dal fuòco dei Caldei. Egli
prése un grande innaffiatóio di tèrra, di quélli che son
pièni di píccioli pertúgi, con cui s'innàffiano i giardíni,
ed empítolo d'ácqua, cólla céra riturò i pertúgi, e di
sópra l'adornò e dipínse di più colóri, accomodándovi la
tèsta d' un vècchio simulácro di Meneláo. Venèndo
poi i Caldèi, ed accostándo il lóro Dío a quéllo di
Canòpo liquefacéndo il fuòco la céra, uscì fuòri l' ácqua
in gran còpia, talménte che spènse tutto il fuòco, e così
rimáse vittorióso il sacerdòte di Canòpo, d' allóra in-

nanzi quel loro Iddio, il quale avea spènto il fuòco e superáto lo Iddio de' Caldèi, onorárono.

D' úno Scultóre.

Disegnándo i cònsoli di Firènze di far una státua, chiamárono Donatèllo, famóso ed eccellènte Scultóre, il quale intéso 'l diségno, domandò per la fattúra cinquánta scudi. I cònsoli sènza proférirgli nulla, la dièdero a far ad un altro Scultóre mediòcre. Costúi, fatta che l' èbbe il mèglio che sèppe, ne domandò ottanta scudi. Maravigliátisi i cònsoli, gli díssero che questo èra un burlársi di loro, giacchè Donatèllo, uòmo tanto illústre, non avéva domandáto per farla più di cinquánta. In sómma non potèndosi accordáre, rimísero la cáusa ad ésso Donatèllo, il quale sentenziò che i cònsoli dovéssero pagáre settánta scúdi. Del che alterátisi, ricordándogli ch'égli medésimo di cinquánta s'èra volúto contentáre : Donatello graziosaménte disse ; E' vero, mi potévo contentáre, perchè avrèi fatto la statua in méno d' un mése : ma questo pòvero uòmo che a pena potrèbbe èsser mio scoláre, vi ha lavoráto più di sei mési. Così Donatello si vendicò argutaménte dell' ingiúria ricevúta dai cònsoli.

Una Paróla mal intésa.

Gli O'ddi fuoruscíti di Perúgia, e capi della parte avvèrsa ai Baglióni, entrárono una nòtte cólle gènti lóro furtivaménte in Perúgia, e con tanto spavènto de' Baglióni, che già perdúta la speránza del difèndersi, cominciávano a méttersi in fuga ; e non diméno perdérono per uno inopináto e mínimo caso quélla vittòria, che non potéva tòrre più lóro la possánza dei nemíci, perchè essèndo già pervenúti sènza ostácolo a una delle bócche della piázza principále, e volèndo uno di lóro, che a quésto effètto avéa portáto una scure, spezzáre una caténa, la quale secóndo l' uso delle città fazióse, attraversáva la strada, impedíto a distèndere le braccia da' suòi medésimi, che calcáti gli èrano intórno, gridò con alta voce, *addiètro*, acciocchè allargándosi gli déssero facoltà di adoperársi, la qual vóce replicáta di mano in mano, da chi lo seguitáva, e intésa dagli altri cóme incitaménto a fuggíre, mise sènza altro impediménto in fuga tutta la gènte, non sapèndo alcúno da chi cacciáti, o per qual ragióne si fuggíssero; dal qual disórdine préso ánimo, e riméssisi insième gli avversarj fécero di lóro grandíssima carneficína.

A SHORT INTRODUCTION TO ITALIAN POETRY.

The Origin of the Italian Language and Poetry, together with a Treatise on the different Species of Italian Verses and their Combinations.

Having now to speak of the different measures adopted in Italian Poetry, it may not be displeasing to the reader to find here some idea of the origin of the Italian Language and poetry. It is, according to the most general opinion, derived from the alteration and total corruption of the Latin idiom, and the immediate co-operation of the dialects of the barbarians, who successively inundated Italy. There have also been many words obtained from the Celtic languages of Italy, the ancient Teutonic, the French, the Spanish, and some few from the Arabic and the Greek.

Various documents prove, that at the commencement of the eleventh century, the writers of Italy began to make use of the new language in poetry. It was then called *Romance*, to indicate that it was spoken in the country of the ancient Roman empire.

The Tuscan people were the first who began to use the new language of Italy, and the first works composed in it were poetic. It was indeed poetry itself which freed the nation from barbarism, and at the same time the Italian language from obscurity.

The commerce of the thirteenth century had raised Italy to the apex of greatness. Its riches were immense, and the beneficence of princes towards literary men and artists were suitable to their power. At this fortunate period, Dante, Boccaccio and Petrarch, with their rare talents, and their learning, raised the Italian Language, Poetry and Literature, to the highest pitch of perfection.

The *Divina Commèdia* of Dante, which is a treatise

of profound philosophy, has long preserved the highest rank in the most enlightened universities. The *Decamerone* of Boccaccio became the model of the Italian language from its elegance of style, and purity of diction. At last the *Cansoniere* of Petrarch revived the muses of Pindar, of Anacreon, of Catullus and of Ovid.

These few remarks may suffice, with respect to the origin of the Italian language and poetry; as a longer examination would exceed the necessary limits in treating an object entirely devoted to literature.

I. OF ITALIAN VERSIFICATION.

Italian verse consists of a certain number of syllables and rhyme. But they have also their blank verse.

There are eleven syllables in the heroic verse, which is used in epic poems, theatrical pieces, sonnets, &c.

> *Varcár ti converrà l'onda funèsta.*

Beside the heroic, there are lesser verses, consisting of ten syllables, as,

> *Sazierète la fame de' còrvi.*
> *Mercenárie falángi di schiávi.*

Or of nine, as
> *Ben mi rivòlgo al dolce loco.*

Or of eight, as
> *I pensièr mandiámo in bando.*

Or of seven, as
> *Innamoráto spirto.*

Or of six, as
> *Le féde giuráta.*

Or of five, as
> *Chi può mirárvi.*

Or of four, as
> *In due mòdi.*

The Italian verse, of whatever number of syllables it consists, has always the accent on the penultima, except it be what they call *versi sdrúccioli*, or slippery verses, which are accented on the antepenultima; but then they have a syllable more than the ordinary sort of verse. Thus if the ordinary sort of verse has eleven syllables, the *sdrúcciolo* belonging to it has twelve; as,

L' arco ripíglia il fanciullín di Vènere.

If the ordinary verse has eight syllables, the *sdrúcciolo* will have nine, and so on.

The *verso tronco* is of ten syllables; as

Monte Pulciáno d' ogni vino è il re.

The heroic verse, or that of eleven syllables, is divided into two parts; the place where this division is made, is called the *cesúra*. The *cesura* is not always equal; that is, the first hemistich or half verse does not always contain the same number of syllables; for this depends on the predominating accent, as the *cesura* is always at the end of the word on which you find this accent. Now this accent may be either on the fourth, or on the sixth syllable of the verse, which occasions several sorts of *cesuras*; the best are those on the fifth or seventh syllable.

On the fifth,

Giúnger già pármi, e dírle, o fida Clòri.

On the seventh,

Quálche nuòvo sospíro imparerái.

Whenever a word ends with a vowel, and the next word begins also with a vowel, this admits an elision, as

Prèsso è il dì, che cangiáto 'l destin río.

Sometimes a concurrence of syllables forms but one syllable, whether in the same or in different words; as

Disse, e ai vènti spiegò véle, ed andònne.

Diphthongs form but one syllable in the middle of a verse, and two in the end, as

Ed io del mio dolór minístro fui,

where *io* and *mio* form each but one syllable, and *fui*, two. Whereas in the following verse,

Fávola fui gran tèmpo, onde sovènte,

fui, on account of its being in the middle of the verse, makes but one syllable: so in the following verse,

>   *Odo 'l rispónder dolce: O Tirsi mio:*

mio, as being at the end of a verse, makes two syllables. This is to be particularly observed.

Verses consisting of ten syllables are accented on the third and sixth syllables, as

>   *Almo sóle che in Cièlo risplèndi*
>   *Col settémplice ràggio fecóndo.*

Verses of nine syllables have the accent on the third and sixth, as

>   *Col nemico sul mar s'affrónta.*

Or on the second and fifth, as

>   *Non vi véde ognóra ascóso.*

Or on the fourth and sixth, as

>   *Bèn mi rivòlgo al dólce lòco.*

Verses of eight syllables are accented on the third, as

>   *Quándo accènde un nòbil pètto*
>   *E' innocènte un puro affètto.*

Verses of seven syllables, besides the accent on the penultima, have no other regular accents; but if the accent is on the fourth, the verse will be harmonious; as

>   *Ninfa di còr feróce.*

Verses of six syllables are accented on the second, as

>   *Délle Api ingegnóse*
>   *Il bióndo licór.*

Verses of five syllables have the accent on the first, sometimes on the second, or on the third, as

>   *Sei fra i perfètti*
>   *Bèi bambolétti.*

Verses of four, three and two syllables, are accented on the penultima.

II. OF THE RHYME.

The Italian Rhyme begins from the vowel of the penultima : hence *amánti* does not rhyme to *dirti*, but to *sembiánti*, and so on.

The Italians do not rhyme, as we do, in couplets, but make several combinations of their rhymes : and these form their different compositions in verse.

III. OF THE DIFFERENT COMPOSITIONS IN VERSE.

The Italians compose their heroic poems of stanzas of eight verses, which they call octaves.   In these the first verse rhymes to the third and fifth, the second to the fourth and sixth, and the seventh to the eighth, as

Cinta di vivo fonte, ónde discénde
  Onda mormoratríce in suo viággio,
  S' èrge forèsta, che del sol contènde
  Nell' ánno ardènte ivi l' entráta al ràggio ;
  Dóppio sentièr che s'intersèca fènde
  In quattro parti il bèll' orrór selvággio,
  E di bell' ácque cristallíne e chiáre
  Ha ciascúna nel grèmbo un picciol mare.

CHIABRÈRA.

There are other sorts of stanzas, called *sestíne*, consisting of six verses, the first of which rhymes to the third, the second to the fourth, and the two last to each other, as

Dive che 'l sacro ed onoráto fónte
  Dóve glòria si béve in guárdia avéte,
  Dal vòstro ombróso e solitário monte
  Un tèmpio méco a fabbricár scendéte ;
  Un tempio ov' immortál pòscia s' adóri
  Quésta dònna de' Galli, e dèa de' còri.

MARÍNO.

The Italians have a third manner of disposing their heroic verse, which they call *tèrza rima* or *terzétti*.

They put three verses in every stanza, the first and
third rhyme to each other; the second rhymes to the
first and third of the second stanza; and the second of
the second stanza to the first, and third of the third
stanza. But at the end of the canto or poem there
must be a stanza of four verses, in order that every
verse may have its rhyme; as

> Gli ánni son al volár sì lièvi e prèsti,
> Ch' al fine altro non è ch' un vólger d' òcchi;
> Questo che poi vi láscia afflitti mèsti.
> Però pría che l' offésa in noi trabócchi,
> Armáte 'l pètto incóntro alla fortuna,
> Che vano è l' aspettár che 'l colpo scócchi.
> Così dicèndo, al raggio de la luna,
> Che gli òcchi mi fería, rivòlse il viso,
> Poi salutò le stélle ad úna ad úna;
> E lièto se n' andò nel paradìso.
>
> SANNAZAR.

There are also tèrza rima in verse, called sdrúcciolo,
or slippery; as,

> Quantúnque Opico mio sii vècchio e cárico
> Di sénno e di pensièr, ch'in te si cóvano,
> Deh piángi or méco, e prèndi il mio rammárico:
> Nel móndo òggi amíci non si tròvano, &c.

A fourth manner of arranging heroic verse in Italian,
is what they call quarta rima, when the first rhymes to
the fourth, and the second to the third.

Example.

> Cóntra gli assálti di Nettún spumánti,
> Quándo Áustro a sdégno ed Aquilóne il mòve;
> E cóntra i lampi e 'l fulminár di Giòve
> Ha l' ingégno mortále, ónde si vanti.
> Ma cóntra i colpi della falce oscúra
> Che arma di mòrte l' implacábil mano,
> Inváno ingégno s' affatíca, inváno
> Stame di vita contrastár procúra.
>
> CHIABRÈRA.

S

But the Sonnet is the favourite composition of the Italians : it is divided into two *quadernarj*, consisting each of four verses ; and two *terzétti*, each of three verses. The two *quadernárj* are ranged two different ways : the first and most usual is, when the first rhymes to the fourth, fifth and eighth, and the second to the third, sixth and seventh. The other, less usual, when the first rhymes to the third, sixth and eighth ; the second to the fourth, fifth and seventh.

There are also two different sorts of arrangement, in regard to the two *terzétti*, or the six last verses ; one is, to make the three verses of the first *terzétto* of three different rhymes, and the last *terzétto* answering to those three rhymes in whatever order you choose ; as,

> *Sólo e pensóso, i più desèrti campi*
> *Vo misurándo a passi tardi e lènti.*
> *E gli òcchi pòrto per fuggíre intènti,*
> *Dóve vestigio umán l' arèna stámpi.*
> *Altro schèrmo non tròvo, che mi scámpi*
> *Dal manifèsto accòrger de le gènti :*
> *Perchè ne gli atti d' allegrézza spènti,*
> *Di fuòr si lègge, com' io déntro avvámpi.*
> *Si ch'io crédo omái, che mónti e piágge,*
> *E fiumi e sélve sáppian di che tèmpre*
> *Sia la mia vita, ch' è celáta altrúi.*
> *Ma pur sì áspre vie, nè sì selvágge*
> *Cercár non so, che amór non vènga sèmpre,*
> *Ragionándo con meco, ed io con lui.*
>
> PETRÁRCA.

The other arrangements of the two *terzétti* are, to make the first verse rhyme to the third and fifth, and the second to the fourth and sixth ; as,

> *Quándo il gran Scípio dall' ingráta tèrra*
> *Che gli fù pátria e 'l céner suo non èbbe*
> *Esule egrègio si partía, qual dèbbe*
> *Uom che in suo còr maschio valor rinsèrra ;*
> *Quei che seco pugnándo andar 'sottèrra,*
> *Ombre famóse onde sì Itália crébbe,*
> *Arser di sdégno, e il duro esèmpio incrébbe*
> *Ai Genj della pace e della guèrra*

E seguírle fur viste in atto altèro
Sull' indégna fremèndo offésa atróce
Le virtù antíche del Latino Impèro.
E allor di Stíge sulla negra fóce,
Di lui che l' Alpi superò primièro
Rise l' invendicáta ombra feróce.

FRUGÓNI.

In the two preceding sonnets the two *quadernárj* are arranged alike, that is, the first verse rhymes to the fourth, fifth and eighth. We shall give here an instance of the other sort of *quadernárj*, where the first verse rhymes to the third, sixth and eighth; the second to the fourth, fifth and seventh.

Example.

Gittò l'infáme prèzzo e disperáto,
L' álbero ascése il venditór di Cristo.
Strinse il láccio, e col còrpo abbandonáto
Dall' irto ramo penzolár fu visto.
Cigoláva lo spirto serráto
Dentro la stròzza in suòn rabbióso e tristo,
E Gesù bestemmiáva e il suo peccáto,
Ch' empia l' avèrno di cotánto acquisto.
Sboccò dal varco alfin con un ruggito,
Allór giustízia l' afferrò, e sul mónte
Nel sángue di Gesù tingèndo il dito.
Scrisse con quello al maledétto in fronte
Sentènza di mortál pianto infinito
E lo piombò sdegnósa in Acherónte.

MONTI.

There are likewise other compositions, consisting of an intermixture of larger and small verses, which may be infinitely varied; some stanzas consisting of twelve or thirteen, some of seven, eight or eleven verses. The most common are of twelve, which frequently consist of two sorts of verse, viz. those of eleven or seven syllables.

Sul punto di mia mòrte,
Occhi, d'un guárdo non mi siáte avári,
E sia di quéi che sóno a vói men cari.

s 2

Con sollécito stúdio amór non tèrga.
I rái di sua beltáte,
E col riso, e col giòco, e col dilètto,
Nè di quella dolcézza égli l' aspèrga,
Nè di quella pietáte,
Che altrúi ragióna i fréddi cor nel pètto ;
Solo un giro neglètto,
Nè fian morèndo i mièi sospír amári.

CHIABRERA.

There is also a singular beauty in stanzas of seven, eight or eleven verses; examples of which may be seen in the Lyric Poets. CHIABRÈRA particularly abounds with a great variety in his *canzonétte.*

Examples.

Occhi armáti di splendóre,
Onde amóre
Per beáre arde le gènti,
Se la giòia del mirárvi
Giústo parvi
Che costár dèbba torménti.

Or,

Poichè amór fra l' èrbe e i fióri
Tra dolcézze, e lièti canti,
Per temprár del cor gli ardóri,
Scòrti avéa gli accési amánti ;
Ne' sembiánti
Lièto anch' éi con lor s'assíde
Sull' erbétta, e schérza e ríde.

Or,

Còre di sélce alpèstra,
Fervido ad innasprir gli altrúi torménti,
Con nuòva crudeltáte !.
Omái stanca è mia dèstra
In sulla lira ad iterár gli accènti
Usi a svegliár pietáte ;
Nè femminil beltáte
Spèra, prègio sembiánte in Elicóna,
Se di quéi vaghi fiór tèsse coróna
Per tuo gentíl valóre.

Or,

Vani desíri
Co' rèi martíri
Non più ci stíeno intórno;
Che pómpa ed òstro?
Il víver nòstro
Puòssi chiamár un giórno.
Cíngiti Clòri di bèl mirto adórno,
E di rubíni
Cospèrgi i críni,
Vie più che lúcid' òro, a mirár cari.

Or,

Quando l' Alba in oriènte,
L' almo sol s' apprèsta a scòrgere,
Su dal mar la veggiám sórgere,
Cinta in gònna rilucènte,
O'nde lampi si diffóndono,
Che le stélle in cièlo ascóndono.

The Italians are celebrated for their *madrigals* and *epigrams*, which are composed of all sorts of verse, long and short, according to the fancy of the poets, as

Di se stessa invaghíta, e del suo bèllo
Si specchiáva la ròsa
In un límpido e rápido ruscèllo,
Quando d' ogni sua fòglia
Un aura impetuósa.
La bèlla rosa spòglia.
Cádder nel río le spòglie : il rio fuggèndo,
Se la porta corrèndo.
E così la beltà
Rapidissimaménte—oh ! Dio sen va.

LEMENE.

Fábio, se quando in púbblico ragióni
Una spietáta tosse ti molèsta,
Non ti prènda timor de' tuòi polmóni,
Che la sède del male è nella tèsta.

BERTOLA.

They have also their *vèrso sciòlto*, or blank verse of eleven syllables, where the measure is observed, without rhyme, as the following :

> *Ahi che al sólo pensárlo entro le vene*
> *Di fòco un fiume mi trabócca, e tutti*
> *Trèmano i volsi combattúti e l' òssa !*
>
> MONTI.

This verse is used in tragedy, and often in Epic poems.

IV. OF THE POETICAL LICENSES.

The Italians use very great liberties in their versification ; not only their poets adopt several words which are not allowed in prose, but they likewise make frequent use of elisions ; these elisions are introduced for the sake of variety, but are never permitted at the end of a verse.

They not only drop the final vowel before words beginning with a vowel, but even before those that commence with a consonant, as, *fier dragóni*, for *fiéri ;* and sometimes they drop the consonant that precedes this final vowel, *animái* for *animáli.*

They likewise lengthen a great many words that have a grave accent on the final, by adding an *e* or an *o*, as *fúe* for *fu*, *féo* for *fe'*, *potéo* for *potè*. It is customary with them also to have recourse to contractions and syncopes, as *pórre* for *pónere*, *pònno* for *pòssono*, *vo'* for *vògliono*, *u'* for *ove*, and others which may be learnt by reading the poets. They write some words in a particular manner, as *súi* for *suoi*, *núi* for *noi*, *serúte* for *ferite*, *fóro* for *fúro*, *spène* for *spème*, &c. In short, there is hardly a language, not even excepting the Greek, that uses more figures or changes of words in their poetry than the Italian.

A COLLECTION OF BEAUTIFUL PASSAGES

FROM THE

MOST CELEBRATED ITALIAN POETS.

CÈRBERO.

Descritto dal DANTE.

Cèrbero, fièra crudèl, e divèrsa,
    Con tre góle, caninaménte latra,
    Sóvra la gènte, che quívi è sommèrsa.
Gli òcchi ha vermígli, e la barba unta ed atra,
    E 'l vèntre largo, ed unghiáte le mani :
    Gráffia gli spìrti, gli scuòia ed isquárta.

Bellézza di Láura. PETRARCA.

In qual parte del Cièl, iu quale idèa,
    Era l' esèmpio, onde natúra tòlse,
    Quel bèl viso leggiádro, in che ella vòlse
    Monstrár quaggiù, quanto lassù potéa ?
Qual ninfa in fónti, in sélve mai qual Dèa,
    Chiòme d'òro sì fino all' aúra sciòlse ?
    Quando un cor tante in sè virtúti accòlse ?
    Benchè la sómma è di mia mòrte rea.
Per divína bellézza indárno mira,
    Chi gli òcchi di costèi giammái non vide
    Cóme soaveménte élla gli gira.
Non sa cóme amór sana e come ancíde,
    Chi non sa come dólce ella sospíra,
    E come dolce parla, e dolce ride.

La Vérgine. ARIÒSTO.

La verginèlla è símile alla ròsa,
  Che 'n bèl giardín, sulla natíva spína,
  Méntre sola e sicúra si ripòsa,
  Nè grégge, nè pastór se le avvicína :
  L' áura soáve e l' alba rugiadósa,
  L' ácqua, la tèrra al suo favór s'inchína ;
  Gióvani vaghi, e dònne innamoráte,
  'Amano avére e séni e tèmpia ornáte ;
  Ma non si tòsto, dal matèrno stèlo
  Rimòssa viène, e dal suo céppo vérde,
  Che quanto avéa dagli uòmini, e dal cièlo
  Favór, grázia e bellézza, tutto pèrde.
  La vérgine che 'l fiór, di che più zèlo
  Che de' bègli òcchi e della vita avér de',
  Láscia altrui còrre il prègio che avéa innánti,
  Pèrde nel cor di tutti gli altri amánti.

Solilòquio d' Amarílli, nel Pastór Fido di GUARÍNI.

O Mirtíllo, Mirtíllo, ánima mía,
Se vedésti quì déntro,
Cóme sta il còr di questa
Che chiámi crudelíssima Amarílli !
So bèn, che tu di lèi
Quélla pietà che da lèi chièdi, avrésti.
O ánima in amór tròppo infelíce !
Che gióva a te, cor mío, l'èsser amato ?
Che gióva a me l' avér sì caro amánte ?
Perchè crudo destíno,
Ne disunísci tu, s'amór ne strínge ?
E tu perchè ne stríngi,
Se ne parte il destín, pèrfido amóre ?
O fortunáte voi fère selvágge,
A cúi l'álma natúra
Non diè légge in amár se non d'amóre !
Légge umána inumána,
Che dái per péna dell' amár la mòrte !

" Se'l peccár è sì dólce,
" E 'l non peccár sì necessário, o troppo
" Imperfètta natúra,
" Che repúgni alla légge!
" O tròppo dura légge,
" Che la natura offèndi!"
Ma che? pòco ama altrúi, chi'l mórir tème :
Piacésse pur al cièl, Mirtíllo mío,
Che sol péna al peccár fósse la mòrte!
Santíssima onestà, che sóla sèi
D'alma bèn nata inviolábil Nume,
Quest' amorósa vòglia,
Che svenáta ho col fèrro
Del tuo santo rigór, qual innocènte
Víttima a te consácro.
E tu, Mirtíllo, ánima mía, perdóna
A chi t'è cruda sol dove pietósa
L'èsser non può : perdóna a questa sola
Ne' détti e nel sembiánte
Rígida tua nemíca; ma nel còre
Pietosíssima amánte.
E se pur hái desío di vendicárti,
Deh! qual vendétta avér puòi tu maggióre
Del tuo pròprio dolóre?
Che se tu se' 'l cor mío,
Come sèi pur malgrádo
Del cièlo e della tèrra,
Qualór piángi e sospíri,
Quelle lágrime túe sóno il mío sángue,
Que' sospíri, il mío spirto ; e quelle pene,
E quel dolór che sènti,
Son mièi, non tuòi torménti.

Il Mattíno. PARÍNI.

Sórge il mattíno in compagnía dell' alba,
Innánzi al Sol che di poi grande appáre,
Su l'estrèmo orizzónte a rènder l[i]ète
Gli animáli, e le piante, e i campi e l'ónde.
Allora il buòn villán sorge dal caro
Lètto, cui la fedél sposa e i minóri,

s 5

Suòi figliolétti intiepidír la nòtte;
Poi sul còllo recando i sacri arnési,
Che prima ritrovár Cèrere e Pale,
Va col bue lènto innánzi al campo e scuòte
Lungo il pícciol sentièr da' curvi rami,
Il rugiadóso umór, che, quasi gèmma,
I nascènti del Sol raggi rifrànge.
Allora sorge il fabbro, e la sonánte
Officina riápre, e all' òpre torna
L'áltro dì non perfètte . . . .

A Dante.   ALFIÈRI.

O gran padre Alighièr, se dal cièl miri
  Me tuo discépol non indégno starmi,
  Dal cor traèndo profóndi sospíri,
  Prostráto innánzi a' tuòi funèrei marmi,
Piácciati deh! propízio ai be' desíri,
  D'un raggio di tua luce illuminármi;
  Uòm che a primièra etèrna glòria aspíri
  Contro invídia e viltà de' stringer l' armi?
Fíglio, i' le strínsi, e assai men duòl, ch' io dièdi,
  Nóme in tal guísa a gènte tanto bassa
  Da non pur calpestársi co' mièi pièdi!
Se in me fidi, il tuo sguárdo a che s' abbássa?
  Va, tuòna, vinci: e se fra' piè ti vedi
  Costór, senza mirár sovr' essi passa.

Descrizióne d'un Cristo legáto alla Colónna.
(*Madrigále.*)

  Di marmo è la Colónna,
Di marmo son gli émpj minístri, e rèi!
E tu pure, Signór di marmo sèi!
Marmo ella è pur natúra,
Marmo quéi per durézza,
Tu marmo, per costánza e per fortézza;
Ed io, che di pietáde e di cordóglio
Spettatór ne rimángo,
Marmo son, se non piángo.

Bègli Occhi. GUARÍNI *ne' suòi Madrigáli.*

Occhi, stélle mortáli,
Minístri de' mièi mali ;
Che'n sógno anco mostráte,
Che'l mio morír bramáte ;
Se chiúsi m' uccidéte,
Apèrti che faréte ?

Amóre. LUÍGI ALAMÁNNI.

Chi vuol dar légge all' amoróso nòdo
Non sa bèn qual sía la sua nátura :
L'un d'una còsa, ed io dell' altra gòdo,
Chi ama lo spírto, e chi sol la figúra,
Chi dilètta la vista, chi l' udire,
Chi sfóga ógni desír solo in servíre.

Amánte Pèrfido. ARIÒSTO.

L' amante per avér quel che desía,
Sènza guardár che Dio tutt' òde e véde,
Avvilúppa promésse, giuraménti ;
Che tutti spárgon pòi per l'ária i vènti.

Amánte Tímido. TASSO.

Ei che modèsto è sì, com' essa è bèlla,
Brama assái, pòco spèra, e nulla chiède ;
Nè sa scoprírsi o non ardísce : ed ella
O lo sprèzza o no 'l véde, o non s'avvéde,
Così sin' ora il mísero ha servíto,
O non visto, o mal nòto, o mal gradíto.

s 6

La Lusinga. BONDI.

Da gran tèmpo i malì mièi,
Col morír finíto avrèi ;
Ma la crèdula speránza
Mi tien vivo, e sèmpre dice,
Che men trísto ed infelíce,
Sarà fórse il nuòvo dì.
Ma il dì nuòvo che succède,
Infelíce ancór mi vede,
E la spème che mi avánza,
Non mi láscia nel patíre ;
Nè il coràggio di moríre,
Nè di vívere così.

Dònna Timida. ARIÒSTO.

Con cor tremánte, e con tremante pième
Fugge la tapinèlla, e non sa dove :
In ciò ch'intórno ascólta, in ciò che véde,
Vede di nuòvo orrór sembiánze nòve ;
Lième arboscèl, cúi débil áura fiède,
Lieve fòglia che cade, o che si scòte,
Di terrór dóppio, il dúbbio cor percòte.

GUARÍNI *nel Pastór Fido.* *Atto I. scèna IV.*

La mísera tacèndo
Per sovèrchio desío tutta si strúgge ;
Così pèrde beltà, se'l fòco dura,
E perdèndo stagión, pèrde ventúra.

Il Simulácro d'Amóre scolpíto da Canòva.
GHERARDO DE' ROSSI.

Fu bugiárdo, o Canova, il tuo scalpèllo
Effigiándo Amóre ;
Se avésse il vólto sì gentíle bèllo,
Avría sì crudo il còre ?

CONCETTI POETICI.

Giuòco di Paròle.

Nel mio primièro ci si véde chiáro,
Curva il secóndo, e più nol troverái;
L' intéro è sacrosánto a tutti caro,
Ne párlan sèmpre, e non si véde mai.

———————

Amóre assomigliáto all' Ape.   TASSO, *nell' Aminta.*

Pícciola è l' Ape, e fa col pícciol mòrso
Pur gravi, e pur molèste le feríte;
Ma qual còsa è più pícciola d'amóre
Se in ógni brève spázio éntra e s'ascónde
In ógni brève spázio ? or sótto all' ómbra
Delle palpèbre, or tra minúti rivi
D'un bióndo crine, or déntro le pozzétte,
Che fórma un dólce riso in bèlla guáncia;
E pur fa tanto grandi, e sì mortáli,
O così immedicábili le piághe !

———————

GUARÍNI *nel Pastór Fido.*   *Atto IV. scéna II.*

Se le paròle míe
Fósser ánime tutte,
E tutte al vòstro onóre
Oggi le consacrássi alle dovúte
Grázie, non basterían di tanto dóno.

———————

Dònna Pícciola.   TASSO.

Picciolétta Isabèlla,
Pícciola o grande nominár degg' ío
La tua beltà ch' infiámma il mio desío ?
Che pícciola la fronte, il crin, le cíglia,
Picciolétta hai la man, la bócca, il piède,
I passi, le fattézze, i bèi sembiánti,
Gli ábiti, il velo, i guánti,

La camerétta, il letticciuòl, la sède;
Ma pur gran maravíglia!
Fra tante còse pícciole si véde
Che quel che rimirándo io sènto al còre,
Non è pícciolo ardóre.

Descrizióne d'un Cespúglio. ARIÒSTO.

Ecco non lungi un bèl Cespúglio, vede.
Di spin fioríti, e di vermíglie ròse,
Che de le líquid' ónde a spècchio siède,
Chiuso dal sol fra l' alte quèrce ombróse;
Così vòto nel mèzzo, che concède
Frésca stanza fra l'ómbre più nascóse;
E la fòglia coi rami in mòdo è mista,
Che'l sol non v'éntra, non che mínor vista.
Dentro lètto vi fan tènere erbétte,
Ch'invítano a posár chi s'appresènta.

A Diana. FANTÓNI.

Vérgin dell' arco nella cáccia fòrte,
  Face del Cièlo, quando Fèbo dòrme,
  Spème di spòse, che rapísci a mòrte,
              Diva trifórme.
A te consácro questo pin, che inálza
  Fra l'árdue nubi la chiomáta fronte,
  E i negri lecci della curva balza
              Fíglia del mónte.
Strage del grégge, e dei pastór spavènto,
  Schièra s' annída d'affamáti lupi,
  Che van predándo cènto capre e cento
              Per quéste rupi.
Se mai di víta il bráccio tuo le priva,
  Se nell' insídie tu a cader gli adéschi,
  Appènder vòglio alla magión votíva,
              Gli òrridi tèschi,

Il Sógno. VITTORÈLLI.

Ascólta, o infída, un sógno,
  Della trascórsa nòtte.
  Parévami le gròtte
D'Alfesibèo mirár:
D'Alfesibeo che quando,
  Alza la verga bruna,
  Fa pállida la luna,
  Fa tempestóso il mar.
Padre, io gridái, nel fianco
  Ho una puntúra acèrba;
  Con qualche magic' èrba,
  Sánami per pietà.
Rise il buòn vècchio, e dísse:
  Fuggi colèi che adóri;
  Erbe per te miglióri
  Alfesibeo non ha.

I Castèlli in Aria. BERTÒLA.

Una séra al focoláre,
  Si sedéan Doríllo e Nina;
  Ei dicéa: Vedér regína,
  Ti vorrèi, di tèrra e mar:
Di supèrbe vèsti adórna,
  E di gèmme prezióse . . . .
  Ma perchè, Nina rispóse,
  L' impossíbile bramár?
Se formár desíri gòdi,
  Brama il prato ognór più erbóso,
  Brama il grégge numeróso:
  Lello al fin che aver si può.
A che pro, l' altro rispóse,
  Se provái finór bramando,
  Che il piacér vièn meno quando
  L' alma ottièn quel che bramò.

Bèlle Guáncie. CHIABRÈRA.

Bèlla guáncia che disdòri
  Gli almi onóri,
  Che sul viso ha l' alma Auróra;
  Onde il prègio ad ogni volto
  Ella ha tòlto,
  Che sul Cièlo oggi s'onóra.
Te vo' dir guáncia fioríta,
  Coloríta
  Del più bèl ch' èbbe natúra;
  Te vo' dir, che non hai fióre,
  Che nel còre
  Sáppia darmi una puntúra.
Che fai tu, se mi dai segno
  Di disdégno?
  Mi ti mòstri più vermíglia,
  Per tal mòdo sei cortése.
  Nelle offèse
  D'una nòbil meravíglia.
Nevi cándide cosparte,
  Con bell' arte
  Infra pórpora sì bèlla;
  Ben vorrèi lodárvi appièno,
  Ma vièn meno
  La virtù della favèlla.
Vòstra glòria da' mièi detti
  Non s'aspètti,
  Chi ciò brama in van desíra:
  Come no? se per dolcézza,
  Di bellézza
  Divièn muto chi vi mira.

Le dònne che non invècchiano. GHERARDO DE' ROSSI.

Io so ben che le pudíche
  Donzellétte a Cíntia amíche,
  Ad Amór tagliándo l' ali,
  S' involárono a' suòi strali;
  Di Ciprígna affè le amáte
  Vaghe ancèlle innamoráte,
  Per non créscer negli anni,
  Han tarpáto al tèmpo i vanni.

Epitáffio per un Parasito.   G. de' Rossi.

Il céner fréddo del cantór Melítto
   Questa brev' úrna in se racchiúder può,
Appéna una Pirámide d' Egítto,
   Racchiúdere potría quanto mangiò.

La Speranza.

ARIÉTTA DEL METASTASIO.

Perchè gli son compagna,
   L' estívo raggio ardènte
   L' agricoltor non sente,
   Suda, ma non si lagna
   Dell' opra e del sudor;
Con me nel carcer nero
   Ragiona il prigionièro,
   Si scorda affanni e pene,
   E al suon di sue catene
   Cantando va talor.——

ODE TRIONFALE, DELLO STESSO.

CORO.

Lodi al gran Dio, che opprèsse
   Gli empj nemíci suòi,
   Che combattè per noi,
   Che trionfò così.

GIUDÍTTA.

Venne l' Assíro, e intórno
   Con le falángi Pèrse
   Le valli ricopèrse,
   I fiumi inaridì.
Parve oscuráto il giórno,
   Parve con quel crudèle
   Al tímido Israèle
   Giunto l' estrèmo dì.
          CORO, &c.

GIUDITTA.

Fiamme, caténe e mòrte,
    Ne minacciò feróce ;
    Alla terríbil voce
    Betúlia impallidì !
Ma inaspettáta sòrte
    L' estínse in un moménto,
    E come nébbia al vènto,
    Tanto furór sparì.
                   CORO, &c.

GIUDITTA.

Dispèrsi abbandonáti
    I bárbari fuggíro ;
Si spaventò l' Assíro,
    Il Mèdo inorridì :
Nè fur gigánti usáti
    Ad assalír le stelle ;
    Fu Dònna sola, e imbèlle,
    Quella che gli atterrì.
                   CORO, &c.

Effetti della Pace.

DELLO STESSO.

In prato, in forèsta,
    Sia l' alba o la sera,
    Se dòrme talór,
    Non turba, non desta
    La tromba guerrièra
    Dal sonno il pastór.
Le madri sicúre
    D' insídie e perígli,
    Se i tèneri figli
    Si stríngono al pètto,
    Impúlso è d' affètto,
    Non più di timór.

ARIA, DELLO STESSO.

Nella face, che risplènde,
    Crede accòlto ogni dilètto,
    Ed anèla il fanciullétto
    A quel trèmulo splendór.
Ma se poi la man vi stènde,
    A ritrárla è pronto inváno,
    Che fuggèndo allor la mano,
    Porta seco il suo dolor.

———

DELLO STESSO.

Sarò qual madre amante,
    Che la dilètta pròle
    Mináccia ad ogni istante,
    E mai non sa punir.
Alza a ferír la mano,
    Ma il colpo già non scénde,
    Chè amor la man sospènde
    Nell' atto del ferir.

———

DELLO STESSO.

Plácido zeffirétto,
    Se trovi il caro oggètto,
    Digli che sèi sospíro,
    Ma non gli dir di chi.
Límpido ruscellétto,
    Se mai t'incóntri in lei,
    Dille che pianto sei,
    Ma non le dir qual cíglio
    Créscer ti fe' così.———

———

DELLO STESSO.

León piagáto a mòrte
    Sente mancar la vita,
    Guarda la sua ferita,
    Nè s'avvilísce ancor.

Così fra l' ire estrème
Rugge, mináccia e freme,
Che fa tremar morèndo
Talvòlta il cacciator.

DELLO STESSO.

Leon ch' errándo vada
Per la natía contrada,
Se un agnellin rimira,
Non si commòve ad ira
Nel generoso cor.
Ma se venir si vede
Orrida tigre in fáccia,
L'assale, e la minaccia,
Perchè sol quella crede
Degna del suo furor.

Contro l' Ingratitudine.
DELLO STESSO.

Benchè di senso privo
Fin l' arboscèllo è grato
A quell' amico rivo,
Da cui riceve umor:
Per lui di frondi ornato
Bella mercè gli rende;
Quando dal sol difènde
Il suo benefattór.

Ode sopra la Virtù.
DELLO STESSO.

Se bramate esser felíci,
Alme belle, è in questa schièra
L' innocènte, la sincèra,
La fedel felicità.

Quel piacer fra noi si gode,
 Che contènta, e non offènde,
 Che resíste alle vicènde
 Della sorte, e dell' età.
Qui la sfèrza del rimòrso,
 Qui l' insulto del timóre,
 Qui l' accúsa del rossore,
 Come afflígga il cor non sa.
Del piacer, che i folli allètta,
 E' il sentièr fiorito e verde ;
 Ma tradisce, e vi si perde
 Di tornar la libertà.——

TITLES AND HONOURABLE APPELLATIONS

USED IN ITALIAN LETTERS.

It is not my design to instruct in the epistolary art, for in this every one follows his fancy: but to make the learner acquainted with the titles and honourable appellations, used in Italian to persons with whom we keep an epistolary correspondence.

Observe that the Italians put the date in the last line of the letter, and none but familiar friends or merchants and tradesmen put it at the top.

To the Pope.—*Alla Santità di nòstro Signóre Pio sèttimo.*—In the beginning of a letter, and in the discourse, *Vòstra Santità* or *V. Beatitúdine.*—In the conclusion, *e con ógni umiltà le bácio i santíssimi pièdi. Di V. Stà*([37]), *Umilíssimo, Devotíssimo, ed Ossequiosíssimo Sèrvo.*
　　Di Parígi, il primo di Gennáio, 1823.

To a Cardinal.—*All' Eminentíssimo e Reverendíssimo Signór Cardinál* * *.*—In the beginning of the letter, *Eminentíssimo Signóre, e Padróne Colendíssimo.*—In the middle of the letter, *V. Eminènza.* —In the conclusion, *E per fine, a V. Eminènza bácio la sacra pórpora, e da Dio le implòro ógui maggiór grandézza e felicità, rassegnandomi, Di V. Eminènza, Umilíssimo, Devotíssimo ed Obbligatíssimo Servitóre.*
　　Di Napoli i 3, &c.

Observe, that when the Princes Cardinals are at

See at p. 412 how the titles, &c., are generally abbreviated.

Rome, they are called by the title of *Eminence*, and not
Highness; Pope Innocent X. having so ordered it.

To a Patriarch, an Archbishop,. a Bishop, a Nuncio, a
Prelate.—*All' Illustríssimo e Reverendíssimo Signóre Prōne mio Colendíssimo, Monsignóre di * *,
Arcivéscovo* or *Véscovo di * *.* In the conclusion,
*E con profóndo rispètto, e somméssa riverènza le
bacio le sacre vèsti. Di V. S. Ill͞ma e Rev. Umilíssimo e Divotíssimo Servitóre.*

If it be a cardinal that is a bishop or archbishop, you
are to make use of titles belonging to such cardinals as
are not princes.

To a Regular Abbot.—*Al Reverendíssimo Padre, Prōne
mio Colendíssimo, il Padre D. * * Abate di N. * *
* In the beginning, Reverendíssimo Padre e Prōne
Colendíssimo.*—At the end, *Reverenteménte ba-
ciándo le mani a V. P. Rͫᵃ, la prègo per singolár
grázia volérsi ricordár di me nelle sue preghière.
Di V. P. Rev., Umilíssimo ed Obbligatíssimo Scr-
vitóre.*
        Di . . . .

To a Canon, a Curate, a Priest.—*Al Reverendo Signóre,
e Prōne Colendíssimo, il Signór * *. Canònico,
Arciprète,* or *Curato di,* &c.

If it be a person of distinction you must say, *all' Ill͞mo
e Revdͫo Sigʳᵉ. Padróne Colendíssimo.*

To a Prior, Rector, Guardiʋn or Superior.—*Al Mólto
Reverèndo Padre e Prōne Osservandíssimo il Padre
N * *. Prióre, Rettóre,* or *Guardiáno,* &c. *de' * *.
In the beginning, Mólto Reverèndo e Prōne Osser-
vandíssimo.*—At the conclusion, *E mi rasségno.
Di V. P. molto Rev., Umilíssimo ed Obbligatíssimo
Servitóre.*

To a Friar Priest.—*Al molto Reverèndo Padre, il
Padre * * dell' órdine di San * *.*—In the begin-
ning, *Molto Reverèndo Padre.*—At the conclusion,
E per fine a V. P. bácio con ógni affètto le mani,

e mi raccomándo alle sue orazióni. Di V. P. molto Rev., Umilíssimo ed Obbligatíssimo Servitóre.

To a Lay Brother.—*Al molto onorándo Fratèllo in Cristo fra' Agostíno * * nel Convènto di P. P. di, &c.*—In the beginning, *Molto Onorándo Fratèllo in Cristo*([26]).

To the Emperor.—*Alla Sacra Cesárea ed Imperiále Maestà dell' Imperatóre.*—At the head of the letter, *Sacra Cesárea Maestà.*—In the course of the letter, *Vostra Maestà.* At the end, *E per fine a V. M. bácio umilissimaménte le mani, pregándo Dio, che la cólmi di tutte le maggióri e più desiderábili felicità. Di V. Cesárea Maestà, Umilíssimo, Devotíssimo, ed Ossequiosíssimo Servitóre.*

To a Roman Catholic King.—*Alla Cristianíssima Maestà del Re di Fráncia.*—In the discourse, *Vostra Maestà* or *Sire.*—At the end, *Colmi Dío Nostro Signore le felicità presènti della Maestà Vostra, d'altre nuòve nell' avvenire. Or, Consèrvi Iddío lungamente V. M. a quélle prosperità, che sótto il felicíssimo, e gloriosíssimo suo govèrno, Ella fa godére a' suoi pòpoli. D. V. M. Crist.; Umilíssimo, Divotíssimo, ed Ossequiosíssimo Servitóre.*

To other Kings.—*Alla Sacra Reál Maestà del Re d' Inghiltèrra, di Prussia, d'Olanda, &c.* In the beginning, SIRE.—At the end, most as above.

To the Dauphin of France.—*Al Serenissimo Príncipe Delfino di Francia.*—At the beginning, *Serenissimo Príncipe.*—In the middle, *V. A. R. (vostra altezza reále).*—At the end, *Consèrvi Iddio per lunghíssimo tèmpo quel bène alla Fráncia, che le ha dato in dar la Serenissima di lei Persóna, a cui con profónda riverènza m'inchino. Serenissimo Príncipe,* or *di V. A. R.; Umilíssimo, Devotíssimo ed Obbligatíssimo Servitóre.*

---

[26] A variety of forms of concluding Letters may be seen at p. 410.

To a Prince of the Blood.—*All' Altézza Serenissima del Signór Duca d'Orleans.—All' Altezza Serenissima del Signor Príncipe di Condé.*

To Reigning Dukes.—*All' Altézza Serenissima del Duca di Parma; di Mèdena, &c.*—In the beginning, *Serenissimo Príncipe.*—At the conclusion (³⁸).

To Secular Electors of the Empire.—*All' Altézza Serenissima Elettorále del Signor Duca di Bavièra, Príncipe Elettorále del Sacro Románo Impèro.*

To Ecclesiastical Electors of the Empire.—*All' Altézza Serenissima Elettorale del Signór Arcivéscovo di Colònia, Príncipe Elettorale del Sacro Romano Impèro.*

To Dukes who are not Sovereigns.—*All' Illustrissimo ed Eccellentissimo, il Signór Duca * *.*

To Ambassadors.—*A sua Eccellènza il signór * *, Ambasciatóre di sua Maestà Brittannica.*

To an Earl, a Marquis, or Baron.—*All' Illustríssimo Signóre, il Signóre Conte * *, Marchése * *, Baróne * *.*

To a Governor.—If he is an ecclesiastic, as those of Italy,—*All' Illustríssimo e Reverendíssimo Signóre Prōne Colendíssimo Monsignór * *, Governatóre di Roma.*—If he is not an ecclesiastic, *All' illustríssimo Signóre e Prōne mio Colendíssimo il Signor * *.*

To a Privy Councillor.—*All' Illustríssimo Signóre e Prōne mio Colendíssimo il Signór * *, del Consiglio di Stato di sua Maestà Cristianíssima.*—In the beginning, *Illustríssimo Signóre Prōne mio Colendíssimo.* At the end, *Di V. S. Illma, &c.*

To a President.—*All' Illustríssimo Signóre, e Prōne Colendíssimo il Signór * *, Presidènte nella corte Sovrána del Parlaménto di * *.*

To an Ecclesiastical Counsellor in Parliament.—*All' Illustríssimo e Reverendíssimo Signóre, il Signór Abate * *, Consiglière nella corte Sovrána del Parlaménto di * *.*

T

To a Counsellor of Parliament.—*All' Illustrissimo Signore Padrone mio Colendissimo il Signór * *, Consiglière nella corte Sovrána del Parlaménto di * *.*

To a Counsellor of the Court of Aids.—*All' Illustrissimo Signore Padrone mio Colendissimo, il Signor N. Consiglière nella cámera de' sussidj di * *.*

To a Doctor of Law or Physic.—*Al molto Illústre ed Eccellentissimo Signor * *, Dottóre di Legge, or Dottor di Medicina in * *.*

To a Professor, or Language Master.—*Al mólto Illústre, e Signóre Professore * *, Lettóre di Teología nel collègio di * *. If he is a Language Master, All' Ornatissimo Signor * *, Prof. di Lingua e Letteratura Italiana, Francese, &c.*

To an Advocate, an Attorney.—*Al molto Illustre e Colendissimo Signóre, il Sig. * *, Avvocáto or Procuratore del Parlaménto di * *.*

They generally address to a gentleman of good birth, *Al Molto illustre Sig. * *.* To a nobleman without a title, *All' Illustríssimo Signór * *.*

To a Tradesman.—*Al Signór * * libraio, sartóre, fornáio, macelláro,* &c.

DIFFERENT FORMS OF CONCLUDING LETTERS.

The following are the forms, which, in epistolary collections, most frequently occur.

E per fine a V. S., or a V. S. Illustríssima, or a V. Eccellènza, or V. A. or a V. Eminènza, or a V. Maestà bácio umilissimaménte le mani.

E le bácio affettuosaménte le mani, e mi creda costantemente di V. E. Umilmo Ser.

E baciándole affettuosissimaménte le mani, le áuguro ógni bène, e contènto.

E per fine mi rasségno con ógni maggiór riverènza, &c.

E per fine mi protèsto con tutta la stima, &c.

E le bácio le mani.

E con quésto passo a sottoscrívermi di V. S. Illīma, &c.

E con pari, e congiuntíssimo affètto auguriamo a V. S. Illīma, e tutti di casa sua, ogni bene, mentre ci protestiamo, &c.

Mantèngami V. S. in sua grázia che io mi confermo, &c.

Mi saluti la signóra sua consòrte, e mi creda, &c.

E per fine nélla buòna grázia di V. S. mi raccomándo, e resto, &c.

E raccomandándomi cordialménte alla sua bontà, passo a rassegnármi, &c.

E baciándole le mani, alle sue orazióni mi raccomándo, e mi dico, &c.

E per fine salúto V. S. ed ella si compiacerà a nome mio baciáre le mani di * * mio cugino, ed alla Signora * * sua consòrte, mentre resto, &c.

E riverenteménte a V. Eccellènza mi dico, &c.

Ed a V. Eccellènza fo umilíssimo inchino.

Ed a V. Eminènza riverenteménte m' inchino.

Ed alle sue orazióni mi raccomándo.

E le bácio con la dovúta riverènza le mani.

E rèsto facèndole umilíssima riverènza.

The forms most used at present are:

E rassegnándole la mia servitù, fo a V. S. or le fo umilissima riverènza, e me le rassègno, &c.

E con tutta la stima mi dico, &c.

E con tutto l' ossèquio mi do l' onóre d' assicurárla del mio profondo rispètto, mentre sono, &c.

E pregándola de' di lèi stimatissimi comandi mi prègio d' èssere, &c.

E rèsto con tutto 'l desidèrio di potér incontrare qualche occasióne di servírla, mentre mi fáccio un prègio di dirmi, &c.

Sono, con tutta la stima ed il rispètto che le dèvo, &c.

E per fine mi do l' onóre d' offrirle la mia debolíssima servitù, protestándomi.

E sia persuása, che sono e sarò sèmpre dispósto ad obbedirla, mentre mi vanto d'èssere, di V. S. Illīma, Umilīmo, Devotīmo Ser. * * *

How the Titles or Honourable Appellations are generally abridged in addressing or subscribing Italian Letters.

A. I. e R.	Altézza Imperiale e Reale.
V. A. R.	Vòstra Altézza Reále.
Affmo	Affexionatíssimo.
Amatmo	Amatíssimo.
V. E.	Vòstra Eccellènza.
Carmo	Caríssimo.
Carma	Caríssima.
Colmo	Colendíssimo.
Devotmo	Devotíssimo.
Eccelmo	Eccellentíssimo.
Eccelma	Eccellentíssima.
Eminentmo	Eminentíssimo.
Illmo	Illustríssimo.
Illma	Illustríssima.
S. M.	Sua Maestà.
V. P.	Vostra Paternità.
Obblmo	Obbligatíssimo.
Prone	Padróne.
Prona	Padróna.
Revdo	Reverèndo.
Revdmo	Reverendíssimo.
Ser.	Servitore or Servo.
Sigre	Signóre, m. sing.
Sigra	Signóra.
Siggd	Signóri.
V. S.	Vossignoría.
V. S. Illma	Vossignoría Illustríssima.

LETTERE MERCANTILI.

Al Sigr. N. N. a Venèzia.

Londra,
ai 2 d' Agósto, 1826.

Stimatíssimo Signóre:

Avendo risolúto col nome di Dio d'erígere casa di negòzio in questa Città (*or* Piazza) sotto 'l nome mio, con facoltà e govèrno tale da potér intraprèndere qualúnque onorévole negòzio, e tenèndo voi nel número de' più cari e parziáli Amíci, ve ne do avvíso con questa mia, acciò nelle vostre occorènze possiáte valérvi dell' òpera mia, sì per provvisióne o mercanzíe, per le quali ho mòdo di farvi godér ogni vantàggio, come in Cambj ed altro che vi pòssa di quà bisognáre. Sicúro di riportárne òttimi e leáli trattaménti, esibèndovi la mia servitù, colle sòlite e consuète provvisióni, con che vi dichiariáte prónto ad una recíproca corrispondènza. In tanto faréte nòta di non prestár fede che alla mía firma, cólla quale sarà la presènte sottoscrítta, e mi diréte cóme dovrò contenérmi per voi, per isfuggíre ogni erróre. Attèndo l'onóre de' vostri stimatíssimi comándi, per farvi sperimentáre il piacére particoláre che ho della vostra grata corrispondènza, accertándovi che alle occasióni sarò per ricórrer a' vostri favóri, mentre affettuosaménte salutándovi, vi bácio le mani.

Al Sig. N. N. a Veróna.

Amsterdam.

Per mancánza d' occasióni non vi abbiámo più scrítto; servirà questa óra per caraménte salutárvi e dirvi, che per órdine del Signor N. N. di Roma vi abbiámo in Condótta di questi SS. N. N. spedita franca, e bèn condizionáta una Balla con fuòri marca e número con-

tenènte Panni d' Olánda, che vi piacerà in tèmpo débito
procurárla, per dispórne a volontà del detto amíco di
Roma, dal quale vi varréte delle vostre spese con avvisáre 'l seguíto. Con questa occasióne v' offriámo la
servitù nostra in tutto ciò che vi potésse occórrere, che
prontíssimi sèmpre ci avréte, e B. L. M.

A Róma.

                                         Amsterdam.

    Sènza le caríssime vostre si sono provvíste le Pèzze
òtto Panni che avete ordináto di perfettissima qualità,
ed una Balla della fuòri marca e número rèsta spedíta
a vostra disposizióne in condótta di questi SS. N. N. ai
SS. N. N. di Veróna, che saréte a procurárla da' medésimi per dárcene a suo tèmpo la ricevúta e soddisfazióne,
come non dubitiámo, avèndovi procuráto fior di ròba,
ed avantaggiátovi al possíbile tanto nella cómpra, che
nelle spese, il che sarà motívo di continuársi in abbon-
danza i vostri impièghi; e come dall' ingiúnto conto .
vedréte, ove abbiámo dato débito per il còsto e spésa
di f... Bco, che di tanti ci daréte crédito, attendèndo
che celi rimettiáte al maggiór nostro vantággio, e sopra
di voi, alla ricevúta del conto colla sòlita vostra puntualità; e favoríteci di nuòvi e maggióri vostri comándi,
che prontíssimi ci avrete con tutto l' affètto, col quale
caraménte salutándovi, B. L. M.

*Ai Sigg*ʳⁱ*. N. N. in Amsterdam.*

                                            Roma.

    Colla gratíssima vostra dei ... ho ricevúto 'l conto
delle Pèzze 8 Paňni d' Olanda che m'avéte provvíste,
e spedíte in Balla N ... ai SS. N. N. di Veróna a mía
disposizióne, che là procurerò da' medésimi.

    Non ho dúbbio che saránno della perfètta qualità che
dite, ed a suo tèmpo vi dirò la ritrováta. In tanto per
farvi valére il vostro avanzo ho ordináto al Sig. N. di
Venèzia di provvedérvi súbito f... Bco, importáre della

detta Balla, che l'effettuerà con ógni puntualità, attendèndo da voi avvíso che sía seguíto, e che mene abbiáte dato crédito a frónte di detta partíta; nel mentre
vi piacerà far nota di provvedérmi Pèzze due Panni di
Berrì per Tabárri che potréte pagáre f. 5 incírca il
bráccio in bianco, e farli tíngere scarlátto come la
mostra; ed in apprèsso vi darò nuòvo órdine per compíre una ballétta, raccomandándovi che detti Panni
síano di buòn còrpo, buòn lanággio e ben copèrti per
darmi ánimo alla continuazióne de' miei impièghi, che
non saránno scarsi, se mi troverò ben favoríto, ed
offerèndomi a' vostri comándi prontíssimo, vi salúto, e
B. L. M.

Ai Sigg. N. N. in Amsterdam.

Venèzia.

Per órdine, e conto del Signóre N. N. di Róma vi
rimétto a uso D ... Banco da N. N. lèttera N. N. a
gròssi ..... ducáto che ne procureréte proméssa, e
pagaménto in tèmpo intendèndovene con detto Amíco
avvisándo 'l seguíto, e pregándovi de' vostri comándi
vi saluto caramente, e B. L. M.

Róma, N. N.

Amsterdam.

Colla vostra caríssima dei .... Corrènte ci rimettéte
da quésto N. N. f. Banco ad uso lèttera vostra; sene
procurerà accettazióne, ed a suo tèmpo ne cercherémo 'l
pagaménto per creditárvene contro la Ballétta tele d'
Olánda mandátavi, e quando altro in contrário non sen-
tiáte, tenéte l'affare termináto. Non ci rèsta, che pregárvi della continuazióne de' vostri stimatíssimi comándi
per i quali prontíssimi sèmpre ci avrete, salutándovi
caraménte vi B. L. M.

Firènze, N. N.
                                        Amsterdám.

E' molto tèmpo che non v'ho scrítto per mancánza
d' occasióni : servirà questa per salutárvi caraménte, e
dirvi che a persuasióne del S. N. N. di Livórno, ho risolúto fare una píccola pruòva della vostra fábbrica, com-
mettèndovi due casse drappi o mantíni di buòna qualità
e de' colóri che vi móstra l' ingiúnta fattúra.   Vi piacerà farne nòta per inoltrárli questa vòlta colla maggióre celerità possíbile per la sòlita Condótta, facèn-
domi alla spedizióne Tratta dell' impòrto, che 'l vostro
cárico incontrerà il dovúto ricòvero : raccomandándovi
che i colóri síano ben viváci, di buòn peso e di perfètta
qualità, così che mi facciáte vantàggio nel prèzzo e
rispármio nelle spese, se desideráte la continuazióne de'
mièi impièghi che saranno di qualche somma, se mi
vedrò ben trattáto, come non dúbito del vostro affètto ;
ed offerèndovi la mia servitù in tutto ciò che quì pòssa
occórrervi affettuosaménte vi B. L. M.

---

*Raccomandazióne d'un Amíco passeggièro, ed Asse-
gnazióne fáttagli de' danári necessárj, &c.*

Mío Signóre ;

Sènza cara vostra, mi rappòrto sopra la mia antecedènte che fu ai 10 del passato.   Questa sèrve solaménte per pregárvi, che se 'l Sig. • • che parte òggi di
quì per N. venísse a riverírvi da parte sua e nostra,
con ricercár i vostri consigli ed aiúti, d' assísterlo nelle
sue occorrènze ; s' egli avesse bisógno di danári, di
fornírgliene sin alla sómma di fl.1,000 monéta corrènte
contro quittánza, e di méttermeli a conto sènza dár-
mene avvíso.   Vi resterò con òbbligo per questo, e per
gli altri favóri che avréte la bontà di far al detto Signore, ch' è molto nostro amíco. Raccomandándovi 'l
ricápito dell' inclúsa, caraménte vi B. L. M.

Sènza cara vostra la presènte sarà per dirvi ch' attèndo abbiáte riscòssa da' Sigg. • • di costì fl——— e
dátomene crédito ed avvíso. In questo mentre vi ri-

métto altri fl——, sopra il Sig. * * pur di costì per
lèttera di questi Sigg. * * di cui vi piacerà di procurar
l'accettazióne e pagaménto a suo tèmpo, ed imborsáti
che gli avrete me ne darete pariménte crédito ed avvíso.
In tanto faréte nòta di provvedérmi le sotto notáte mèrci
e di spedírmele in due Baríli, quando però me le vogliáte
dare al prezzo avvisátovi : in difètto, tralasciate anco di
riscuòtere suddétta riméssa con rimandármene la lèttera :
ma quando avréte risolúto di spedírmi i detti Baríli àl
prèzzo accennáto, saréte rimborsáto súbito del vostro
avanzo, e sarà cáusa di darvi Commissióni di maggiór
sostánza.   Marcheréte i Baríli di Num. 10. 11. colla
sòlita mia marca avánti, e per grazia non vi dimenticáte
della fede di sanità sopra cotésti Baríli, dove si attèsti
che la ròba sia stata costì fabbricáta, e rèsto——

———

Per rispósta della cara vostra de' 22 passáto, gòdo di
sentíre che abbiáte ricevúto ed imborsáto la cèdola di
cambio di fl...... da me riméssivi sopra cotésti Signóri
N. N.   Di grazia, s'egli è possíbile senza vostro pregiu-
dízio, compiacétevi con suddétti fl....... saldárne la
partíta, mentre, come ben sapéte, avete posto la ròba
più cara a me che non avete fatto ad áltri di quì, avèndo
ciò visto con gli òcchi miei proprj, e v'assicúro, che se
mi faréte godére qualche vantággio, non mancherete mai
di Commissióni dalla parte mia, ed in brève ve ne ordi-
nerò 2 Baríli ; ma saldáte s' è possíbile la partíta suddétta, quando però non lo vogliáte fare, avvisátemene,
che súbito vi farò pagare quel poco avánzo che preten-
déte ; ma poi le mie Commissióni saránno scarse, perchè
non è di ragióne ch' io paghi più degli altri ; e caraménte vi B. L. M.

———

Rispondèndo alla gratíssima vostra de' 6 stante ; vi
dirémo, che in questa nostra fièra, già termináta, abbiámo
fatto fine de' due primi Baríli .... e di Baríli sei ....
che ci provvedéste per conto a metà ; del tutto se ne
formerà 'l conto per mandárvelo con altra. Vediamo
ora per detto conto a metà che avete provvísto e spedíto

per Bolzáno al Signor N. a nostra disposizióne altri due
Baríli....e Baríli òtto....dei quali come anco di quelli
che rèstano, procurerémo lo spáccio, il quale seguíto,
vene darémo ragguáglio con mandárvene 'l conto ; come
per tanto l' abbiámo ricevúto del loro importáre, che
rivedrémo per scritturárlo, in mancánza di erróri (di
vostra conformità) abbiámo fatto nota che de' fl. 682
che avanzáte per la nostra metà di suddétte mèrci, ce ne
sarà fatta tratta in fièra pròssima di Bolzáno dai Signori
N. N. di B. laónde vi farémo le disposizióni necessárie,
acciocchè rèsti puntualménte compíta, e secóndo che
s'andrà esitándo, s' ordineránno nuòve provvíste, come
intenderéte, e nel rèsto in che vagliámo a servírvi, co-
mandáteci liberaménte ; e per fine vi B. L. M.

———————

Signor mío ;
Sopra la còpia della nostra última del primo Set-
tèmbre scaduto, e per adèsso vi diamo avvíso che 'l
Signor N. v'ha indrizzáto pel Carrettière N. una cassa
No. I. che abbiámo comméssa per pròprio conto, essèndovi dentro mille nove cento settánta sètte marchi
d' argento, con altre robe di prèzzo, come vedréte dalla
nota qui sotto uníta, e vi preghiámo di farne cèlere
inoltrazióne, e colla minóre spésa che si potrà.   Sèrvavi
l'avvíso, e comandáte dove ci troveréte capaci per rèn-
dervi servízj gradíti, non dubitáte che sarémo sempre
dispósti ad effetuárli con tutta quell' attenzióne che
meritáte, e nella stessa manièra, con cui ci favoríte
sèmpre ; mentre caraménte vi salutiámo, ed augurán-
dovi un felíce viággio, ed ogni vantággio possibile alla
pròssima fièra di N. dove forse qualcúno di noi avrà 'l
piacére di vedérvi ; restiámo, &c.

———————

Il falliménto del Signor N., seguíto in Parigi i 19 del
corrènte, ci ha quasi rovináti, perchè ci ha fatto pèrdere
dódici mila scudi da qualche tèmpo già spiráti óltre un'
altra partíta di quattro mila òtto cènto floríni, che dovrà
maturáre al Natále di quest' anno.   Ma, pasiènza!
Iddío ha volúto così, così sía.   Vi dirémo che tèmpo fa,

demmo órdine al Signor N. d' indrizzárvi un Còllo, quello che anco ci scríve d'aver fatto. Vi piáccia dunque andárlo procurándo a suo tèmpo ben condizionáto, e ce lo rispediréte quanto prima per Lindo a nostra disposizióne. Vi preghiámo di restríngere quanto mai sarà possíbile l' aggrávio della Condótta, non dimenticándo d' unírvi la bolétta di sanità. Avréte visto colla nostra antecedènte un Baríle di Caffè all' indrízzo del Signor N. e méntre siamo entráti nel nuòvo anno, v'auguriámo felicíssimo capo d'esso, colmo d'ogni bène e bramáta prosperità. L'istésso facciámo a quelli che v'appartèngono, e siamo di cuòre, &c.

Prima Lèttera di Cámbio a due mési di data.

Livorno.   Gennáio, 1846, per mille Piástre.

A due mesi di data pagáte per questa prima di Cámbio all' órdine del Signór N. mille Piástre valóre ricevúto contánte dal detto Signóre, e li passeréte secóndo l' órdine di

Al Signór N.
a Cádice.   MICÁLI.

Prima Lèttera a Vista.

Firenze, 10 Marzo, 1846, per 330 Ducáti di Banca.

A vista pagáte per questa prima lèttera di Cambio all' órdine de' Sigg. N. N. Fratèlli, trecènto Ducáti di banca, valóre ricevúto da' détti Signóri, che passeréte secóndo l' avvíso di

Al Signòr N.
a Venèzia.   EMANUELLE FENZI & Co.

Fòrmula d' Assegnazióne.

Signor Filippo N. vi preghiámo di pagáre contra nostra Assegnazióne al Signór Danièle N. ad Ordine,

dugento Scudi quaránta cinque Crucíferi in monéta che
passeréte come per avvíso di
Francofòrte, 4 *Febbráio,*
       1846.   CARLO R.

Scúdi 200. 45, *Crucíferi Monéta.*

Fòrmula di Quetánza.

Confesso e dichiáro per la presènte d' avér ricevúto
òggi dal Sig. N. N. di * * la Sómma di quaranta cínque
Scúdi, che mi dovéva dopo la Fièra passàta per divèrse
mercanzíe.
Sinigáglia, i 9 *Novèmbre,*
       1845.   FERDINÁNDO N.

Fòrmula di Ricevúta.

Ho ricevúto dal Signór N. N. mílle fioríni a Cónto di
quanto mi dève fino a questo dì.
Argentina,
gli òtto Dicèmbre,   ANTÓNIO N.
       1844.

Altra Ricevúta.

Ho ricevúto dal Signór R. un plico di P. per il
Signor Príncipe L. che m' òbbligo di fargli tenér in
mani próprie, a mio rísico e perícolo.
Firènze, 4 *Agósto,*
       1843.   LUIGI MOLINI.

Lèttera di condotta per Tèrra.

Francofòrte, 15 *Mággio,*
                    1846.

     Signóre :
     Alla guárdia di Dío e condótta di Michèle
Vetturále di questa Città, riceveréte un Còllo
B. T. di Mercánzie marcáto cóme in márgine, pesánte
duemila cènto cinquánta líbbre, il quále avèndo

ricevúto ben condizionáto, ed in tèmpo débito, gli pagheréte per il suo traspòrto a ragióne di dúe Scúdi per Quintále, come per avvíso del

Vòstro umil^{mo} Sèrvo,
N. N.

Lèttera di condotta per Acqua.

Venèzia, 20 Agósto,
1845.

Signóre :

Vi mándo per la Nave (o barca) di Giovánni N. Barcaruòlo di V. quattórdici Casse di Zuc-

D. P. chero marcáte come in márgine, le quali avèndo ricevúte ai 25 del corrènte in buòno stato, gli pagheréte per il suo transito a ragione di un tállaro per Cassa, ma solamente la metà, se non le conségna al detto tèmpo. Sono

Vòstro umil^{mo} Servitóre,
N. N.

LETTERE DI CIVILTA'.

Ad un Professore.

Illustríssimo Signóre,

Le rèndo mille distintíssime grázie per tutt' i favóri usáti vèrso mío fíglio, méntre è stato Collegiále in cotesta sua règia Accadèmia, dóve mi pare ábbia fatto non mediòcre profítto. Può V. S. Illustríssima, star ben cèrto, che mi farò sèmpre un prègio di servírla ogni qual volta vorrà onorármi de' suòi pregiatíssimi Comándi, per testificárle l'indelèbile gratitúdine che conservár dèbbo vèrso l' innáta sua gentilézza, ed in mancánza mia, lo stésso mio fíglio, che si dichiára da lèi favoritíssimo, non ometterà mái di compíre l'òbbligo suo, per non rèndersi immeritévole della di lèi continuáta protezióne. Gradísca frattánto in ségno della mia servitù e divozióne un forniménto di bottóni dell' última mòda, venúta solaménte la settimána scórsa da Lóndra; nè voglia far attenzióne alla qualità del dóno, al di lei mèrito in nessún mòdo adequáto; ma al cuòr del Donatóre, che fin alle Céneri, si dirà

Di V. S. Illma.

Nápoli, ai 7 *Agósto,* 1845.   Devot^{mo} ed Umil^{mo}
Servitóre.

Ad una Nobil Dama.

Illustríssima Signóra,

Per farle vedére quanto stimo l' onóre de' suòi pregiatíssimi Cénni, al riceviménto dell' última sua in data dei 15 Mággio, ho pregáto 'l Giúdice di questa nostra Città, Amíco mio strétto, affinchè spedísca la sua cáusa ventilánte nel suo Tribunále, e m' ha promésso che lo farà il mese pròssimo, di manièra tale che mi dà a sperare che V. S. Illma sarà servíta sènza fallo, e le dico per suo ripòso, che le manderò a suo tempo Còpia délla sentènza, con che potrà ella interaménte assicurársi, che vivo impazientíssimo d'obbedírla, e rènderla persuása délla venerazióne e della stima con cúi ho l' onóre di protestármi.

Di V. S. Illma,

Firénze, i 14 *Lúglio,* Divotíssimo ed obbligatíssimo Ser.
1844.   GIOVANNI DA SCARPERIA.

P. S. Sua Fíglia gòde assái buòna salute, grázie al Cièlo e per èsser dégna fíglia d'una degníssima Madre, viène stimáta ed amáta non solaménte da tutte queste Religióse, che quasi l' adórano, ma da tutti quelli che hanno luogo di conóscerla.

Lèttera del Sereníssimo Príncipe Leopòldo, al Sig. Egídio Menágio.

Signór Menágio,

Gli amorévoli sentiménti che V. S. mi signífica di compatiménto e di duòlo per la mòrte del Serenissimo

:ipe *M.*, mio fratèllo, di felìce memòria, sóno proprj
ánimo suo cortése, esperimentáto da me in tante
ióni : ónde li ricévo io con affettuósa parzialità, e
ndo grázie ben grandi ; desiderándo di potér corri-
lere alla cordialità di V. S. colla pienézza della
in tutto ciò che sia di suo gusto. Ed in tanto le
ro dal Cièlo tutte quelle prosperità più perfètte che
áppia bramáre.   Firènze, ai 25 Novèmbre.

IL PRÍNCIPE LEOPÒLDO.

---

*ra del Sig. Menágio alla Signóra Contéssa della
Faétta.*

no obbligatíssimo alla gentilézza di V. S. Illma
 grazia singoláre che s'è compiaciúta di farmi cólla
cortesíssima lèttera. Che veraménte è fare una
a singolare agli assènti, avérgli in memòria in così
ιο luògo, qual' è la Villa di *Frèsne* ; ed in com-
ía di così amábili persóne, quali sóno Madáma *du
iis* e Madamigèlla *le Gendre:* tutte cose capacíssime
upare interaménte l' ánimo suo, per grande che sía.
ιt' a me, non dirò già a V. S. Illma che ógni dì
ιe fiate anch' ella mi torna a mente, noh essèndone
partíta ; le dirò bène che sòno a *Vitrì*, luògo altresì
ιo, dove fra dòtti Pastóri, e vaghe Pastorèlle, si
) tutt' i balli e giuòchi che si scrívono del paése di
dòne e d'Astrèa : ma che ogni luògo m'attrìsta dov'
on vedo V. S. Illma, e che in questo ameníssimo
) vo fuggèndo tutt' i piacéri e passatèmpi di così
ιrdévoli Pastóri e Pastorèlle.

> *Solo e pensóso i più desèrti campi
> Vo misurándo a passi tardi e lènti.*

ιdi può ben conóscere V. S. Illma, ch'io non son
) adèsso delle di lei virtù e gentilézze invaghíto,
 n'èra allóra che dimorándo ella in *Angiù* nella de-
ιíssima Villa di *Ciampirè*. Tornerò a Parígi, súbito
ιlla vi sarà tornata.   Fra tanto le mando il Madri-

gále Italiano, da me fatto per Madama di *Sevigné*, ad imitazione di quello del Guaríni, *Occhi stelle mortáli, &c.* tanto stimato e tanto lodato da V. S. Illustríssima.   E per fine le áuguro ogni più desideráta felicità.

MADRIGALE DEL MENAGIO.

Pianto di bèlla Dònna.

Ah! del Regno d' Amór prodígio tristo!
Spárger lágrime amáre
Que' dólci lumi ho visto;
Là tra le Grázie assíso
Soléa scherzáre il riso,
Spargéan di pianto que' bègli òcchi un mare;
Ma pur co' raggi ardènti
Spargéan fiamme cocènti:
E quel fatále ardore
Tòsto m' accése il core.
* O mísera mia vita!*
Occhi, lumi immortáli,
Deh qual per i mièi mali
Pòsso speráre aíta?
Se nubilósi ardéte,
Seréni che faréte?

GILBERT & RIVINGTON, Printers, St. John's Square, London.

Lightning Source UK Ltd.
Milton Keynes UK
UKOW03n0624070813

215001UK00001B/25/A